# EXTRAORDINARY PRAISE FOR
## *UN*fair

A Greater Good Favorite Book of 2015
An Amazon Best Nonfiction Book of the Month
A Goodreads Best Book of the Month

"In this important, deeply researched debut, [Benforado] draws on findings from psychology and neuroscience to show that police, jurors, and judges are generally guided by intuitive feelings rather than hard facts in making assessments.... The new research challenges basic assumptions about most key aspects of the legal system, including eyewitness memory, jury deliberations, police procedures, and punishment.... An original and provocative argument that upends our most cherished beliefs about providing equal justice under the law."

—*KIRKUS REVIEWS* (STARRED REVIEW)

"As gripping as a Grisham novel, only it isn't fiction. With captivating cases and razor-sharp science, Adam Benforado puts the justice system on trial and makes a bulletproof argument that it's fundamentally broken. This extraordinary book is a must-read for every judge, lawyer, detective, and concerned citizen in America."

—ADAM GRANT, WHARTON SCHOOL OF BUSINESS,
AUTHOR OF *GIVE AND TAKE*

"In *Unfair*, Adam Benforado makes us aware of all our many imperfections when it comes to the judgment of others in our midst. He does so gently and with astonishing knowledge. Learning so much about our subconscious biases and the judicial system that exploits them is fascinating—and deeply troubling. But he goes further: he offers obtainable solutions, ones that we should race to effect, both within our own minds and in the human fates on which we bring our minds to bear."

—JEFF HOBBS, AUTHOR OF
*THE SHORT AND TRAGIC LIFE OF ROBERT PEACE*

"This book suggests that criminal justice in the United States is not a system at all but a set of dysfunctional units that deliver biased decisions that make society less safe. Benforado deftly analyzes actual cases and recent studies in psychology and neuroscience to argue for broad-based reforms.... A stimulating critique of today's criminal justice system with applications to recent cases in Ferguson, MO, and elsewhere . . . authoritative and accessible."

—*LIBRARY JOURNAL* (STARRED REVIEW)

"Adam Benforado has written a book that will make you rethink everything you believe about crime and punishment. He gracefully blends science and storytelling to make a powerful case that our failure to bring the realities of human psychology into the courtroom has led to profound injustice. Enthralling and unsettling in equal measure, *Unfair* might be the most important book you read this year."

—DANIEL H. PINK, AUTHOR OF *DRIVE*

"This thoughtful and penetrating study raises many deeply troubling questions, and even more important, offers humane and very reasonable approaches to cure some of the ills of a system of 'criminal injustice' that should not be tolerated."

—NOAM CHOMSKY, PROFESSOR EMERITUS, MIT

"In *Unfair,* [Benforado] argues that most errors in criminal justice stem from the failure to take into account the frailties of human cognition, memory and decision-making. . . . This is a book everyone in the legal profession should read, and the rest of us too, for it is as much about the confounding idiosyncrasies of everyday behaviour as inequity in law."

—*NEW SCIENTIST*

"Systems of justice are built by human brains. As such, they're subject to all the foibles of human psychology, from biased decision-making to xenophobia to false memories. With the eye of a scholar and the ear of a storyteller, Benforado marshals the burgeoning research to illuminate the nexus between law and the mind sciences."

—DAVID EAGLEMAN, DIRECTOR OF THE INITIATIVE ON NEUROSCIENCE AND LAW, AUTHOR OF *INCOGNITO*

"*Unfair* is beautifully written, painstakingly researched, profoundly illuminating, and deeply disturbing. As evidence mounts that our criminal 'justice' system abounds with injustices, Benforado lays bare the systemic and psychological sources of its failures, weaving together compelling narrative and recent insights from the mind sciences. *Unfair* is must-reading for anyone who cares about justice and, more important, for anyone who does not."

—JON D. HANSON, ALFRED SMART PROFESSOR OF LAW, FACULTY DIRECTOR OF THE PROJECT ON LAW AND MIND SCIENCES AND THE SYSTEMIC JUSTICE PROJECT, HARVARD LAW SCHOOL

"Benforado makes a compelling case, backed with reference to extensive scientific research, for [his] point of view in *Unfair*. . . . Over and over again, Benforado demonstrates that basic assumptions underlying the criminal justice system are not supported by scientific evidence. . . . [He] also reminds us of how far the practice of criminal justice has drifted from its ostensible goals. . . . He is hopeful, however, that the system can be reformed, and the information in this book is offered in part toward that end. *Unfair* offers an excellent overview of an important body of information."

—*POPMATTERS*

"*Unfair* is a beautifully written book that manages to be both engrossing and important—a fascinating blend of psychological insight, legal know-how, and compelling storytelling. If you've ever wondered why the legal system doesn't work as well as it should, Benforado's intelligent take on the relationship between human psychology and the law will enlighten you—and leave you hopeful that we're capable of doing better."

—ADAM ALTER, NYU STERN SCHOOL OF BUSINESS,
AUTHOR OF *DRUNK TANK PINK*

"*Unfair* is an engaging, eye-opening read. By weaving together the latest findings in psychology and neuroscience with real-world stories of justice gone wrong, *Unfair* sheds new light on how easy it is for unconscious biases to wreak havoc on the criminal justice system and the steps that can be taken to make the system fairer."

—SIAN BEILOCK, PROFESSOR OF PSYCHOLOGY, UNIVERSITY OF CHICAGO,
AUTHOR OF *CHOKE* AND *HOW THE BODY KNOWS ITS MIND*

"Benforado is part of a rising chorus of academics, politicians, and those of us who work in the criminal justice system who are appalled by the fact that this country spends $60 billion a year on prisons and boasts the dubious honor of incarcerating more persons per capita than any other nation. In *Unfair*, Benforado does a wonderful job of describing the scope of the problem and of thinking creatively about how we can improve our criminal justice system."

—*THE FEDERAL LAWYER*

"*Unfair* is an incisive look at the problems that arise in the legal system because of the way people think as well as the prospects for meaningful reform. Adam Benforado has written an engaging and masterful book on one of the most important issues society has to face."

—ART MARKMAN, PROFESSOR OF PSYCHOLOGY, UNIVERSITY OF TEXAS,
AUTHOR OF *SMART THINKING* AND *SMART CHANGE*

"In this provocative critique of the American criminal justice system, Adam Benforado demonstrates beyond a reasonable doubt that unfair outcomes aren't tragic exceptions—they're the rule, and human psychology is to blame. Bringing together cutting-edge research with insights from real-life cases, Benforado shows us how our hidden biases undermine our guarantee of fairness and equality under the law, and offers much-needed solutions."

—PHILIP ZIMBARDO, AUTHOR OF *THE LUCIFER EFFECT*

"Insightful . . . one of the most important books written in a very long time."

—DOUGLAS A. BLACKMON, PULITZER PRIZE—WINNING AUTHOR OF *SLAVERY BY ANOTHER NAME*, HOST OF *AMERICAN FORUM*

"Benforado's book is simply chock-full of eye-opening research and practical suggestions for improvement. . . . Hopefully, [*Unfair*] will push us to take a step in [the right] direction."

—*GREATER GOOD*

"It's surprisingly easy to look back at high-profile criminal proceedings and see the flaws, while taking the overall system for granted. Adam Benforado looks across the whole canvas, elucidating through empirical data and scientific research how our own legal structures measure up—or, more accurately, don't—to our values of justice and fairness. Criminal law in the United States is far from perfect, and Benforado's thorough, thought-provoking examination is a welcome step in identifying and preventing institutionalized injustice."

—JONATHAN ZITTRAIN, GEORGE BEMIS PROFESSOR OF INTERNATIONAL LAW, HARVARD LAW SCHOOL

"In this fascinating book, Adam Benforado sheds new light from just about every angle on our criminal justice system. Practitioners, policy makers, and everyday citizens will learn much about a subject that demands greater public debate."

—TOM PERRIELLO, FORMER U.S. REPRESENTATIVE

"Unlike fields such as economics or philosophy, judicial theory and practice have largely ignored relevant findings about the human mind coming out of behavioral neuroscience and social psychology. This timely and important book can help us bring our criminal justice system into the twenty-first century."

—EDWARD SLINGERLAND, CO-DIRECTOR OF THE CENTRE FOR HUMAN EVOLUTION, COGNITION, AND CULTURE, AUTHOR OF *TRYING NOT TO TRY*

# UNfair

## THE NEW SCIENCE
## OF CRIMINAL INJUSTICE

## Adam Benforado

B\D\W\Y
BROADWAY BOOKS
NEW YORK

Originally published in hardcover in the United States by Crown,
an imprint of the Crown Publishing Group, a division of Penguin
Random House LLC, New York, in 2015.

Photograph on page 20 reprinted from "Believing Is Seeing: The
Effects of Racial Labels and Implicit Beliefs on Face Perception," by
J. L. Eberhardt, N. Dasgupta, and T. I. Banaszynski, 2003, *Personality and
Social Psychology Bulletin* 29: 360–70. Reprinted with permission.

Photograph on page 117 (left) by Stuart Franklin/Magnum Photos.

Library of Congress Cataloging-in-Publication Data
Benforado, Adam.
Unfair : the new science of criminal injustice / Adam Benforado.—First
edition.
    pages cm
1. Criminal justice, Administration of—Psychological aspects.
2. Discrimination in criminal justice administration—Psychological
aspects. 3. Criminal psychology. I. Title.
    HV7419.B46 2015
    364.3—dc23

                    2014041693

ISBN 978-0-7704-3778-7
eBook ISBN 978-0-7704-3777-0

PRINTED IN THE UNITED STATES OF AMERICA

Cover design by Christopher Brand

10 9 8 7 6 5 4 3

FIRST PAPERBACK EDITION

FOR BROOKE AND MIRA

# Contents

# Introduction

The water in the vat was untroubled and deep.

It had been prepared earlier for the brothers, Clement and Evrard. But they were still in the church, standing in front of the assembly, waiting like stalks for a breeze.

It was the winter of the year 1114. The days were getting shorter; the rain was coming to northern France. Clement and Evrard, who were peasants, lived in the small village of Bucy, a few miles east of Soissons.

The charge was heresy. That is why they now shifted barefoot before Bishop Lisiard, Abbot Guibert, and all the rest. But the brothers were not the type of heretics who openly defended their false faith—who, though poison-tongued and cancerous, wore their treachery on their faces. No, they were emissaries of the evil that "spreads secretly," the evil that was "condemned to everlasting whispers"—a snake slipping through cracks in the community wall, striking feeble and unwary minds. Into idle ears these heretics spewed their wickedness: Jesus' birth was not divine at all, marriage was a farce, baptisms of young children were void. And in the shadows, with their bodies, they breached the laws of God and man.

As Abbot Guibert recorded, they did not set apart their cemeteries as sacred ground, refused to eat food produced by "sexual generation," practiced homosexuality, and engaged in perverse rituals. Indeed, rumor had it that their religious meetings were held "in underground vaults or secret cobwebby places" where wild orgies took place and where any child conceived in the chaos was then made into bread and eaten "as a sacrament."

Such were the men brought before Bishop Lisiard to answer for their crimes.

The brothers had been betrayed by their neighbors: a woman Clement had purportedly been brainwashing for months, driving her mad, and a deacon who had heard Clement make statements against the Church.

But these accusers now failed to appear. And when questioned by the lord bishop and Abbot Guibert, the men "gave most Christian answers" and denied the charges against them, which presented a problem endemic to all systems of justice: a strong suspicion of guilt without solid evidence.

In twelfth-century France, however, there was a ready solution.

Following the celebration of Mass, the lord bishop and Archdeacon Pierre led Clement and Evrard to the vat. As they appeared before the water, the lord bishop spoke out the litany and delivered the exorcism. Tears rolled down his face. And Clement and Evrard, seemingly moved, gave an oath that they were not heretics and had never followed, nor taught, gospel contrary to the faith.

It was at this moment that Clement was thrown into the water.

This was not some ritual cleansing. This was the critical moment in the adjudicatory proceedings and the most important moment in Clement's life. This was the trial—"the ordeal of exorcised water"—and it all came down to buoyancy. Would Clement bob on the surface, or would he sink like a sack of stones?

As the ninth-century theologian Hincmar of Rheims explained, the man who "seeks to hide the truth by a lie, cannot be submerged in the waters above which the voice of the Lord God has thundered." Baptismal water was pure and would naturally reject the bodies of those who were infected by falsehood.

Murders, adulterers, and heretics would float; innocents would be enveloped.

An accused person like Clement would generally have been stripped of his clothes and bound with cords before being pushed into the pool. According to Hincmar, the reason was twofold: first, to prevent the guilty man from cheating justice by placing weights in his clothes or pulling himself under, and, second, to allow the innocent man to be quickly drawn up before he drowned. In some versions of the trial, the accused needed to sink to a certain distance—to the length of the hair on his head, for example—with a knot tied in the rope to assist with measuring.

In Clement's case, though, no knot was needed. All could see. He "floated like a stick."

To the men, women, and children who gathered at Soissons, this ordeal was no travesty: this was true, fair justice. Here were the most esteemed and respected members of society—cornerstones of the religious hierarchy—presiding over the ordeal as part of the official sacred Mass. And here was a neutral process that seemed to avoid the biases that came from other potential means of deciding cases. Witnesses could lie and judges could bow to political pressures, but God's judgment was true and incorruptible. In an era in which the divine permeated every aspect of life, the various hot and cold ordeals—fishing a ring out of a boiling cauldron, carrying an iron straight from the fire, or being plunged into a vat of water—would have seemed quite rational and quite fair.

To achieve the proper result, all-seeing God, who controlled the natural elements, would direct those elements to behave in an unusual manner: hot iron would fail to burn the innocent hand; cold water would prevent the guilty from sinking. So, if you *did* sink, that was an answer the community could accept. With no dominant governmental authority to manage the conflicts of the scattered small communities of Europe through much of the Middle Ages, the legitimacy of human action in matters of law was always contestable. But godly action was not.

Moreover, with an ordeal like Clement's, the righteousness of the judgment was available for all to see and immediately understandable to a largely illiterate society. For people seeking order—and consensus—in a disordered world, and justice in an unjust time, the ordeal would have seemed a blessing: not only acceptable but the best possible way to settle disputes and clear up mysteries. How else might a community assess concealed guilt when hard proof—concrete evidence, reliable witnesses—was lacking? There was no apparent alternative.

Today, with nine hundred years of perspective, it is easy to spot the flaws in the system. In ordeals of fire and water, the mechanism of deciding guilt was not grounded in fact. Innocent men and women could of course be burned by hot irons and boiling water. And what determined whether someone sank in a vat was largely a matter of the amount of air in the lungs and, more fundamentally, the percentage of body fat. Women and heavyset men were naturally—and unfairly—at a disadvantage.

Even if the process had been valid, the ordeals were not administered with any type of true consistency. When were the suspect's answers under questioning good enough that the trial could be avoided altogether? How long did the iron have to sit in the coals? How bad did the hand have to look when it was unwrapped to be deemed clear evidence of guilt?

And for those of us living in Western democracies today, the idea of religious leaders overseeing criminal proceedings seems fundamentally misguided—as does punishing the crime of heresy at all. What interest does society have in prosecuting those who decry the baptism of children "not yet of an age of understanding"?

Most glaringly, how strange to think you can look inside a

man's head and discover his blasphemous thoughts by tossing him into a pool of water! It verges on comedy. In a scene from *Monty Python and the Holy Grail*, a village mob drags a purported witch before Sir Bedevere the Wise, who explains the process of adjudication as follows: both witches and wood burn, both wood and ducks float; therefore, if the woman weighs the same as a duck, she is most definitely a witch. The joyous crowd rushes off to the nearest set of scales. We laugh because this is so plainly absurd. It is shockingly unjust. It is shockingly irrational.

But how will someone nine hundred years from now view our current system of justice?

The truth is that our descendants will be no less surprised by the routine and systematic unfairness we tolerate today than we are by our ancestors' trials by ordeal. They will look back at our judges and juries and see biases that are just as obvious as the ones we now perceive in the bishops and abbots who presided centuries ago. They will look back at our criminal code and see laws as wrongheaded and illegitimate as the prohibition on heresy. They will examine our processes and procedures—how strictly we followed them, how heartily we trumpeted them as bastions of integrity and accuracy—and laugh at our naïveté just as we laugh today at the mumbo-jumbo justice of Sir Bedevere the Wise. If there is a Monty Python of the thirtieth century, its members will write skits that look an awful lot like episodes of *Law & Order.*

We feel confident that we know our judicial system. We know why people commit crimes, how to identify the guilty, and what makes a good judge. And we know where we still have work to do. We acknowledge the rough edges, the lingering imperfections—the lying cops, racist jurors, lazy investigators, corrupt judges, biased witnesses, and self-aggrandizing lawyers—that threaten to unbalance our scales of justice.

Our intuitions are so ingrained that it's hard to imagine they might be wrong. But in fact the forces we believe decide cases and determine outcomes form, at best, a badly incomplete list of concerns. At worst, they are largely irrelevant. Even if we quashed all the familiar problems that can derail a case, even if our system operated exactly as it was designed to, we would still end up with wrongful convictions, biased proceedings, trampled rights, and unequal treatment. Injustice is built into our legal structures and influences outcomes every minute of every day. And its origins lie not inside the dark heart of a bigoted police officer or a scheming D.A. but within the mind of each and every one of us.

In this book I draw on new research from psychology and neuroscience to expose the hidden dynamics undermining our criminal justice system. What these insights reveal is surprising and counterintuitive, even deeply unsettling. Peering into the black box of the brain, scientists have discovered that we do not understand ourselves very well at all and are much less in control of our actions than we imagine. At the exact moments when we believe we are guided by reason and willpower, we are frequently propelled by automatic processes. Even as we feel that we are bending the environment to our ends, it is often the other way around, with seemingly insignificant elements in the world around us powerfully shaping our behavior.

Take our ability to accurately assess risk, which is at the heart of our legal system. We think we understand the factors that determine whether a cop draws his gun, where police departments and prosecutors allocate precious resources, how high a judge sets bail, and if legislators pass a tough new crime bill. We assume that the likelihood of an event and the seriousness of the consequences drive our appraisals, and that people with the same information will make the same risk calculations.

But a growing body of scientific evidence suggests that we are not the consistent, rational number crunchers that we suppose. In one study, researchers asked two sets of experienced forensic clinicians to determine whether a particular mental patient with a violent history, Mr. Jones, ought to be released. Both groups were provided with a "state-of-the-art assessment" by a respected psychologist. The only difference was whether the psychologist chose to express the risk Mr. Jones posed to the public as a probability ("Patients similar to Mr. Jones are estimated to have a 20 percent probability of committing an act of violence") or as a relative frequency ("Of every 100 patients similar to Mr. Jones, 20 are estimated to commit an act of violence"). One might assume—quite logically—that the choice is of no consequence: the information is exactly the same and easy to understand in both cases. Yet it had a huge effect on the experts. Those who considered the risk in terms of 20 dangerous perpetrators out of every 100 were *twice as likely* to keep Mr. Jones confined in the mental hospital as those who pondered the 20 percent chance that he would engage in violence upon release. When the researchers probed more deeply, they found that people had a pretty benign picture of Mr. Jones with his future dangerousness conveyed as a probability, but if it was expressed as a frequency, they immediately thought of "some guy going crazy and killing someone"—and that potent image made them see Mr. Jones as more of a risk.

The actual likelihood of the threat is often not what matters most. If we have strongly negative feelings about something— like an assault by a pedophile—we will treat it as a significant risk regardless of how likely it is to occur. A one-in-five-million chance and a one-in-five-thousand chance look exactly the same to us. And it's not just that we ignore probabilities; we can be insensitive to raw numbers as well. Indeed, sometimes when more people are in peril, we may actually care less. Mother Teresa was right: "If I look at the mass I will never act. If I look at the one, I will." Research suggests that you're significantly more likely to convince a lawmaker to support a new bill that will indefinitely detain certain sex offenders after they complete their sentences if you tell him about a specific child victim than if you explain that it will save a thousand statistical lives. It's no coincidence that major pieces of legislation—like Megan's Law and the Adam Walsh Act—have been motivated by the murder of a single child.

We assume that assessing risk is an activity largely devoid of emotion, but much of the time our assessments are guided by intuitive feelings rather than hard facts. Fear can play a particularly important role. And the problem is that we often fear things that are not in fact major threats while ignoring things that present a significant danger. We scour the online sex-offender registry, worried that our son will ride his bike by a predator's house on the way to the pool, but pay little heed to the danger of driving him instead. Yet the risk that your child will be kidnapped and killed by a sexual deviant is as low as the risk that he will be struck by lightning, while car accidents and drowning are among the leading causes of death for kids. The pedophile threat, though, taps into the very things that trigger fear: it seems uncontrollable, unfamiliar, and dramatic. So we invest heavily in registries and other harsh measures, despite research suggesting that such efforts have no significant impact on rates of reoffending and, in fact, threaten our core values of fair treatment.

The news media further distorts our perceptions because our threat-detection system tends to rely heavily on whatever is within easy reach. Incidents that are prominent in our memories end up taking on an outsize role. And how easily we can recall an event influences not only our sense of how frequently that event occurs but also our sense of how important it is. It makes a difference, then, that there is far more coverage of serial rapists and child kidnappings than of diabetes deaths. Likewise, the disproportionate number of stories on the local news about crimes committed by young African American men increases people's fear of black men and leads to an overvaluation of the threat they pose, which may in turn affect how police officers, prosecutors, judges, and jurors treat them.

At present, our legal system is largely oblivious to the existence and impact of these psychological processes, and many more. In the pages that follow, we will use real cases and events to explore the nature of the criminal mind, eyewitness memory, jury deliberations, police procedures, and intuitions about punishment. What could lead an otherwise upstanding attorney to conceal a critical piece of evidence from the other side? Why would a person under no physical duress confess to a crime she didn't commit? Can the presentation of mug shots alter a witness's memory of her attacker? Is it possible to predict the severity of someone's sentence based on his appearance? Will we soon be able to tell whether a criminal will offend again by looking at a scan of his brain?

As we uncover the secret world of detectives, judges, prisoners, and others, we will confront challenging questions. What if our legal rules and practices not only are blind to the real influences on human behavior but serve to actively perpetuate myths that neuroscientists and psychologists have revealed to be false? What if the structures and frameworks of criminal law that we have adopted to eliminate bias actually make matters worse? And if most people are unfamiliar with the complexities of our hidden minds, might there be powerful players out there taking advantage of this knowledge to stack the cards in their favor at the expense of the weakest?

I was drawn to these issues in the early days of law school, as I began to realize that the way we understand the thinking and behavior of our legal actors is incorrect—and, frequently, harmful. The more I read and thought about things, the more convinced I became that we need a new model, grounded in the science of the mind, for our legal system to be truly just. In the last decade I've dedicated my professional life to exposing the flaws and pointing the way forward.

The supporting evidence in this book includes research I've conducted with other legal scholars and psychologists as well as studies I cover in my law school courses and outside lectures. Although the science is powerful, we need to handle it with care. Among other things, we need to remember that the laboratory can be different from the real world, that correlation is not causation, and that not all findings are equally established and robust.

There is a danger when lawyers, judges, and policymakers start making changes to our legal system based on a flawed understanding of the relevant science or on unsubstantiated research.

But we also need to be conscious, right from the outset, of the immense cost of failing to consider potentially relevant scientific insights until they have reached the level of dogma. As we wait five or ten or fifty years for a finding to become incontrovertible, people's lives are being upended by legal rules, principles, and norms that often have *no scientific basis at all.*

Many academics and journalists voiced grave misgivings when Judge Luisa Lo Gatto of Como, Italy, reduced the sentence of Stefania Albertani from life in prison to twenty years, based, in part, on structural images of her brain showing that two areas, the anterior cingulate gyrus and the insula, contained less gray matter than those of the average healthy woman. Stefania had pled guilty to murdering her sister, burning the corpse, and later trying to kill her parents. Critics of the reduced sentence made compelling arguments that the neuroscience linking deficiencies in these parts of the brain to reduced inhibition and increased aggression was far from fully developed and that it was a real leap to use it to explain a particular individual's actions. Moreover, they noted, Stefania's brain had been compared with the brains of just ten other women.

These are legitimate concerns. Yet few who sounded the alarm thought to question the basis of Stefania's initial sentence.

It seems obvious that a person who chooses to force-feed her sister lethal quantities of psychotropic drugs before setting her on fire deserves severe punishment. But what research is there to demonstrate the underpinnings of that intuition—that "guilty minds," evil, free will, and so on actually exist? Our thoughts, beliefs, and actions are simply the product of roughly 100 billion neurons, each with its associated synapses, sending out and receiving neurotransmitters. If some of these electrochemical reactions don't occur in the normal way, because of, say, a tumor or a traumatic brain injury, a person may lack empathy, or hear voices, or have trouble remembering things. Be born with the wrong set of genes, which lead to the wrong set of electrochemical reactions, and your chances of committing a crime skyrocket. Where do notions of personal volition and blameworthiness fit in?

Skepticism is critical to building a better legal system, but some of the skepticism about the latest research seems to reflect fear of change and blind faith in the status quo as much as it reflects a careful weighing of the science. We must not be so cautious that we end up tacitly sanctioning a system that rests upon superstition and myth.

Our judicial system is flexible enough to respond to new developments in the mind sciences that reveal flaws in our laws and processes. There are solutions and remedies within our reach. Some of these solutions, like reconceptualizing which behaviors we punish, are grand and ambitious and must be the focus of long-term efforts. But many others, directed at police training, rules of procedure, courtroom design, and our legal code, can be implemented in the near future. Whether we choose to pursue them will have less to do with our natural limitations and much more to do with the robustness of our commitment to equal justice under the law.

Are we willing to look into the deep recesses of our brains as we seek to root out unfairness, even if it means learning things about ourselves that we wish were not true—and transforming practices that have been around for centuries?

Do we care that the path through our system is greased for some and tarred for others, owing to the cognitive biases of police officers, jurors, and judges? Does it matter if certain people are disadvantaged from the outset simply because of the structure of their brain or the shape of their face?

How troubled are we by the thought that, this very day, men and women are sitting on death row for crimes that they did not commit—one in every twenty-five, by the best estimate?

The development of DNA testing in the 1980s has given us a glimpse of the problems that beset our justice system. But it is as if we lit a single match in a vast, dark mansion. The dim light has allowed us to see that our criminal process can be horribly flawed—over three hundred people have been exonerated based on genetic mismatches since that time, more than 95 percent of them wrongly condemned as murderers and rapists. "The ghost of the innocent man convicted" is no "unreal dream," as the esteemed jurist Learned Hand once assured us.

Yet the magnitude of the crisis is many times larger. Still in the shadows are the vast majority of cases in which potentially exonerating DNA evidence wasn't available, no good lawyer could be found, or an erroneous conviction just wasn't worth fighting. Beyond the room in which we stand are the guilty who went free, the victims who were ignored, the prisoners suffering silently, the innocent men pushed up against walls and patted down. There are corridors of injustice we've never thought to inspect. And were we to finally descend to the pitch-black basement, we would find the weight of everything above us resting in sand—the key assumptions that our legal system makes about human nature, good and evil, honesty and dishonesty, without much real-world support at all.

There is no way to appreciate the grievous unfairness in our house of law or fashion a remedy until we understand the human psychology that is driving it. That is the goal of this book. It is time to turn on the lights.

# PART I

# Investigation

# 1

## THE LABELS WE LIVE BY

### The Victim

Jerry Pritchett had stepped out in the cold January night. It was Friday, a little past nine, and Jerry was wearing his slippers. He was just fetching something from his car. But he paused.

There, between the bare ginkgo trees, was a pale, gray-haired man flat on his back in the dim light of a street lamp. The sidewalk that lined the neat brick houses on the north side of Gramercy was empty, save for the body. As Jerry approached, it was clear that something was wrong, but the man couldn't speak. When Jerry asked him a question, he only groaned in reply. He wasn't carrying a wallet, but Jerry saw a wedding ring and a watch.

Jerry's wife, Claude, made the 911 call and then joined her husband. She noticed that the man seemed disconnected: his eyes wouldn't meet hers, and when she spoke he didn't seem to understand. He was trying to move himself into a sitting position, but because he was using only the left side of his body, his strength kept giving out, causing his head to pitch back against the concrete. Jerry placed one of his slippered feet under the man's skull.

Less than ten minutes after the emergency call, four D.C. firefighters pulled up to the house. Almost as soon as they started to attend to the man, he began to vomit.

Claude thought that the man had suffered a stroke, but the firefighters smelled booze. This wasn't a stroke or heart attack: as one of the firefighters remarked, "Nine out of ten times it's alcohol-related." The engine driver found a little blood on the man's head above the right ear, but there wasn't any noticeable swelling, and a little pressure applied with a gauze pad stopped the bleeding. They decided not to perform a complete assessment or record the man's heartbeat, breathing, or blood pressure.

When one of the responding police officers arrived on the scene and asked the firefighters what was wrong, they said that the man was "possibly intoxicated," that he "fell and hit his head." As a result, the cops kept to the periphery. According to protocol, they should have worked to secure the scene and begun a preliminary investigation to figure out whether a crime had occurred, but here it didn't seem necessary: this was just a drunk.

The ambulance carrying emergency medical technicians finally arrived, twenty-three minutes after it was dispatched. "What we got?" the crew leader asked, and one of the firefighters replied, "ETOH," which is short for ethyl alcohol, the alcohol in wine, vodka, and other spirits. She wasn't pleased: "We came all this way for an ETOH?"

The firefighters had noticed a few things that didn't quite add up—the constriction of the man's pupils, for instance—but they didn't pass that information along. And neither of the EMTs asked; the man's condition was as obvious as the foul stench of vomit on his coat. Consequently, they loaded him onto a stretcher without a backboard or neck collar. Given her advanced training, the crew leader was supposed to take charge of the patient, but she got in front to drive without examining the man.

As the assistant EMT did a neurological assessment in the back, he found that the man was barely conscious—scoring a 6 on the 15-point Glasgow Coma Scale, which called for a Priority 1 designation. The assistant, though, classified him as a Priority 3, meaning that he was stable. The man's inability to form words, his diminished eye and motor responses, just came down to intoxication—nothing to worry about. The assistant skipped the other cognitive tests and left the run sheet blank.

Although Fire and Emergency Medical Services policy requires transporting patients with altered mental status to the closest appropriate facility, the EMTs decided to take the man to Howard University Hospital. It was twice as far away as Sibley, but the crew leader needed to run some personal errands, and Howard was more convenient. The patient could sleep it off in the ambulance just as well as he could at the hospital.

When they arrived at Howard, the EMTs moved the man onto a gurney and told the triage nurse that he was drunk. He was pushed into the hallway and left there; fifteen minutes passed, then thirty, then an hour. The hospital staff didn't know about the low Glasgow Coma Scale score or any other details about the man, and they, too, took the diagnosis of intoxication at face value. As the triage nurse later explained, she assumed he'd been talking to the EMTs and was now sleeping, so she "just let him sleep."

No one at the hospital performed the required intake assessments, and when the triage nurse discovered that the man had an abnormally low temperature, she disregarded the information and moved on. After all, it was a cold night. She didn't check his pupils because that would wake him up, and sometimes when drunks woke up, they became belligerent and tried to leave the hospital. Shining a light in his eyes would just mean taxing an already short-staffed hospital. "I saw he was not in distress so I did not wake him," she later explained.

When she passed the man off to the charge nurse, the triage nurse said, "We have another ETOH." And when the team leader for the C and D corridors of the ER was told the same thing, she just "left it alone." He was not having respiratory problems, so he "was not a priority at that time." With no reason to rush, the doctor elected to wait for the man's vomit to be cleaned up before she examined him.

Then something happened that changed everything.

At around 11:30 p.m., another nurse came by to help the team leader sanitize the patient in hallway D. As they were moving the gurney, she noticed that the man's breathing was different: he now seemed to have a growling snore. That was sometimes a bad sign, so they gave him a sternum rub to check his responsiveness, and the patient "flipped his arms and legs inward." They repeated the rub, and he reacted the same way.

The nurses couldn't believe it: he was "posturing," a common indication of a head injury. But wasn't this an ETOH? No one had said anything about a head injury.

The doctor saw the posturing from the nurses' station, and they immediately moved the man to the resuscitation room and called the trauma team.

What had seemed, a moment earlier, to be a routine case of over-imbibing had suddenly become a life-or-death emergency. They intubated the man and now began to discover more cause for concern. His pupils were unequal and did not react normally to light; his breathing was shallow; and they found a small bump and some blood on the side of his head.

They had been looking at things all wrong. The symptoms he exhibited were caused by a neurological injury, not intoxication. And they had wasted hours.

The man was taken in for surgery at 5:50 a.m., more than eight hours after he was first evaluated by emergency medical personnel. It would be for naught.

David Rosenbaum, the award-winning *New York Times* journalist, died the next day of a brain injury when a blood clot caused his brain to swell. The sixty-three-year-old had retired a month earlier after nearly four decades at the paper's Washington bureau covering the Capitol's defining political battles. He had a wife, Virginia; two children, Dorothy and Daniel; and two granddaughters. He lived right around the block from Jerry and Claude Pritchett, on Harrison Street.

---

How had David injured his head?

The major breaks in the case came down to luck. The lead officer on the scene Friday night when David was put into the ambulance just happened to stay on after his regular shift and answer a radio call about a missing person. When he visited the home and looked at a photograph of the husband who hadn't returned from his evening stroll, it clicked: this was the same "man down" from earlier in the night on Gramercy Street.

However, it wasn't until well into Saturday, when credit-card companies called about several suspicious purchases on David's accounts, that the police realized the extent of their mistake. This was a possible robbery and assault, and they hadn't even secured the crime scene. The perpetrator or perpetrators had been given almost an entire day's head start.

But they caught a break. After seeing coverage of David's death on the news, Michael Hamlin, a twenty-three-year-old maintenance worker, walked into the Seventh District police station to tell his story. Hamlin later claimed that it was out of remorse—the incident was "bearing on his conscience"—though there was some evidence that he thought he might be able to talk his way out, or at least avoid deeper trouble.

According to Hamlin, he had picked up his cousin, Percy Jordan Jr., that night in his green Cadillac. He noticed the hard plastic pipe that Jordan, forty-two, had in his backpack and asked what it was for, to which Jordan shot back, "You know what it's for." As they drove, Jordan said, "Let's go get someone," adding that they should "go into some of the nice houses they got up there," by which he meant David Rosenbaum's northwest D.C. neighborhood. After they parked, they spotted a man with headphones walking down the street, and Jordan went to hide behind a tree right in front of the Pritchetts' house. When David passed by, Jordan grabbed him, hit him in the head and waist with the pipe, and said, "Give it up, old man." The force of the blows cracked two of David's ribs and fractured his skull. With David on the ground, Hamlin ran over and grabbed the wallet out of his back pocket.

It was a good score: around $270 in cash, which Jordan and Hamlin split, along with various credit and debit cards. Leaving the area, they used one of the cards to fill up the gas tank and purchase some snacks. They were back in the car, eating chips and sipping juice, before David was even discovered by the Pritchetts.

Lady Justice wears a blindfold. Visit the Supreme Federal Court of Brazil in Brasilia or the Shelby County Courthouse in Memphis, Tennessee, and you will see her: sword in one hand, balance in the other. As the great champion of liberty William Penn once explained, "Justice is justly represented blind, because she sees no difference in the parties concerned. She has but one scale and weight, for rich and poor, great and small." That is as true for victims as it is for suspects and defendants. The identity of the victim does not influence police work, prosecutions, or sentences. Every man or woman is the same in the eyes of the law.

At least, that's what we're told. When seventeen-year-old Trayvon Martin, an African American, was shot and killed by George Zimmerman, a neighborhood watch leader, in a gated community just outside Orlando, Florida, many around the country expressed outrage that Zimmerman had not been arrested immediately. It seemed to be a clear case of racial bias: when young black men are killed, no one cares. But the special prosecutor, Angela Corey, pushed back: "We only know one category as prosecutors, and that's a 'V.' It's not a 'B,' it's not a 'W,' it's not an 'H.' It's 'V,' for victim. That's who we work tirelessly for. And that's all we know, is justice for our victims." Ask any D.A., any police captain, any judge, and that's the official line.

But how accurate is this narrative of equal justice?

Consider the case at hand. It can be divided neatly into two distinct periods: the time when the victim was John and the time when he was David. When his nametag read JOHN DOE ETOH, firefighters, EMTs, nurses, and doctors neglected rules and procedures, ignored responsibilities, and went through the motions. The police, for their part, did not interview potential witnesses, try to identify the victim, canvass the neighborhood, collect any evidence, or question why an apparently intoxicated person had no wallet. The headphones that were found next to John's body in the grass were simply left at the scene. When the lead officer was asked whether he had filled out the mandatory incident report, he replied, "No, not for a drunk."

Once "the drunk" was identified as David Rosenbaum, however, things swung in the opposite direction. There were suddenly newspaper stories and official investigations of the emergency response. When the media and the police realized that the victim on Gramercy Street had been a reporter and editor at the most prestigious paper in the United States, when more than seven hundred people showed up at the memorial service—including Arlen Specter, Orrin Hatch, and Ted Kennedy—and when David Pryor, the former Arkansas senator, remarked that "the echo of [David's] footsteps and the pounding of his noble heart will be heard for generations to come," it became, quite simply, a different case.

Indeed, with David in the role of the victim, the D.C. government was prompted to consider sweeping changes to emergency and police procedures. And prosecutors, now under great pressure to serve up justice, convinced Hamlin to plead guilty to the lesser charge of second-degree murder, in exchange for testifying against Jordan. Hamlin was sentenced to twenty-six years; Jordan received sixty-five after a first-degree conviction.


If Lady Justice swung her sword for David, why did she sit idly by for John as he moaned for help? The problem is not, as the playwright David Mamet once glibly suggested, that justice is also deaf; it's that even as she genuinely believes in her blindness, her eyes are actually taking in quite a lot of information. And once she has a picture of you in her head, that picture has a profound impact on how she goes about her job.

Recent research in psychology sheds light on this process and helps explain the central mystery of David's case: how so many different professionals—police officers, firefighters, nurses, doctors, and EMTs—specifically charged with helping people and saving lives, made so many errors, from the second David was found lying on the ground to the moment he was transferred to the trauma team at the hospital. It isn't a story of a few weak links. In the words of the D.C. inspector general's sixty-nine-page report, prepared in the wake of the incident, there was "an unacceptable chain of failure." What propelled responders to forgo established protocols, overlook obvious concerns, cut corners, and disregard evidence? The answer lies in how we assess a victim in the wake of a crime. The common assumption is that we gather information through our senses and then, after careful evaluation, reason our way to a complete picture of the person. We use that picture where it is relevant (for example, in coming up with a profile of a serial killer) and put it aside when it is not (determining how much effort to dedicate to securing the crime scene).

In fact, we are not such cool and deliberate detectives; rather, we are masters at jumping to conclusions based on an extremely limited amount of evidence. The automatic processes in our brain (commonly referred to as System 1) quickly take in the scene and then reach a conclusion about the victim based on what is right in front of us, without considering what we might be missing. Ambiguity and doubt are pushed to the side.

In certain circumstances, our more deliberative and effortful mental processes (System 2) can override those initial impressions—and raise the specter of uncertainty—but often, they do not. The less we know, the easier it is for us to produce a coherent story, and it is the consistency of the narrative that predicts how much confidence we will have in our assessment. The unfortunate result is that we may become overconfident precisely when we have limited or weak evidence.

Consider the following two sentences:

> When an elderly woman gets on the train, Carl immediately gives up his seat.
> When an elderly woman gets on the train, Alex remains in his seat, reading his book.

Which man is likely to come to the aid of a passenger having a heart attack? Easy, right? It is obviously Carl.

But now look back at the sentences. They tell us almost nothing that would help us accurately forecast each man's future actions. Carl might not have seen the woman at all; he might have given up his seat after suddenly realizing it was his stop, or to move away from a crying child. And Alex might have remained seated because there were many open seats on the train, or because someone else offered the woman a seat and she refused, or because his back was turned. We took a few bits of information and then quickly filled in what was missing, so that we had a coherent story that allowed us to divine the men's characters and predict how they would behave. We do this hundreds of times a day.

Before you finished reading about the events on Gramercy Street, your mind, too, was busy filling in the details, elaborating scenes and conversations, sizing up the characters, and solving the case. We all fancy ourselves expert sleuths, and we have the credentials to back it up: six Grisham novels, dozens of episodes of *CSI*, hundreds of news stories on murders and rapes. But just like the professionals responding to a 911 call, we often come to conclusions about the victim's identity and the nature of the crime based on the limited—and largely irrelevant—information directly in front of us.

Ask people to evaluate the academic aptitude of an elementary school student after playing them two video clips—one of her outside of school and the other of her taking an oral test—and the responses will shift based on the scenery in the first clip. When the student is shown in an urban, low-income setting, individuals view her inconsistent performance—getting some hard questions right and some easy questions wrong—and rate her ability as below grade level. When the *exact* same student is shown in a suburban, middle-class setting, they rate her ability as above grade level. Same girl, same performance, different conclusions. We hand out IQ points based on the size of her house and the number of trees in her neighborhood.

We can see the influence of the immediate situational context on how people assessed David. Finding him lying on the sidewalk in her upscale neighborhood, Claude Pritchett described him as "dressed nicely and not unkempt." Yet, three hours later, the Emergency Department physician described David, now slumped in a hospital hallway, as "very disheveled, unkempt, his hygiene wasn't the best. He looked dirty. He looked like our typical alcoholic."

This also helps explain why the police officers didn't give much thought to the possibility that the incoherent man lying on the sidewalk might have been the victim of a serious crime. The patrol service area that includes the 3800 block of Gramercy, with its generously spaced homes and landscaped yards, is one of the very safest in D.C. and had not recorded a single homicide the previous year. Although there were more than four thousand robberies in the forty-five patrol service areas in D.C. each month, David's neighborhood averaged only two.

In the mad dash to understand the scene in front of us and decide how to react, a victim's clothing, haircut, skin color, glasses, and perfume can all serve as signposts. In David's case, one of the most significant cues was the vomit on his jacket. When interviewed after the fact, almost every person—from the Pritchetts, to the firefighters, cops, and EMTs, to the hospital staff—brought it up. And it seems to have had an immediate impact on people's evaluations of him by triggering one of our most powerful emotions: disgust.

Disgust guides our lives to a surprising degree, altering our steps as we navigate the sidewalk (don't step in that!) and steering us to certain seats on the subway. While different people experience disgust differently (interestingly, those with more conservative moral beliefs tend to be more sensitive), it's a universal emotion. Disgust a Kazakh, Peruvian, Vietnamese, or your neighbor down the street, and chances are you'll see the same telltale facial expressions: wrinkled nose, raised lips, open mouth. Disgust responses appear in kids at about the same age across cultures. In experiments, a two-year-old will generally eat what appears to be dog poop (actually a mixture of peanut butter and strong cheese), but a four-year-old will not.

If your stomach turned as you read about feasting on feces, you are not alone—the mere *thought* of something disgusting can produce the effect. And, in fact, disgust can be directed at a whole bunch of things beyond the physical world of maggot piles, pus-filled sores, and rancid hot dogs. We cringe at the thought of having sex with a pig, a child being beaten, or cannibalism at the Jamestown settlement some four hundred years ago.

Many scientists believe that disgust evolved to help our ancestors avoid parasites and microbes that were transferred through physical contact, primarily with food. But it also proved useful for navigating our social worlds, telling us which people and actions were appropriate and which to avoid. As a result, today we see evidence of both "core" disgust (triggered by rotting meat, rat droppings, and the like) and disgust aimed at social offenses (a wealthy man stealing from a church collection plate) in almost all cultures. Both help us stay "uncorrupted" or "pure." But because the same areas of the brain may be recruited for both responses, sometimes things get mixed up: what starts as core disgust can result in feelings of moral disgust and vice versa. The implications for how we assess other people are jaw-dropping.

Imagine walking into a psychology laboratory to fill out a survey judging the appropriateness of various actions, like a friend lying on a job application, consensual sex between first cousins, or survivors of a plane crash killing and eating a mortally wounded fellow passenger. The desk you are asked to work at is sticky, and there is a plastic cup that appears to contain the remnants of a smoothie and a chewed pencil. Dirty tissues and greasy pizza boxes spill out of the overflowing trash can. If you are like most people, you would probably be a little annoyed and think that the university sponsoring the research should fire its cleaning crew. But surely the mess wouldn't affect your answers on the survey— our sense of right and wrong, we assume, is fixed.

Yet when scientists conducted an experiment along these lines, they found that the filthiness of a room (or, in another version, the smell of fart spray) made people's moral judgments significantly more severe. Disgust at the lab conditions generated disgust at the starving plane-crash victims.

Turning back to David's case, we begin to see how this tendency might have come into play. The disgust that people felt upon smelling and seeing the vomit on his body may have caused them to keep their distance (remember the responding police officers who decided not to get involved, and the doctor who refused to work on David until he had been cleaned up). Assessing David's injuries required close inspection, as did catching the clues that suggested a crime had been committed. No one who kept him at arm's length was in a position to reach the conclusions that might have saved his life and quickly brought his attackers to justice.

Just as critically, the vomit may also have led the firefighters, EMTs, police officers, nurses, and doctors to engage in *moral* distancing. The physical disgust they felt may have generated an explanation for David's condition that involved lack of discipline and poor character—drunkenness—rather than another potential cause: a stroke, seizure, diabetes, head injury, or drug interaction. And once the ETOH label was attached, David was in trouble.

The labels we give victims can make a big difference in how their cases are handled. Is this a poor person or a rich person, a black man or a white woman, a retiree or an infant? It matters every step of the way, from the dispatch call up through the trial.

Suppose David had not been the only one lying on the sidewalk when the emergency responders first arrived. Imagine that there was a ten-year-old girl next to him and that both she and David were in such critical condition that only one could be saved. If you were one of the firefighters, would you just flip a coin? Or would you choose to help one victim over the other?

Despite what we say about giving equal respect to all victims, most of us would save the girl. A ten-year-old is at the peak of her perceived value, and participants in experiments involving tragic tradeoffs tend to choose saving her over both older individuals (like sixty-three-year-old David) and babies. Privileging the young seems to be grounded in an understanding that old people have had a chance to live a fuller life and that young people have more years left to contribute to the world. But clearly there is a limit: infants and toddlers have not had as much invested in them as their preteen counterparts, and their social relationships are not as significant, so people don't perceive their deaths to be as costly.

The greater value we place on young people's lives carries through to another context: we are also more motivated to seek justice on their behalf when they are killed. When an older man is murdered, research suggests that police officers will be less driven to track down his killer—even in situations where the murderer did not choose his particular victim and put everyone at risk, as with a remotely detonated bomb.

In David's case, though, his age may have been far less damaging than another label patted down on his chest as he was transferred from the firefighters to the EMTs to the hospital staff:

alcoholic. In most people's minds, being addicted to drugs or alcohol is not like having an aneurysm or being hit in the head with a pipe by a stranger. It seems "chosen," and that makes it much harder for us to want to help substance abusers. When researchers had people assess a fictitious person infected with AIDS, participants were significantly more sympathetic to the man when they were informed that he'd contracted the disease through a blood transfusion than when they were told that he'd gotten the virus as a result of shooting up.

Compounding the issue is that once David was labeled an alcoholic, it was more likely that he would be seen as morally disgusting, even by those who didn't notice the vomit. This is often the case with "outgroup members": in different times and places, women have been treated as unclean, Jews likened to cockroaches, Gypsies characterized as disease-ridden, and gay men and lesbians reviled as the scum of the earth. Such associations can be particularly damaging because moral disgust is linked to dehumanization.

In one demonstration, people reported strong reactions of disgust after looking at images of homeless people and addicts, which aligned with observed brain activity in the insula and amygdala. More interesting, though, was what wasn't activated: the medial prefrontal cortex, which is involved in the assessment of people and social interactions. It lit up when participants looked at photos of Olympic athletes, middle-class Americans, and disabled people. But for those viewed as neither warm nor competent because of their perceived moral failings, there was comparatively little brain activity, akin to the pattern seen when people looked at an overflowing toilet or vomit. Passing a homeless drunk, we do not see a human being with a mind, feelings, needs, and ideas; we see him as if he were a mound of rags and trash, and that influences how we treat him. A pile of garbage can be left in the hallway for hours; it doesn't merit a police investigation; it doesn't need to be handled gently as it is lifted from the sidewalk. The dehumanization is all the easier when the victim lacks a name and cannot communicate, aside from the occasional moan.

Beyond affecting how we treat a victim, the identity we assign also influences how we answer the question "What happened?" In one classic experiment, researchers discovered that they could alter the way people judged the culpability of a rape victim simply by changing how she was identified. Given that our law eschews such distinctions, that was a surprising finding, but the truly astonishing part of the study was in how the identity mattered. When the scientists described the victim as "a virgin" or "a married woman," she was viewed as *more* responsible for her rape than when she was described as "a divorcée." Take a moment to ponder that: the victims seen as most socially respectable were assigned more blame for the sexual assault they experienced than the victim viewed as least respectable.

To unlock the mystery, we need to understand our true motivations, in particular our drive to see the world as a fair place where people receive their just deserts. When confronted with an example of a seemingly "good" person, like a virgin, suffering a terrible outcome, we experience a strong dissonance. And we eliminate that discomfort—and maintain our perception of justice—by finding fault with the victim. We trick ourselves into thinking that she must not be that innocent after all. She must have done something that contributed to this bad event.

A former co-worker of my wife's was recently shot in the neck as he walked home from watching *Monday Night Football* at a bar a couple of miles from where we live in Philadelphia. It was horrible, shocking news, and my immediate reaction was to find some way to explain it away by identifying a flaw in his behavior that night. He shouldn't have walked home so late—that was courting trouble. He must have resisted giving the robber his money; why else would the guy shoot him? I couldn't face up to the truth: that there are dangerous people looking for victims at all hours of the day who will pull the trigger before you even have a chance to reach for your wallet.

What is surprising about this tendency is how robust it is: I think about these things for a living and I still didn't realize what I was doing until my wife pointed it out. Indeed, the power of the dynamic can lead us to blame even the most innocent of victims: children. When charges of child sex abuse were made public against the former defensive coordinator for Penn State football, Jerry Sandusky, one might have expected a uniform outpouring of sympathy for the victims, but that's not what happened. Penn State students rioted after the firing of Joe Paterno, the head coach, who had failed to stop the abuse after being told directly about an incident in which Sandusky was caught raping a ten-year-old in the locker-room showers. Another victim, who courageously came forward to recount assaults by Sandusky that started when he was just eleven or twelve—and is credited with initiating the investigation that eventually led to Sandusky's imprisonment—was so bullied in the aftermath that he had to leave his high school.

We may see child abuse as worse than abuse of an adult—or the rape of a virgin as worse than the rape of a divorcée—but the greater harm means that harshly punishing the perpetrator isn't sufficient to restore a "just world." To do that, we may need to cast the victim as partially responsible.

Clearly our labels can change when we are strongly motivated to revise them, as when a person initially categorized as innocent or good suffers a terrible crime. Why, then, do most labels prove so difficult to peel off?

Research suggests that once we have summed someone up, we search for data confirming that identity and disregard or minimize evidence conflicting with it. Of course, it doesn't feel that way. It feels as though we are just dispassionately sorting through the details. But really our minds are bending the facts, sawing off inconvenient corners, and tossing away contradictory information so that everything can be fit into our ready-made boxes.

Say you learn that a friend's roommate is a waitress. Without any conscious effort, that label will prompt you to remember things about her appearance, behavior, and lifestyle that are consistent with her occupation—and distinct from what you'll remember if you're told she's a librarian. And if you know she's having a phone interview in the next room, the words and phrases you'll pick out through the wall are completely different from the ones you'll pick out if you think she's speaking with her lawyer. In an experiment along these lines, those listening to a degraded audio recording of what they believed to be a criminal suspect were significantly more likely to hear the statement "I got scared when I saw what *it'd* done to him" as "I got scared when I saw what *I'd* done to him" than when they thought they were listening to a job candidate.

Labels have an amazing way of reinforcing themselves even when that seems impossible. In a great demonstration, two groups of students were asked to draw a young man's face *while looking at his photograph*, but one group was told he was black and the other was told that he was white. What is incredible is that the label influenced certain people's depictions: those who believed that traits like race are immutable and useful in predicting behavior drew portraits that distorted features to align with the racial category they had been given (see page 20).

The consequences of this drive for coherence and confirmation can be disastrous. Medical research suggests, for example, that one of the major causes of physician error arises from the fact that doctors come to a conclusion very early in their assessment of a patient and then stick with their judgment even as they encounter contradictory evidence. Unfortunately, the impact on our criminal justice system is no less severe. "Tunnel vision" is an endemic

Ambiguous Target Face

"Black" drawing

"White" drawing

problem in the investigative world, corrupting even seemingly objective judgments like fingerprint analysis.

In fact, DNA testing—the shining jewel of the forensic world—appears to be susceptible to confirmation bias. It's hard to believe: in television dramas filled with hunches and subjective judgments, the matching of DNA is portrayed as the cut-and-dried part of the case. You've got a feeling a suspect is lying to you; you enter his DNA into the FBI's Combined DNA Index System (CODIS), which has DNA profiles for some twelve million convicts and suspects and about half a million crime scenes; and after a short commercial break, you know for sure.

But the reality is more complicated. In one recent study, researchers gave experts a DNA sample, telling them that it was part of a gang-rape case in which one of the perpetrators had accepted a plea deal and was testifying against the others. They needed to confirm that one of the suspects who denied any involvement had, in fact, taken part in the rape. As expected, the experts found that his DNA matched the sample, corroborating the witness's account and the prosecution's case. However, the researchers then took the same biological evidence and gave it to seventeen other DNA analysts without providing any backstory. What happened? Only one of the seventeen experts agreed with the original group that the DNA was a match. Nucleotides do not rearrange themselves to fit the prosecutor's frame, but that doesn't mean there is no room for bias. Someone has to interpret the results. And the first set of analysts couldn't help but be swayed by the information they had already been given.

Confirmation bias likely played a central role in the case of David Rosenbaum. Once David was labeled a drunk, the responders and medical professionals appeared to focus on finding evidence that supported that description. Interestingly, the first people to encounter David, the Pritchetts, did not smell alcohol on David's person. Why not? Well, perhaps because they weren't looking for it, since their theory was that the man on the sidewalk had suffered a stroke. For those assuming that this was an ETOH, though, the odor was very noticeable. As one of the firefighters recounted, "I could smell the alcohol reeking from him, like it was coming out of his pores."

This, in turn, reinforced the notion that the cause of the man's condition was intoxication, when in fact the smell of alcohol is not very diagnostic at all. According to the U.S. Department of Health and Human Services, well over half of adults in the District of Columbia count themselves as active drinkers. After dinner on a Friday night, there are thousands of people in the city who, like David, have consumed some alcohol in the previous four or five hours. You could sit in the emergency room at Howard during the night shift and find scores of patients—victims of heart attacks, gunshot wounds, allergic reactions, pneumonia—with the faint odor of booze on their breath.

But the problem wasn't just that the responders engaged in a biased search for clues; it's that they evaluated the evidence they did uncover in a selective fashion—treating facts that supported their existing understanding of the case as highly persuasive, while dismissing those that did not. For example, one of the firefighters reported that he immediately ruled out the possibility that he was dealing with a diabetic because he looked for a medical identification bracelet, which he often does "when people can't talk," and didn't find one. The lack of a bracelet seemed to reinforce the intoxication explanation, but it doesn't actually preclude a diabetic reaction at all: the victim might not own a bracelet, might have taken it off, or might not yet have been diagnosed.

Likewise, the Pritchetts and the initial cadre of cops, firemen, and EMTs all noticed that David was wearing an expensive watch and wedding band. According to Commander Robert Contee of the Second Police District, it followed that "there was no reason to think it was a robbery." But, of course, that's incorrect. The robbers could have taken his wallet and either been scared off at that point or not noticed his ring and watch.

Indeed, if responders had gone in with the assumption that they were dealing with a crime, they most likely would have uncovered powerful evidence within minutes of arriving, like a witness down the street who'd seen David's attackers just minutes earlier and noted that they looked suspicious (going so far as to write down the first digits of their license plate number). With a different starting frame, they might have noticed that the back pocket of David's pants was torn—a potential sign that his wallet had been ripped out during a robbery. As it was, the first person to spot the tear was a nurse at Howard cleaning David up. And she wasn't in a position to make the connection because she didn't know the circumstances in which David had been discovered.

A big part of why labels stick to victims is that, in many cases, we aren't even aware that we are operating with a label or that it might be wrong. We never revisit our initial assumptions to test whether they still hold (if they ever did). Numerous people who saw David accepted the label of drunk without questioning the frame. And they did so in the face of strong counterindications. If the man was a drunk, where was the booze, and how had he gotten so intoxicated without a wallet or any money? How had he come to rest on the sidewalk in a wealthy residential neighborhood when he wasn't able to lift himself off the ground on his own? There was actually plenty of evidence suggesting that this was a much more serious condition than ETOH: the man's inability to speak, his failure to respond to oxygen, his vomiting, his extremely poor motor control, his pinpoint pupils, his elevated pulse, his bleeding head, and his inability to use the right side of his body, among other things. But each one was ignored or minimized because the established narrative didn't accommodate it.

The failure to appreciate counterevidence was almost certainly exacerbated by the fact that the responders did not make independent assessments of David. If they had each come across him separately and attempted to determine the cause of his condition, they might well have reached different conclusions, and that could have led them to discover the head injury much more quickly. The lack of independent assessment is puzzling because police departments, with all their experience conducting eyewitness interviews, are well aware that when one person, for whatever reason, makes public his observations and conclusions very early on in the process, others feel pressured to conform. This is why when, say, six people witness a bank robbery, detectives usually elicit statements and conduct lineups with each one individually.

In the end, it's hard not to ask the "what if" questions in David's case. What if the criminals had used a knife instead of a pipe? What if David had been carrying his ID? What if his wife had gone looking for him and had been there when the ambulance arrived, or met the hospital staff at Howard? What if the

Pritchetts had driven David to the hospital and then conveyed their observations directly to the triage nurse?

All of these things might have radically altered the course of events the night David was attacked, but they didn't happen—and it doesn't just come down to bad luck. The errors were predictable and preventable. That fact makes David Rosenbaum's death especially tragic, but it also offers a glimmer of hope—one that David's family seized upon. They decided to offer the District of Columbia a deal: they would drop their lawsuit against the city if it created a task force to reform the Department of Fire and Emergency Medical Services to help prevent similar tragedies in the future. A number of these reforms, like ensuring that both EMTs and firefighters are fully prepared to carry out medical protocols and that they are held accountable for their performance, can help future responders avoid the critical mistakes that were made in David's case. But we need to go further to get at the root of the problem: preventing damaging labels from taking hold in the first place.

When we know that extraneous elements can lead to harmful labels, we should consider intervening to counteract them. Controlling the influence of disgust, for example, may be as simple as providing first responders with menthol salve to put under their noses to neutralize the smell of vomit, feces, or a dead body. We also need to take action when we know that victims with particular personal characteristics—the elderly, minorities, homeless people, addicts—tend to be devalued and receive substandard treatment. We could start by introducing more empathy training designed to get police officers, EMTs, and ER nurses to see members of these groups—who are overrepresented in 911 calls—as human beings worthy of compassion and careful treatment.

Perhaps most important, responders should conduct their own blind assessments of victims—whether that involves giving a cognitive evaluation, searching the crime scene, or conducting a forensic test. Data ("His eyes are not dilating properly, and his pulse is abnormal") should be shared; labels ("He's a drunk") should not.

Treating someone based on a label—such as ETOH—should always be a last resort. When we act upon a single label, we almost always lose vital nuance. With the power failing and the floodwaters rising as Hurricane Katrina made landfall, the medical chairman at Memorial Medical Center in New Orleans had to make an evacuation plan. He used a shortcut to help sort the patients: those who possessed do-not-resuscitate orders would be given lowest priority in leaving the hospital. In that panicked moment, the choice seemed justifiable—as he explained later, these folks seemed to have the "least to lose"—but, in retrospect, using that label as a sorting mechanism was a grave mistake. It did not help doctors distinguish between those who were going to die anyway and those who could be saved; nor did it divide those willing to die from those holding hard to life. A DNR simply informs medical professionals not to engage in CPR if the person stops breathing or her heart ceases beating; the order is not meant to affect the delivery of other medical care. Moreover, a person may choose to have a DNR whether or not she is seriously ill. Using the label, however, gave the chairman the illusion of objectivity.

The patients abandoned on the seventh floor were never just one label. They carried an almost infinite array of tags—recovering, terminal, insured, elderly, forty-something, mother, son, fat, handsome, combative, kind. A few of these were written on their charts, or read from their faces, coughs, and trembling hands. But most were invisible.

No one deserves to be summed up in a word. And no one should die because of an acronym.

# 2

# DANGEROUS CONFESSIONS

## The Detective

The back door of the apartment had been bashed open with a blue mop. Someone had washed bloody hands in the sink. And if you walked right up to the front staircase and bent down, you could see where those same hands had brushed the wall near the banister—streaks of red fresh against the white.

Dawn Engelbrecht knew that something was wrong as soon as she saw her five-year-old boy walk into the bar where she worked. Holly Staker was supposed to be watching him and his younger sister, but there he was, little Blake, standing in front of her. A neighbor had noticed him playing outside in the dark and had brought him by.

No one picked up when she called the house, but she got through to Holly's mother, and the two of them met at 442 Hickory Street.

The house is on the north side of Waukegan, Illinois, a classic brick two-flat set close to the neighboring houses. Most people would call it a nice street, though it has known better times. The houses have steps cut across the wide green verge between the street and the sidewalk. But 442 is different from the others: the footpath follows the left side of the house around to the back. You have to jog right if you want the front door.

It was locked, as Dawn had left it. But when she finally turned the key of the second-floor apartment, she found the television on. A single white tennis shoe lay on the floor. A chair in the dining room was turned over.

They called for Holly, but there was no answer. Taylor, the two-year-old, was fine, though—safe and sound, lying on her brother's bed. Maybe Holly had just gotten bored and left?

It was not until the police arrived that Dawn thought to look behind the bedroom door.

Eleven-year-old Holly was curled in the fetal position, her hands up by her face, her black stretch pants cast aside, the missing white shoe tangled in one of the stirrups. She had been stabbed twenty-seven times and raped.

A year later, twelve jurors fixed their gaze on Juan Rivera, the man accused of the crime. Juan—a petty criminal, barely twenty—sat motionless. They had heard the evidence, the alibis, the reports, listened as each witness and expert gave his or her account. They had seen the pictures of the bedroom and of Holly's face, and it was time to decide.

Guilty.

And so it went at the second trial as well, ordered by the Appellate Court of Illinois after Juan's initial conviction was overturned. Different jury, same result.

For a man like Juan, sentenced twice to life in prison without the possibility of parole, to get a third chance before a jury is as rare as a snowflake in June. But his lawyers found a way: DNA evidence.

It had always been there, those twelve years Juan sat in prison. A vaginal swab had been collected at Holly's autopsy. But after being labeled, it sat in an evidence locker until 2005, when it was finally tested.

The results of the analysis were startling. The semen in the sample belonged to a single man, and that man was not Juan Rivera.

Proof. Vindication. After so long in the dark, it felt as if someone had lit a lantern inside his body. He would walk out of that prison. He would be reborn. There was life to live.

It took four more years to reach that third trial, but the moment finally came—the opportunity for science to redeem the failures of the past and save this condemned man. With the lab test offering exoneration and with no physical evidence linking Juan to the crime, the outcome seemed like a foregone conclusion.

But something curious happened once proceedings got under way. The prosecution didn't back away; it doubled down, advancing two explanations for the autopsy evidence: either the DNA sample had been contaminated or Holly had had sex with someone else before she was raped and killed by Juan.

The problem for the prosecution was that there was nothing to suggest that the swab had been compromised, and the experts were in agreement that the semen had been deposited shortly before the victim was killed. Semen tends to drain into underwear, but no sperm was found on Holly's clothes. That meant that the prosecution had to convince the jury that an eleven-year-old girl had sex with a mystery man directly before being violently attacked by Juan Rivera, who managed to leave the mystery man's semen completely intact in the girl's body and to provide no trace of ever having touched her himself, let alone of having been inside the apartment where she was found. The account seemed implausible, to say the least.

Once more, twelve jurors retired to the deliberation room to ponder the tragedy at 442 Hickory Street. When they returned, they were met with the gaze of Holly's twin sister, Heather, and Juan's brother, Miguel. Juan, on the threshold of exoneration, was silent and ready.

Guilty.

It was a verdict that Juan's lawyers described as "unfathomable," but it had happened. Again.

The defense had provided many facts to raise a reasonable doubt in the eyes of the jury. It wasn't just that none of the copious forensic evidence at the crime scene—blood, fingerprints, hair, and semen—matched Juan. There were also phone records and data from an electronic leg monitor Juan was wearing (a condition of bail for an earlier charge of stealing a car stereo) corroborating his parents' claim that he had been home the night of the murder, talking to his mother in Puerto Rico. Yet, despite Juan's alibi and the lack of either eyewitness testimony or physical proof, the prosecution got the conviction it sought because of evidence so damning that it made everything else in the trial seem superfluous: a signed three-page confession.

As Holly's sister later put it, "Why would you confess? If I'm getting charged with murder, I am not going to fess to something I did not do and then explain the whole night and how I did it and why I did it and everything like that if I didn't do it." Innocent people just don't confess. Indeed, the esteemed father of evidence law, John Henry Wigmore, once declared that false confessions were "scarcely conceivable." The potency of this assumption overpowers doubt, even when there is exonerating evidence or indications of police coercion.

We expect people to be consistent; we assume that someone who has signed a confession believes what it says. In a famous study documenting this phenomenon, researchers asked people to evaluate essays written about Fidel Castro. Despite being told that the authors of the essays had been assigned their respective positions, for or against, participants disproportionately believed that the writers of the pro-Castro essays actually held pro-Castro views. They placed too much faith in outward conduct as a window on inner belief and underestimated the power of the situation to shape behavior. The expectation was that—assignment or no assignment—a person's views on Castro would remain constant: *semper fidelis.*

Another reason we find it hard to accept that some confessions are false is that we assume that our system has eliminated the cruel tactics that once led people to admit to crimes they didn't commit. There is a long history of harsh coercion directed at suspects. As Supreme Court Justice Hugo Black wrote in 1940, "The rack, the thumbscrew, the wheel, solitary confinement, protracted questioning and cross questioning . . . left their wake of mutilated bodies and shattered minds along the way to the cross, the guillotine, the stake and the hangman's noose." Indeed, before the 1930s, it was common to get suspects to confess by subjecting them to what was known as the "third degree"—including significant physical pain. But that has been abandoned in the back room of history.

Juan Rivera, though, did falsely confess—and he is not alone. False confessions and incriminating statements are the leading contributors to wrongful homicide convictions, present in over 60 percent of the known DNA murder-exoneration cases in the United States. More broadly, they appear to have been a factor in about 25 percent of all post-conviction exonerations.

These cases tend to confound our expectations: physical coercion is rare, the confessions are often rich in detail, and multiple innocent suspects may confess to acting together. Indeed, in one of the most famous examples—the so-called Central Park Jogger case—five teenagers all admitted to participating in the brutal rape of a woman only to be exonerated by later DNA analysis. While some who falsely confess do come to believe that they committed the crime, most are completely aware that they are innocent. And researchers are beginning to understand how this baffling behavior can come about.

Front and center is the common approach to questioning suspects. The generally accepted gold standard, the Reid Technique of Interviewing and Interrogation, which has been used to train more than half of the police officers in the United States, not only fails to guard against false confessions but actually appears to encourage them.

Using the Reid approach, when someone like Juan is brought in for questioning, detectives determine whether he is telling the truth through a nonconfrontational interview, and then, if he appears to be lying and his guilt is "reasonably certain," they proceed to an aggressive interrogation designed to extract a confession. Unfortunately, as we will explore in detail later, police officers are no better than the rest of us at detecting deceit. And far from correcting officers' erroneous intuitions about lying, the Reid technique relies heavily on unreliable gut instincts and dubious cues to deception.

This means that a significant number of the people who end up being subjected to the harsh interrogation phase of questioning under the Reid approach are actually innocent. Indeed, it is innocent people who are more likely to waive their rights to remain silent and to have a lawyer present in the first place. They tend to assume—as we all do—that what they themselves know to be true will also be readily evident to outsiders. Since they didn't commit the crime in question, there is little risk of talking to the police in an open way; if anything, clamming up or requesting an attorney would imply guilt. But, in reality, once the interrogation phase is under way, innocence is off the table: investigators are advised to repeatedly accuse the suspect of having committed the crime and prevent the suspect from offering denials or alternative explanations. All efforts are directed toward gaining the coveted confession. To this end, the Reid manual heartily embraces lying about the evidence in the government's possession. If you want to get a hardened criminal to admit to a crime, you can't just play nice.

As a result, the environment is one of maximum psychological coercion: the suspect is completely isolated in a windowless room and may be harangued and berated for hours on end. Many who falsely confess later say that they admitted to committing the crime simply to escape the abuse. And experimental evidence suggests that people often downplay the potential long-term consequences of confessing to illegal activities when an admission appears to provide relief from short-term discomfort. When we have an opportunity to end the stress, fatigue, and fear we are feeling in the moment, we find it hard to appreciate the ruinous repercussions that may result from admitting to something that we did not do.

Police interrogations take full advantage of our cognitive myopia. According to the nine steps of the Reid technique, the investigator is meant to hammer on the suspect's unquestionable guilt and emphasize the futility of denials in light of the damning evidence, while at the same time offering sympathy and potential justifications that encourage the person to see confessing as more acceptable. The officer might suggest that the crime wasn't a big deal ("You know, the victim kind of had it coming, if you ask me; I'd probably have done the same thing as you in that situation") or offer a potential narrative that lessens the moral role of the offender ("You weren't planning to kill him, I bet, you just needed some money, and it was only when he suddenly started to attack you that the gun went off").

Empirical evidence suggests that both of these approaches— commonly referred to as minimization and maximization—can contribute to false confessions. And the effects are not small: in one study, when minimization was used with students accused of cheating ("I'm sure you didn't realize what a big deal it was"), the rate of false confessions tripled. When the interrogator added a subtle suggestion of leniency in exchange for confessing ("Things could probably be settled pretty quickly [with a signed confession]"), the rate increased sevenfold.

Despite these serious concerns, judges have been reluctant to reform interrogation practices. While the Supreme Court has formally prohibited confessions obtained through violence or threats, as well as those gained through direct or implied promises, lower courts have regularly turned a blind eye to many coercive practices. Further, the justices have explicitly sanctioned interrogator tricks, like pretending to possess fingerprint evidence and lying to a suspect about the results of a polygraph test, which encourage innocent people to confess to crimes that they did not commit.

In one of the most tragic cases, seventeen-year-old Martin

Tankleff awoke one morning to find his mother stabbed to death and his father badly cut and clinging to life. Investigators suspected that Martin was the perpetrator, and so, during questioning, one of them pretended—within earshot of Martin—to talk on the phone with an officer at the hospital where Martin's dad had been taken. After the fake conversation, he told Martin that his father had come out of his coma and said "Marty" had done it. The father, in fact, never came to and died shortly thereafter, but Martin admitted to the killing and served seventeen years in prison before he was exonerated.

What's worse is that Martin's false confession was predictable. His case involved two of the basic elements we know lead to disaster: a suspect particularly susceptible to coercion and a grueling interrogation. A disproportionate number of verified false confessions have come after unusually lengthy interrogations—lasting twelve hours, on average—with suspects who were under eighteen or suffering from mental illness or disability.

The interrogation of Juan Rivera fits the pattern perfectly. At the time of his arrest for Holly Staker's rape and murder, Juan was nineteen years old, had an IQ of 79 (well below the average of 100), and read at a third-grade level. Among other mental illnesses, he suffered from major depressive disorder and had made several suicide attempts. Despite these warning signs—disclosed to the police early in the process—officials proceeded to engage in a long, high-pressure interrogation.

It took four days of questioning and polygraph tests, but eventually Juan began to backtrack on his initial account of the night of Holly's death, in which he said he'd been at a party near the scene of the crime and seen someone there acting suspiciously. There are many reasons that a suspect like Juan might not be truthful when first questioned by detectives: among other things, he might fear that the truth does not sound believable, or he might suppose that a little lie will allow him to avoid more intensive and unpleasant treatment. But the police, as they often do, took the inconsistencies in Juan's story as a clear sign of guilt and decided to switch to aggressively seeking a confession. Although the polygraphs administered at Reid & Associates, the company that developed the Reid technique, had been inconclusive, the detectives had the polygrapher lie, directly accusing Rivera of raping and murdering Holly.

Rivera immediately became upset and denied involvement in the crime, but the detectives took him back to the Lake County Jail and continued to push for a confession. At around midnight, more than twelve hours after the day's questioning had begun, Rivera broke down sobbing—crying so hard that he completely soaked his clothes. He wasn't able to get the words out, but when the sergeant laid into him once again—"Juan, you were in that apartment with Holly Staker, weren't you?"—Juan nodded.

Over the next few hours Juan would provide the police with a full confession. By 3 a.m., the officers had what they needed and went to type it up. Rivera, left on his own, began to slam his head against the wall. Moved to a padded cell, he fell into an acute psychotic state. The nurse on duty described him as incoherent (in her words, he "sounded like the people who talk in tongues" and was "not in touch with the reality of what was going on around him"). When she checked back a couple of hours later, he had pulled out pieces of his hair and scalp and was curled in a fetal position.

Returning in the early morning, the detectives crouched down on the floor where Juan was lying (still handcuffed and shackled), read him their summary account of his confession, and had him sign at the bottom.

The document, though, was so inconsistent and riddled with factual errors (for example, Juan described Holly as wearing a nightgown) that the State's Attorney's Office told the detectives it was unacceptable. The interrogation had to continue. The two detectives, however, were too exhausted to go on, so two new detectives stepped in.

These interrogators focused on "clarifying" the problematic and inconsistent parts of Juan's first confession. After a few more hours, they got the improved version they wanted, but, unsurprisingly, a number of their inquiries had been highly suggestive. Questions like "She had a multi-colored shirt on, right, Juan?" provide insight into how so many false confessions come to contain specific details about the victim and crime scene. Information that only the real perpetrator could know is often inadvertently (and sometimes deliberately) revealed to a suspect over the course of an investigation. Juan Rivera discussed the crime with no fewer than ten law enforcement personnel over the four days he was interrogated, and on the second day the detectives took him on a "ride along" to the crime scene. Moreover, at least fifteen of the fifty-four purportedly "unique" facts in Juan's confession had appeared in local newspapers. Lamentably, these are just the types of details that end up being highlighted as strong proof that a confession is genuine.

While a more rigorous interrogation protocol might have made a difference for Juan, he would still have had to contend with investigators' assumption of guilt. As we've seen, once people form an initial impression of someone, they find it hard to change course. This can be problematic when it comes to police questioning, given that the whole reason a suspect is brought in for an interview is that the investigators have a hunch that he was involved in the crime.

Beginning the process with a theory of guilt leaves investigators predisposed to view the suspect's ambiguous behavior as demonstrating deceit and to be overconfident in that assessment. This, in turn, can lead them to switch to the hard-nosed interrogation phase prematurely and to chart a more aggressive course once there. One study found that mock interrogators could be encouraged to ask more biased questions, take a more unyielding stance, and lie to a suspect about nonexistent evidence against him, simply by being led to believe at the outset that the suspect was responsible for the crime. The results were stark: participants who started off with a guilt mindset were more than 20 percent more likely to confirm guilt than those who started off with an innocence mindset.

We can see these psychological forces at work in Juan's case. As is common in false confessions, Juan provided many facts to the police that contradicted what was known about the crime (he described changing the diaper of a baby in the room, although the baby was not in diapers) or what was plausible (he described eleven-year-old Holly as coming at him with a knife in a rage after he refused to continue having sex with her). Yet these clear discrepancies did not prompt police or prosecutors to doubt his guilt; they simply meant that the detectives had to go back and clean things up in a later round of questioning.

And once a confession is extracted, everyone—investigators, lawyers, jurors, and judges—starts to view the whole case through the lens of guilt, so other evidence can become more compelling than it actually is. This is confirmation bias on a grand scale. A hazy eyewitness identification suddenly appears reliable. A jail-house informant angling for a deal suddenly seems credible. In turn, your defense attorney may not work as hard to fight for your innocence, the trial judge may be tougher on you, and the prosecution may stake out a stronger position with respect to a plea bargain. Perhaps most important, a confession can cause detectives to stop investigating. In one particularly egregious case, a lab technician discovered that the suspect's blood type did not appear to match the crime-scene evidence and requested that the samples be sent to the FBI for DNA testing. He was turned down, however, on the grounds that the police already had a confession.

Even when a DNA sample tested before trial excludes the suspect, he may still be unable to break free from the shackles of his confession. In eight of the first 250 DNA exoneration cases, a suspect confessed to a crime that pretrial lab results showed he did not commit, and in all eight of these cases, police, prosecutors, judges, and jurors ignored what the DNA said. The only reason these men were eventually freed was that the biological evidence from the crime scene was finally matched to someone else. As remarkable as it is, Juan Rivera's case is not unique.

And Juan is not the only person who could have been steered into falsely confessing to Holly Staker's rape and murder. Hardnosed interrogations are particularly common when there is an absence of other clear evidence and immense pressure to solve a serious crime. Failing to gain a confession may result in an investigator not closing a major case, disappointing the family of the victim and the broader community, and damaging his own reputation as well as that of the police department. By the time Juan was brought in for questioning, the case was growing cold, and one can't help but think of all the other potential suspects—mentioned in initial police reports—who might have stepped into Juan's shoes: The high school student with a picture of Holly hidden in his wallet? The guy who decided to brag to his friends about how many times he had stabbed her? The man around the corner who had a conviction for sexually assaulting his eleven-year-old stepdaughter? One of the other sex offenders, drifters, or addicts living within blocks of Holly's house? They were all treading water at the outer edges of the whirlpool. Juan was simply caught in the vortex first.

Juan's story has a happy ending. In December 2011, the Illinois Court of Appeals overturned his conviction. But it would be foolish to see the case as a triumph of our judicial system. It is, instead, a story of terrible failure. When Juan Rivera was freed in January 2012, he had spent half his life in prison for a crime he did not commit—nineteen lost years in the Stateville Correctional Center that he will never get back. He finally made it out, but it took the tireless efforts of lawyers with the Center on Wrongful Convictions at Northwestern University, a Stanford law professor, and a team of bright, dedicated students all working without pay. It took Juan keeping faith that the truth would emerge and maintaining his innocence even as he was repeatedly asked to plead guilty in exchange for a reduced sentence. It took newspaper articles, radio interviews, and television coverage. It took three full trials, three dozen jurors, and three appeals. It took nineteen years. And all that time the real killer was roaming free—and roams free to this day. In a deeply troubling twist, in June 2014 this mystery man's DNA profile was matched to a murder committed nearly a decade after Holly was attacked.

Juan felt the sting of injustice every morning he awoke in his cell, but the unfairness of his case burned beyond the walls of Stateville Correctional Center. It deprived the Stakers of the closure they sought. It scarred the Riveras and the town of Waukegan.

And it stands as a warning to all of us. We have been lulled into thinking that discarding the rack and the back-room brute was enough. But all we have done is change the form of our coercion. The wounds and scars are now hidden, which leaves us in a far more precarious position. How do we spot a coerced confession when there are no bruises or welts? How do we know to sound the alarm bell when no one wears the torturer's cowl or beats out a confession, innocence be damned?

During the closing argument of Juan's third trial, the prosecutor Mike Mermel asked jurors, "Is there anything in the makeup of any of [the police officers involved in the case] that would lead you to believe that they were the kind of people who had dedicated their lives to this profession, yet just decided to just frame this poor innocent Juan Rivera because they were tired of investigating and wanted to go home?" If the answer was no, it followed, Juan must be guilty.

But the science tells us that this is dead wrong. A person can end up admitting to a crime he did not commit when everyone is trying desperately to do their best, when justice is sought, when no detective rolls up his sleeves and puts a fist into the suspect's gut. It wasn't that the thirty-six jurors were stupid or apathetic. It wasn't that Judge Starck or the prosecutors were corrupt. It wasn't that Juan had incompetent lawyers. Members of the media and others have advanced all of those explanations, but they miss the real reason why Juan was sentenced to life in prison.

Juan lost his third case because professionals and concerned citizens striving to do the right thing could not see the coercive forces behind his confession. We cannot afford such blindness. As I will show in the final chapter, empirically tested questioning techniques that avoid the pitfalls of the Reid approach are already being used in other countries and could be used here. But we must also ask ourselves the broader question of whether seeking an admission of guilt is a proper approach for a just legal system.

In the United States today, the vast majority of people charged with a crime are presented with a choice: say you did it and receive leniency, or maintain your innocence and suffer the consequences if a jury doesn't agree. Ninety to ninety-five percent admit guilt, which means no one ever has to come forward with any proof that the defendant is actually responsible, no jurors ever consider the evidence, and the trial process is completely short-circuited.

Let that sink in: nine out of ten prisoners are being punished based solely on their own admission of guilt.

We've put away the breaking wheel, yes, but how far have we really come?

Suppose you were told that the victims of a carjacking had identified you as their assailant and that you had two choices: (1) plead guilty to the charge and spend two years in prison or (2) try your luck at trial, with a potential sentence of twenty-five years to life. If you knew you were innocent, would you take the risk? Twenty-year-old James Ochoa faced this very choice and decided that he couldn't bear the chance that an Orange County jury would believe the victims' mistaken identification. He took the plea and spent sixteen months in prison, during which time he was stabbed by another inmate, before the police caught the actual perpetrator on an unrelated carjacking and got a DNA match.

The Supreme Court believes that such cases are rare, but the experimental evidence suggests otherwise. In one recent study extending over several months, college students were given a choice: admit that you knowingly cheated on a logic test, avoid a trial before the Academic Review Board, and give up the participant payment you were supposed to receive; or proceed to the trial, risking loss of the payment, assignment to a mandatory ethics course, and discipline from your faculty advisor. Over half of innocent participants falsely admitted to cheating.

If we really believe in transparency, freedom from coercion, and justice grounded in proof, we cannot continue to operate a system based on plea bargaining. Despite the bluster of the prosecutors in Ochoa's case, they were holding a weak hand: Ochoa had a strong alibi, eyewitness identifications were inconsistent, and the bloodhound that purportedly led the police to Ochoa's front door had been improperly handled. Most critically, the sheriff's crime lab had eliminated Ochoa as a source of the DNA and fingerprints left in the car and on the gun. But the real cards were never revealed, and no one ever evaluated the actual facts.

That is the madness of the plea. And given that fewer than 10 percent of criminal defendants ever make it to trial, it would seem that the plea bargain should be the overwhelming focus of reform efforts. But its failings are interwoven with those elsewhere in the criminal process: the reason so many people elect to plead out is that they dare not take their chances with the rest of the system. If police investigations, trials, and punishments weren't subject to the serious flaws taken up in the remaining chapters, innocent men and women would never plead guilty. They could put their faith in truth, justice, and equality and know it would see them through.

# 3

# THE CRIMINAL MIND

## The Suspect

Prisoner Records 1884–1889 New Zealand Police Museum Collection

Can you spot evil in a face?

Look at the men above. Which one was convicted of raping an eight-year-old girl? Which one was a tightrope walker caught for larceny? Which one was sentenced for killing a sheep?

Our gaze traces the arch of an eyebrow, the crookedness of a nose, the jutting ear. We look at the lips: are they clenched, calm, frightened, angry? Are those the hands of a pedophile?

We cannot help it. There is something about a mug shot that grabs us by the collar and pulls us in for a second, and then a second more.

I find it hard to read about a crime without inspecting the accused. When a suspect was recently apprehended for the brutal murder of a young doctor in her home just up our street, the first thing I did was type in his name so that I could look at his face.

It was almost automatic—a necessary step in the process of encountering a harm, examining its contours, trying to make sense of it. And as I began writing this book, I spent hours poring over photographs like these four, taken in New Zealand between 1887 and 1890.

I am not alone in feeling the magnetic pull of these images. There are books and gallery exhibitions, government databases and private collections, eBay auctions, CNN slideshows, and dedicated websites all devoted to mug shots. They are ubiquitous: our most wanted and our least wanted.

Part of the allure is pure voyeurism, of course. The Internet provides a titillating assortment of "hot mug shots" and "weepy mug shots" and "face tattoo mug shots"—and separate pages of celebrities and people with strange haircuts and people who have felt the strong arm of the law. We can gape at their eyes, painted up Cleopatra-style or swollen shut. But there is something more to it, I think.

These faces—and bodies—offer the possibility of uncovering the signs and causes of criminality.

When something awful has happened, we search for the harbingers that might have warned us away. And we seek the origins of the harm: we want to know what could lead a person to light a home on fire, shoot a man in the back, or sexually abuse a child.

Look again at the four New Zealanders. The rapist was the man on the far left, Frank Masters. The others in the lineup committed simple property crimes: from left to right, John Powell (sentenced to two years in prison for killing a sheep in order to steal the carcass), Alick Evan McGregor (one month for larceny), and William Johnston, the tightrope walker (three months for larceny). Masters was a serial sex offender, having been convicted at least four times between 1885 and 1888 for indecency—more specifically, "indecent exposure in the presence of young girls."

Though all of those affected by Masters's crime—the victim and her parents, the jurors, the judge, the surrounding community of Wellington—are long since dead, the rape of a child still unsettles us. What drove this man Masters? What was wrong with him? We burn to know, but there are few avenues to pursue.

Even if we could trade places with the Crown Prosecutor back in December 1889, we still wouldn't have access to what Masters was thinking when he committed the crime. His real motives, his capacities, his impulses—they remain today as they were then: shrouded behind a bearded face, dark eyes, a bald head.

At trial, Masters's explanation for his terrible acts was one of compulsion, but the evidence before the judge and jury was difficult to parse. During his fourth trial for indecency, Masters had asserted "that he was not master of himself when he committed the offences, and knew nothing about them until he was arrested." And at the suggestion of his lawyer, the Court ordered that Masters "be medically examined as to his sanity." Nonetheless, Dr. Johnston, the Gaol Medical Officer, "found him to be . . . sane, but of filthy habits."

So, despite Masters's pleas to the Court "to have steps taken to prevent him from doing such things again," he was not long thereafter released, and promptly went out and raped a child.

At his sentencing for that crime, Masters launched into "an extraordinary and wandering statement, speaking in lachrymose tones for upwards of 25 minutes," according to the newspaper report. "He couldn't help himself [he said], for he must be a lunatic—a thorough madman." In addition to "suggesting that he should be 'chained hand and foot' in a lunatic asylum, [he] proposed a drastic remedy that would effectually prevent his repeating the crime." He wanted to do good, "to get married and lead a proper life, and not go on in this way," but there was something— his nature, his destiny—that brought trouble into his life again and again. The reporter who recounted the trial thought Masters was putting on a show: "That he was acting a part there could be little doubt." But the judge was less sure: "Whether the prisoner was insane or not he could not tell."

In this context, it's easy to see the appeal of tools, practices, and rules of thumb that promise to expose what is hidden: the true cause of behavior, proof of guilt, or a corrupted soul. The "trial by ordeal" described at the beginning of this book was just such a mechanism. It made interior evil manifest. A heretic might claim innocence, but submersion in water revealed the truth.

Of course, we have not always needed elaborate rituals to unmask criminality. Indeed, for most of history, we've relied on nothing more than our own eyes. We all have intuitions about what criminal faces, postures, and behaviors look like. And we employ them every day, as we decide whether to count our change, how to respond if someone cuts in line, and when to cross the street as we walk home. As you gazed on the four accused New Zealanders, these unconscious associations were guiding your choice. We really do judge books by their covers—although it may be hard to articulate exactly what it is that we see and why it seems to point to criminality. "He just looks like a rapist," we say, as if that explained everything.

The idea that a person's facial traits offer a window into his character dates back to antiquity, but it was not until the nineteenth century that "physiognomy" was developed and organized to understand crime. To contemporaries, it felt like a moment of true revolution, a time to shed myths and backward practices. The message in the wind was that the world could be classified and explained, and that scientific and technological advances could be employed to improve society. Darwin, Edison, and Daguerre had shown the way. If the curve of a finch's beak revealed its preference for a particular type of seed, why shouldn't the slope of a man's nose reveal his inner motives, good or bad? And if someone could design a machine to accurately compare noses, what was to stop society from creating a classification system for criminals? Eliminating crime seemed a real possibility.

One of those swept up in the bluster of excitement was a professor at the University of Turin, Cesare Lombroso, who had previously been the director of the mental asylum in Pesaro. The Lombrosians were convinced that through a scientific approach, the origins of any criminal act could be identified. They were particularly interested in the possibility that those who committed crimes might be biologically different from the rest of the population.

One of Lombroso's epiphanies came during the autopsy of a notorious criminal, in which he was struck by how similar the anatomy of the head before him resembled a "savage" or "ape": "At the sight of that skull, I seemed to see all of a sudden, lighted up as a vast plain under a flaming sky, the problem of the nature of the criminal—an atavistic being who reproduces in his person the ferocious instincts of primitive humanity and the inferior animals." Here before him on the table was an explanation for the plague of crime. Those among us who seemed to have "an irresistible craving for evil for its own sake," who sought to "extinguish life," who were sexually depraved, or whose "excessive idleness" led to fraud and theft, were different in mind and body. They were "born criminals"—more like animals, for which these actions were normal. In order to identify those "degenerates" predisposed to engage in delinquent behavior, one had only to identify their bodily anomalies—"the stigmata," in Lombroso's words—that revealed a reversion back to a less evolved, animalistic state. It was not an entirely new notion—others had considered the connection between men and beasts centuries earlier (as the seventeenth-century woodcut on page 46 suggests), but Lombroso brought a rigor and focus to the endeavor. He and his followers set about carefully identifying and measuring various bodily features and proportions—from the existence of tattoos to the shape of the cranium—in an effort to map criminal degeneracy.

Take out a mirror and you can begin to see yourself as the Lombrosians would have. Pointy head? Strong jaw? Pathetic beard? Receding brow? These were all on the list of criminal traits.

Lombroso's project was greatly facilitated by an array of new technologies. There were devices to record a person's skull capacity and form; his blood pressure; his senses of touch, smell, and sight; his sensitivity to pain and temperature; and the way he spoke, among numerous other things. Perhaps my favorite invention is Louis Frigerio's "otometer," an instrument to measure the diameter of the ear and the angle at which it meets the head—the ear being, according to Frigerio, among the most critical of organs in signaling degeneracy. Frigerio claimed that criminals and the insane possessed large, flat ears that jutted out from the head, which made sense, he said, since these types of ears were also common in apes and other "inferior animals."

In the quest to record the physical state of the criminal for the purpose of objective comparison, no device was more promising than the camera. Although mug shots were initially used simply as a means of tracking criminals—with police departments assembling "rogues' galleries" to help them spot known offenders—those interested in physiognomy had grander plans. One British innovator, Francis Galton, a cousin of Charles Darwin, developed an approach that involved taking various images of criminals and overlaying them in a single photograph. What does a hotel thief look like? Galton would take the pictures of six known hotel thieves and combine them into one archetype. Conceivably, a person could then identify a rogue destined to be a pickpocket before he had ever reached into an overcoat. A new dawn seemed upon the horizon: knowing the signs of criminality and its animalistic causes, one might reduce crime—or perhaps eliminate it altogether.

But it was for naught. The work of Galton, Lombroso, and others turned out to be almost entirely incorrect. And far worse, their crackpot theories fed racist ideologies and were used to justify eugenic movements aimed at eradicating degeneracy by controlling who could have children.

It seems we have come a long way from the calipered past: our soldiers opened the gates of Dachau, after all. We teach the forcible sterilizations of the first half of the twentieth century as a tragic failing. And we laugh at people who still believe it's possible to divine a person's nature from his body. Those, like Sylvester Stallone's mother, Jackie, who offer such theories—Jackie being a preeminent "rumpologist"—end up fodder for standup bits.

But much of our progress is an illusion. Having purged explicit, open physiognomy, we remain *closet* physiognomists, unaware that we are appraising a person based on the color of his skin, the thickness of his lips, or his uneven ears. That these assessments are implicit makes them all the more destructive. Working toward an objective and falsifiable system of classification, Lombroso and Galton put their claims into the public domain for inspection, testing, and appraisal. Our judgments, by contrast, are subjective and rarely scrutinized.

Just as problematic, in considering *why* a person committed a crime, we tend to rely on a specious "mug shot" notion of criminality: we focus on a paper-thin, one-sided conception of the perpetrator, at the expense of the surrounding situation. As a general matter, we're inclined to believe that a person's actions reflect a freely made choice based on a set of stable character traits, preferences, and beliefs. And when we hear about some horrible event, like a murder, we immediately produce a metaphorical "mug shot" of the perpetrator: an evil person who chose to disregard our most vital social norms to serve his own desires. We tend not to pay much attention to the potential impact of other causal factors—like exposure to lead as a child or the pressures of being in a gang—unless they are utterly glaring (like someone forcing the perpetrator to act with a gun to his head). Normally, we stick with our simple "mug shot" account, which leads us to expect people's behavior to be consistent across circumstances. Once a murderer, always a murderer.

Sometimes that turns out to be right, but often it is not—and even when people act as we'd predict, it's largely a coincidence. Our "mug shot" approach to explaining tragic events is skewed and unfair. By imagining most criminals as autonomous, rational actors deciding to pursue greedy, lustful, or hateful ends, we underestimate the significance of forces in the world around us and dynamics in our brains over which we have little control. Once again, we are paying attention to all the wrong things.

The soft tissue of the brain is the starting point for everything we do.

What is allowing you to perceive the words of this sentence, understand their meaning, remember the contents of the previous section, feel the pages or device you hold in your hands, and decide to continue on to the next paragraph?

The answer is nothing more than neurons, synapses, and neurotransmitters. Take away these electrochemical interactions and that's it: no thoughts, no emotions, no choices, no behavior.

Even for those with no religious inclination, it doesn't feel that way. It feels as if we have something like a "soul"—independent, purposeful, and rational—directing our actions. How could that *thing* be nothing more than neurons generating electrical impulses, triggering chemical signals carried to other neurons? It seems improbable, impossible even. But that is the truth.

There wasn't some villainous spirit commanding Masters to assault that eight-year-old girl; his behavior arose from the three-pound lump of cells nested in his skull. A useful starting point in deciphering the causes of criminal behavior, then, is to consider how the brain of a criminal like Masters might differ from a "normal" brain.

Even back in Masters's time, there was some appreciation of the fact that particular areas of the brain might be involved in regulating particular behaviors. Perhaps the most famous example was that of a twenty-five-year-old supervisor for the Rutland and Burlington Railroad in Vermont, Phineas P. Gage.

Gage's fame all came down to a tragic and miraculous event one day in 1848, when he decided to pack explosive powder into a rock using a metal rod. His actions (perhaps not unexpectedly, to our cautious modern eyes) triggered a sudden explosion, and the thirteen-pound piece of iron was driven up through his left cheek and straight out of the top of his head.

In an amazing bit of luck, despite horrible damage to his prefrontal cortex and other areas of his brain, Gage survived with most of his physical and intellectual capacities preserved. But as his friends quickly noticed, Gage was "no longer Gage." Respectful, pleasant, and dutiful before the accident, Gage became lazy, boorish, and foul-tempered. The injury to particular parts of his brain seemed to change particular aspects of his behavior.

But there is no evidence that Gage ever engaged in truly criminal behavior, and perhaps a more relevant case to Masters's is one reported in the *Archives of Neurology* more than 150 years after Gage suffered his injury. Indeed, many of the facts seem to echo the reports on Masters.

In 2000, a married forty-year-old Virginia schoolteacher, Mr. Oft, who had never had abnormal sexual urges, suddenly began collecting child pornography and, soon thereafter, attempted to molest his prepubescent stepdaughter. As a first-time offender, the man was diverted to a twelve-step inpatient program for treatment of his sexual addiction. Any serious slip-up and he would be sent to prison. Even though he understood that risk, did not want to be incarcerated, and seemed to know that what he was doing was wrong, he began to solicit sex from the staff at the rehabilitation facility.

Oft was kicked out of the program, of course, and was set to be sentenced the next day, when he developed an intense headache. It was so bad that he had to go to the hospital. But no sooner had his neurological examination begun than he was propositioning the women in the room and openly discussing his fear that he would rape his landlady.

With his bad behavior in clear evidence, the doctors might have written off the headache as a mere ruse to delay going to prison, but instead they ordered a brain scan. What they found was staggering: a tumor, as big as an egg, in the right orbitofrontal area.

The surgery to remove it provided similarly stunning results: with the tumor excised, Oft lost all interest in pornography and easily completed the Sexaholics Anonymous program that had previously been such a struggle. Seven months later, he was permitted to return home.

Oft's apparent recovery, however, did not last. By October 2001, his headache had reappeared—as had his secret collection of explicit materials. Were the two again connected? Sure enough, when doctors ordered another brain scan, they found that the tumor had grown back. And with a second surgery, in February 2002, the sexual deviance vanished once again.

Cases like these provide vivid illustrations of how deficits in the brain can produce profound changes in behavior. But it is important to understand that such clear examples are rare, and anecdotes get us only so far. Most of the time, we have a person like Masters—someone who has done something atrocious without anything like a large tumor or hole in the skull to go by. A better approach for revealing the neural origins of crime is to compare the brains of many individuals.

Existing incarceration data has given us a clue about where to focus our attention. Our prisons, for example, contain a disproportionate number of people with significant mental illness, including psychopathy and antisocial personality disorder (a related but broader condition listed in the American Psychiatric Association's *Diagnostic and Statistical Manual of Mental Disorders*). Psychopaths have just the traits you'd expect to find in people behind bars: selfishness, superficial charm, impulsivity, dishonesty, irresponsibility, and lack of empathy or concern for others. And though they make up only 1 to 2 percent of the general population, they represent a whopping 15 to 25 percent of those incarcerated. The evidence related to traumatic brain injuries is similarly stark: while less than 9 percent of those outside of prison have experienced such trauma, roughly 60 percent of those in prison have had at least one such injury.

Although the basic approach of criminal neuroscience shares a lot with early physiognomy, our tools have come a long way from Frigerio's otometer. Computed tomography (CT) and magnetic resonance imaging (MRI) scans capture the structure of the brain at a moment in time. You can think about the images they produce as a snapshot of the contents of our skulls: an interior brain Polaroid. Their primary value comes in revealing trauma, disease, or abnormality: they can show whether a person has an egg-sized tumor or an abnormally small amount of tissue in a particular area of the brain. A functional magnetic resonance imaging (fMRI) scan, by contrast, reveals which areas of the brain are recruiting more oxygenated blood *over time*—that is, it gives us a sense of where neural activity is concentrated when a person is being asked a question or looking at a series of images (such as sexually explicit pictures of adults and children). This neuroimaging technology has allowed us to identify correlations between brain structures, on the one hand, and activities and behaviors, on the other.

Take the prefrontal cortex. Pathological liars, highly aggressive people, and those with antisocial personality disorder tend to have less gray matter in this area. There are also links between violent behavior and injuries to the prefrontal cortex, and between having a criminal record and reduced blood flow in this part of the brain. This aligns with other research showing that the prefrontal cortex plays a crucial role in impulse control, including a person's ability to make prudent long-term decisions, delay gratification, and adhere to rules.

One of the strangest aspects of prefrontal cortex dysfunction is that someone with damage in this region of the brain may understand the difference between right and wrong but nonetheless be unable to act in a moral fashion. Mr. Oft's case would seem a prime example: he was aware that his actions were reprehensible even as he reported being powerless to control them.

Given the complexities of antisocial behavior, it is not terribly surprising that other parts of the brain also influence criminality. The amygdala, for instance, is thought to play an important role in regulating aggression. Neuroscientists have identified this area as critical for understanding the beliefs, intents, desires, and emotions of others. When it is not functioning properly, a person may be at an increased risk of committing violence, because it is the ability to appreciate the shock, fear, and distress of others that helps prevent us from harming people. We have known for a long time that psychopaths have significant empathy deficits—and sure enough, their amygdalae are less active than those of people in the general population.

Although we've been considering them in isolation, the parts of the brain are interconnected, and deficits in multiple areas may contribute to a particular criminal behavior. Pedophilia, for example, seems to involve an array of deficits at the neural level, including problems with the amygdala *and* frontal cortex that interfere with how a person processes emotional cues and sexual stimuli.

But the location of the abnormality or dysfunction may affect the nature of the crime that a person is disposed to commit. Those who have deficiencies in their prefrontal cortex appear more likely to commit crimes that demonstrate impulsivity and emotional arousal (smashing someone in the head with a bottle after being ridiculed, for example). By contrast, those with demonstrated abnormal activity in their amygdala—but fairly unexceptional activity in their prefrontal cortexes—appear more likely to engage in calculated, directed, and emotionless aggression (gathering tools and stalking someone for weeks before brutally murdering her to steal her jewelry). Both dysfunctions might lead to murder, but they involve different neural structures and processes.

Some researchers have argued that this may explain the contrasting behaviors associated with "acquired psychopathy," which tends to involve reactive aggression brought on by immediate dangers or frustrations, and "developmental psychopathy," which tends to involve instrumental aggression directed at accomplishing selfish ends. Those with acquired psychopathy have suffered an injury to their prefrontal cortex that makes it hard for them to regulate their emotional responses, while those with developmental psychopathy have dysfunctional amygdalae that prevent them from properly processing signals of distress.

Television shows and movies lead us to regard psychopaths either as pure evil (think Michael Myers in the *Halloween* slasher films) or as hyper-rational actors who simply choose to do horrible things (think Hannibal Lecter), but the science offers a very different explanation for their behavior: they have abnormal brains that leave them without critical tools that the rest of us take for granted. As we'll explore later, we are reluctant to embrace this biological account because it makes it harder for us to justify our harsh treatment of criminals. But it's what the best evidence suggests. And the case against our simplistic "mug shot" view of defendants is made even stronger when we consider what causes brain dysfunction in the first place: genetic and developmental factors that are mostly beyond the control of the person they affect.

Some scientists have claimed that roughly half of the variability in antisocial traits across the population comes down to the genes that people are born with. All things being equal, if you have a Y chromosome, you are several times more likely to engage in violent criminal behavior. And psychopaths and pedophiles are both disproportionately men. But it can be hard to separate out the impact of genes from social factors: after all, men and women are subjected to very different arrays of experiences and expectations.

A good example of the interplay between genes and environment is the enzyme monoamine oxidase A (MAO-A), which breaks down certain neurotransmitters and is encoded on a single gene. Scientists have suggested that if you happen to have a version of this gene that produces less of the enzyme, your likelihood of committing a violent crime by age twenty-five is increased several hundred times, but only if you've *also* experienced early childhood abuse.

On a more general level, the environment can play a powerful role in how our brains develop, particularly during the prenatal, infant, and early childhood periods, with a resulting impact on future criminality. There are head injuries, yes, but also experiences that shape us and may increase our likelihood of eventually breaking the law.

Some of those experiences have to do with missing out on key things that our bodies need to build a healthy brain. A wealth of evidence, for example, shows that nutritional deficiencies in the womb and during childhood can lead to cognitive dysfunction. Even micronutrients appear to matter: several studies link low levels of trace elements like zinc and iron with increased aggression.

Exposure to certain toxic substances can also play a role. If your mother smokes during pregnancy, you are approximately three times more likely to commit a crime in adulthood. And similar patterns emerge with respect to alcohol abuse. Particularly disturbing are the elements outside a mother's control: if you're born in a certain neighborhood in a certain country at a certain time, you may be exposed to heavy metals linked to violent behavior every time you drink a glass of water or breathe.

There is growing evidence, for instance, that lead poisoning from gasoline may have been a major contributor to the sharp rise in violent crime between the 1960s and 1990s. The theory is that kids were exposed to airborne lead dust from car emissions in the 1940s and 1950s, which led to reduced brain volumes and dysfunction, particularly in the frontal cortex (again, the part of the brain that frequently shows abnormality in violent populations). As a result, two decades later, those with high exposure had a reduced ability to regulate their emotions and impulses, with criminal consequences.

Other critical experiences come from interpersonal interactions. It matters what your parents, siblings, friends, and neighbors are like. Having a mother and father who are abusive or neglectful, being an outcast at school, and falling in with delinquent friends all seem to increase one's likelihood of committing a crime.

And many of these risk factors appear to have a multiplicative effect: a hyperactive ten-year-old with a low IQ living in poverty with an antisocial single mother who engages in harsh discipline and frequent abuse—all known predictors of delinquency—is several times more likely to commit a violent crime by age eighteen than a ten-year-old who simply has a low IQ.

Even when genes and environment leave a person at a low risk of criminality, being in a certain age group may bump it up. We know that people in their late teens and early twenties are disproportionately represented in the rolls of criminal offenders. A recent survey from Great Britain found that people between sixteen and twenty-four were behind more violent crimes than *all other age groups taken together.*

Part of the explanation is that our brains *develop*, just like the rest of our bodies—but in fact more slowly than the rest of our bodies. The frontal lobes, particularly the areas that regulate judgment, decision-making, and self-control, may not completely mature until people are well into their twenties. As you'd expect from looking at their brains, adolescents tend to be less adept at considering the consequences of their actions. Lacking the fully formed quick-decision-making structures that steer adults away from potentially dangerous criminal activities without needing to deliberate, adolescents sometimes get lost trying to figure out how risky something is: Should I pull the gun out of my pocket? Should I throw this bottle at that car? Should I inhale this drug? According to one theory, part of the problem may be that while the prefrontal cortex is a late bloomer, the amygdala—which deals with emotional reactions and reward processing—is a precocious debutante, leaving those in their late teens very susceptible to the allure of criminal actions and the sway of their emotions.

From an evolutionary perspective, the adolescent brain's characteristics and its lengthy development seem baffling, but some scientists believe that the distinctive features of the adolescent brain that spawn risk-taking and novelty-seeking may actually have been adaptive in our ancestral past, encouraging adolescents to move out into the world, develop new social connections, gain valuable new experience, and take the chances necessary for success in a competitive environment. We may get caught up considering the current costs of a youthful mind—measured in alcohol and drug overdoses, car accidents, fights, and arrests—and miss the benefits of an adolescent brain: the willingness to experiment, to meet new people, the endless desire for learning, feeling, and knowing what the world has to offer.

One bright sign is that in recent cases a majority of Supreme

Court justices have seemed to accept the scientific evidence that there is a fundamental difference between juvenile minds and adult ones. In both *Graham v. Florida,* which eliminated sentences of life without parole for juvenile offenders who did not commit homicide, and *Roper v. Simmons,* which abolished the death penalty for those under eighteen, the Court noted that young people are not only more vulnerable to peer and other outside pressures but may also lack the psychological development to act responsibly. We need to extend this new understanding to all people, young and old, whose brain function leaves them at special risk.

Yet convincing the Supreme Court and the broader public that crimes often reflect neural deficits is just half the battle against the "mug shot" view of criminality. To eliminate the myth that poor character or an evil soul is behind criminal behavior, we also need to establish that even those *without* brain abnormalities are subject to powerful situational influences that shape the decision to break the law. Genetic, biological, and experiential factors leave some individuals at a vastly higher risk of committing a crime, but most people's moral identities are never set in stone. The particular circumstances in which we find ourselves can make all the difference.

Two seeds from the same pod can grow into very different trees. Just look at the Bulger boys: James (nicknamed Whitey) and William (called Bill).

They were raised in South Boston, two of the six children of James and Jean Bulger. The elder James had lost part of his arm after an accident and struggled to find steady work, so the family lived in Old Harbor, the first public housing project built in New England. Whitey and Bill shared a room with their younger brother, Jackie, until Bill was a sophomore in high school, while the girls were together in a room down the hall. Though the project has since been taken over by drugs and despair, back then

Old Harbor was a community of two-parent households, poor but striving. The Bulgers did not have much, but they had their family and they had their dignity.

In early adolescence, however, Whitey's and Bill's lives would take very different turns.

Whitey stayed local and fell in with the gangs down on Mercer Street. The boys he hung out with skipped school and got into fights and sometimes worse. Whitey was fourteen when he was first arrested for stealing. In short order he would be picked up for larceny, forgery, battery, assault, and armed robbery.

Age fourteen was similarly pivotal for Bill: it was then that he decided to head across town to Boston College High School rather than sticking with his friends at South Boston. While Whitey was brawling and getting into trouble, Bill was doing his homework and working at John and Mary Karp's meat market for tuition money. Later, while Bill was immersing himself in the scholarly world of Boston College, Whitey was robbing banks, a pursuit that eventually landed him a major prison sentence.

The further the brothers walked, the more their paths diverged.

Bill went off to law school and made law review, which set him on a road that would see him grow into a powerful and effective politician: a state representative and Massachusetts Senate president. As a legislator, he fought against child abuse and for education and welfare reform, among other issues. He was later appointed the twenty-fourth president of the University of Massachusetts and would go on to collect more than twenty honorary degrees.

And Whitey? After he was released, following nine years in prison, he rose to be the major organized-crime boss in Boston—and the inspiration for Jack Nicholson's character in Martin Scorsese's Oscar-winning movie *The Departed*. When Osama bin Laden was killed, Whitey moved into his spot as America's most wanted man. After authorities finally caught him, he was convicted of participating in eleven murders, along with drug trafficking, extortion, racketeering, and other crimes, and given two life terms in prison plus five years.

All that said, we shouldn't overstate the case: Bill, like many twentieth-century Boston politicians, did not have a career free of controversy, and he remained staunchly loyal to Whitey, refusing to assist authorities in catching him. Still, cronyism and hardball politics are quite different from murder and drug trafficking. And whatever affection he maintained for his older brother, Bill's love of scholarly endeavors, his professional experiences, and his everyday life set him in a wholly different sphere.

It is possible, of course, that Whitey and Bill were different genetically—they were not identical twins, after all; they were just brothers. It is also possible that in one of those teenage fights Whitey suffered a traumatic brain injury that led to problems with impulse control. But the most plausible explanation is simply that the brothers inhabited two very different environments at critical moments in their lives. Our surroundings often exert such a powerful influence that they all but erase the effects of disposition.

Consider a modern-day Whitey. He is sixteen years old, wearing a mask, and his hand is on a gun inside his jacket. As part of a gang initiation, he is supposed to rob the first person who walks by the graffitied alley he's standing in. He does—shooting and killing the man, a father of three, in the process.

Reading this brief description, most of us already have a causal story in mind that focuses on the flawed character and poor choices of the boy. But what role might the situation have played in the terrible crime?

As a starting point, let's rule out some of the elements of the situation that clearly could not have played any sort of causal role—the mask he was wearing, for example. The conventional account of the criminal's mask is that bad people who want to commit bad acts cover their faces in stockings or wear balaclavas so that they can do what they want—burglarize, rob, rape, or murder—without being identified and caught. It is a tool employed by a person to assist him in accomplishing his chosen end.

That seems uncontroversial enough, but researchers have found that the mask itself can be the *source* of harmful behavior. In one experiment, a group of elementary school students at a Halloween party played games—first wearing their normal clothes, then their costumes, then their normal clothes again. In the "anonymous" second set of games, students were significantly more aggressive, but that aggression disappeared when they removed their masks for the final games. It seemed to be the costumes and not the children's inherent character that mattered—a finding that some have connected to anthropological research showing that societies in which warriors mask or change their appearance during battle are far more likely to also kill and torture their victims.

As a follow-up, the researchers decided to look at whether the anonymity of wearing costumes could encourage kids to commit an actual crime. In the experiment, young trick-or-treaters entered a home where there was a bowl of candy and a bowl of coins. The person who greeted the children told them that they could have one piece of candy each and, if they asked, told them that the money was for charity.

So what did the kids do as soon as the greeter left to go into another room?

Well, lots of them stole candy, as well as money. Some groups took the entire bowl of treats. But there was an interesting twist: in one condition of the experiment, the woman first asked the children for their names and addresses. These kids didn't steal. The anonymity effect of the mask had been neutralized.

Now consider another of the tools used in the modern-day Whitey's crime: the gun. We have all heard the expression "Guns don't kill people; people kill people." Even for those who view the NRA with deep distrust and contempt, this bumper-sticker wisdom has a certain logic: guns are inanimate objects, after all. They don't have the power to influence someone's behavior.

Except that research now suggests they do.

Clutching a weapon can change us. In one set of studies, participants were each given either a toy gun or a non-weapon, like a ball, to hold while images of different people appeared on a screen. Participants were told that when the picture showed someone with a gun, they should quickly point the object they were holding at the screen; when the image revealed someone with a phone, wallet, or shoe, they should aim at the ground.

The results were astounding. The simple act of wielding a gun biased participants' assessment of how dangerous someone was. With a gun in hand, participants were significantly more likely than those holding benign objects to aim at people on the screen. Moreover, simply having a gun conspicuously visible inside the laboratory did not have a significant effect; participants had to be holding it.

The best explanation is that using a gun as a pointer leads people to perceive ambiguous objects as guns because perception and action-planning employ shared processes in the brain. And that suggests that having a gun at your fingertips can make the world seem a far more threatening place, with potentially deadly consequences.

Even the surrounding landscape—the spray-painted alley, the trash in the gutter, the abandoned row houses—may influence a modern-day Whitey's actions. Back in the early 1980s, George L. Kelling and James Q. Wilson advanced a "broken windows" theory, which asserted that potential criminals took cues from their environment: "If a window in a building is broken and is left unrepaired, all the rest of the windows will soon be broken. . . . One unrepaired broken window is a signal that no one cares, and so breaking more windows costs nothing." For a long time, the notion that litter, rundown buildings, and burned-out cars could encourage criminal behavior was based mostly on anecdote, but recent empirical work has begun to bolster Kelling and Wilson's ideas.

In one set of experiments, researchers in the Netherlands found that by making very minor changes to the visible disorder in a real neighborhood, they could alter people's behavior. When there was more graffiti, significantly more people stole a five-euro note (visible inside a letter perched in the slot of a post office box). When the experimenters illegally locked bikes in plain view, more than triple the number of people trespassed in an area clearly marked NO THROUGHWAY.

On a positive note, green space in cities may have the opposite effect. Crime, it turns out, does not lurk in the bushes. Indeed, in my hometown of Philadelphia, a recent study found that areas with trees, shrubbery, and grass experienced less crime, in particular fewer robberies and assaults.

Even accepting that the backdrop can play a causal role in human dramas, it seems hard to believe that elements in our situations could ever lead a person to commit a truly atrocious act—say, killing a man. But, in fact, the most famous series of experiments in psychology came remarkably close to proving just that. The question that sparked it all was a straightforward one: What percentage of the population would deliver a potentially lethal shock of electricity to another human being simply for getting a question wrong on a test?

Although logic suggested that only a sadistic person would flip the switch, Stanley Milgram found that 63 percent of experimental subjects delivered the full 450 volts when an experimenter instructed them to. What was even more interesting was that Milgram could get compliance rates to vary between zero and 92.5 percent just by changing minor elements in the environment. Did the participant first see two peers refuse to obey orders? If so, obedience plunged. Did the instruction to continue the experiment come from a scientist in a gray lab coat or a lay administrator? With a scientist, compliance shot up. Was the location of the experiment Yale University or a private facility in Bridgeport, Connecticut? In the Bridgeport lab, the number of committed shockers plummeted.

We want to believe that atrocious crimes are always caused by atrocious people who are very different from us. But that is simply not the case. There is psychological truth behind Hannah Arendt's famous characterization of evil as "banal." Arendt was writing about the trial of the Nazi Adolf Eichmann for the *New Yorker*, and in observing the proceedings she was struck by how utterly ordinary Eichmann seemed. Here was someone who had done monstrous things—overseeing the Final Solution—yet he did not appear to be a monster. Although subsequent research has revealed that Eichmann may have been a more enthusiastic executioner than he let on, Arendt's broader message has endured.

The implications are hard to accept: we may all have the potential to harm, to be criminals. But the threat to our self-esteem is actually graver than that. Acknowledging the science means losing vital cover. If situational factors play such a powerful role in offending, we can no longer claim to be outside observers. When we decide not to regulate weapons, when we elect to leave swaths of our neighborhoods blighted or cut nutrition programs for women, infants, and children, when we provide young inner-city men with few options but to join gangs, we become implicated in the crimes that eventually result.

The major effect of knocking down the "mug shot" view of criminals, then, is to eliminate the barrier that stands between us and those we lock up. This is difficult, but it's critical to achieving a just legal system—a topic we'll return to at the end of the book. When we appreciate that a person's likelihood of committing a crime drastically increases with the wrong genes or a blow to the head, it makes it easier to feel empathy for those who have done wrong, to forgive them, and to offer help rather than hurt. And when we understand that the power of our environments can lead us all to commit terrible acts, we suddenly have a reason to change those conditions to ensure that no one is led astray.

Without a "mug shot" notion of crime, we'd look at the photographs of Frank Masters, John Powell, Alick Evan McGregor, and William Johnston with different eyes. Real mug shots would no longer be objects of amusement and curiosity. We'd see them for what they are: reminders of the work still left to be done.

# PART II

# Adjudication

# 4

## BREAKING THE RULES

### The Lawyer

It isn't just murderers who make deathbed confessions. Sometimes prosecutors do, too.

Gerry Deegan was dying of cancer. He had worked for the D.A. in Orleans Parish, Louisiana, since law school, battling to put bad men away. Now his number had come up, and he wanted to tell his friend Michael Riehlmann something. Riehlmann was a former prosecutor himself—same parish. He listened.

Nine years earlier, Deegan had done something he now regretted.

It all started with Raymond T. Liuzza Jr., the son of a well-known New Orleans businessman, bleeding to death in front of his house in the early morning of December 6, 1984. The only witness to the shooting described the assailant to police as a six-foot-tall African American with "close cut hair." But that didn't narrow things down much, and the police were casting about until the Liuzza family announced a $15,000 reward for information leading to the conviction of Raymond's murderer.

The money lured Richard Perkins out of the depths: "I don't mind helping [you] catch [the perpetrator]," he told them, "but I would like [you] to help me and, you know, I'll help [you]."

According to Perkins, two men were behind the crime: Kevin

Freeman and John Thompson. The police snagged Freeman first, then kicked in the door to Thompson's grandmother's house. Thompson's two sons were there, and his girlfriend, his mom, his brother and sister, and his grandmother. They watched as the police, guns drawn, took Thompson away. He was twenty-two years old.

Freeman matched the description the witness had given: tall, with closely cropped hair that had earned him the nickname Kojak. But it was Thompson—four inches shorter and hair in a large Afro—who would catch the charge.

His photo in the paper had attracted the eye of a father whose three children had recently been involved in a seemingly unrelated incident—an attempted carjacking. Now, looking at the Afro in the photograph, the children thought they were staring at the carjacker once again. And when they went down to the station, they picked out the same newspaper photo from an array of mug shots.

The D.A.'s office had their man. What's more, Freeman had turned quick and easy and was ready to be the key witness in a murder trial against Thompson. All they had to do was think about strategy: they had been dealt a strong hand for the death penalty, but they had to play their cards right.

The opening move was to try Thompson on the armed robbery of the kids, because a conviction would discourage Thompson from testifying in his own defense during the more critical murder trial. If he chose to testify, the rules of evidence would allow the prosecution to introduce his robbery conviction to impeach his credibility—a potentially devastating hit. And without Thompson's testimony, the defense would have a much harder time presenting his side of the story and reducing the impact of the testimony against him. Just as important, a prior violent felony on Thompson's record could help secure an execution verdict in the second case.

Deegan was enlisted to assist James Williams on the armed robbery case, while Williams and Eric Dubelier handled the murder case. And Deegan and Williams knocked it out of the park: Thompson was sentenced to 49.5 years in prison without the possibility of parole on the robbery charge based on the identifications of the three victims, which set the stage for a clear win for the prosecution in the murder trial. Thompson was going to be executed. Harry F. Connick Sr., the district attorney for Orleans Parish (and father of the musician and actor of the same name), had a signature victory—a sign that, even in the sometimes-troubled Big Easy, justice eventually came to the wicked.

John Thompson was sent to prison and then to death row in the Louisiana State Penitentiary—the infamous Angola, Alcatraz of the South. He was sitting there now, as Deegan and Riehlmann spoke.

So what did Deegan want to get off his chest?

He hadn't done right in the first trial. During the carjacking, the eldest child had injured the assailant, and the man had bled onto his pants. A crime-scene investigator had taken a swatch of the bloody fabric, and the crime lab had run a pretrial test of the swatch, which had conclusively identified the blood type of the assailant. But Thompson's lawyer never knew about it because the report had not been handed over, and Deegan himself had checked the swatch out of the evidence room on the first day of trial and never returned it.

He had kept all of this to himself for nine years: he had suppressed blood evidence.

Back in 1963, in the case of *Brady v. Maryland*, the Supreme Court made clear that prosecutors must turn over evidence that is favorable to the defendant and material to issues of guilt or punishment. Failing to do so—in common parlance, committing a *Brady* violation—is a contravention of the constitutional right to due process.

Riehlmann suggested that Deegan reveal what he had done—come clean. It was the right thing to do. But when Deegan elected to keep his mouth shut, so did Riehlmann.

For five more years Thompson sat in his isolation cell, waiting for the day he would die. His execution had been scheduled six times. Each time it was delayed for an appeal, but the appeals had run out. His seventh and final date was May 20, 1999.

In a last-ditch effort, Thompson's lawyers hired a private investigator to look through the evidence one final time. It was less than a month before the execution. There wasn't much hope the P.I. would turn up anything, but nonetheless she scanned through the microfiche of the crime lab archives. And then there it was: a copy of the lab report with the carjacker's blood type.

B, it said.

Thompson had type O blood. He was innocent.

His conviction for the armed robbery was vacated, which led to a reversal of his murder conviction. Thompson was finally able to testify in his own defense. At the new trial, Thompson presented evidence that the man who had been the government's key witness against him in the first trial—Kevin Freeman—was actually the murderer. It took the jurors only thirty-five minutes to find Thompson not guilty.

After more than eighteen years in prison, Thompson walked out of Angola on May 9, 2003.


How does such an atrocity—there is no other word for it—occur? What could lead someone to hide evidence that could potentially save an innocent man's life?

The Supreme Court has given us an answer. Prosecutors are mostly upstanding people, but there are few bad ones mixed in, as in any profession. Our existing legal regime adequately trains lawyers on their ethical obligations, but, at the end of the day, lawyers make their own choices. Prosecutors know their legal responsibilities; when a troubling incident like this one occurs, it's because someone decided to disregard his duty and act in a dishonest way. And in the Court's view, not much can be done to prevent it, because the problem lies with individual moral compasses, set years earlier, rather than with institutional and other situational pressures.

After being released from prison, Thompson successfully sued District Attorney Connick on the grounds that he had acted with deliberate indifference to the need to train prosecutors in their responsibilities to disclose exculpatory evidence, like the blood evidence that was kept from Thompson's attorneys. But when the case made it to the Supreme Court, Justice Clarence Thomas, writing for the majority, overturned the $14 million in damages Thompson was set to receive—$1 million for each year he was on death row—relying on the above reasoning. In the majority's opinion, ethical legal training is effective, the prosecutor's role is clear, and there just wasn't proof that Gerry Deegan's actions were anything but an isolated incident.

Similarly, Justice Scalia, in a concurrence joined by Justice Alito, characterized the withholding of evidence as the result of the actions of a lone "miscreant prosecutor" who had committed "a bad-faith, knowing violation." Deegan, in this framing, was a rogue agent—a loose cannon "willfully suppress[ing] evidence he believed to be exculpatory, in an effort to railroad Thompson." To suggest that broader forces within the D.A.'s office might have contributed to the deprivation of Thompson's rights was ludicrous. If you had a large barrel of apples, a few rotten ones were unavoidable: "the inevitability of mistakes over enough iterations of criminal trials" was something that society just had to accept.

This aligns with our common sense, although many of us would go even further. Yes, we should expect there to be good and bad prosecutors, but we also think there is something unsavory about lawyers in general. They are sharks or hired guns, ready and willing to do whatever it takes to win.

Despite the pervasiveness of these stereotypes, explanations of dishonest behavior that focus on the bad character of certain lawyers *or all lawyers* are largely inaccurate. Lawyers do cheat and lie. They do break the rules and cause immense suffering. When Deegan failed to turn over the blood test to Thompson's defense and hid the actual sample, he was violating the law and, more fundamentally, breaching basic moral tenets: a man's life was at stake, and Deegan kept him from learning of evidence that could have saved him. That is all true. The big question is, why? Until we have an accurate picture of what is driving things, we won't make serious progress in eliminating attorney misconduct.

If you spend time studying dishonesty, you will quickly notice a strange paradox: although most of us care about being moral and ethical, we step over the line all the time. Our behavior can be baffling.

On the one hand, we are rule-following creatures. We stop at red lights and pick up after our dogs even when no one is around; we do not shout curse words when visiting elementary schools or reach our hand into the tip jar at Starbucks or grope passing strangers or hunt other humans for sport. And we celebrate our rules of moral living in our religions, in our professions, and in our schools. We have monuments to the Ten Commandments and mandatory ethics seminars and criminal codes. To be labeled as unethical is to be tagged with a badge of ignominy.

On the other hand, take a look around: we are swimming in a sea of dishonesty. At this very moment there are people right in front of us—strangers and those we know; our idols, our enemies, and our friends—behaving badly: employees lying on their time sheets or padding their expense accounts; athletes feigning fouls to win penalties or taking performance-enhancing drugs to gain an edge; cheating spouses and partners; men and women engaging in insurance fraud and tax fraud and defrauding their elderly relatives; millions of Americans downloading billions of songs and videos that they did not pay for.

There is evidence of pervasive cheating at nearly every stage of life. In light of recent data, it may be time to retire our romantic notions of youthful innocence. Cheating by students is rampant: over half of high school students admit to cheating, and the numbers appear to be just as bad or worse at the college level. Graduate students cheat, too, with business students leading the way (56 percent admit to doing so) and aspiring lawyers actually below average (45 percent). What's more, top students appear just as likely as the rest of the bell curve to violate academic rules. In recent years, significant cheating has been revealed at the elite Stuyvesant High School in New York, the Air Force Academy, and Harvard.

In truth, people dodge and skirt, hustle and scam on Beggars Row and Wall Street and every avenue between. Watch your children, your spouse, your students, your co-workers, your employees, and you will see the game being played.

So what's driving it all? Why do people cheat? And what is it about our legal system that makes prosecutors particularly vulnerable?

If dishonesty doesn't come down to just a few people with bad characters, might the underlying commonsense model of why people cheat still be correct—that is, that people choose to cheat whenever the benefits outweigh the costs of potentially getting caught and punished?

Researchers decided to test that theory by paying people to solve number puzzles and varying the factors that we assume influence dishonesty. What they found was baffling. Making it less likely that participants would be caught lying about the number of matrices they had solved did not significantly increase the level of cheating—nor did increasing the amount of money that participants were paid for correct answers. Indeed, when the researchers increased the payout up to $10 per matrix, cheating actually decreased.

Our dishonesty, then, is not a simple matter of cost-benefit analysis. Lots and lots of people engage in dishonest behavior, but even when provided with the chance and incentives, they don't generally cheat "big."

In one study documenting this phenomenon, behavioral scientists gave people the opportunity to cheat without getting caught on a multiple-choice test that awarded money for each general-knowledge question they got right. And sure enough, a very large number of study participants did. But each person cheated by a relatively small amount—only 20 percent of the amount he could have gotten away with.

It's as if there is something inside of people limiting how fast the dishonesty engine will turn. According to researchers, that mechanism may be our own egos. We are each strongly motivated to maintain our image as a virtuous person—and that motivation can act as a powerful constraint on our self-interested actions. We want to believe that we are honest and ethical, and when we cheat, we endanger that rosy self-view. The more an instance of cheating threatens to darken our picture of ourselves, the less likely we are to act.

In an interesting demonstration of this dynamic, a group of experimenters presented participants with an opportunity to earn money from cheating by lying about how many times a coin they had flipped had come up heads. Although all participants were aware that they could cheat without getting caught, some participants were told, "Please don't cheat," while others were told, "Please don't be a cheater." It's hard to imagine that such a subtle linguistic cue would have any effect at all, but the researchers found that it did. When the verb "cheat" was used, some people still cheated, but when the self-relevant noun "cheater" was used, participants' identities were suddenly implicated, and there was no cheating.

To feel good about ourselves, the obvious answer is to swear off dishonesty or keep it small. Cheating on a few questions in a psychology experiment doesn't make us feel like a bad person, nor does failing to report a small gambling win on our taxes. But there's another way to address the inner conflict that arises when our actions are at odds with our positive self-image: trick ourselves into thinking we're not behaving so badly after all.

So, although 51 percent of high school students in one study admitted to having recently cheated on a test, and 61 percent admitted to having lied to a teacher, and 20 percent admitted to having stolen something from a store, 93 percent of those surveyed reported that they were "satisfied with [their] own ethics and character." Likewise, while taxpayers end up defrauding the government of some $385 billion each year—often by failing to report income—well over 90 percent of the public agrees that "it is every American's civic duty to pay their fair share of taxes" and that "everyone who cheats on their taxes should be held accountable." Though we are reluctant to acknowledge it, we all have this capacity for self-deception.

If we want to understand why people act dishonestly, we need to look at the factors that determine how easy or difficult it is to rationalize dishonest behavior. When justifying our actions is a struggle, we find it more difficult to break the rules. And therein lies the key to prosecutorial misconduct: most lawyers aren't consciously trying to cheat defendants; they're just extremely good at deceiving themselves.

One of the most promising strategies that people use to rationalize an ethical breach is to downplay the causal link between the dishonest action and any associated harm. If I can convince myself that my behavior is unlikely to be damaging, it becomes much easier for me to justify it and maintain my positive self-view. And the greater the distance—and the more intervening elements—

between what I'm thinking about doing and any clear detriment, the less motivated I'll be to choose the honest option. For example, scientists have found that people will cheat about twice as much when they are cheating to earn tokens that can be exchanged for money as when they are cheating to earn money directly.

To understand why this is relevant to prosecutorial misconduct, consider two attorneys. One, like Deegan, is deciding whether to hand over a potentially exculpatory report on blood evidence found at the scene of the crime; the other is deciding whether to pay a $10,000 bribe to a wavering juror to gain a conviction.

Research would suggest that the second prosecutor is much less likely than the first to take the dishonest action, because it is harder for him to see his actions as innocuous. After all, they come right at the critical moment of decision. And there are no other apparent interveners who can be blamed. By paying off the decision-maker, the second prosecutor is determining the outcome.

The first prosecutor, by contrast, is operating at a safe distance from any harmful consequences. Even if he doesn't hand over the report, the defendant's lawyers are likely to uncover additional evidence to vindicate him—if he is innocent—on their own. As a result, they should be able to present a convincing case to the jury, which should acquit. So the blame for any wrongful conviction would fall squarely on the defense attorneys and jurors.

In the Thompson case, the fact that Deegan was working on the robbery trial, not the murder trial, would have made it even easier for him to distance his actions from Thompson's death sentence: after he completed his own role in the prosecution, there was still an entire additional trial that had to take place.

The nature of the adversarial system, which places the burden on lawyers to zealously advocate for their positions but does not charge them with the task of being the ultimate decision-makers, may itself promote dishonesty by allowing attorneys to feel less responsible for the consequences of their actions. And the earlier in the trial process it is, the more attenuated the connection to any eventual harm is likely to seem. All other things being equal, we ought to expect more dishonesty in the weeks leading up to trial than in the time after a jury is impaneled and proceedings have begun. Once a conviction has been attained, the process ought to reverse itself: new dishonest actions that simply maintain the status quo (for example, denying the defendant a fair appeal or a parole hearing through a dishonest act) should become easier to rationalize.

Since Thompson was on death row when Deegan revealed to his friend Riehlmann that he had withheld potentially exonerating evidence in Thompson's case, it would seem harder for Riehlmann to justify not passing on the information to Thompson's lawyers. But unlike Deegan, Riehlmann had not worked on the case and hadn't failed to hand over evidence. He had only *heard* about the violation. Just as important, Riehlmann had learned about it well after Thompson had already been convicted and put on death row. And given that Thompson's blood type was not known, it would not have been clear to Riehlmann that passing on the information to Thompson's attorneys would make any difference at all. Indeed, it was possible that even if the report had been handed over, the defendant might have turned out to have the same blood type as the perpetrator, which would have made him *more likely* to be convicted, not less. Although we can't know for sure what led Riehlmann to keep Deegan's confession secret for five years as Thompson's life hung in the balance, it seems plausible that someone in his position might do so without feeling much responsibility at all.

Note, too, that omissions and commissions are viewed differently. It is easier to see the harm in a commission (the hypothetical prosecutor bribing a juror) than in an omission (Deegan failing to turn over the lab report). An omission does not seem to upset the "natural" course of things, whereas a commission seems to steer events onto a different path. And omissions tend to be more readily justified because there are almost always benign reasons for not doing something: "I didn't understand it was my responsibility," "No one told me," or simply "I forgot."

So, the fact that *Brady* violations involve a prosecutor not doing something that she is supposed to do may make them particularly likely to occur. Other common types of prosecutorial misconduct involve omissions as well: for example, failing to alert the court when you know your witness is lying on the stand, or turning a blind eye to a law enforcement officer concealing or destroying evidence.

It can also feel like we're not taking action if there is someone (or something) else we can characterize as controlling our behavior. If our boss made us do it, we are not responsible for what happened. Attorneys in the criminal justice system are often acting at the behest of another: an assistant D.A. will be very aware that he is working for the D.A., just as a public defender will be aware that it is his client who ultimately calls the shots. As a result, the establishment of rigid hierarchies and chains of command may provide a sturdy ladder for misconduct.

Another way we manage to justify bending the rules is through social comparison. Of the dishonesty I've witnessed in my life, it's uncanny how many of the incidents involved groups of people rather than lone individuals. One person crossed the line and then suddenly three others were right there with him. Being in a group seems to alter people's moral compasses, aligning the dials and leading people who would otherwise act ethically toward trouble. Researchers have begun to look more deeply at this seemingly infectious aspect of dishonesty. Rather than viewing our behavior in absolute terms ("Is it moral or immoral to cheat on this test?"), we measure our actions against those of people around us ("Are my best friends sharing answers on the exam?").

In a recent study, psychologists had a group of people complete a test in which the better each person performed, the more money he earned. One of the "test-takers," who was actually working for the experimenters, was instructed to cheat very publicly by standing up, just sixty seconds into the test, and announcing that he had finished, had gotten everything right, and would therefore be getting the maximum payment. The question was whether this behavior would encourage other people to cheat. It did, but only when the cheater seemed to belong to the same group as everyone else in the room—that is, when he was wearing a T-shirt from the university where the experiment was being administered. When he was wearing a rival university's T-shirt, cheating actually *dropped* significantly below the control condition.

In an adversarial legal system, lawyers have especially strong group identifications—it's the prosecution versus the defense—and under such circumstances they should be particularly susceptible to moral cues from their compatriots. It is revealing in this regard that episodes of prosecutorial misconduct are often not isolated, as we would expect if it were a simple matter of rogue agents pursuing their own corrupt ends.

Responding to Justice Scalia's characterization of the prosecutorial misconduct in Thompson's case as "a single *Brady* violation by one of [Orleans Parish's] . . . prosecutors," Justice Ruth Bader Ginsburg, in a blistering dissent (which she read from the bench), pointed out that there were actually "no fewer than five prosecutors" who had acted to deprive Thompson of his rights and had "kept from him, year upon year, evidence vital to his defense." As she described, this "was no momentary oversight, no single incident of a lone officer's misconduct": "Throughout the pretrial and trial proceedings against Thompson, the team of four engaged in prosecuting him for armed robbery and murder hid from the defense and the court exculpatory information Thompson requested and had a constitutional right to receive."

Bruce Whittaker, the prosecutor who had initially approved the armed robbery indictment for Thompson, had received the crime lab report showing that the perpetrator's blood was type

B and had placed it on the desk of James Williams, an assistant D.A. who was trying the case. But neither man turned it over to Thompson's counsel—despite an official request for all information "favorable to the defendant" and germane "to the issue of guilt or punishment," including "any results or reports" of "scientific tests or experiments." Then Deegan, who was working with Williams, transferred all of the physical evidence from the police property room to the courthouse property room, but left out the bloodstained swatch. Neither Williams nor Deegan mentioned the swatch or the crime lab report during the trial—and the swatch was never seen again.

There were other critical materials that the prosecution team (including Eric Dubelier, who was partnered with Williams on the murder case) had failed to pass along to the defense. Thompson's attorneys might have seriously undermined the testimony of Richard Perkins, the man who first provided the police with Thompson's name, if they had been able to show that he lied under oath when he said that he had no knowledge of reward money before coming forward, but the prosecution did not pass along the audiotapes of Perkins's discussion of the cash prize with the victim's family. Likewise, the defense team might have shown the inconsistencies between the testimony of the prosecution's key witness, Kevin Freeman, and what Freeman purportedly told Perkins about the murder, but the defense team never received the police report containing Perkins's recollections. And, critically, Thompson's attorneys were never able to point out the discrepancy between the eyewitness's initial description of the murderer's "close cut hair" and Thompson's Afro, because they were never given the relevant police reports.

All of this suggests a *culture* of dishonesty—and indeed there is now significant evidence of prosecutorial misconduct within the D.A.'s office over a period of years. As Justice Ginsburg put it, "Disregard of *Brady*'s disclosure requirements were pervasive in Orleans Parish." District Attorney Connick himself had been indicted for withholding a crime-lab report in a different case, and several other convictions had been overturned by Louisiana judges based on prosecutors' failing to disclose *Brady* material while Connick was in charge.

As the tragedy of the New Orleans prosecutor's office shows, dishonesty can spread like a plague when given the right conditions. We take cues from those around us in deciding which behavior is acceptable and which is not—and when the norm is to bend the rules, it will be hard for most people to resist. On a broader scale, the negative stereotype of lawyers as cutthroat, manipulative, and amoral may actually *cause* unethical behavior, because it suggests pervasive and egregious dishonesty in the profession. Everyone else is doing it, so why not me?

Clearly, we take cues for our moral actions from those around us. But we also take cues from our own past behavior. This explains, in part, how we can start with a very minor act of dishonesty and gradually shift to more serious transgressions over time. Should I cheat on this math test or not? Well, I copied my algebra homework from my friend last night and this is pretty much the same thing, so it really isn't going to make a difference in how I feel about myself. Take a few steps down the path of dishonesty and you may soon find yourself miles away from the person you thought you were.

It is not just that small infractions often lead to bigger ones; scientists have also shown that greater dishonesty can be induced by simply altering a person's moral self-view. In one of my favorite experiments, researchers had participants take a test while wearing sunglasses that they were told were either genuine designer models or counterfeits. You might expect that the fake shades would make no difference at all, but in fact the percentage of people cheating more than doubled in the counterfeit condition. According to the researchers, the participants wearing the counterfeit glasses suddenly saw themselves in a new light: with the badge of dishonesty on their face, it was easier to cheat. And they also viewed their peers differently, predicting a significantly higher rate of cheating than did the people wearing "authentic" sunglasses.

It is easy to see how the slippery slope might affect a prosecutor. Initially, a colleague or superior might pressure him to bend a minor ethical rule (say, deliberately failing to mention a relevant case in an evidentiary motion because it undermines a key argument). Awareness of that transgression may then lead him to adopt a more lenient moral standard. After the initial breach of ethics, acting a bit more dishonestly (say, failing to provide the defense with a witness's description of the perpetrator that only partially matches the defendant's features) would not have a major impact on the prosecutor's overall sense of self-worth. Making matters worse, the research predicts that the more the prosecutor cheats, the more he is likely to believe that others—his colleagues and his opponents on the defense team—are also cheating, further promoting his dishonest actions. It's a dangerous cascade, especially when lives are at stake.

As improbable as it sounds, one of the most effective ways to rationalize our ethical lapses involves reframing our bad actions as *good*—a means of restoring order or serving justice. A wrong committed to remedy a wrong can become a right. Indeed, research suggests that a major driver of dishonest behavior is a desire to even the scales.

In one experiment, scientists looked at what would happen when a customer was treated rudely by a coffee shop employee and then given back more change than he or she deserved by the same employee. What they found was that people who were mistreated kept the money at a much higher rate than those who had not been mistreated. Customers on the receiving end of rudeness seemed to have been given a great excuse to justify keeping the shop's money.

It is likely that lawyers who feel that the other side has been given an unfair advantage by a judge (for instance, after a motion has been denied or evidence has been kept from a jury), or who believe that attorneys across the aisle are using underhanded tactics, are more inclined to engage in dishonest acts. The chip on your shoulder can be both a motivation and a justification for bending the rules in your favor. And that's true even where the perceived imbalance does not come from anything that the opposing attorneys or the judge has done. For a prosecutor, the chip may simply be a feeling that she is at a disadvantage because she has to work particularly long, grueling hours at lower pay than lawyers in the private sector or has an unreasonable boss or didn't go to a fancy law school. We might also imagine a new attorney feeling that she is a step or two behind other prosecutors in the office and concluding that she just needs to cheat a little bit until she catches up. Deegan was the least experienced of anyone on the prosecution team—he'd been with the district attorney's office for less than a year when he was assigned to the Thompson case.

Along similar lines, one way to convince ourselves of the righteousness of our actions is to disparage the person we're lying to or cheating. If we are hurting someone who is himself in moral disrepute, our actions suddenly become more justifiable. And it's particularly easy to see ourselves as serving moral ends when the victim has already been arrested and charged with a crime.

Deegan could readily cast himself in the role of a defender of justice. There was a very real possibility that if Thompson's blood had not matched the sample taken from the victim of the carjacking, Thompson would not have been convicted of the robbery, and without that conviction he might have been able to dodge the murder charge altogether. If you firmly believed he was guilty of brutally killing Raymond T. Liuzza Jr., it might seem quite acceptable to break the rules to ensure that Thompson got what he deserved. Moreover, there is a sense among those who work on the side of the government that most criminal defendants have already gotten away with numerous crimes in addition to the ones they are charged with. If you speak with prosecutors candidly, you will be surprised at how many, when pressed on a time they bent the rules a bit, will offer up the same excuse: "Well, even if he wasn't guilty of this crime, he was guilty of *something*."

So, in many cases, it may be the impulse to do *right*—to act altruistically—that causes us to cut corners. In a startling finding, scientists have shown that people may actually cheat more when their cheating benefits others but not themselves. If we are acting solely for others, it is hard to see ourselves in a negative light and much easier to rationalize unethical acts. People who work for nonprofit foundations, schools, or other public benefit organizations may be relatively more inclined to bend the rules because the charge of enhancing social welfare seems to justify the dishonest behavior.

If this theory is correct, both prosecutors and public defenders might well be particularly vulnerable to rationalizations of this kind. In a sense, a prosecutor who does not bend the rules is letting many people down: the victim's family, the police officers who worked the case, his fellow prosecutors, and society as a whole (including future victims who would otherwise be protected). He may also be letting down all of the people who expect him to excel in his career—his partner, his children, his parents, his friends. Ironically, then, it is caring deeply about other people, not a callous lack of empathy, that can set in motion some acts of dishonesty.

It's clear that rationalizing dishonesty is part of human nature. Still, some people are more honest than others. How can we tell which individuals are more likely to cheat?

Some of the personal characteristics that scientists have identified might be expected. Guilt-prone people, for example, are less likely to commit ethical transgressions. Other discoveries are more novel.

Sparked by intriguing findings that pathological liars have considerably more white matter (the cells that transmit signals between different areas of the brain) in their prefrontal cortex than the rest of the population, and knowing that white-matter structures have been shown to be associated with creativity, researchers decided to look at whether differences in creativity across the population might influence levels of cheating. Their hypothesis was that people who were more creative would find it easier to come up with convincing stories to justify unethical behavior. Sure enough, in their experiments, the most creative participants were also the most dishonest. Moreover, the researchers found that they could increase cheating across the board by priming people to get them into a creative mindset. Interestingly, general intelligence doesn't appear to be relevant; it's specifically creative capacity that matters.

All of this would lead one to expect that the more creative lawyers would be more likely to engage in dishonest behavior, but— perhaps more crucially—it also raises the possibility that lawyers may be particularly susceptible as a group. Much of what lawyers are trained to do, of course, is to come up with justifications, reasons, and arguments for various actions or events. They are in the business of creating plausible stories that help advance their position. One might even say that creativity, above all else, is what separates successful from unsuccessful lawyers. It is unsettling to think that a prosecutor's ability to knit together a compelling narrative that ties a defendant to a crime might also allow him to come up with a convincing story to justify breaching the defendant's rights.

And with frequently vague ethical rules and considerable room for discretion, lawyers often find themselves operating in zones of ambiguity, where creativity tends to have the biggest impact on dishonesty. Almost all of the most common acts of prosecutorial misconduct can be recast. Are you suppressing potentially exonerating evidence or keeping an immaterial report from confusing the jury? Are you making an improper closing argument or being a zealous advocate? Are you badgering and manipulating a witness or ensuring that the truth is revealed through rigorous cross-examination? Are you encouraging erroneous testimony or providing an opportunity for the jury to hear all sides?

Lawyers may be especially good at rationalizing their dishonest acts, but they're also put in situations that make the behavior particularly tempting. It made a difference that Deegan could simply check out the blood swatch from the police property room. It also mattered that the blood test report was sent to the prosecutor's office, which could then fail to turn it over to the defense. That took literally no effort at all. We should worry, then, about the enormous control that prosecutors have over the state's evidence and witnesses: they are the ones who decide if and when the defendant's team will receive the ballistics report or the DNA report or a copy of the witness statement or the initial police write-up. Give even the most upstanding fox the keys to the henhouse and see what happens.

In addition, research suggests that we are particularly likely to act dishonestly when we've already used up our reserve of self-control. According to some psychologists, willpower is a limited resource, and, unfortunately, lawyers often work under conditions that seriously deplete their store. A prosecutor faces the same challenges as the rest of us: trying to stick to his New Year's resolution and go running before work, attempting to control his emotions in the face of an unreasonable boss, fighting to pay attention during a boring conference call, struggling not to lose his temper with a rebellious teenage son. But he may face other stresses as well. Up against tight deadlines, an assistant D.A. frequently has to stay on top of multiple cases at the same time, which means juggling court opinions, statutes, facts, and other details. Moreover, he must work to satisfy the needs and desires of multiple constituencies whose interests may conflict. Figuring out how to please the victim's family, the public, the judge, and his boss, all while trying to achieve justice and fend off attacks from the other side, inevitably leads to major mental fatigue—and, far too often, dishonesty.

Given the likely frequency of prosecutorial misconduct, it seems strange that it is so rarely investigated or disciplined. The main reason is that it's hard to detect. Many of the cases over the last two decades were brought to our attention only when a DNA exoneration prompted an examination of how an innocent person had come to be convicted. Concealing evidence, one of the most common kinds of misconduct, is particularly hard to spot, because the defendant has no way of knowing what's being kept from him. And all too often attorneys do not even recognize that they have done anything wrong. Deegan eventually came to regret his decision, but in some cases, even when our immoral actions are front and center, we are able to delude ourselves into believing that the benefits of our dishonesty were rightfully earned. In one set of experiments, people who cheated on a test by using an answer key and received a high score tended to interpret that score as evidence of their high intelligence! It seems likely that prosecutors who use dishonest means to gain an edge and end up winning will later ascribe their success to their hard work, skill, and wisdom. Winning effectively wipes the slate clean.

Most of the dishonesty in our legal system, then, is going to remain invisible. But that doesn't mean there's nothing to be done. Our moral flexibility is a two-way street: while cheating can be contagious, the people around us can also promote doing the right thing. We need to tap into the positive effect we can have on one another by changing how government lawyers see their role. Research suggests that the more prosecutors are focused on winning, rather than on achieving justice, the more likely they will be to act dishonestly. Unfortunately, they receive many subtle (and not-so-subtle) cues that what really matters is their scorecard. In one

notorious example, prosecutors in Cook County, Illinois, partici-
pated in what was known as the Two-Ton Contest, with the prize
going to the first attorney to convict defendants whose combined
weight exceeded four thousand pounds. But leadership within a
prosecutor's office can turn things around by introducing robust
ethical norms and ensuring appropriate monitoring.

Growing experimental evidence suggests that knowing that
we are being watched can help us behave in the right way. Indeed, contrary to the Supreme Court majority's belief that Connick's supervisory shortcomings were not to blame for Thompson's
wrongful conviction, there is good reason to think that effective
oversight in the D.A.'s office might have prevented the injustice
Thompson suffered. Had Gerry Deegan been working in an office
that took *Brady* seriously, with colleagues keeping an eye out for
ethical breaches, he might very well have decided to pass along
the critical blood evidence to Thompson's attorneys.

We know such a cultural shift is possible because it's happening now. In 2006, Dallas County District Attorney Craig Watkins
created a new unit to address wrongful convictions by having a
team on the prosecution side reexamine cases in which the defendant's guilt was in question. Watkins argued that prosecutors
have a major interest in pursuing claims of innocence—not only
because that can lead to catching the real perpetrators, but also
because prosecutors have a responsibility to clean up their mistakes. The initiative has been extremely successful, helping to
exonerate thirty-three people since it began. Its accomplishments
have prompted the creation of similar programs in Cook County;
Wayne, Minnesota; Brooklyn; and Santa Clara, California. The
message to government attorneys in these jurisdictions is powerful: ensuring the integrity of the criminal justice process is at the
core of the prosecution's role, and there are smart, diligent people
checking your work.

Establishing new mechanisms of supervision and redefining
attorney roles requires a significant commitment to change. But

there are smaller measures all offices can take to encourage honesty. In the laboratory, even subtle moral cues have been shown to help. For instance, asking individuals to sign an honor code—or just try to write down as many of the Ten Commandments as they can remember—can greatly reduce or even eliminate cheating on a test. More astonishing, the benefits of these ethical reminders persist even when individuals do a poor job of actually recalling the Commandments and when the honor code is completely made up. MIT, for instance, doesn't have an honor code, but researchers found that it didn't matter: they could effectively quash cheating by having students sign a fake one ("I understand that this experiment falls under the guidelines of the MIT honor code").

This research suggests that we ought to install moral reminders for lawyers that help interrupt the process of rationalization and self-justification that occurs in moments of temptation. One idea might be to have prosecutors recite an oath—or write down what they believe their particular moral or ethical responsibilities to be—prior to the proceedings each day of trial. Likewise, to encourage attorneys to turn over exculpatory evidence to the defense team, we could ask prosecutors not only to sign a statement promising that they had complied with their *Brady* duties, but also to articulate in a few sentences why refusing to turn over such material is immoral. As scientists have discovered, the key is making the reminders a regular part of the process without having them become so routine that they're invisible.

It's a simple formula: to get prosecutors to follow the virtuous path, we must point them where we want them to go, set up signposts, and regularly check their progress. We can't sit back and wait, counting on others to right the course. After prosecutors have already broken the rules, it's too late.

Look again at the miracles needed to save Thompson's life: the two Philadelphia lawyers who took over his case free of charge after he'd sent hundreds of letters to others with no response; the law firm willing to pay for one last-ditch effort after all the appeals had run out; the investigator who—at the last possible moment—found the carjacking blood test on a piece of dusty microfiche. It reads like fiction. We've got to face reality: there are no guardian angels for most of the Thompsons of this world. With limited resources and heavy caseloads, few defense attorneys are up to the role, and there is rarely money for special investigations. It is an open question whether jurors or judges might act the part, demanding more from prosecutors and seeing through to the true facts—topics to be considered in the chapters to come. But it seems foolish to test our luck, when we can intervene before innocent men like Thompson are ever brought into the courtroom.

# 5

# IN THE EYE OF THE BEHOLDER

## The Jury

Given the great human longing for power—our dry-throated thirst for control, our teeth-baring fury to protect even the feeblest charge over the most limited domain—I have always been baffled by the effort people devote to getting out of jury service. For many of those summoned to the courthouse, it is not an exaggeration to say that being impaneled is the greatest authority they will wield in their entire lives. Not only do jurors get to decide guilt or innocence, to command the resources of the state to change the direction of a person's life, but they also enjoy the seemingly supernatural ability to determine history after it has already occurred. Serving on a jury means getting to decide what happened. Jurors are the authors of the facts. And you, who just last night got in a heated argument with your wife over who got to manage the volume on the television remote, gave it all up by *lying to a judge*, no less, about your "very serious" back pain.

People are strange, which raises the broader question of why we trust laymen, who possess no special qualifications or legal training, with such immense responsibility in the first place.

In fact, for centuries, many in the legal elite—judges and scholars—have not. There is a long tradition of doubting the capacity of a jury to accurately determine the facts of a case, and as a result a lot of effort has gone into fashioning various mechanisms to constrain the jury's power. Today, the debate over jury authority has been raised anew in the context of emerging technology. When we have a videotape of the critical events, do we really need a jury to tell us what happened?

An unusual recent case brought this question to the fore.

Deputy Clinton Reynolds was sitting in his cruiser along Highway 34, southwest of Atlanta. It was a damp Thursday evening in late March. The cars would catch a glimpse of him and ease onto the brakes. He kept an eye on the radar gun. A Cadillac came up doing 73 in a 55, so he flicked on his blue lights. He was going to let it go—everyone speeds. He wasn't even going to pull out.

But the Cadillac didn't slow as it passed. In fact, as soon as he turned onto the two-lane road, the driver accelerated.

Reynolds radioed in the license plate and reported that he was in pursuit. He didn't request assistance, but another officer, Timothy Scott, was listening in and soon joined the chase. When the Cadillac turned into a shopping center parking lot, Scott sped ahead to try to block the exit. He thought he'd boxed the driver in, but the Cadillac made a sharp turn at the last minute, lightly colliding with his cruiser before heading southbound on Highway 74.

Rejoining the chase, Scott told Reynolds to give way and pulled into the lead position: "Let me have him . . . my car's already tore up."

The six-minute pursuit had covered two counties, and Scott had had enough. He radioed in for permission to "PIT" the vehicle. A Precision Intervention Technique maneuver involves hitting the back of the fleeing car in order to spin it to a stop. And though it's known to be hazardous at high speeds, Scott got his answer, crackling across the radio: "Go ahead and take him out." The cars had reached a narrow stretch of the road, with no shoulder, but Scott saw his chance and took it. He hit the gas and rammed the Cadillac's rear bumper.

The result was dramatic: the Cadillac swerved and then swung to the right shoulder, careened down an embankment, and flipped over. Scott yelled into his radio, "It's a 10-50 [police code for an accident]. It's gonna be a bad 10-50. Bad." White smoke poured from the wreckage. The officers ran down to the car and pulled desperately on the doors. Scott looked through the window and could tell that the driver "did not have his seatbelt on. His head was beneath the brake pedal, his torso was across the seat, and his legs were bent over the back of the seat."

One of the officers said what they all were thinking: "He ain't gonna make it."

Victor Harris, nineteen, the youngest of nine children, beat the odds and survived. But the cost of the accident was severe: in the hospital, Victor learned that he was paralyzed from the neck down.

Taking stock of the events that led to his injury, Victor decided to sue Officer Scott under the Fourth Amendment of the Constitution, which prohibits unreasonable seizures. Victor's argument was that just as the Constitution forbids a police officer from shooting a shoplifter in the back as he runs away, it also bars an officer from using a potentially lethal bumping technique to cause an individual's vehicle to spin out when the initial offense was simply driving a few miles over the speed limit.

The government, for its part, contested the notion that Officer Scott's actions were unreasonable, which raised some important factual questions. Perhaps chief among them were just how serious a risk the chase posed and who was to blame—Victor or the police—for the hazards that it created.

Had the accident taken place ten or twenty years earlier, those weighing Victor's claim and determining what happened would have had to piece together a narrative from the testimony provided by the parties, various witnesses, and experts. But in 2001, Coweta County, Georgia, was running dashboard cameras in its squad cars. To determine whether Victor created a significantly dangerous situation in fleeing from the police that justified Scott's

PIT maneuver, the chase did not have to be re-created; it could simply be watched.

The case eventually made its way to the Supreme Court. And it was clear from the oral argument that the justices were skeptical of Victor's position. They had all seen the video, and it had left a powerful impression. As Justice Scalia explained, Victor "created the scariest chase I ever saw since *The French Connection*."

The issue, though, was what a jury would think. Was it possible that a reasonable juror might watch the video and disagree with Justice Scalia? If so, the justices would have to send the case back for a full trial; if not, then Victor's attempt to gain relief was over.

The Supreme Court majority found this an easy question to answer because the videotape provided such a clear picture of what actually happened. According to the Court, after watching the tape, no reasonable juror could possibly believe that the chase was anything but extremely dangerous and no reasonable juror could possibly imagine that the police were at fault for Victor's paralysis. As Justice Scalia wrote in the opinion, Victor's "version of events" was "utterly discredited" by the videotape. The Court was so sure of itself that it took the unprecedented step of posting a link to the video online and inviting members of the public to watch.

There is a difference, however, between being sure and being right.


Each of us believes that we see the world exactly as it is and that other reasonable people will see things similarly—that is, correctly. This is true whether we are watching a referee throw a flag at a football game, discussing the state of the economy with a friend, or sorting through evidence with fellow jurors. Was that a late hit on the quarterback or wasn't it? There is only one right way to view the play, and the person sitting next to us in the stands ought to see it just as we do.

We operate under the illusion that reality enters our brain through our senses unfiltered. We acknowledge the potential for bias when we hear about what happened from another person— say, when a friend describes a referee's call to us after the fact—but not when we are watching the game ourselves. That's true even if our experience is being mediated through technology. When we watch a video, listen to a recording, or look at a photograph, we feel as if we are viewing things in an objective, neutral manner.

But then, not everyone does see things the way we do.

When we come across those with conflicting viewpoints or beliefs, we experience a strong dissonance that we seek to resolve. One option would be to reassess the evidence and question our own objectivity, but we rarely take that route. Rather, we look to dismiss the other person's views by finding a character flaw that explains her contrary position. Those with conflicting viewpoints or beliefs, it stands to reason, have something wrong with them that is distorting their vision: they are biased, they are ideological, they are stupid, they are uneducated.

If you happen to believe that climate change is real and largely a result of human activity, think about how you feel when you read about a senator calling global warming a myth. Does it cause you to wonder if your belief is, in fact, correct? Or is your immediate reaction to think, "Oh, he's just in the pocket of the oil lobby," or "What an idiot"?

If you go to the movies and your date says afterward that the film was terribly boring when you thought it was great, do you stop to question the objectivity of your perspective? Do you think, "Maybe I'm wrong" or "Both of our positions are reasonable"? Or do you start to reassess going on the date in the first place—"This guy just isn't very smart" or, more charitably, "Maybe he needs more exposure to independent cinema"?

The process of maintaining our own viewpoints by discrediting anyone who disagrees with us is largely automatic. But whether we're at a Giants game or a protest rally, most of our disagreements don't arise from the character flaws of those who see things differently. Rather, they reflect the realities of cultural cognition: our shared backgrounds and experiences shape how we perceive seemingly objective facts. Watching an Eagles linebacker deliver a hit on the Giants quarterback, we cannot help but be influenced by our allegiance to the Giants as we determine whether the referee was right to throw a flag. It feels as though our assessment is totally neutral, but it's not. At any given moment, our race, gender, age, profession, politics, religion, and countless other identity-defining characteristics and affiliations are coloring what we see.

In a powerful demonstration of this phenomenon, a group of law professors decided to test the Supreme Court's conclusion that "no reasonable juror" could watch the footage of the chase that left Victor Harris paralyzed and see Victor's evasion of the police as anything but extremely dangerous and the cause of the eventual crash. Did "the videotape . . . speak for itself," as Justice Scalia suggested? The researchers asked a diverse group of 1,350 Americans to watch the video and then offer their impressions.

What they found were clear rifts in perception along ideological, cultural, and other lines concerning the key issues in the case: Was the chase worth the risk? Did Victor pose a lethal danger to the police and public? Were the police justified in terminating the chase by using deadly force? Who was more at fault—the police or Victor?

Each participant in the study watched the same footage, but they did not see the same thing. A less affluent, liberal, highly educated African American woman with egalitarian and communitarian views was far more likely than a wealthy, conservative white man supportive of existing social hierarchies and individualism to see Officer Scott and the police as the primary culprits.

It was not that some viewers lied about what they had seen,

failed to pay attention, or did not understand the questions they were being asked. It was that their identities and affiliations acted as tinted glasses, filtering out certain details and bringing others into sharp focus. Contrary to the Supreme Court's conclusion, there was not just one "reasonable" view of the facts. There were many. The retired white businessman from Scottsdale, Arizona, literally saw something different in the flashing lights and spinning tires from what the black college student from Philadelphia saw.

The participants, though, didn't feel that their identities were shaping their take on events. And the fact that the true source of our disagreement remains hidden from us can result in very serious problems. As the research team pointed out, it was this blindness that led the Supreme Court to reach the wrong conclusion—preventing a jury from considering the case on the grounds that there was only one legitimate way to understand what happened—and, in the process, to stigmatize all those who viewed the facts differently from Justice Scalia's majority. According to the Supreme Court, such people were "unreasonable" and were rightly barred from participating in the judicial process.

Of course, the faith we have in our own perceptions and our cynical discrediting of those with whom we disagree can create trouble even when a jury does get to consider the case. As jurors, we are often oblivious to how our own preexisting commitments, beliefs, and biases shape our impressions, but we quickly and easily spot them influencing others.

In the play (and 1957 film) 12 Angry Men, it is Juror #10 who most clearly lacks objectivity: he wears his prejudice against the Hispanic defendant on his sleeve, ranting about how Hispanics are "dangerous" and "wild"; how they're "real big drinkers" and inborn liars. "Most of 'em," he explains, "it's like they have no feelings! They can do anything!" And, yet, after saying many explicitly racist things about the defendant, it is Juror #10 who most clearly expresses his sense that others who don't see things as he does are the ones who are biased or naïve: "I don't understand you people! I mean all these picky little points you keep bringing up. They don't mean nothing. You saw this kid just like I did. You're not gonna tell me you believe that phony story about losing the knife, and that business about being at the movies."

Juror #10 is no anomaly: when there is disagreement within the jury over the facts of the case, it can be very difficult for jurors not to blame the imagined character flaws of the people with whom they disagree. Judges frequently receive notes about certain members of the jury being "difficult" or "unreasonable," and gridlock is not uncommon. In such circumstances, judges often urge jurors to continue their work, and when consensus is finally reached, it is held up as a triumph of group decision-making—the outliers were made to see sense. Yet there is reason to be skeptical. In *12 Angry Men*, Juror #8 (played memorably by Henry Fonda in the movie version) starts out as the lone dissenting voice and ultimately convinces the other eleven jurors to change their votes and acquit the defendant. In real life, though, it is often the Henry Fondas of the world who give in. They may not see the facts the way the rest of the jurors do, but they are eventually browbeaten into acquiescing to the majority view. Even when their divergent views are entirely legitimate, they may come to believe the other jurors' claims that they are being unreasonable. Recent research suggests as much: the best way to predict a jury's ultimate verdict is to look at what the majority of jurors favor before deliberating, because that aligns with the outcome 90 percent of the time.

In truth, none of us are immune to these dynamics of perception and judgment. They influence every player in the courtroom. And they shape the public response to jury verdicts. When O.J. Simpson was acquitted of murdering his ex-wife, Nicole Brown Simpson, and her friend, Ronald Goldman, the reaction of many was to find a flaw in the jury. Why did they acquit? Well, nine out of the twelve jurors were black, and they must have voted based on racial allegiance, consciously disregarding all the evidence. Or maybe it had to do with intelligence—after all, only two of the jurors had college degrees; they probably didn't understand the scientific evidence or were easily manipulated by the masterful con men led by Johnnie Cochran. Few people were willing to entertain the notion that other people might simply look at the same evidence, develop a genuine "reasonable doubt," and feel that the prosecutors had failed to prove their case.

If different people with different backgrounds and identities can look at the same events and see very different facts, is it also possible that the same person can look at the same events and see very different facts depending on how information is presented? It seems highly doubtful—as long as we are looking at "reality," the frame shouldn't matter. A human witness can forget, get confused, or lie, but we assume that a photograph or video provides us with an accurate record of exactly what happened.

It was precisely this confidence in the objectivity of videotape that led the Supreme Court to decide *Scott v. Harris* on its own. As Justice Scalia explained, by presenting a neutral, unfiltered account of events, the video of the police chase revealed Victor's version of events to be a "visible fiction." And the dawn of the "video age" has been hailed by many people across the political spectrum as a clear path toward improving accuracy in our legal system: finally, juries will be able to see key interactions with their own eyes. Even Marge Simpson has weighed in: "You know, the courts may not be working anymore, but as long as everyone is videotaping everyone else, justice will be done."

But are Marge and Justice Scalia right?

Unfortunately, the latest scientific evidence says they are not. Unless you're a film critic or an artist, you don't tend to think about how the particular camera angle or viewpoint influences the way we make sense of the scene in front of us. We get caught up in what we are seeing, without considering *how* we are seeing it or what we might be missing. But all of our seemingly neutral media hold the potential to bias assessments of what transpired and who was to blame.

Over the last few decades, researchers have conducted a number of experiments showing how this happens. When we view events as if standing in the shoes of the person experiencing them, we are much more likely to attribute the actor's behavior to forces and constraints in the surrounding environment than when we adopt the perspective of an outside observer, in which case we tend to make attributions that focus on the individual's disposition and character.

Imagine that you are impaneled on a jury and have to decide whether the defendant's confession was voluntary or coerced by the police. As luck would have it, the entire interrogation was recorded, and you are provided with a videotape from one of three cameras in the room: a camera directed at the interrogator, a camera directed at the defendant, or a camera positioned to the side, showing both parties. It would seem reasonable to assume that regardless of the footage you were shown, you would come to the same conclusion, since all three cameras capture the exact same scene. When scientists conducted a number of studies using such a setup, however, they found that perspective made a big difference. By simply shifting the point of view from the person being questioned to the interrogator, researchers were able to significantly reduce the number of people who thought the resulting confession was coerced. Watching the interrogator through the eyes of the suspect, it was a lot easier to see—and feel—the menace and pressure. Those who watched the videotape that showed both sides made assessments that fell in between the two conditions.

Camera perspective bias can also influence our assessments of whether the defendant is guilty and how severely he should be punished. In one experiment, moving from a confession videotape showing both the suspect and the interrogator to one focused solely on the suspect doubled the rate of conviction. What's more, the bias seems to occur both for minor offenses like shoplifting and for more serious crimes like burglary, rape, and manslaughter. And it's surprisingly sticky: greater expertise (being a law enforcement officer or a judge), increased accountability, and judicial instructions aimed at encouraging people to be more mindful of perspective bias all appear to be largely ineffective. People just cannot see what they are missing.

Could camera perspective bias have played a role in the outcome of Victor Harris's case?

Justice Scalia thought he had rooted out any potential unfairness by noting that "there are no allegations or indications that this videotape was doctored or altered in any way," but he and the rest of the majority were wrong.

The video camera mounted in Officer Scott's cruiser seemed to offer an unfiltered lens on the core facts of the case. But it didn't just record a high-speed chase; it recorded a chase *from the perspective of the lead police officer involved in the pursuit.* Watching the tape, we sit where he sat and hear what he heard: from the taillights of the suspect's Cadillac reflecting off those wet Coweta County roads to the crackling voice of the dispatcher telling us to "take him out." Having adopted the officer's physical perspective, it becomes extremely easy to share his assessment of the situation and understand why he acted the way he did.

What if the Supreme Court had watched another, different videotape—say, a clip taken by a pedestrian standing at an intersection or footage from a news helicopter hovering above? What if there had been a recording taken from inside Harris's car, looking back at the police cars hot in pursuit? Each of these tapes would be a true, accurate depiction of the police chase, but the research suggests that we would reach very different conclusions about the level of risk the chase created, whether deadly force was reasonable under the circumstances, and who was to blame for putting the public in danger.

Seeing events through Victor's eyes would have put his actions in a whole new light. Viewers might have considered what it must feel like to be a nineteen-year-old black man in Georgia being pursued late at night by multiple police cars with lights flashing and sirens blaring. It might have triggered feelings of empathy and raised challenging questions: "How would I have responded under the circumstances, after making that initial mistake of not pulling over, knowing how officers tend to treat those who flee, and seeing no witnesses to intervene if things got out of hand?" With such a video, it would have been easier to see Victor as a young man influenced by powerful situational pressures.

At the time of the accident, Victor was working at a temp agency to support himself as a full-time student at Griffin Technical College. He had left home at four in the morning and had been working all day. By 11 p.m. he was completely exhausted and was not paying attention as he passed the speed trap. When he suddenly saw the lights in his rearview mirror, he "panicked." His license had been suspended for unpaid tickets, and he was afraid he'd go to jail. Running from the police is the last thing many Americans would ever do, but for young African American men—for whom the threat and fear of harassment, capture, and incarceration is ever present—it can be a basic instinct, learned as a kid. There is no expectation that things will work out, that you'll get a fair shake, that you can trust in the police and the system. For many black teens, when you see a cop, you just go.

In a fateful instant, Victor pressed down on the gas. As he explained later, "It wasn't my intention to put anyone's life in danger or to scare anyone. My only plan was to get home.... As I was running, I saw other police cars that were blocking off the streets, and I felt like I was being trapped.... I couldn't believe this was actually happening to me.... The last thing I wanted to do was hurt myself or anyone else. I was nineteen years old and I was scared."

———

Victor Harris made a terrible error in judgment that rainy night, but he did not deserve to be paralyzed, and he did not deserve to have his case taken away from a jury. The system failed him because of the psychological limitations of the people who operate it—limitations we all share. We see, in the words of the Bible, the speck in the eye of our brother but fail to notice the beam in our own eye. We blindly trust in the objectivity of our technologies because they seem to deliver reality, when, in truth, they may distort our perspectives.

Reasonable jurors can differ radically in how they perceive a case, and if you draw the "wrong" panel, you might be convicted of a crime when twelve other jurors would have found you innocent. Similarly, efforts to protect suspects from police abuse, like taping all questioning, can, paradoxically, have the effect of unfairly tipping things in favor of the prosecution if the camera happens to always be placed behind the interrogators.

Moving forward, both of these concerns warrant dedicated reforms.

With respect to perspective bias, the time to act is now. Every year, more squad cars are outfitted with dashboard cameras, more jurisdictions require interrogations to be taped, and more officers are wearing recording devices on their bodies as standard procedure. Most of these recordings will show events from the perspective of the police, and each one will hold the potential to sway those who watch it later, whether that is a prosecutor deciding whether to charge a suspect with resisting arrest, an internal-affairs detective reviewing the conduct of an officer, a juror trying to figure out who the aggressor was, or an appellate judge reviewing a case.

But the solution isn't to eliminate cameras altogether. Used in the correct manner, cameras may offer ways to make our system fairer.

In 2012, a program was introduced in Rialto, California, to place small cameras on the bodies of police officers (in this case, on their sunglasses). Over the next year, both the number of complaints filed against officers and the number of incidents where officers used force decreased by well over 50 percent. Knowing that they were being watched seemed to encourage cops and members of the public to behave more civilly.

The proliferation of video footage may also help us to avoid certain biases (for example, by eliminating the need to rely on faulty eyewitness memory to identify a suspect). And once we understand how footage can influence perception, we can change how we use cameras to address that distortion. Since camera angles that offer a third-party perspective can eliminate biased assessments of whether a confession was coerced, that should be the first choice. Since it's often not possible to employ dashboard cameras—or those attached to an officer's glasses—in a neutral manner, such video footage shouldn't be used in a conclusive fashion, as it was by the Supreme Court. We should be particularly careful when footage doesn't show all parties in the frame or when it captures only some of the key events. Alternatively, we might allow it to be entered into evidence only with the consent of the defendant.

Unfortunately, controlling for the influence of each juror's unique background and set of experiences presents a more vexing puzzle. The Sixth Amendment provides the defendant in a criminal trial with the right to "an impartial jury." It's a promise that we do not keep and may never be able to deliver. Still, we can do better.

Shifting more responsibility for determining the facts to judges has always been a possibility. But when judges usurp the jury's role on the grounds that something appears clear and uncontroversial, as the Supreme Court did in *Scott v. Harris*, they run the risk of simply substituting their own backgrounds and experiences for those of the jury.

Rather, we should focus on jury composition. If different jurors perceive the key facts and legal issues of a case differently, then juries ought to be diverse. It is not fair that certain groups—such as white Americans—are currently overrepresented in jury pools while other groups are underrepresented. That is not fair to prospective jurors from disadvantaged groups, and it is not fair to people like Victor Harris who would face better odds in court with more inclusion. To treat the problem, we need to look hard at why—decades after reforms were put in place to address the exclusion of certain groups—jury diversity continues to be an issue. Multiple reforms may be in order, including paying jurors (or employers) enough to ensure that no one loses income, providing transportation and childcare to those who need it, and rethinking how we screen jurors.

Under our current system, during the *voir dire* process prior to trial, the lawyers and the judge attempt to remove certain people from the jury pool whom they expect to be biased toward one side or the other. The challenge, as I'll explore in greater detail later, is how to get *voir dire* to serve its intended purpose as we learn more about how particular identities, experiences, and values may influence juror perceptions and judgments at trial.

Imagine a case of check fraud against a forty-two-year-old obese African American mother of six living on welfare. How should we go about sorting through potential jurors?

Recent research suggests that a person's weight can influence juror assessments, with male jurors more likely to reach a guilty verdict when the accused is an overweight woman than when she is thin. Female jurors, by contrast, do not exhibit this body-size bias, nor do men who are judging other men. What's more, slim men appear to be particularly skewed against heavy female defendants: they are not only significantly more likely to conclude that an obese woman meets the criteria for the crime than a slender woman, but also inclined to judge her more likely to reoffend.

In light of this, we could prevent all men from sitting on this particular jury, or bar all the skinny guys. Or we could ask the men more detailed questions to try to further differentiate within that pool. But if we care about fair treatment, doing nothing seems negligent.

It is hard, though, to know where to stop. There are many other variables that may bias certain jurors and not others, including—in this fraud case—the age, race, and socioeconomic status of the defendant. If we have limited resources, which ones should we pay attention to and which should we ignore?

Emerging technology may allow us to gain an increasingly nuanced understanding of how cultural cognition operates in the jury box. Implicit association tests are already able to capture the strength of the stereotypes and general attitudes individuals have about different groups, including racial minorities, poor people, and the obese. The basic idea behind the tests is that people will be quicker to group things that they already associate with each other (such as a picture of a thin person and the word *good*) than things that they don't expect to go together (such as a picture of an obese person and the word *good*). When an image or word appears on the computer screen, you hit the "e" key if it belongs in the category on the left of the screen (thin faces/positive words) and "i" if it belongs on the right (obese faces/negative words). Then the categories are changed around (thin/negative and obese/positive). Measuring the speed of responses in milliseconds allows scientists to tap into automatic—and often unconscious—biases, which may be particularly useful in getting at jurors' hidden partialities. When it comes to obesity, for example, people show strong implicit *and* explicit weight bias, since it is culturally acceptable to express negative feelings about obese people, but a different pattern emerges for biases against blacks and the poor. In these cases, many people show strong implicit biases, but relatively few are aware of their proclivities or willing to admit to them.

To date, the researchers who have developed these tests have warned, on ethical grounds, against using them for anything other than educating jurors. But, as we will discuss later, sophisticated, individualized juror assessment is already offered by trial consultants and sanctioned by our legal system. The time may come when scientific screening is a standard part of *voir dire*. And breakthroughs in neuroscience may even make it possible to detect certain proclivities in individual jurors based on neural activity. The initial work has already begun. In a recent fMRI study, scientists found that the amount of money that mock jurors awarded to a black victim could be predicted by their brain activity as they looked at black and white faces. Rather than filling out a questionnaire, an arriving juror might someday be presented with pictures or descriptions of various people, situations, or events and then be dismissed (or perhaps "balanced out") if his brain responses exhibit patterns associated with biases relevant to the case at hand. Whether this seems like a dangerous form of government intrusion or a huge leap forward probably depends on your feelings about the current system.

The challenge will always be to determine whether a measure of implicit bias or particular brain activity is a reliable enough predictor of behavior to be grounds for intervention. How sure do we have to be that a juror is more likely to side with the police regardless of the facts of the individual case?

But that's really not a new question. It arises in nearly every trial—implicitly or explicitly. What we have to decide is whether we want to answer it with the aid of science or without. The car is on; the wheels are turning; we are driving forward no matter what. We can look at the best map available—imperfect though it may be—or we can navigate by instinct. The choice is ours.

# 6

## THE CORRUPTION OF MEMORY

### The Eyewitness

"Do you see a person in the courtroom here today that was the person who came in your apartment that night?"

The victim looked around the room.

"Yes, sir."

The Meriwether County prosecutor chose his words carefully. This was a pivotal moment in the trial: an opportunity to tip the case. If he played it for maximum theatrical effect, the Georgia jury would be his.

The woman on the stand waited and they watched—this elderly woman, who had been hurt so badly that a rape kit could not be used; whose face, partially paralyzed, still carried the frozen terror of the crime.

"If you would, please, ma'am, come out of the witness stand, and if you would just go point out that person."

She stepped down, just as he asked, and, in full view of the entire court, raised her hand.

"That's him."

John Jerome White was convicted and sentenced to life in prison.

At trial, White had been adamant that he was not the man who had broken into the woman's house in the early morning hours of August 11, 1979, beaten her, and sexually assaulted her. He was not the one who had then rifled through her purse for seventy dollars in cash, yanked the telephone cord out of the socket, and walked out the back door. "I know I didn't rape that lady," he insisted.

Had the case turned only on the physical evidence, White might have convinced the jury to let him off. The prosecution didn't have much—a criminalist at the Columbus Branch of the State Crime Laboratory had testified that there was "sufficient similarity" between hairs collected on bedding from the crime scene and hairs belonging to White "to conclude that they could have had the same origin." But under cross-examination, the analyst was forced to admit that his level of certainty was quite low: the hair collected in the victim's house "could have" come from White, by which he meant nothing more than "it's more likely it did than didn't."

The prosecutor, however, had a trump card in his deck.

The victim had identified White as her attacker, not once but three separate times. As any D.A. will tell you, producing a positive ID by the victim is one of the most effective ways to lock a man up. In the words of Supreme Court Justice William J. Brennan Jr., "There is almost nothing more convincing than a live human being who takes the stand, points a finger at the defendant, and says, 'That's the one!' "

But John Jerome White was not the one. DNA tests conducted in 2007 on those same crime-scene hairs excluded him as the perpetrator.

By the time White walked out of Macon State Prison in December of that year, the victim had long since died, but the finger she raised some twenty-eight years earlier had left a jagged scar. Without her error, White wouldn't have spent almost half of his life in prison. It was that simple and that cruel.

Yet there was a still darker twist to this case. With White identified, the file was closed. The authorities never looked for the real perpetrator and had no idea how close they had been to catching him—not decades later, after he had raped another Meriwether woman, but way back in 1979. It was then, just a few weeks after the assault, that the victim had stood at the police station in front of the five men pictured below.

White appears in the middle of the lineup wearing ripped jean shorts and a white T-shirt. He is rail thin, with a relaxed, almost feminine pose—legs together, elbows in, hip slung to the side. He looks directly at the camera.

The victim had no trouble picking him out—the one holding the number 3. As she explained, she was "almost positive" that he was the perpetrator.

It was an awful mistake. But it was only half of the story. As it turned out, she made *two* fateful errors that day. Standing before her, just two spots to the right, was her real attacker: James Edward Parham, number 5, round-faced in jeans and a striped shirt, glancing off to the side. At the police station, she had looked upon the true perpetrator and picked out an innocent man.

Parham's inclusion in the lineup had been a mere coincidence.

The police were focused on White. Parham just happened to be locked up for an unrelated offense at the moment the victim was brought in for the identification, and he was pulled in as a "filler." The police had no idea that he was actually the person they were looking for. And it would be almost thirty years before anyone would connect the dots.

White's case is unusual, but it is not isolated. Even among the limited number of DNA exoneration cases that have been catalogued by researchers, there are at least two other instances in which a victim was given the opportunity to identify the true assailant and selected an innocent man instead.

In one of those cases, a twenty-two-year-old college student, Jennifer Thompson, was raped at knifepoint in her apartment. She was determined to help the police catch her attacker, and when she was presented with a photo array, and then a lineup, and then an in-court identification, she named the same man, Ronald Junior Cotton, each time. Thompson was "completely confident," and Cotton was given a life sentence. But then another man in the prison wing where Cotton was locked up, Bobby Poole, began bragging that he was actually the one who had attacked Thompson. At Cotton's retrial, Poole was brought into the courtroom: "Ms. Thompson, have you ever seen this man?" Without hesitation she responded, "I have never seen him in my life. I have no idea who he is." Cotton was sentenced again to spend the rest of his life in prison. But, just like White, he turned out to be innocent, and the guilty party—matched through DNA—was none other than Poole. As Thompson wrote later, "I was certain, but I was wrong."

These tragedies bring the problems with witness memory into stark relief. If a person who was face to face with her attacker for an extended period of time can fail to identify him and instead implicate another man, what about all the other cases, the vast majority, in which a witness catches only a passing glimpse of the perpetrator, and that person does not appear in the lineup down at the police station?

While there are other ways to identify a suspect or piece together events, including surveillance footage and DNA evidence, witnesses provide the most common means of figuring out what happened. Some witness memories, like the face of the perpetrator or the make of his car, are critical to solving a case. Others are important for determining *how* events transpired, which can reveal a motive, establish a necessary element of a crime (for example, that the killing of the victim was premeditated), or eliminate a self-defense claim (the victim pulled out a knife only *after* the suspect pointed a gun at him). But nearly every case turns on the memory of a witness at some point, whether it's steering a police officer toward evidence, encouraging a reluctant prosecutor to press charges, convincing a juror to convict, or influencing a judge at sentencing. To cite just one statistic, each year in America some 77,000 people are charged with crimes after being identified by eyewitnesses in police lineups.

Our dependence on witness memory would not be so troubling were it not for the clear picture that emerges from the thousands of studies on memory, experiments with mock witnesses, and real-life cases.

There is, for instance, compelling evidence that eyewitness identifications are frequently inaccurate. When the actual perpetrator appears in a lineup along with several innocent fillers, witnesses fail to pick anyone out about a third of the time. And of those witnesses who do choose someone, one third select a filler. This is great news if you're guilty, because it means that your chance of being identified in a lineup is only about 50 percent. But even more disturbing is what happens when the perpetrator does *not* appear in the lineup: in that situation, people select an innocent filler about half of the time (rather than correctly declining to select anyone). Moreover, people who successfully pick the suspect in a lineup turn out not to be so reliable after all: when those individuals are shown an identical lineup *without* the suspect, roughly half of them simply select someone else—an innocent person.

It is no surprise, then, that erroneous eyewitness identifications are one of the leading causes of wrongful convictions. Of the first 250 DNA exonerations in the United States, 190 of them appear to have involved mistaken identifications.

The mystery is how such horrible injustice can arise when, in many cases, no one intended to mislead or deceive. Victims tend to be strongly motivated to identify the people who actually committed the crimes against them. The vast majority of other witnesses who come forward want to help solve cases. And police, prosecutors, jurors, and judges have powerful incentives to catch and convict true perpetrators. There is nothing in John Jerome White's case, for example, to suggest that the police set him up or deliberately bent the rules; they were simply trying to bring a rapist to justice. After his exoneration, White himself was reluctant to attack the people whose actions had deprived him of freedom for so long. It wasn't a story of some evil conspiracy, just a case in which "some people made some mistakes."

White was right, but he also missed something important: the mistakes were neither random nor unexpected. As we'll see, they were the predictable outcome of a criminal justice system that exacerbates the limitations and frailties of human memory.


Most of us have strong intuitions about how our memories work. One of the most widely shared notions is that they are basically like video cameras: over the years, our brains capture thousands of images and clips that we can retrieve whenever necessary. Sure, sometimes we forget where we stored things, or the image was blurry to begin with, but when we do successfully retrieve one of those stored pictures or videos, we are viewing an authentic and accurate record of what was once before our eyes.

Not only do a large majority of us report that we have excellent memories, but we also expect other healthy human beings to perform basic memory tasks with accuracy and consistency. As a result, we have great faith in the power of memory as a tool in the criminal justice system.

Part of that faith is quite warranted. In some ways, our memories are indeed the amazing crime-fighting tools we believe them to be. We have an uncanny ability, for example, to remember certain faces.

But we also all know that our memories fail on a regular basis. I regularly cannot recall the names of people I have just been introduced to, crossword puzzle clues I read seconds earlier, and grocery items I assured my wife I did not need to write down. How is it possible that I can readily remember a useless fact I came across back in college, like the year *On the Origin of Species* was first published (1859), but not the last four digits of the phone number I was just given for the dermatologist? How is it that years later in a Tube station in northeast London I easily recognize the woman who had a locker next to me my freshman year of high school, but I struggle to place the student who sat in my class just last semester when I run into him at a bar near campus?

The answer is that our memories aren't really like video cameras at all. To begin with, our real memories are severely hampered by limits in perception and attention. We are simply incapable of processing the incredible amount of material we encounter every second of every day. Just seeing or hearing or smelling something does not create a discrete memory that we can readily recall.

As a demonstration, I'd like you to describe a person whose image you have seen thousands of times. Indeed, chances are high that you are carrying at least one copy of his picture with you at this very moment.

Imagine that I'm a sketch artist and tell me about the man who appears on the front of the ten-dollar bill—without looking, of course.

Is his hair, curly, wavy, or straight? Does it cover his ears? Does he have a dimple in his chin? Is he wearing a bow tie? Are his eyebrows bushy? Does his jacket have a small collar or a big collar? What type of nose does he have? And, finally, what is his name?

Now turn the page and take a look at the man on the bill. How close did you come?

For many of you, this task was extremely difficult, but it could have been much worse. I could have asked you about the signatures that appear to the left and right of Alexander Hamilton's neck, or about what appears on the reverse side of the bill.

We don't generally take notice of elements in our field of vision if we aren't focused on them. The details of Hamilton's face are largely irrelevant to our use of the ten-dollar bill. When we pull one out, our attention is on completing a purchase; all we need to know is that it's a ten in our hand and not a five, a one, or a twenty. It doesn't matter how many times we've seen it or even how important it is. Indeed, we sometimes overlook things that are critical to our lives.

In one study, researchers found that only 24 percent of the faculty, staff, and students with offices in the Psychology Department building at UCLA recalled the location of the nearest fire extinguisher—despite the fact that each extinguisher was clearly visible and no more than 25 feet away. Many of the people in the building had been exposed to them every day for years, but that didn't matter. The fire extinguishers were not germane to their day-to-day goals and experiences.

On the bright side, when we are encouraged to pay attention to something, our memories tend to oblige. When the experimenters returned to the UCLA office building two months later and asked the same participants about the location of the nearest fire extinguisher, everyone knew, because the earlier interaction had brought the location of the bright red objects to the forefront. The

challenge for criminal witnesses is that many times the relevance of an object or person does not become clear until well after the incident. We are much less likely to remember the idling van and the bearded passerby if we have no reason to note them at the time.

Imagine, though, a situation in which you are aware that you should make a mental note of everything around you—say, you witness a brutal assault in an alley. Unfortunately, even then our memories do not perform as we expect them to. They lack the permanence of photographs or videotapes; over time, we simply lose the ability to recall a lot of what we experienced. And the process is rarely uniform. We tend to be best at remembering the gist of what happened (two men were arguing, and the tall one picked up a pipe and hit the short one in the head) and are much less successful in remembering verbatim details (the tall man said, "You told Bill to leave the money in the cellar"). The specifics are also the fastest to slip away, with the exact words of a conversation being particularly delicate. Events that elicit strong emotion—like violent crimes—may enhance our memory of the core essence of what transpired while leaving us unable to remember many of the surrounding facts: Did the tall man have a backpack? Was anyone waiting in a car along the street by the alley? Were there any lights on in the building across the street? These are often the very details that allow investigators to solve crimes.

The trouble with relying on memory is not just that we fail to encode certain things or that we forget over time, but also that our memories record what we encounter through the lens of our motivations, expectations, and experiences. As a result, two people will not have exactly the same memory of the same event.

And once formed, memories are far from immutable. They are subject to revision, alteration, and reconfiguration. Memory is a constructive process perhaps best likened to creating a collage: we piece together various fragments and then fill in the inevitable white patches with our background knowledge, desires, and beliefs until we have something that is complete and usable. When we go to retrieve a memory, we are not simply rummaging through an old filing cabinet for a snapshot; as we search, we may in fact be arranging the image.

The malleability of our memories has been documented in a number of experiments, including one in which participants were shown either an iconic image of the 1989 Tiananmen Square protest in Beijing (below, left) or a doctored image of the same scene (right). The alteration of the photograph affected people's reported memories about the event: those who saw the doctored image recalled the protests as much larger than did those who viewed the original photograph.

Presented with new information about an event, we may readily incorporate it into what we remember. We can even remember things that we never experienced or saw. One study found that

40 percent of British participants reported having seen footage of a bus exploding during the 2005 London terrorist attacks, although no such footage existed, and 35 percent of that group recounted particular details from the imaginary video. Contrary to what we'd expect, false memories are often highly specific, which makes them all the more believable both to the people who carry them and to third parties (including police officers, jurors, and judges).

In most cases, our false memories are not made out of whole cloth but are instead logical extensions of what we would expect or want to have happened. We may remember having expressed doubt to a colleague about a project that eventually failed or recall hearing slurred speech from someone who got into a drunk-driving accident later that evening. Conjuring these memories provides us with a narrative that makes sense and affirms what we want to believe.

If we look across experimental studies, people's recollections of events are about 80 percent accurate. Put differently, roughly every fifth detail is false. But the problem is not just that we remember events mistakenly; it is also that we do so with great surety—one study showed that a quarter of inaccurate memories were given with total confidence. The victim who identified John Jerome White, remember, was "almost certain" he was her attacker.

How did she get things so wrong? Some of the reasons are obvious in retrospect. She was seventy-four years old and not wearing her glasses when she was attacked. The only light came from the closet in an adjoining room. And before leaving, the perpetrator gave her a pillow and told her, "Hold this to your face until I get out." Research shows that a witness's eyesight and age, the viewing duration and distance, and the lighting all play a role in whether a memory is encoded accurately.

But many of the findings are less intuitive. For instance, one study showed that a person's identification of someone they saw under full moonlight was only as accurate as flipping a coin—which is to say, not at all. And, overall, the factors that play a role in our encoding of a memory are much more influential than we'd imagine. Simply by altering the conditions in which a witness viewed a person, researchers were able to boost identification accuracy to 86 percent or drop it to 14 percent.

The legal system amplifies the problem by treating many of these important variables as entirely irrelevant. In White's case, for example, one source of the victim's misidentification may have been that the victim was white and her attacker was black. Research suggests that people are 50 percent more likely to make an error in identifying a person from another race, although individuals who have a lot of contact with the other race tend to be more accurate. The same is true of identifying someone of a different age. But because of its commitment to nondiscrimination, the law generally doesn't acknowledge or address this reality—and most police officers, judges, and jurors don't even know it's an issue.

Researchers have also shown that our memories can be affected by mental or physical stress. It's difficult to simulate the fear and anxiety associated with being the victim of a real crime, but scientists have gotten creative, drawing upon other experiences that may generate similar feelings. In one study, for example, participants were taken on the "Horror Labyrinth" tour of the London Dungeon, in which they passed through a dark maze with a screaming skeleton, frightening music, disorienting mirrors, and an actor in a dark robe who blocked the path of visitors. Participants who did not find the experience distressing were more than four times better at identifying the actor out of a nine-person lineup than those who reported high levels of anxiety and had increased heart rates.

So, when a criminal uses a gun in a robbery, it doesn't just encourage his victim to comply; it also makes it less likely that she'll remember his face. There is more to it, though, than generalized fear; our poor memory also comes down to where our attention is drawn during a holdup (remember the ten-dollar bill). When a weapon is aimed at us, it tends to dominate the scene, and if our eyes are glued to the barrel, we are going to struggle to identify the suspect later on.

Our memories may also be compromised by significant physical exertion, as when a victim fights off an attacker or a cop chases down a suspect. In one simulation study, police officers who punched and kicked a three-hundred-pound hanging bag to the point of exhaustion were far less successful at memory tasks than officers who remained idle. Not only did they struggle to recall briefing materials they had received beforehand, but they were also half as likely to correctly identify a suspect they encountered after hitting the bag.

This seems backwards—we would expect that fighting off an attacker would make us *better* at remembering that person, but that's just not the case. One implication is that when police officers and other witnesses make errors in recalling particular details after a strenuous encounter with a criminal, we need to resist our gut instinct that they are lying or trying to protect the perpetrator. It's likely that they just don't remember.

As influential as it is, the legal system usually has no control over the conditions in which we encode our memories. If a witness is far away or standing in the dark at the time of the shooting, there is nothing a police officer, prosecutor, or judge can do. Yet these officials have significant command over the period when a memory is retained and later retrieved. And the processes and practices we use to handle eyewitnesses are often just as critical to identifying the true perpetrator and learning what really happened.

It's strange, then, to discover how haphazard and variable the approaches to eyewitnesses are across the twenty thousand or so law enforcement departments in the United States. A large majority of officers have not received any formal training on how to properly interview a witness or conduct an identification, and many police departments lack guidelines altogether. Those that do often employ faulty procedures that seriously imperil the likelihood of a just and effective investigation.

The flawed handling of the victim in White's case was evident from the start.

It is routine stuff in any TV crime drama. Frequently, when the police don't have leads, they first bring the victim in to help them come up with a composite image of the criminal. The picture is then put up around town and circulated to officers, and eventually the perpetrator is recognized (just in time for the credits to roll).

The real-life rape case followed the script. When a Georgia Bureau of Investigations agent saw the sketch of the rapist, he thought it looked a bit like someone he was investigating on an unrelated burglary: John Jerome White. Great story, except that White wasn't the perpetrator.

And, in fact, the overall track record of composites is weak. Those who view a composite image are only slightly better at picking a suspect out of a lineup than someone guessing randomly. That wouldn't be so bad if the creation of the composite didn't have adverse consequences in itself. But the very process of working with an artist or computer technician to construct an image may actually alter the witness's initial memory. In certain instances, the composite may even come to *replace* the initial memory.

In White's case, any distortion of the victim's memory was almost certainly exacerbated when the police brought her back in to look at a photographic array.

On the positive side, photo arrays (or photographic lineups, as they are sometimes called) are more accurate than the most common identification procedure—the "show-up," in which the police ask the witness to observe a single suspect, often at the crime scene. Cops like show-ups because of their speed and convenience, but they are highly suggestive and often lead to erroneous identifications: when you see someone sitting on the curb handcuffed, the clear implication is that the police must be fairly certain that he is the culprit. The array, which provides simple headshots of multiple people, is an obvious improvement, but it brings its own serious problems.

For one thing, when witnesses are shown a photo array, they naturally assume that the perpetrator is included. After being told that they chose an innocent filler, over half of witnesses will go ahead and pick out someone else. The good news is that if you expressly tell a witness that the perpetrator may or may not be present, this stems the tendency, but police officers routinely fail to offer any caution at all.

Perhaps the biggest problem with the photo array employed in White's case was simply that it occurred so long after the attack—some six weeks later. Time is the enemy of eyewitness accuracy, so if you go into the police station the night you witness a crime, you are likely to be far more accurate than if you wait a month or more. Indeed, the most precipitous drop in accuracy appears to occur after about seven days. In one study, witnesses who identified a perpetrator a month after an incident were only half as accurate as those who did so after just a week.

Of course, the photo array was not the only identification procedure the police used in White's case; a week later, the victim was brought back to do a live lineup. Although it's less common than some of the alternatives, the live lineup tends to be the most accurate eyewitness identification tool. A lot depends on how the lineup is constructed and administered, however, and in White's case there were major problems.

One of the basic principles of creating a valid lineup is ensuring that the people in it all match the initial description provided by the witness so that the suspect does not stand out. Lineups in the United States tend to have five fillers, and when only some of the fillers match the initial description, those who do not match become irrelevant. So a lineup may really present only two or three potential perpetrators—or sometimes just one.

In White's case, the victim initially described her attacker as a stocky, well-built man with a round face. She said he had short hair and was clean shaven. Flip back to the photograph and you immediately notice a problem with the lineup: White has a skinny body and narrow face and could never be called well built. Moreover, his hair is fairly long, and he has a mustache. The two men shown to the left of White and the first man to the right are also slender, with longer faces. Indeed, the only man who seems to meet the victim's initial description is the man on the far right— the true perpetrator, James Edward Parham. In a very unusual twist, however, this deeply flawed lineup did not focus attention on Parham because a completely different police error produced an even more powerful distortion: the victim had seen and picked out an image of White just one week earlier.

There is substantial evidence that people regularly confuse individuals in their memories, in part because they lose track of the source of a recollection. The process of retrieving memories, remember, is a constructive process: sometimes we cut out some-one's face or body and paste it into a completely different setting. This unconscious transference can arise without any police inter-vention at all; a witness might point the finger at someone who was merely a bystander at the scene of the crime, or someone who worked at the McDonald's where the witness ate that morning. In fact, there is some evidence that merely seeing a person's image previously on a social media site can corrupt an identification pro-cedure.

More often the problem arises when police departments ask a witness to view a suspect multiple times. Experimental evi-dence confirms that having come across a person's face in a book of mug shots significantly increases the likelihood that a witness will select that person at a later lineup, even when the actual perpetrator—someone else—is present.

The use of multiple identification procedures is generally born of good intentions: the police really want to make sure they have the right person. In White's case, the second procedure was organized because the victim was not completely sure of her initial identification with the photo array, and the police were worried that perhaps the photo did not actually look like White. What they did not realize is that by making White the only person who appeared in *both* the photo array and the lineup, they were actually *increasing* the risk of misidentification. The victim may have felt considerably more certain when seeing White in the flesh—in fact, she stated as much—but exactly what was she remembering? The face of the man who brutally attacked her in her home almost two months before, or the face of the man in the photograph she had picked out a week earlier?

As a case like this proceeds, a witness commonly becomes more and more certain of her identification, but that certainty often fails to correspond to a rise in accuracy. That is because a witness's level of confidence may be inflated by factors that are completely unrelated to the memory itself. When a police officer offers a supportive statement like "Nice work—you chose the guy we picked up," witnesses tend to express less doubt in their identification and greater confidence that they saw the perpetrator clearly.

In fact, of all the factors we've discussed, the comments made by other people may have the biggest impact on a witness's memory. After a witness observes a crime, she is often exposed to additional information about what happened. Some of this information may come from news reports or chatting with other witnesses; other details may be picked up from interactions with the police. There is, of course, the potential that this additional information may make a person's memory more accurate, but often it appears to be the other way around.

In one recent study, participants were shown slides of a man taking a woman's wallet and then concealing it in his jacket pocket. After looking at the photos, participants listened to a description of the slides that contained misleading information like "Then the man hid the wallet in his pants pocket." When participants were asked to recall details from the pictures they had seen, a significant number made errors based on the misinformation, including claiming that they had observed the man hide the wallet in his pants.

Even a single word choice by a police officer can alter an eyewitness's memory. In another study, two groups watched a film of a car accident and were then asked to estimate how fast the vehicles were traveling when they either "smashed" or "contacted." When the word *smashed* was used, the average estimate was nine miles an hour faster. Participants in the "smashed" group were also more inclined to recall shattered glass at the scene, although there wasn't any in the actual footage.

Young children and the elderly appear to be particularly susceptible to misinformation effects, as are those with low IQs, those who are sleep-deprived, and those strongly driven to please others.

Perhaps most shocking is that suggestion can create false *autobiographical* memories. A number of studies have shown how easy it is to plant false memories—everything from receiving a painful enema to meeting Bugs Bunny at Disneyland (which is impossible, because Bugs is a Warner Brothers character). One group of researchers found that they could get 50 percent of participants to remember all or part of a childhood hot-air balloon trip that never happened after showing the person a doctored photo of the event along with other real photos from the person's youth.

The research is sobering. And it makes the manner in which officers interact with witnesses critical. Both verbal and nonverbal cues can jeopardize the accuracy of witness statements and identifications, regardless of the good intentions of the police or the awareness of the witness.

Imagine you're a cop administering a photo array. The witness begins to say something like "I'm pretty sure it's this guy," pointing to the photograph of someone who is unquestionably innocent. You know how much harder it will be to clear the case if she picks the wrong person, so you respond, "We are in no rush here. Take your time and just be sure you're certain." You haven't told her whom to pick or not pick, so there's no problem, right?

It seems like good advice and harmless, but this is just the type of shepherding that can encourage a mistaken identification. And a simple cough, sigh, or gesture may be just as powerful. In one study, when an experimenter merely stroked his chin, people were three times as likely to report that a man in a video they had watched had a beard, when in fact he was clean shaven. In most cases there is going to be no record of a suggestion this subtle: the witness is nudged, and no one will ever know.

Interviews are especially fraught: it's difficult to conduct one without influencing the witness. Since most officers have very little training in the interview process, they often end up employing approaches that hinder the task of recovering complete and accurate memories. Among other things, they fail to gain a rapport with the witness, they interrupt too much, and they ask questions that are either highly suggestive or too narrow. When they reach a dead end, they often continue to probe, urging the witness to work a bit harder to uncover the details that must certainly be there. This may be effective on occasion, but in many cases it can lead the witness to remember things that never happened—either spontaneously, in an effort to fill in missing details, or because of specific information provided by an interviewer ("Do you remember a smell of smoke on his clothes?"). And the more that detectives repeat questions and conduct multiple interviews in hopes of cracking a case, the more confident the witness grows in her memory, regardless of its accuracy.

These distortionary factors might not be so harmful if the ultimate decision-makers in criminal cases were aware of them and could adjust their expectations accordingly. However, research suggests that most judges and potential jurors place too much faith in witnesses' memories. And they are often oblivious to the things that can reduce accuracy and reliability, which makes them bad at determining how much weight to give to, say, a particular eyewitness identification.

Compounding the problem is that not only do jurors fail to appreciate the significance of poor witness viewing conditions or biasing lineup procedures, but they also depend on dubious factors to decide whether an identification or account is accurate. For instance, attending to the confidence of a witness right after she's encountered the perpetrator and made an identification is wise, but a witness's confidence may also be misleading, particularly weeks, months, and years after the crime. Overall, jurors are two to three times as trusting of extremely confident witnesses as they are of less confident ones, and these impressions affect their behavior: the more confident the witness, the more likely it is that a jury will convict. When a woman like the victim in the White case has the courage to come forward to identify the man who raped and beat her and says she's certain, we feel assured that we have the right man.

Jurors appear to be particularly impressed by in-court identifications, in which they can actually observe the drama of the perpetrator being pointed out. Yet these identifications might be the most troubling of all: in many cases, the witness has already viewed the defendant multiple times and is under enormous pressure to be consistent. Had the victim in the White case stepped out of the witness box and failed to point out her attacker, not only would she have seemed incompetent, but she might also have derailed the whole case, undermining weeks of work by the police officers and lawyers trying to help her receive justice. Prosecutors commonly have eyewitnesses carry out this farce on the stand because they know how convincing such performances are to the jury. And judges almost never intervene because they operate with the same mistaken notions about memory. They believe that standard legal tools like the defense's ability to cross-examine eyewitnesses is sufficient safeguard, without realizing that such a tool may be largely useless—most witnesses have no idea that their memories have been corrupted.

In his 1908 book, *On the Witness Stand*, the pioneering psychologist Hugo Münsterberg recounted a famous meeting of a German "scientific association, made up of jurists, psychologists, and physicians." On the night of the convention, there happened to be a public festival out in the street. All of a sudden, in the midst of the proceedings, the doors to the hall were flung open and "a clown in highly coloured costume" burst in, followed by a man carrying a revolver. The men shouted at each other and began to wrestle, at which point the gun went off. A few moments later the intruders ran out of the room. Given that a criminal investigation was a near certainty, the president of the association asked the forty people in attendance to carefully write down, individually, exactly what they had seen. Unbeknownst to them, the entire scene was an experiment in eyewitness observation and memory, staged by the president.

The results were disheartening: the statements were filled with false details and omitted numerous key facts. According to Münsterberg, when considered alongside his own memory experiments on Harvard undergraduates, the poor showing served as a "warning against the blind confidence in the observations of the average man." Indeed, "in a thousand courts at a thousand places all over the world, witnesses every day affirm[ed] by oath . . . mixtures of truth and untruth, combinations of memory and of illusion, of knowledge and of suggestion, of experience and wrong conclusions."

More than a century later, that indictment still feels fresh. Look what happened after John Jerome White was finally exonerated in 2007. In the direct aftermath, there was a push in Georgia to seriously reform the eyewitness identification procedures across the state with best practices and mandatory officer training. But other than the creation of a voluntary training program for police officers handling eyewitness identification procedures, significant research-based reforms have not been adopted. In the vast majority of jurisdictions across the country, the story of entrenchment is no different, and the Supreme Court has failed to intervene meaningfully at the national level.

Of course, *some* progress has been made in the decades since Münsterberg first applied psychological insights to the law. In the last thirty years, more than two thousand studies have been published on eyewitness identifications alone. With more rigorous scientific methods and a greatly expanded understanding of memory, we are now in a much better position to make lasting changes in the way our criminal justice system approaches eyewitnesses.

The first step is to convince the majority of those inside and outside the legal system that there is a problem and that justice demands we address it. As Münsterberg put it, "If the time is ever to come when even the jurist is to show some concession to the spirit of modern psychology, public opinion will have to exert some pressure."

We need to start thinking about witness mistakes in the way that we think about other types of errors that individuals, groups, and institutions make. As I mentioned, studies of actual police lineups show that eyewitnesses select innocent people more than 30 percent of the time. Would we as a society tolerate the sale of a car whose brake lights malfunctioned on every third trip, or a hospital that handed out the wrong medicine to every third patient? Obviously not; we would demand immediate change. So why do we accept the claim that the legal system works just fine as it is?

It's true that, much of the time, when a witness picks out an innocent filler from a lineup, that person does not go on to be convicted of the crime. But given the tens of thousands of witness identifications annually, even a low percentage of truly consequential errors can produce an egregious level of harm. And consider that someone could offer the same rosy account of the hospital that gave every third person the wrong prescription: in most cases the patient would either notice before taking the medication or swallow it without experiencing any significant ill effects. But would we say to those who did suffer serious adverse reactions—or to the families of those who lost their lives—"It's a shame about the error, but since our system works pretty well in general, we're not going to change it"?

We also need to keep in mind that the wrongfully convicted are not the only ones who end up suffering from flawed witness procedures. When an innocent person is locked up, the police stop looking for the true offender. Indeed, we know of at least 230 misidentification cases like White's, in which an innocent person was exonerated and the real perpetrator eventually identified through DNA. In almost half of those cases, the perpetrator committed other crimes after the investigation was closed.

When memories are distorted and erroneous details about a crime are passed to the authorities, police officers and prosecutors lose days, weeks, and months investigating false leads and building cases against the wrong people. They fail to attain justice for victims and waste limited resources that are desperately needed elsewhere. Improving witness procedures does not pit the interests of defendants against law enforcement; it serves our common goal of achieving fairness and efficiency in criminal law. Indeed, many police officers are actually quite supportive of reforms. As a spokesman for the Georgia Bureau of Investigations explained at the time of White's exoneration, "Nobody in law enforcement wants to arrest the wrong person."

Although states like Virginia, North Carolina, Connecticut, and Ohio have all had success in introducing new eyewitness procedures, New Jersey provides the most notable example of fearlessly embracing the latest research. In 2001, the attorney general of New Jersey issued new eyewitness guidelines that required, among other things, recording the identification procedure and having someone other than the primary investigator handle the process. The police are also instructed to use sequential lineups for both photo and live identifications, and to record the interactions. Ten years later, the New Jersey Supreme Court took a similarly bold step forward. Writing of the "troubling lack of reliability in eyewitness identifications" and stating unequivocally that "the possibility of mistaken identification is real," the court outlined a framework for regulating their use at trial, including placing a burden on the state to show that an identification is reliable if a defendant offers evidence that the witness might have been impermissibly influenced. Even when disputed evidence is allowed to come before the jury, a judge must provide adequate information to jurors concerning the risks—the ones discussed in this chapter—related to misidentification. Reformers hope that New Jersey can act as a model for other states in the years to come.

Promising solutions may also be found abroad. One of the best existing tools for improving accuracy and completeness in eyewitness recollection, the cognitive interview, is already being used by the police in the United Kingdom, New Zealand, Australia, Canada, and Norway. Based on insights from cognitive and social psychology, the approach focuses on establishing a good rapport with the witness, who then provides her account with a minimal number of open-ended questions and few interruptions. Studies have documented that this technique elicits between 25 and 50 percent more correct information.

One of the reasons that the cognitive interview is so successful is that it goes to great lengths to preserve a witness's original
memory, rigorously avoiding suggestive questioning and discouraging witnesses from guessing. The benefits of that approach
suggest that we need to fundamentally rethink how we handle
eyewitness evidence. A memory of the perpetrator's face is just as
susceptible to adulteration and misuse as a hair sample or partial
fingerprint taken from a crime scene, but we don't treat it that
way. We don't worry that it will get corrupted or lost or misre-
ported. We don't subject it to careful monitoring or objective assessment. That needs to change. As Hugo Münsterberg argued,
it makes little sense that a court should make "the fullest use
of all the modern scientific methods when, for instance, a drop
of dried blood is to be examined in a murder case, [while] the
same court is completely satisfied with the most unscientific and
haphazard methods of common prejudice and ignorance when a
mental product, especially the memory report of a witness, is to
be examined."

Münsterberg thought that the path forward was to rely more
heavily on a different kind of witness: experts. It's an intriguing possibility. If geneticists are the stewards of DNA evidence in
court, should psychologists act as stewards of memory evidence,
from the moment a witness is identified up through that witness's
testimony at trial? Are experts the best hope for bringing objectivity, consistency, and accuracy to our troubled system of criminal justice?

# 7

# HOW TO TELL A LIE

## The Expert

There is damning evidence, and then there is the infamous Rodney King video.

Woken up by the drumbeat of a circling helicopter, George Holliday had stepped out on his balcony with his new Sony camcorder and pressed RECORD. Though it was almost one in the morning, the scene in the video is flooded with sharp light from the squad car high beams. Bodies are already in motion. In the first seconds of the tape, King, surrounded by a dozen or so police officers, gets up from the ground, takes a couple of steps, and is smashed in the face with a metal baton. He's got Taser darts in his chest; you can see the glint of the wires. Over the next minute and a half, King is hit fifty-six times, as the officers swing their clubs like baseball bats—repeated "power strokes" to the head and shoulders. He falls and they kick him as hard as they can. He rolls on the ground in apparent agony and they don't stop—not until they've got him hogtied, his hands and legs lashed behind him, face in the asphalt. They drag him to the side of the road and leave him in a pool of blood to wait alone for an ambulance.

It's as brutal a police action as you will see. Twenty-four years later, it is still hard for me to watch.

King's skull was fractured in nine places, his eye socket and cheekbone were shattered, and his leg was broken. He suffered a concussion, injured both knees, and sustained damage to nerves in his face. The officers claimed that he must have been on PCP—an explanation, they hoped, for their harsh responses—but no PCP was found in his system. And though it was speeding that had initiated the police response, King was never charged with any crimes.

The tape was played over and over on major networks around the country. And before the trial of the three patrolmen and the supervising sergeant directly involved in the beating, polls revealed that more than 90 percent of Los Angeles residents who had watched the footage thought that the police had used excessive force. The details that emerged in the weeks that followed only made the actions seem worse. Earlier in the night, one of the cops had described his last call, a domestic disturbance involving African Americans, as "right out of 'Gorillas in the Mist.'" And after nearly killing King, another had gleefully crowed, "I haven't beaten anyone this bad in a long time." In the hospital emergency room, they taunted a barely conscious King: "We played a good game of hardball . . . we hit quite a few home runs." What it all added up to seemed clear: a bunch of racist white cops brutalizing a black man for sport.

Political leaders on both sides of the aisle reached a unanimous verdict. According to Tom Bradley, the mayor of Los Angeles, the officers had, "with the use of their batons and with their feet, left no doubt in anybody's mind about the charges that should be levied against them." President George Bush, whose law-and-order platform had earned him wide support from police departments, offered a similarly stark assessment: "Those terrible scenes stir us all to demand an end to gratuitous violence and brutality. Law-enforcement officials cannot place themselves above the law that they are sworn to defend. It was sickening to see the beating that was rendered and there's no way, no way in my view, to explain that away. It was outrageous."

The evidence was so clear and so egregious that it prompted the Justice Department to review all complaints of police brutality against the government in the previous six years. Police departments around the country began using the video in training as an example of what *not* to do. And Darryl F. Gates, the police chief of Los Angeles, was forced to resign.

If ever there was a slam-dunk case, it was this one.

But the trial didn't go as everyone expected. On April 29, 1992, all four officers were acquitted.

People poured into the streets of South Central. Stores were looted, motorists were dragged out of their cars, dozens of fires burned. More than fifty people would die; more than one thousand buildings would be destroyed; more than two thousand people would be injured; and more than twelve thousand people would be arrested.

How had this happened?

The acquittals that set off the deadliest riots of the American twentieth century are generally credited to the performances of two men at trial: Sergeant Stacey Koon, the lead officer at the scene of King's beating; and Sergeant Charles Duke, the defense's chief expert, who testified that every baton blow, Taser shock, and kick captured on Holliday's tape was justified under official protocol.

The removal of the case to a predominantly white suburb gave the defense a chance, but it was these particular men, according to the conventional account, who produced the victory. Their testimony was indeed pivotal—but the standard story misses the reason why.

The real reason that Koon, Laurence Powell, Theodore Briseno, and Timothy Wind left the Simi Valley courthouse free men in the face of seemingly conclusive evidence has less to do with the special talents of the two sergeants than with what we might term our justice system's "expert paradox." We ought to defer to experts when they are more qualified to assess matters than we are, but we often get things backwards: we rely on our own skills of analysis where they are deeply flawed, and we embrace expert evidence when it is misleading and unhelpful. King was denied justice in the state court trial because jurors were both too trusting of their own ability to determine whether Koon was lying and too accepting of the dubious framing provided by Duke.

They watched Koon on the stand, in his white shirt and striped red tie, the bright light bouncing off his bald forehead. They looked at his relaxed body, slightly hunched, and his eyes blinking slowly and occasionally asymmetrically, the right eye closing just before the left. They listened to his measured voice, his direct and precise responses, the way certain words revealed a lisp. They watched how he'd look up to his right to remember things whenever asked to recollect. They met his gaze as he turned toward them to explain his fear that King was on drugs, and watched him stare down the prosecutor, unwavering as he stated that every action his officers took was "reasonable and necessary using the minimum of force": "Sometimes police work is brutal. That is just a fact of life." They took it all in, right down to the pout his lips made in silent anticipation of the next question. But what they believed to be the telltale signs of truthfulness turned out to be red herrings.

Likewise, the jury ate up Duke's narrative of officers dutifully and cautiously going about their business because he fit the image of an expert. Duke, a former LAPD self-defense instructor with over twenty years of experience, had a commanding presence in the courtroom as he stood in front of the jury with his microphone and pointer stick. Barrel-chested with a brown mustache and the squinty eyes of a veteran officer, he exuded authority and coolheaded objectivity. "I never form an opinion until I get all the facts," he told the prosecutor. Was he shocked by the tape? No. The officers were following established policy and procedure; this was precisely what handling a dangerous suspect looked like.

Just as important, Duke seasoned his account with the requisite sprinkling of scientific legitimacy. The power of the videotape of the King beating arose from its dynamism and immediacy. As we've seen, film provides us with the feeling that we are there, experiencing things as they happen. Duke, trading on the power of framing, defused the impact by breaking the video down into its constituent parts—stills of the blows directed at King—and the defense attorney teed up his analysis of each one: "When he is in this position here, at 3:36:19, would it be appropriate to hit Mr. King with a baton?" It seemed like an entirely natural move for an expert seeking to help us gain a true understanding of what was going on—after all, breaking something down to understand it is a basic part of the scientific method. And the particular techniques Duke relied upon—slowing the speed of the tape, inspecting blown-up images—are just the type we expect: experts use special tools to reveal the hidden truth beneath the surface. Duke's air of objective authority was only enhanced by the time-coded stamps and superimposed grids added to the video stills.

He seemed to be exposing the real story of what happened, but all Duke really did was bias jurors in favor of the defense. Kicks that once seemed brutal, out of control, and visceral became frozen, sterile, and distant; an atrocity, complete and easily identified, was fractured into a pile of jagged-edged shards. Even more masterful, Duke managed, by not showing live action, to recast King as the aggressor. His approach focused the attention on what King was doing in each frame—on how the officers were simply responding to King's "cocked" arm, the way his leg was "coming up," how he was moving into a "rocking position." Duke was fastening blinders to jurors' heads, when they assumed he was fitting them for new glasses.

There is a fundamental problem, then, with our handling of expertise. To understand why, we need to look at the circumstances in which we keep experts at bay and place our faith in our own knowledge and abilities, as well as the situations in which we come under the spell of expert witnesses and—critically—their special tools. Consider the most essential task for any criminal justice system: separating truth from untruth. Jurors in the Rodney King trial were trying their best to sort the two out as they watched Koon and Duke on the stand. How and why did well-intentioned men and women get so tripped up?

We have all had a lifetime of practice in detecting lies. Think of how many times a day you get to hone your skills: Did your son actually brush his teeth? Does the mechanic really need to replace your brakes? Does your spouse really mean she's sorry? Is your student's grandmother actually sick? We assume that the result of all of these encounters is that, by adulthood, most of us have developed finely calibrated instruments for catching lies both big and small. When it comes to assessing truthfulness, we are experts.

Our legal system shares this notion. In the law's estimation, the twelve Simi Valley jurors were fully capable of observing Sergeant Koon's blinking, listening to his even-toned responses, and making the call. The Model Criminal Jury Instructions in the Third Circuit, for example, which encompasses the federal courts in Delaware, New Jersey, and Pennsylvania, make it clear that jurors are the gatekeepers of truth: "You are the sole judges of the credibility of the witnesses. Credibility refers to whether a witness is worthy of belief: Was the witness truthful? Was the witness' testimony accurate? You may believe everything a witness says, or only part of it, or none of it."

Before trial, Third Circuit judges explain to jurors that there is nothing special about assessing credibility in court: "You may decide whether to believe a witness based on his or her behavior and manner of testifying, the explanations the witness gave, and all the other evidence in the case, just as you would in any important matter where you are trying to decide if a person is truthful, straightforward, and accurate in his or her recollection."

The message to jurors is that they have all the tools and knowledge they need to decide questions of credibility. As they sit in their chairs in the gallery watching each witness, they should go with their gut. Detecting lies isn't rocket science or brain surgery: "Remember to use your common sense, your good judgment, and your experience."

All of this fits into a more general faith in the ability of laypeople to discern the reality of a case: what happened, who was responsible, what the key players were thinking at key moments. We do not use a panel of criminal law professors to answer these questions; in fact, qualifying for jury duty requires no familiarity with law, forensic analysis, or psychology. Jurors don't even have to have a high school degree. Our system of justice celebrates the talents of the amateur, giving him or her the vital role of determining the facts of the case and applying the relevant law.

Those officially designated as experts, by contrast, are the conduits of scientific, technical, and specialized knowledge: as a general matter, the scientific evidence we've discussed—from DNA to fMRI—comes into the courtroom only through their testimony. But their role is a subservient one. When an expert witness testifies, we do not tell jurors to simply defer to the good doctor. In the Third Circuit, for example, the opinions of experts are to be given "whatever weight you think appropriate." In fact, a juror "may disregard the opinion(s) entirely" should he so choose.

If we embrace the power of an ordinary person to sort out falsehood and inaccuracy, what *is* the common sense of lie detection? What are the "tells" we live by?

Every year when I teach my Law and Mind Sciences seminar, I start off the class on deception by asking my students to judge whether I am being truthful as I explain how I spent the previous evening: cooking a meal of tapas for friends, going out to a bar to watch *Monday Night Football*, and so on.

I always tell the truth, but every year, like clockwork, almost all of the students think I'm lying. They point out that I didn't look them in the eye and that I seemed to be gesturing "too much," or maybe it was that I was speaking faster than normal. The behavioral cues they focus on turn out to align quite well with general folk wisdom. In experiments and surveys, gaze aversion, for instance, is by far the most commonly cited factor in determining that someone is lying. Police officers and others in the criminal justice system focus on many of the same things, which isn't surprising given their training and instructions.

If you remember, with the Reid technique, before an officer begins interrogating a suspect to gain a confession, he first has to determine whether the suspect is lying. And to do that, the Reid manual explains, an investigator must pay attention to "nonverbal behaviors that reflect comfort versus anxiety, confidence versus uncertainty, and a clear conscience versus guilt or shame." So, for example, "a suspect who does not make direct eye contact is probably withholding information." Knowing the signs of deceit—like jittery legs and lint picking—allows a police officer to identify liars with confidence.

Similarly, in evaluating the believability of in-court testimony, judges often direct jurors to focus on the witness's demeanor— how she acts, as opposed to what she says. In the Third Circuit, for example, jurors are explicitly encouraged to consider "the witness' appearance, behavior, and manner while testifying." Indeed, we have such faith in these judgments that we allow them to decide outcomes. If a jury watches a defendant and decides—based solely on her body language—that she has perjured herself, the jury can use that as affirmative evidence of guilt.

The problem is that when researchers have looked at these commonsense cues, they have found that most have nothing to do with whether or not someone is lying. The handful that are somewhat predictive tend to involve verbal elements (like the tension in one's voice or a lack of detail in one's responses) rather than visual ones. Numerous studies have shown, for example, that people who are lying are actually less likely to move their arms and legs (not more likely, as observers tend to assume), and averting one's gaze is not related to deceit. Even worse, when people are under a lot of pressure to appear trustworthy, that often exacerbates the behaviors that observers wrongly associate with lying. A truthful person who will calmly look you in the eye when discussing matters in her own home will stare down at her restless legs when called upon to defend herself in court.

The believability of a witness can also be boosted by completely irrelevant factors. Put the affable and handsome George Clooney on the stand, and people are much more inclined to believe what he says than if you call up someone viewed as unattractive or unpleasant. Likewise, tell observers that a witness is a prize-winning poet or cancer survivor (an immaterial positive detail), and they are significantly more likely to trust his statements than if you tell them that he flunked out of dental school or hates dogs (an extraneous negative detail). Some of these cues are downright bizarre. Initial evidence suggests, for instance, that people are inclined to be more trusting of men with brown eyes than of men with blue eyes, except when the blue eyes appear on someone with a broad face. According to the researchers, people with brown eyes tend to have rounder faces, so it is actually the shape of the men's faces that is doing the work: round faces are perceived as happier, and happy faces are linked to trust (untrustworthy faces, by contrast, are perceived to be angrier).

Overall, it turns out that we are quite bad at ferreting out deception. In a recent analysis of more than two hundred studies, participants were able to identify lies and truths correctly just 54 percent of the time, only marginally better than chance. And the elements that we would imagine have a big impact on our ability to detect lies—whether we are judging a long-term acquaintance or a stranger, whether the lies involve high or low stakes, whether we are interacting with the person or observing from a third-party perspective—don't move detection rates more than a few points in any direction. Moreover, the people one might expect to have special talents at judging deception—police officers, judges, psychiatrists, auditors—aren't any better than the rest of us at sorting out lies from truths.

Yet just like my students, experimental subjects tend to be very confident in their lie-detection performance. And, unfortunately, those who are most confident in their judgments aren't generally more accurate than those voicing greater doubt. Although it would be nice if moving from the laboratory to a real-world setting brought an improvement in lie-detection performance, there is reason to think that it just gets worse in the courtroom. First of all, while study participants are generally permitted to focus on whatever they think is most helpful in judging deceit, jurors are explicitly told to zero in on elements likely to lead them astray, in particular the witness's demeanor. And being unable to attend to visual cues—on account of blindness—is considered a valid reason for exclusion from a jury during *voir dire*. Ironically, contrary to the assumptions of many courts, the blind may often be in a *better* position to assess truthfulness than jurors focused intently on body language, because they are less likely to be misled by downward stares and shaky limbs.

Furthermore, during an actual trial, witnesses are likely to be considerably more nervous—even if they are innocent or telling the truth—than in a laboratory experiment, and signs of nervousness are frequently misconstrued as evidence of deceit. Meanwhile, some dishonest witnesses do not show telltale signs of lying, which may be a simple reflection of the fact that they have undergone extensive practice with attorneys: when it comes to lying, research suggests that practice really does make perfect. Finally, it is hard to see how a juror might be able to make use of the few cues that appear to have some diagnostic value. How is she supposed to see from across the room whether a defendant's pupils are dilated, or decide which of hundreds of behaviors to focus on, all while trying to pay attention to what the witness is saying?

So, you might be saying to yourself, there is a gap between our intuitions about lying and the actual scientific evidence, but at least there are proven techniques out there that can make up for our shortcomings. There is a *science* of lie detection.

And herein lies the paradox. Logic would suggest that the great confidence we have in our own ability to detect deception would make us particularly unreceptive to outside experts. Besides, everyone knows that, for the right price, an expert can be found to defend any side of an issue. But as we saw with Sergeant Duke's analysis of the video footage, we can lose this perspective in the heart of a trial when there are experts in front of us, using the trappings of science. Their methods and tools erase our concerns, in part, because they seem to eliminate subjectivity and bias. The result is that we often put too much faith in the science and technology that experts bring into the courtroom.

Nowhere is that more clear than in the case of assessing deceit. The fact that we expect lying to produce bodily manifestations has left us ready to accept an array of dubious lie detectors that seem to offer objective analysis. A parade of "experts" have convinced generation after generation that their vats and techniques and machines can expose what was previously hidden: the secret mendacity revealed in a floating torso, trembling hands, quivering eyelids, beads of sweat, or blotchy skin.

The heart has received special attention over the centuries. Daniel Defoe, the author of the novel *Robinson Crusoe*, suggested in a 1730 essay on combating crime that guilt and innocence might be assessed by checking a potential thief's blood circulation: "a fluttering heart, an unequal pulse, a sudden palpitation shall evidently confess he is the man, in spite of a bold countenance or a false tongue."

Some two hundred years later, in 1923, William Marston would attempt to bring results from his lie detector—which measured changes in systolic blood pressure—into an actual criminal proceeding. Like Defoe, Marston pursued endeavors in both fact and fiction—a coincidence, no doubt, but a fitting one, for Marston's "systolic blood pressure deception test" was almost as fanciful as the magic lasso that his comic-book character, Wonder Woman, wrapped around villains to force them to speak the truth.

Yet there was nothing fictive about the events of 1923: the deception test was being introduced in the trial of a real man, James Frye, who stood accused of robbery and murder. The court ultimately refused to allow Marston to testify as an expert, on the grounds that his lie-detector method had not been generally accepted by the broader scientific community. But his efforts laid critical groundwork for the first modern polygraph, which measured a subject's pulse, blood pressure, and breathing. And it was Frye's case that established the standard for the admissibility of expert testimony in the United States for the next several decades and, in some states, to this day.

Despite widespread use by intelligence agencies, businesses, police departments, and even private individuals—with several hundred thousand tests administered each year—the polygraph has never won over scientists, so polygraph results are generally not admissible as evidence against criminal defendants. As the Supreme Court put it in 1998, there is "simply no consensus that polygraph evidence is reliable." Part of the problem is that even the most sophisticated polygraph is only measuring physiological responses—such as cardiovascular, respiratory, and electrodermal activity—and these responses may or may not be closely correlated with deception. People regularly lie without sweating and sweat while telling the truth.

More recent developments, like Neuro Linguistic Programming–based lie detection, which is grounded in the notion that those who are right-handed tend to look up to their left when visualizing a real event that they experienced and look up to the right when visualizing an imagined event, have run into the same problem. It's appealing to think that Koon's rightward glances on the stand really meant something, but there's no evidence to support the notion that eye movements can be used to detect deception. More generally, methods and technologies designed to use a person's nonverbal behavior to uncover deception have turned out to be about as effective as measuring a person's skull to assess his criminal propensities.

These failures have motivated efforts to capture lying at its source—the brain. Until very recently this approach was impossible, but breakthroughs in neuroscience, including the EEG and fMRI, have finally allowed us a glimpse into the black box. We now have the potential to ask a person whether he murdered his wife or show him an image of a bloody bathroom sink while we observe what is happening inside his head.

The implications of these neuroscientific advances have not been lost on the world of lie detection. And there has been a mad dash by private companies, law enforcement and intelligence agencies, and others to develop specific applications. In 2011, the Defense Advanced Research Projects Agency (DARPA) oversaw a budget of almost $250 million focused on cognitive neuroscience research, and national security entities have invested millions more in the last decade to develop effective lie-detection technology. Today, even private citizens can gain access to some of the latest tools. Want to "prove" that you've never had an affair or stolen from your workplace? For a few thousand dollars a pop, there are at least two companies that will assess your brain activity using fMRI or EEG equipment.

It was only a matter of time before lawyers tried to bring EEG and fMRI into the courtroom. From the outset, however, scholars and judges have questioned whether these new technologies are up to the challenge, particularly for criminal matters. It is one thing to permit someone to undergo a brain scan in an attempt to verify her marital faithfulness and quite another to allow a jury to use lie-detection evidence presented by an expert as the basis for acquitting an accused murderer.

In 2012, Judge Eric M. Johnson, of the Montgomery County, Maryland, Circuit Court, had to make just such a decision about the expert testimony of Frank Haist, an assistant professor of psychiatry at the University of California, San Diego. Haist had been hired by No Lie MRI to study the brain of a man accused of a brutal murder. What he and the company promised was remarkable and tantalizing: an opportunity to reveal the secret truths inside the defendant's head.

The prosecution alleged that Gary Smith, a former Army Ranger, had spent a routine night drinking beer and playing pool at the VFW before fatally shooting his roommate and fellow veteran, Michael McQueen.

When the police had arrived at the men's Gaithersburg apartment, they'd found Gary covered in blood, vomiting outside. He was the one who had called the cops, crying to the dispatcher, "Oh my God, help me. . . . I dropped him off at the house, and I came back, and he had a big hole in his head." Sure enough, when the officers had entered the house, they'd found Michael's body. But, curiously, there was no gun.

Gary had proceeded to try several stories on the police. He'd come home and found Michael dead, but the weapon and shooter were gone. No, the gun was there—Michael had killed himself. No, wait, Gary *had* been in the apartment. He had panicked because it was his gun that Michael used. He had thrown it into a lake.

It was this strange series of lies that was at the crux of the case. What had really happened that night?

Gary hoped he could clear things up with the help of experts from No Lie MRI. Technicians asked Gary a series of questions as he lay inside the MRI machine. He was told to lie on certain questions that were demonstrably true—like whether he had ever served in Iraq—to establish a baseline for when they got to questions about the murder, where he was told to be truthful.

"Did you shoot Mike McQueen?"

Gary responded that he had not.

Professor Haist then reviewed the different fMRI images. Knowing which areas of the brain tend to be highly active when people are lying, and having a sense of Gary's brain state when he lied, Haist could look critically at the images of Gary's brain when he answered questions about Michael's death.

In Haist's opinion, the images taken when Gary was known to be lying could be clearly distinguished from those taken when he answered questions about the murder. Even the uninitiated would see the difference: the scans show far more red and yellow patches at moments when Gary is known to be lying. The clear implication, then, was that Gary must be telling the truth about his roommate's death.

If only it were that simple.

First of all, we do not yet have the data to tell whether lie-detection approaches using fMRI, EEG, and other brain-scan technologies actually work well enough for us to rely on them in a legal setting. Some technologies have virtually no independent, peer-reviewed research to stand upon; they rest instead on the largely unsubstantiated claims of their promoters. One company, Brainwave Science, offers an EEG-based tool, Brain Fingerprinting, which is purportedly "over 99% accurate" in "scientifically detect[ing] whether specific information is stored in the brain—or not—by measuring brainwaves." According to the Brainwave Science website, "Many seasoned criminals have discovered ways to beat a polygraph. Deception is much more difficult with Brain Fingerprinting. When the subject recognizes the stimuli, an involuntary MERMER (brain wave response) occurs. It's about as foolproof as it gets." The benefits are apparent: "Investigators can identify or exonerate suspects based upon measuring brain-wave responses to crime-related photos or words displayed on a computer screen." Convinced? Neither are most scientists.

The technique that has the most empirical support is fMRI lie detection, which connects lying with oxygenated blood flow to certain areas of the brain, but the relevant research has been plagued by a lack of standardized methods, small sample sizes, and inconsistent results. One of the biggest problems has been that participants are generally aware that they are taking part in an experiment and have been told to lie or tell the truth. Is a person trying to cover up shooting his roommate really the same as someone instructed to lie about a playing card that he picked out of a deck? Is a college student paid to take part in a study comparable to a habitually lying psychopath with a history of drug abuse facing the possibility of the death penalty? And could that psychopath cheat the test if he wanted?

We've known for a long time that polygraphs can be gamed, and it turns out that countermeasures are also very effective when it comes to fMRI. You can render the data unusable just by moving your head slightly, swishing your tongue, curling your toes, or holding your breath. Changing what you are thinking about during questioning (trying to remember state capitals, say, or counting down from a hundred by threes) may also muddy the results. Much fMRI lie detection is based on the idea that because it is cognitively more difficult to lie than to tell the truth, lying activates more areas of the brain (thus the greater number of red and yellow patches in the image of Gary's brain when he was known to be lying). But if you make your brain busier when giving an honest answer, it will look more like your brain when you are lying. Conversely, if you carefully memorize all of your lies so they're simple to recall, you may look like a saint.

Despite these problems, it is conceivable that a day may come when a particular lie-detection approach is accurate 80, 90, or even 99 percent of the time. The question then will be whether that level of accuracy is high enough. If humans were able to take the margin of error into account and treat expert testimony as just another piece of evidence, it wouldn't matter. But there is reason to doubt that we are up to the task.

Concerns that juries may overvalue scientific evidence have been around for quite a while. In the 1990s, attorneys, judges, and academics became worried about "white-coat syndrome," the notion that jurors blindly defer to experts without actually evaluating their testimony. A decade later, the fears morphed into the "CSI effect"—the idea that certain television programs (like *CSI, Law & Order*, and *Without a Trace*), along with high-profile cases involving DNA tests, fiber analysis, and fingerprinting databases, had led members of the public to believe that forensic evidence was both widely available and almost infallible.

More recently, researchers have begun looking at how neuroscientific evidence can bias outcomes in criminal trials. Brain scans may have a particularly strong influence on jurors. In one experiment, significantly more participants found a defendant guilty after reading that he had failed an fMRI lie-detection test than when the trial summary included evidence of deceit based on polygraph or thermal-imaging results. One of the reasons fMRI may carry such weight is that we may conflate its use in a criminal context with scanning done to identify medical conditions, like tumors or strokes. Diagnostic imaging, we assume, is diagnostic imaging.

Particularly troubling is the fact that even trained judges do not seem to be immune to the special allure of neuroscience. In one study, 181 state trial judges read about Jonathan Donahue, who, during an attempted robbery of a Burger King, ended up beating a restaurant manager repeatedly in the head with a pistol—causing permanent brain damage—because "the fat son-of-a-bitch wouldn't stop crying." According to testimony from a psychiatrist, Donahue met the criteria for classification as a psychopath. In addition, half of the judges were presented with testimony from "a neurobiologist and renowned expert on the causes of psychopathy" who offered results from a genetic test. The test revealed that Donahue carried a particular gene linked with antisocial behavior—in particular, with brain-development problems that result in the absence of "a normal violence-inhibition mechanism." The other half of the judges did not receive this additional expert testimony.

You might expect that the psychopathy diagnosis would do all of the work at sentencing—it doesn't seem as if knowing the underlying neurological cause would add much. You might also expect that the judges would view the scientific evidence as a reason to lock Donahue up for longer. Psychopaths present a serious future threat, after all.

But you'd be wrong. Bringing in expert testimony on the defendant's antisocial condition turned out to be a double-edged sword. Judges rated the evidence of psychopathy as aggravating overall, as expected, but the additional neurobiological explanation of psychopathy resulted in significantly *reduced* sentences— about 7 percent shorter, on average. The neurobiologist's testimony changed how judges thought about the defendant's condition. With the source of Donahue's behavior located in the brain, he suddenly seemed less in control of his actions and less blameworthy.

The question, of course, is whether the expert opinion here *ought* to be given such weight, and many neuroscientists are concerned, not only because applying general research on genetics and brain function to a particular individual is dubious, given the state of the existing science, but also because it is unclear why explaining the particular biological mechanism of psychopathy ought to have an impact on sentencing. After all, the judges had already been provided with testimony explaining the psychology of psychopathy and how resistant it is to treatment. The key point is that the person has an impairment for which he is not responsible. It should not make any difference whether that impairment is the result of being emotionally abused as a child or possessing a certain gene or experiencing a series of concussions.

During three days of pretrial testimony concerning the former Army Ranger Gary Smith's fMRI evidence, Judge Johnson was presented with some of the research we've just discussed. Now he had to decide whether to allow Professor Haist's findings to come before the jury. It was never going to be an easy decision—here was a man accused of murdering a friend and roommate; his life was in the balance. All he asked was that jurors be able to consider this potentially exculpatory evidence. If you were accused of murder and you had evidence that you were innocent—even if it was based on unsettled science—shouldn't you at least be able to show it to the people deciding your fate?

No, said Judge Johnson, the brain scans had to be kept out of the courtroom. Gary Smith was ultimately convicted of involuntary manslaughter and sentenced to twenty-eight years in prison, with the case now working its way through the appellate courts.

Judge Johnson took the path of caution. But that does not mean that all judges will resist the allure of neuroscience-based lie detection and wait for the field to develop. There has already been a major shot across the bow, half a world away. On June 12, 2008, in Mumbai, India, Judge Shalini Phansalkar-Joshi handed down the first-ever decision convicting someone of murder based in part on a brain scan.

It started as a love story. Aditi Sharma and Udit Bharati met when they were just teenagers. They dated as students at Mahantsingh Engineering College, and after getting engaged they headed off together to business school at the Indian Institute of Modern Management in Pune. But Aditi soon broke off the engagement, having fallen for a fellow MBA classmate, Pravin Khandelwal. Aditi and Pravin dropped out of school and moved to another state—disappointing, no doubt, for Aditi's parents, but nothing out of the ordinary.

Six months later, though, Aditi was back in Pune, allegedly arranging to meet Udit at a McDonald's. Udit would not survive to the next night.

According to prosecutors, Aditi poisoned Udit with arsenic-laced candy that she offered him as the two sat talking. The turning point in the case came when Aditi consented to being hooked up to an EEG after an initial polygraph test suggested her involvement in Udit's death. As she sat with thirty-two electrodes attached to her head, technicians read aloud various innocuous statements, along with first-person statements about key facts in the case: "I bought arsenic." "I met Udit at McDonald's."

According to investigators administering the Brain Electrical Oscillations Signature test (BEOS), the electrical signals coming from the surface of her scalp were damning. When she heard the details of the crime, specific regions of the brain involved in reliving past experiences became active. Aditi had not just heard about the murder; she had "experiential knowledge" of it—she was the murderer. And what is particularly astonishing is that for the investigators to reach this conclusion, Aditi didn't have to say a word.

The BEOS results provided key evidence for Judge Phansalkar-Joshi; she included no less than nine pages in her decision explaining and defending them. Because Aditi was later released on bail by the Bombay High Court pending her appeal (which may take years to work out), it is easy to write this case off as an anomaly likely to be remedied by the existing judicial process. But that would be a serious mistake, because lawyers around the world are currently working to bring in similar evidence in an array of different contexts.

In the United States, courts have resisted allowing neuroscience-based lie-detection technology to come before a jury, but judges have permitted brain images to be used to challenge a witness's testimony and to mitigate a defendant's responsibility for a crime. Over the last decade, criminal defense attorneys have introduced neurological evidence in hundreds of cases, and the trend is increasing. So, for example, when Grady Nelson killed his wife and stabbed and raped her eleven-year-old daughter, his lawyer convinced a Miami judge to allow a neuroscientist to testify about abnormalities in Nelson's brain. That evidence appears to have saved his life. Two jurors who came out against his execution reported that it was the neuroscience that had made them vote as they did. "It turned my decision all the way around," one of them explained. "The technology really swayed me. . . . After seeing the brain scans, I was convinced this guy had some sort of brain problem." If either of those jurors had voted differently, Nelson would have been sentenced to death.

Even when lie-detection technology is barred from the courtroom, it can still have a powerful influence on our justice system. Although the polygraph has been kept out of criminal trials for years, it has managed to play a critical part in many convictions. Polygraphs are regularly used in criminal investigations at both the federal and the local level. As we saw in Juan Rivera's wrongful conviction case, detectives can even lie to suspects about the results in hopes that it will prompt a confession, and because the polygraph has the patina of "hard science," it can have that effect even on those who are innocent. Kevin Fox, for instance, was told by police that he would be cleared as a suspect in the rape and murder of his young daughter, Riley, if he passed a polygraph. The test administrator, however, lied to Fox, allegedly telling him that the polygraph was absolutely reliable and admissible in Illinois state court and that it showed that he was the perpetrator. With that seemingly devastating strike against him, Fox, like Rivera, didn't see any other way forward but to confess to a horrific crime he did not commit.

Polygraphs are a routine part of probation and parole processes, including the regulation of released sex offenders. In New

Jersey, for example, almost all of the state's 5,600 supervised sex offenders must be given at least one polygraph each year. Hooked up to the machine, they may be asked whether they've had any unsupervised contact with minors, abused drugs, or felt attracted to a sixteen-year-old co-worker at the fast-food place where they work. Failing the test can mean losing a job, being required to wear an electronic ankle bracelet, or ending up back in prison. In certain states, they may even be given a "sexual history disclosure examination" that covers their entire life, which could conceivably prompt additional prosecution if other crimes are revealed.

The science-fiction world in which the government tries to read your thoughts is already upon us, and it is no great leap to assume that EEGs and fMRIs will be the next generation of tools to be exploited. These technologies are starting to have an impact on our legal system, and those who stand to gain from using them are not going to wait for approval from the scientific establishment any more than they have with the polygraph.

We need to prepare judges to make the hard calls on admitting new lie-detection evidence. The existing instructions just aren't up to the task. The main problem is not the criteria the Supreme Court has established to guide courts in deciding whether expert testimony should be admissible: Is the research falsifiable and testable? Is it peer reviewed? Has it been accepted in the scientific community? What is the likely or known error rate? These are the proper questions to ask. The problem is that most judges aren't able to answer them. In a recent survey, only 5 percent of state trial court judges were able to explain the meaning of "falsifiability," and an even smaller percentage understood "error rate." Moreover, in an experiment involving Florida circuit court judges, researchers found that the judges' decisions to admit or exclude expert testimony were not based on the quality of the science at all. With numerous legally relevant scientific breakthroughs on the horizon and increasingly sophisticated methods, that is reason for serious concern.

Federal and state judiciaries should commit to the rigorous training of judges in assessing expert testimony. If a forklift operator has to reach a basic level of competency with the standard equipment for his job, why shouldn't a judge? A lack of proficiency can bring devastating consequences in both cases. And making scientific literacy mandatory doesn't demean judges; it's a testament to the importance of what they do. As we'll see in the next chapter, judicial education provides other benefits as well, and there's existing precedent. Indeed, in the last few years, leading researchers have drafted guides to help judges handle neuroscientific evidence, and a handful of seminars have been held around the country. But we need to greatly expand and bolster this work—and we might consider starting earlier, by offering more classes at law schools focused on science in the legal sphere. The first law and neuroscience coursebook was just published, and over twenty schools now have classes—like the one I teach— focused on law and the mind sciences.

Training, though, is only part of the solution. We also have to decide whether there are some kinds of expert testimony on emerging science that judges should not consider. We could very well bar mind-reading testimony from the courtroom altogether, prohibit the police from interrogating suspects using fMRI, or require a special type of warrant in order to "search" a person's brain for memories of a crime.

For centuries, we've espoused a robust commitment to protecting privacy. Under traditional English law, even when authorities had a warrant, the government was not allowed to access a person's private papers. In the United States, the Fourth and Fifth Amendments were designed to protect the privacy of all men and women, even those accused of the most heinous crimes. Yet many of us think differently today about privacy: we willingly share our inner secrets, beliefs, hopes, and emotions on social media to casual acquaintances and often strangers. Many of my students shrug their shoulders when I point out the way corporations now collect and analyze demographic information and personal data on buying habits, Internet usage, travel history, and countless other details of our lives in order to predict our behavior. So what if a company knows that I'm gay or pregnant or considering leaving my husband before I've told anyone else? Revelations that the U.S. government has been widely spying on foreign heads of state and its own citizens have not seriously imperiled those in power. The truth is that many Americans may not see looking into a suspect's or defendant's mind without consent as a "fundamental affront to human dignity," as the ACLU recently characterized it.

But we—all of us, not simply a few neuroethicists—need to stop and consider the matter: we owe it to future generations to make an active choice on the proper balance between privacy and security. Given the different cultural backgrounds that people bring to the table, our best bet may be to think about things from the perspective of someone who knew she would one day be accused of a crime but did not know whether she would be innocent or guilty. With that outlook, we wouldn't go down the road to routine police questioning using brain scans until the science was very settled indeed. We might, however, be supportive of a defendant's right to bring in even imperfect proof of truthfulness. There's no reason that prosecutors and defendants should have to meet the same hurdles when it comes to lie-detection evidence. And in a period of less than absolute certainty, it seems fitting that mind-reading technology should serve as a shield rather than a sword.

# 8

## UMPIRES OR ACTIVISTS?

### The Judge

John Roberts was sitting on the D.C. Circuit Court of Appeals when President George W. Bush nominated him for the Supreme Court in July 2005. It had been more than a decade since the last justice joined the Court, and the stakes were further raised when Chief Justice William Rehnquist died that September. There were now two vacancies, and the president wanted Roberts to fill the preeminent position. Standing in his way were confirmation hearings before the Senate Committee on the Judiciary.

Once upon a time, for a man with Roberts's sparkling credentials—dual Harvard degrees, years of experience as a government lawyer and in private practice, thirty-nine cases argued before the Supreme Court, and a federal appellate judgeship—the Senate would not have presented such a daunting challenge. But the landscape had changed with the failed nomination of Robert Bork in 1987.

Like Roberts, Bork had a distinguished résumé and was sitting on the D.C. Circuit when President Ronald Reagan came calling. He was buoyed by significant conservative excitement—a dream pick, to many. And despite the efforts of liberal groups to discredit him, public opinion was in his favor on the eve of the hearings. But a series of missteps, with the microphone on and cameras flashing, turned the tide. In the end, fifty-eight senators voted no, providing the most decisive loss in the history of Supreme Court nominations.

Roberts and his team were determined not to make similar blunders, and they did not disappoint. Where Bork had appeared humorless and arrogant—stating, at one point, that he wanted to serve on the Supreme Court because it would be "an intellectual feast"—Roberts played the part with humility and charm. Where Bork had weighed in on hot topics—criticizing the reasoning behind *Roe v. Wade*—Roberts avoided taking clear positions on contentious issues. Arguably the savviest move, though, came in how he framed being a judge:

"Judges are like umpires. Umpires don't make the rules; they apply them."

Roberts certainly wasn't the first person to use the metaphor, but in the fall of 2005, it seemed a particularly compelling notion to many denizens of Capitol Hill and their constituents back home. Good judges call balls and strikes. They don't pitch or bat. They put their backgrounds, experiences, and allegiances to the side and apply the clear law to the clear facts. Bad judges, by contrast, let their personal opinions about policy infect their rulings. They are unelected activists, advancing their own ends by "interpreting" things where there is no room for interpretation and by legislating from the bench.

In setting out the two implicit categories and then claiming to be one of the good, objective judges—with "no agenda" and "no platform"—Roberts allayed the fear that had doomed Bork, of seating a conservative "ideologue" with a grand scheme. More important, he engendered a world in which those who followed—Samuel Alito, Sonia Sotomayor, and Elena Kagan—were forced to acknowledge the basic truth of the umpire frame or face the possibility of rejection.

Justice Sotomayor's path through the Senate was made much more tenuous by the simple fact that she had previously voiced her belief that "personal experiences affect the facts that judges choose to see," and that judges might be unable to be truly impartial "in all, or even in most, cases." In Sotomayor's estimation, the law was often ambiguous, making interpretation unavoidable: "Whether born from experience or inherent physiological or cultural differences . . . our gender and national origins may and will make a difference in our judging."

To many in the Senate and in the American public, this conception was utterly unacceptable. As the Republican senator John Cornyn, of Texas, explained, Sotomayor's professional success was not going to carry her through confirmation: "The real question is how she views her role as a judge: whether it is to advance causes or groups or whether it is to call balls and strikes." While a few Democratic senators criticized the analogy for failing to capture the full nature of a judge's role, Sotomayor fell into line, offering reassurance that she was not an activist and would just apply the law.

This was Roberts's master stroke. During his confirmation hearings, he wasn't just playing defense to survive the confirmation battle; he was also establishing an offensive position to reshape the nature of adjudication in the long term. There was a war over what judges could and should do. Establishing the umpire as an ideal would constrain judges who thought that their backgrounds ought to play a role in their decisions, as well as presidents who sought to appoint more women, blacks, Hispanics, Asians, Muslims, and gays to the judiciary. There was no need for diversity on a court of referees. And it would limit others who thought that the law was not neutral, clear, and set in stone, but rather frequently ambiguous and subject to changing meaning with changing times. The umpire judge was necessarily a textualist—a strict constructionist—with no right to look outside his little black book of rules to decide a case.

Chief Justice Roberts's metaphor has maintained its dominance, in part, because breaking the world down into objective technicians and biased ideologues aligns so well with our intuitions and observations about the judiciary. There really do seem to be some judges out there who insert themselves into the game or try to distort the outcome. Indeed, a majority of Americans feel that "judicial activism" has reached a crisis, and some three-quarters believe that justices are sometimes swayed by their political or personal views.

Yet the public doesn't seem to agree on *which* judges are biased. For certain people, Justice Ginsburg is a dangerous activist with an agenda and Justice Scalia is a beacon of objectivity; for others, it is precisely the opposite. Likewise, while 45 percent of conservative Republicans believe that the Supreme Court has a liberal bent and only 9 percent believe that it is conservative, the opposite pattern exists for liberal Democrats: 48 percent believe the Court is conservative, while only 15 percent believe it is liberal.

Clearly, these numbers should give us pause. Something other than the facts is driving our notions of judicial impartiality. A prime culprit appears to be our general tendency to see third parties—including judges, the media, debate monitors, and referees—as more set against our side and more in favor of the opposition than they actually are. In one of the most famous demonstrations of this dynamic, people who identified as either pro-Israeli or pro-Arab were shown major-network television coverage of the 1982 Israeli military operation into West Beirut. Given the impact of cultural cognition (discussed in the jury chapter), it should come as no surprise that although the two groups watched the same clips, they saw different "objective" facts. What *is* surprising is that both groups saw the news as significantly biased against their side.

So, we may be primed to spot judicial bias even when it doesn't exist. And, confident in the accuracy of our viewpoints, when a judge takes a position that we strongly disagree with, we are all the more likely to try to discredit him. The difference, then, between the judge we see as an activist and the one we see as an umpire may have nothing to do with their actual biases and everything to do with whether they share our perspective on the world.

But that's only half of the problem with the umpire frame. In line with Roberts's model, we tend to assume that judicial bias is a conscious choice. That's why we have rules barring members of the judiciary from holding office in political organizations, soliciting gifts from those coming before the court, or allowing personal relationships to influence their decisions. But while there are rare incidents when a judge is found to have taken a bribe or ruled a certain way because a family member asked him to, such explicit, conscious bias is not the major issue that the judiciary faces. And the vessels of partiality are not a limited set of activist judges who have bad dispositions or lack character and integrity. As we will see, all judges are susceptible to numerous unappreciated biases that influence their perceptions of seemingly neutral facts and laws, as well as their ultimate judgments.

While judges are meant to check their identities at the door of the courtroom—in keeping with Chief Justice Roberts's umpire model—they simply cannot. As we saw with jurors, a person's background and experiences necessarily color her perceptions, emotions, reasoning, and judgments. Under oath, Roberts claimed to bring true neutrality to his work, but there are no agenda-cleansed, ideology-free judges. They are a myth, no more plausible than a Supreme Court made up of eight unicorns and a troll.

Although it is hard to find a single judge who would admit to being swayed by her political leanings, researchers who analyzed more than twenty thousand federal court decisions found significant partisan bias in the way judges handled federal agency decisions. Democratic appointees disproportionately struck down "conservative" decisions (in which a corporation, like GM or

Exxon, brought the challenge) and upheld "liberal" decisions (in which a labor union or public-interest group, like the Sierra Club, brought the challenge), while the opposite was true of Republican appointees. What's more, although the charge is more often directed at liberal judges, conservative members of the Supreme Court actually scored higher on their degree of "judicial activism" (assessed by the percentage of agency decisions they elected to overturn). Other studies have revealed a similar link between a judge's political affiliation and the treatment different parties receive, with judges appointed by Democrats more likely to act favorably toward minorities, workers, convicted criminals, and undocumented immigrants, and those appointed by Republicans more likely to act favorably toward big business and the government.

Of course, it is not just political orientation that matters; age, race, and gender, among other factors, all appear to influence how a judge goes about her job, just as they influence jurors. Although she was forced to retreat from her statements about how gender and ethnicity influence judging, Justice Sotomayor was right: identities and personal experiences do "affect the facts that judges choose to see." And that means that those on the bench often prejudge cases. Justice Scalia, in particular, is frequently criticized for taking public stances on issues like gay marriage and then failing to recuse himself in later cases involving those issues. But the fact is that no judge or justice ever approaches a case with a genuinely open mind. They read briefs and hear arguments with brains shaped by Sunday school, military service, summers on Cape Cod, and years as a prosecutor or a parent. Researchers recently found that judges who had a daughter rather than a son were 16 percent more likely to decide gender-related civil rights cases in favor of women's rights. The effect appears to be driven primarily by male judges appointed by Republicans. One theory is that having a daughter helps these judges better understand the challenges that women face on issues like equal pay and reproductive health, giving them a perspective that they wouldn't otherwise have.

All of this makes the lack of diversity on our present courts a major concern. White men, for instance, are overrepresented almost two to one on state appellate benches, with nearly all other groups underrepresented. But it also raises a historical quandary. Our system is rooted in the principle of *stare decisis*—the notion that courts should generally adhere to the law as established by earlier cases—and many criminal statutes also reflect what judges decided many decades ago. What qualifies as rape? What are the elements of a valid self-defense claim? Should victims have to face their accusers in court? The psychological evidence suggests that we should expect very different responses depending on the gender, religion, sexual orientation, and political orientation (among many other things) of the judge or legislator making the call.

Yet the answers we have are largely the creation of a very narrow band of Ivy League–educated Christian men of northern and western European ancestry. The Supreme Court was pumping out precedent for almost 180 years before the first African American had a chance to share his perspective, more than 190 before the first woman left her mark, and 220 before the first Hispanic authored an opinion. So, even if you happen to come before a Latina judge whose background and perspective actually benefit you, she will be operating under an elaborate legal structure built over centuries by individuals whose experiences may be quite foreign to your own.

Judicial decision-making is affected not just by who a judge *is* but also by how she thinks. As we've seen, our decisions are governed by both fast intuitive processes that operate automatically and slower, more controlled deliberation. You might suppose that a judge, because of the nature of her job and training, would rely almost exclusively on deliberative reasoning, but the reality is that judges are frequently—or, some researchers assert, predominantly—intuitive deciders. Like the rest of us, they rely on mental shortcuts when they need to make a judgment, whether that involves allowing a piece of evidence before a jury or sentencing someone to prison.

Sometimes these automatic rules of thumb are quite helpful. When a judge isn't sure whether to overrule an objection, he may take a cue from his previous interactions with the lawyer whose objections are almost always superfluous and the fact that opposing counsel seems exasperated. That can lead to the right decision. Unfortunately, these intuitive processes can also result in systematic errors when they rely on irrelevant cues and dubious connections.

Consider the so-called anchoring effect, whereby an initial numerical value—which is made salient by, say, my asking you for the last two digits of your phone number—ends up informing a subsequent appraisal, like how much you think a bottle of wine is worth. By the mid-1970s, researchers had shown that numerical anchors exert a strong force on people's judgments about things like the percentage of United Nations members that are African countries, but it seemed a significant leap to think that they might influence an experienced judge on a matter of real importance, like how much a car accident victim should be awarded after losing his right arm or how much time a rapist or repeat shoplifter should spend in prison. Yet when researchers took up these questions with real judges, they found clear evidence of the power of anchoring. Asked to sentence a hypothetical defendant, judges were significantly influenced by cues that shouldn't matter: a number provided by a journalist during a recess telephone call ("Do you think the sentence for the defendant in this case will be higher or lower than three years?") or a prosecutor's sentencing recommendation that the judge was told was randomly generated. Shockingly, even rolling a set of dice affected the sentences that judges handed down.

One of the things that was so surprising about this research was that expertise and experience did not act as a tonic. Participants who were experts in criminal law and who had dealt with cases similar to the hypotheticals were just as influenced by the irrelevant numbers as legal professionals with no such background. And while other research suggests that expertise can, in certain circumstances, help judges avoid cognitive pitfalls that befall laypeople, in this case all it seemed to do was make judges feel more confident in their sentencing decisions.

The source of the problem is no secret: judges often have to decide questions under conditions of uncertainty. How does one know for sure where bail should be set, whether a photograph of the defendant is unfairly prejudicial, or when to declare a mistrial? It doesn't help that the evidence judges rely on to answer these types of questions is frequently contradictory, thanks to an adversarial system in which the prosecution and the defense are tasked with marshaling the facts that support their respective positions. As a consequence, judges are susceptible to various false signals that seem to offer a way out. And the legal rules designed to keep judges on course often come up short.

Judges are required, for example, to disregard legally prejudicial and irrelevant facts, like a defendant's arrest, five years earlier, for snatching a purse. While that fact may make the defendant seem more likely to have committed the burglary at issue in the present case, it does not go any distance toward proving his guilt. However, in two separate sets of experiments, researchers found that real judges asked to decide a hypothetical case were often unable to put such information to the side—even when they were explicitly reminded that the facts they had learned were inadmissible.

A similar dynamic is at work when it comes to gender, race, class, and a host of other factors. Judges are well aware that none of these variables should influence decision-making; indeed, they regularly instruct jurors to ignore such differences when assessing witnesses, defendants, and attorneys. But judges are part of a society in which all of these factors carry strong associations, from stereotypes about a woman's role in raising children to feelings about transgender people. And it's not a simple matter of taking off one's prejudices in the robing room.

If judges consistently carry biases, does that mean they are consistent *in* their biases? Interested in this question, a set of researchers decided to look at how judges make decisions over the course of the day. The investigators turned their attention to eight experienced judges serving on two Israeli parole boards.

Overall, these judges rejected 64.2 percent of the requests made by prisoners. But that wasn't what the researchers were interested in: they wanted to know about the judges' decisions at different times of day. Did it matter whether a case appeared before the board in the early morning or right after a midday break? For an umpire judge, it wouldn't matter: a strike is a strike is a strike, no matter the location of the sun. But what about for these real judges?

An analysis of more than a thousand rulings showed that the judges were significantly more likely to grant prisoners parole at the beginning of the workday or after one of the two food breaks—ruling in favor of prisoners about 65 percent of the time—than they were at the end of the day or right before a break, when favorable rulings dropped almost to zero. Moreover, factors like the severity of the crime and the amount of time the prisoner had already served—which should influence judges' decisions—tended not to have an impact on the rulings. The time of day seemed to be the important thing.

How could this be?

The study's authors hypothesize that as the day wears on, judges become mentally depleted, causing them to go the cognitively easy route and stick with the status quo: denying parole. Repeatedly making decisions taxes our mental resources, and to overcome the fatigue we may require rest or increased glucose—literally, food for thought.

What is particularly alarming is that this was not some laboratory experiment. The two parole boards involved in the study process approximately 40 percent of all requests in Israel. And the judges had no idea of the nature or extent of their bias. That's one of the reasons mental depletion can be so dangerous: often you won't feel depleted at all, so you won't see any reason to doubt your judgment.

Judges, of course, want to be consistent. And one of the most disheartening recent findings is that this desire can actually lead us to be more biased. As a professor, I face this problem every semester when I sit down to grade exams. In my Criminal Law course, for instance, I can give no more than 20 percent of the students an A or A−. Although, statistically, it is entirely possible that in a class of eighty I might get three A's in the first five exams, my expectation is that only one of the five will be an A, and that expectation threatens to alter how I grade (in this case, encouraging me to judge the strong exams at the beginning more harshly). Researchers have dubbed this phenomenon "narrow bracketing": those who must make a continuous flow of judgments assess subsets of these judgments in isolation (say, all of the exams graded before lunch, or all of the cases seen in one day) and avoid deviating too much from the expected distribution. According to this research, although a judge should count on occasionally having five great candidates for parole in a row, after four successive grants a judge is less likely to grant the fifth prisoner's request simply because it differs from the pattern he expects (that is, only about two out of every three people being granted parole).

That a judge's decision in one case might influence his next decision, or that the time of day when the case is heard might have an impact on the outcome, is totally antithetical to our conception of a fair justice system. And it is vital that we continue working to better understand the forces that shape judicial decision-making. As the legal theorist and appellate judge Jerome Frank wrote all the way back in 1930, "If the law consists of the decisions of the judges and if those decisions are based on the judge's hunches, then the way in which the judge gets his hunches is the key to the judicial process. Whatever produces the judge's hunches makes the law."

Judges, then, are not much like Chief Justice Roberts's beacons of objectivity, neutrality, and disinterest. But, in truth, neither are real umpires or referees.

While some social scientists have been looking at judicial decision-making, others have been investigating bias in referees. The findings are staggeringly similar: across different sports, referees who appear committed to being neutral and objective end up making skewed calls and managing matches unfairly. Tennis officials, for instance, are subject to perceptual bias akin to the influence of camera perspective on judges and jurors. The spot where an umpire perceives a ball to land is shifted in the direction it is traveling, so he is more likely to call balls out that are actually in than to call balls in that are actually out. Like their judicial counterparts, referees are also swayed by factors that are meant to be irrelevant. White umpires give white batters smaller strike zones than they give black batters, tae kwon do competitors dressed in red tend to be awarded more points than those in blue, and the taller of two soccer players involved in an ambiguous collision is more likely to be called for a foul. In addition, as with judges who expect a certain distribution of parole denials and subconsciously alter their decisions accordingly, basketball refs are inclined to even out foul calls, and baseball umpires tend to reduce the strike zone with two-strike counts and expand it on three-ball counts. Finally, like judges, referees are not always able to ignore the roar of the crowd: home-team biases are robust and pervasive across numerous sports, and the larger the crowd size, the greater the favoritism.

Many of us say that we want an umpire judge, but perhaps what we really want is a robot judge—and presumably not one programmed by humans. Flesh-and-blood adjudicators come with the same limited hardware we all carry in our brains—circuits designed for a Pleistocene past, processors too slow to keep up, and storage drives wanting in capacity.

All of this raises an interesting puzzle: as I've mentioned, judges (and referees, for that matter) rarely, if ever, feel like they are acting in a biased way. Most would vigorously deny that they are being influenced by impermissible and irrelevant elements in their environments or that they are being driven by intuition rather than pure reason. Indeed, most would feel quite confident that they are tuning out biasing factors and focusing on the pertinent details of the case. In light of the growing body of research that makes such rosy accounts of objectivity highly doubtful, how can judges be so blind?

The answer is that introspection and personal observation don't tell the whole story. An appellate judge sitting in her chambers with the text of the Constitution on her left, a pile of cases on her right, and the lower court record on her lap can feel quite sure that she is simply applying the letter of the law to the facts of the case. But *feeling* as if you are reading the text of the Fourth Amendment through unfiltered lenses and applying precedent without bias does not make it so.

Legal training, experience, and the rules and expectations of the job have the potential to help judges overcome certain biases, but they also reinforce a myth of impartiality. For example, part of the socialization of law school involves learning to deal with serious and sensitive legal issues—like when a sexual encounter qualifies as a rape—without becoming "emotional." When students learn to discuss nonconsensual sex without getting upset, they are understood to be looking at matters objectively. But, of course, cultivating a flat affect does little or nothing to eliminate the biases that a person might bring to the issue. And approaching something like sexual assault without emotion is neither objective nor fair and balanced. It only feels that way.

Similarly, over the last hundred years, most law professors have focused their classroom teaching on bringing structure and meaning to the numerous opinions and statutes students are required to absorb. And we assign reading from casebooks that offer up a vision of the law as a set of ordered rules that can be deduced, learned, and applied with consistency and predictability. Certainly, precedent and statutory laws can act as powerful constraints on judges—and may even help eliminate or reduce certain biases—but we professors engage in a damaging charade when we pantomime a legal world in which clear instructions are implemented by dutiful technicians. That world does not exist, but it's what all judges have been trained to expect.

Once they are sitting on the bench, approaches to interpretation that seem to offer judges a way to ensure objectivity help keep the truth hidden. Justice Antonin Scalia's textual originalism, for example, advises the judge to "look for meaning in the governing text, ascribe to that text the meaning that it has borne from its inception, and reject judicial speculation about both the drafters' extra-textually derived purposes and the desirability of the fair reading's anticipated consequences." A judge's decision, then, turns on the text, the text, and nothing but the text. With seemingly no room for personal agendas or political distortions, it's the ideal method for the umpire judge.

But the truth is that a text is rarely confined to just one interpretation, and figuring out the proper historical meaning of a legal source is inherently subjective and conjectural. The Fourth Amendment begins, "The right of the people to be secure in their persons, houses, papers, and effects, against unreasonable searches and seizures, shall not be violated . . ." So what is a "search"? Is using a thermal-imaging device from across the street to see if someone is using heat lamps to grow marijuana in his home a "search"? Is placing a GPS tracking device on a car a "search"? Textual originalism does not dictate a clear answer; it just provides a cover of legitimacy to an inherently biased task.

In situations like this, a judge is free to attach the meaning that supports his preferred outcome and "find" the history that backs up that meaning, all the while feeling certain that it is the text that's doing all of the work.

While textual originalism makes it especially difficult for us to see and acknowledge the biases that judges bring to the table, all judges, whether in the mold of Justice Scalia or Justice Ginsburg, struggle to appreciate the blinders they wear as they go about their work. This is particularly evident in the widespread practice of Supreme Court justices and clerks conducting their own research regarding facts in a case.

The common portrayal is that justices don't find facts; they receive them, applying the law to what was established at trial. But members of the Court actually conduct a significant amount of "in-house" investigation into general questions about the world that are relevant to particular legal and policy issues. Rather than simply relying on the lower court record and the briefs before them, the justices (or their clerks) regularly search Google or Westlaw or the Supreme Court library catalogue to determine the amount of carbon dioxide emissions in the air, whether late-term abortions tend to be pursued primarily by women below the poverty line, or whether most members of the public believe that self-defense is a fundamental right. Indeed, in surveying the 120 most important opinions of the last ten years, one legal scholar found that a majority of cases included citations to one or more outside sources.

On first glance that seems rather unproblematic. If a case comes down to whether fleeing from the police in a vehicle amounts to a "violent felony" under the Armed Career Criminal Act, what's wrong with a justice or clerk doing a little background reading to get a better sense of the number of injuries and deaths from police chases? In *United States v. Sykes*, both Justice Kennedy and Justice Thomas uncovered crash statistics that helped them conclude that vehicular flight is indeed a violent felony. Isn't this precisely what we want when a justice lacks sufficient knowledge about a particular subject or when relevant data does not appear in the record or in the briefs?

The problem, as scholars have pointed out, is not that the justices are trying to become more informed. It's the nature of the information they turn up. In many cases, the "facts" they discover are flawed or misleading.

Judges, just like the rest of us, tend to make gut decisions and then look for supporting data, discarding and dismissing conflicting evidence along the way. It's the same problem we encountered with the police, emergency responders, and medical personnel who focused on the facts that fit the initial conclusion that David Rosenbaum was just a drunk. When judges do research, they already have an idea of what they are looking for and—surprise!—they tend to find it. The underlying drive is to bolster an argument, not discover the truth.

Suppose you are a justice looking, for the first time, at the details of the *Sykes* case. Your immediate instinct (no doubt informed by watching the video of the police chase and fiery crash in *Scott v. Harris* four years earlier) is that of course fleeing the police in a vehicle is a violent felony. But you need a reason to justify that position, and so your brain offers a rationalization: lots of people are injured and killed during pursuits. It seems like that has to be true; you just need to find the data that says so. And so you go online to look for sources and you search until you find just such a study. There: proof that people are injured and killed when police chases occur, which in turn establishes that vehicular flight crimes are indeed violent felonies. It felt like the conclusion was dictated by the facts, when really a gut reaction led you to engage in a narrow, targeted search.

We tend to assume that the more data a person has at her fingertips, the more accurate she'll be. But, in fact, having more information may make it easier to find the necessary support for an erroneous proposition. When a pair of political scientists asked a group of Republicans whether "the size of the yearly budget deficit increased, decreased, or stayed about the same during Clinton's time as President"—it, in fact, decreased—the most politically informed members (those in the 95th percentile) gave a wrong answer more often than less informed members (those in the 50th percentile). A similar effect was found for well-informed Democrats asked about the state of inflation during President Reagan's time in office. With more information on hand to support the intuition that the other side's president had been a failure, it was easier to reach the wrong (but favored) conclusion.

Our analytical skills can be distorted by a similar dynamic: sometimes being more adept at evaluating something can actually amplify our ideological biases. In one set of experiments, researchers looked at how people with different levels of math competency assessed the effectiveness of a skin-rash treatment or a firearm regulation when given basic data. On the skin-rash evaluation, things played out exactly as you might expect: those who were bad at math got the right answer about half as often as those who were good at math. But when participants were asked to determine the effectiveness of the gun ban, something funny happened with the highly numerate. When the data pointed to a conclusion that conflicted with their ideology, they appeared to disregard it. Given numbers suggesting that crime decreased, mathematically adept conservatives got the right answer only about 20 percent of the time, as compared with 85 percent of the time when the data suggested that crime increased. The reverse was true for liberals: about 70 percent reached the correct conclusion when the data pointed to a decrease in crime, but that dropped to below half when the data implied that the ban was ineffective. Despite knowing how to use the numbers to make an accurate determination, those with conflicting ideological positions simply went with their gut. The findings suggest that being a more skilled and experienced member of the bench might not bring the benefits we'd expect.

The situation may be exacerbated by the fact that when it comes to the controversial issues that come before the Supreme Court, there are almost always authorities to buttress any position one might want to take. Indeed, when Justice Elena Kagan sought support for her dissent in *Sykes*—that fleeing the cops in a car is *not* inherently violent and aggressive—she was easily able to find it, citing evidence that a driver might legitimately fear that a criminal rather than a police officer was pulling her over. The fact that justices' research may be driven more by motivated reasoning than by an open-minded quest for information is reflected in the diversity of sources that justices cite. Look at recent opinions and you'll see interest-group sites and blogs alongside esteemed peer-reviewed journals.

It doesn't help that judges are exposed to a surprisingly narrow set of ideas, experiences, and viewpoints in their daily interactions. Sure, judges are not sequestered in ivory towers. They have spouses, children, and friends; they attend cookouts and weddings and plays; they read books, watch movies, and go on vacations. But, like all of us, they fall into routines, sticking to what they already know, prefer, and trust.

Justice Scalia reads two newspapers in the morning: the *Wall Street Journal* and the *Washington Times*. As he told a journalist for *New York* magazine, he "used to get the *Washington Post*, but it just . . . went too far for me. I couldn't handle it anymore." He was tipped over the edge by "the treatment of almost any conservative issue. It was slanted and often nasty. And, you know, why should I get upset every morning?" He "usually" listens to talk radio—that is where he gets most of his news. In the past, he went to dinner parties that had a real mix of liberals and conservatives, he said, but that hasn't happened in a long time.

We all wear blinders fashioned from our limited lives. And if you happen to live in northern Virginia, listen to NPR, and mingle primarily with liberals, you are going to conduct your judicial research accordingly, clicking on certain websites and not others, recalling particular research studies, reading beyond the abstract of this author's paper but not his colleague's. And you may surround yourself with clerks who do the same.

A search engine like Google may seem to offer a way out of the bind. But search engines are themselves deeply biasing. Many of them create filter bubbles by organizing the results based on your particular interests and proclivities, as revealed by the other websites you visited, your Facebook profile, or other personal details. In essence, without your awareness, you are being steered toward the sources that you are likely to find the most persuasive and that are most likely to support your views—and away from those that might cause you to rethink your positions.

Amicus curiae briefs—"friend-of-the-court" filings, widely believed to aid the justices by helping to fill informational gaps—are a dead end as well. Although they often purport to offer impartial counsel, they are advocacy documents with facts chosen to persuade. And members of the Court draw from them—more than a hundred times between 2008 and 2013—with a startling lack of scrutiny, citing amicus facts backed up by e-mails, research funded by the amicus itself, unpublished studies "on file with the authors," and, sometimes, nothing at all. With dozens of amici in certain cases and more each year, it seems as if justices are being given a deep reservoir of knowledge, but all that the system really does is supply an easier way to support preexisting conclusions.

As we have seen, much of the bias that infects a judge's decision-making is subtle and automatic. And in many cases it is small enough or disguised enough to go unnoticed by others.

It is like having a single step that's ever so slightly higher than the others. Until recently, at the 36th Street subway stop in Brooklyn, there was just such a step. Every day it caused numerous people to trip as they ascended to street level. But no one did anything, even those who were most severely affected. The guy who nearly dropped his baby? The woman who fell to her knees? They caught their balance or brushed themselves off and walked on, thinking that it was just bad luck or that they had been clumsy or distracted. Few, if any, blamed the step, and so there it remained, a fraction of an inch off, until someone decided to film the entrance. Suddenly, with a pool of data, the problem was so clear it was comical. In under an hour, the videographer captured seventeen people stumbling on the step. And within a day of the evidence being posted online, New York's Metropolitan Transportation Authority had begun replacing the staircase.

We should embrace a similar approach with respect to our courts. Judges need to know if they are more likely to grant parole in the morning than at the end of the day or show more leniency toward a white petitioner than a black one. They need to be aware of how they conduct research and how often they side with the government and whether female attorneys coming before them fare as well as men. But if no one is keeping careful track of their decisions, how will they see the patterns?

Fortunately, a lot of the monitoring and aggregating machinery already exists. Journalists and academics are in a better position than ever to uncover unequal treatment and distorted outcomes. It was the *Boston Globe*'s analysis of more than fifteen hundred Massachusetts drunk-driving cases, for example, that revealed a gross disparity in verdicts. In 2010, 82 percent of defendants who selected a bench trial before a judge were acquitted (well above the national average); for those who stuck with a jury trial, the figure was just 51 percent. In interviews, the judges themselves seemed surprised at the results—they simply did not realize how tilted they were against the prosecution. It took an outside monitor pulling together all of the data to reveal the slant.

The journalists' work prompted the Supreme Judicial Court to commission its own year-long study of the problem, which made specific recommendations to help reduce the acquittal rate and restrict the ability of defense attorneys to steer their clients to the most favorable judges, among other things. These ongoing reform efforts hold the potential not only to increase fairness but also to save lives.

That said, with the decline of print media—the traditional bastion of serious investigative journalism—and constraints on university research funding, the judiciary itself ought to commit to better recordkeeping aimed specifically at uncovering hidden biases. If the Massachusetts Trial Court had collected data on conviction rates for bench and jury trials, it might have noticed the problem years earlier.

On an individual level, psychological research suggests that judges could also benefit from *self*-monitoring by learning about the biases that influence their behavior, expecting (and accepting) that they are not immune, and then taking stock of how they actually behave. The judiciary could help judges with this process not only by providing training on relevant psychological dynamics (a few seminars have already been offered at the federal level on implicit bias) but also by providing individualized statistics. Judges receive surprisingly little feedback on their decision-making—lawyers rarely offer it, and the appellate review process rarely yields any meaningful information on cognitive biases or errors. How does a judge know, for example, whether race, gender, or age impact her treatment of defendants, or whether the harsh sentences she hands down are effective? Judges usually make calls and move on. But seeing the data could be a powerful antidote.

A judge is always going to have hunches about a case—and when those hunches reflect years of experience, they can be valuable. But since they can also lead to errors, our intuitions need to be carefully examined.

That's equally true for police officers, lawyers, jurors, and witnesses: we need to get all of our key legal actors in the business of second-guessing themselves. That sounds strange, but doubt isn't the enemy of justice—blind certainty is. And, in most cases, healthy skepticism isn't going to develop on its own because there are so many forces pulling the other way.

Former New York supreme court judge Frank Barbaro stands as a prime example of how to interrogate one's instincts and decisions. Everything is stacked against it, but Barbaro found a way: "I had a practice . . . that whenever I made a legal decision, I never let it lie. I ran it through my mind again." There was one case in particular that he kept mulling over. In October 1999, the defendant, Donald Kagan, had waived his right to a jury trial, putting his fate entirely in Barbaro's hands. Kagan claimed that he had acted in self-defense when he shot and killed Wavell Wint outside a Brooklyn movie theater. But Judge Barbaro convicted him of second-degree murder and a weapons charge and sentenced him to fifteen years to life.

Although it had been more than a decade, Barbaro told his wife, Patti, "I really feel I need to revisit this case. I need to get the transcripts. I don't feel comfortable with this. It's been haunting me." And when he pored over the record anew, he was "absolutely horrified": "It was so obvious I had made a mistake. I got sick. Physically sick."

He realized that his own background and experience as a vigorous civil rights advocate had colored his treatment of the case: "When the trial began, I was absolutely convinced that Donald Kagan [who was white] was a racist and was out looking for trouble and fully intended to kill Mr. Wint [who was black]." That frame had caused him to overlook evidence that suggested that Kagan acted in self-defense.

Revisiting the facts, Wint now appeared to have been the aggressor. It seemed Kagan had shown his gun only to ward off a drunken Wint, who'd tried to rob Kagan of his gold chain. Wint's friends had dragged him away, but he'd fought them off and gone right back into Kagan's face. When Kagan pulled his gun a second time, Wint went for it. In the scuffle, the gun fired into Wint's torso. In December 2013, fourteen years after Kagan had been convicted, Judge Barbaro took the witness stand to claim that his own verdict should be overturned: "I believe now that I was seeing this young white fellow as a bigot, as someone who assassinated an African American. . . . I was prejudiced during the trial."

It is almost unheard of for a judge to admit that bias led him to err at trial. And it took real courage: the admission not only revealed an awful mistake—his mistake—to the world, but also opened him up to vicious attacks from prosecutors who portrayed him as a feeble-minded old man. But it seemed to Barbaro that the only way forward is to be fearless about looking back: "[T]he legal system should become very sensitive to the question of have we done justice? Have we made a mistake? And that's what I'm trying to do now."

# PART III

# Punishment

# 9

# AN EYE FOR AN EYE

## The Public

More than five hundred citizens of Falaise had come to the execution. They assembled around the town scaffold, where the Vicomte de Falaise himself presided over the proceedings.

Earlier, the accused had been tried and convicted of a vicious crime: savagely biting a child in the face and arms. And though the child had subsequently died, there was no expression of remorse at trial, no apology to the family. Indeed, the guilty party had not spoken a word since being taken into custody, and she said nothing when a harsh sentence was handed down: she was to be given injuries that matched the child's—wounds in the head and arms—before being garroted and hanged.

The crowd watched with eager eyes as she was brought up the scaffold for all to see. She had been dressed in men's clothes, and a special executioner had been brought in from Paris. It was 1386, and the population of northern France expected a show. But still, the condemned refused to speak.

As the last preparations were made, the assembled men and women waited for the final act. It was, the Vicomte must surely have thought, a righteous punishment for an atrocious act, and after the executioner had done his work and the body of the felon hung limp, he ordered a fresco of the scene painted in the

Church of Holy Trinity in the town. When, some three decades later, Henry V and his British compatriots destroyed much of the church, the people of Falaise came together to have the fresco repainted, where it remained for more than four hundred years.

Though the fresco has not survived—it was whitewashed by the church in 1820 during a renovation—today we know for certain why the condemned never spoke.

She was a pig.

The events at Falaise were far from an anomaly. Trials and punishments of animals were common for centuries. Judicial proceedings were brought against rats and locusts that infested villages and destroyed crops. Mastiffs were guillotined for assaults. Murderous bulls were seized, tried, and convicted. Horses were burned by court order for their transgressions.

The prosecution of animal crimes was not just a matter of backwoods folk practice; it was written into legal codes and religious sources. It was official and sanctified. There were processes and procedures to be followed. In some cases, lawyers were even appointed to represent the accused.

According to Plato, in ancient Greece, "If a beast of draught or other animal cause homicide, except in the case when the deed is done by a beast competing in one of the public sports, the kinsmen shall institute proceedings for homicide against the slayer; [and] on conviction, the beast shall be put to death and cast out beyond the frontier." The trial was to take place not in some country barn or nameless field but in the Prytaneum of Athens, the social and cultural center of society.

Likewise, by the mandate of the Old Testament, "If an ox gore a man or a woman, that they die: then the ox shall be surely stoned, and his flesh shall not be eaten; but the owner of the ox shall be quit [that is, not held responsible]."

Many of the recorded examples of animal prosecution and

punishment come from the European subcontinent, but there is evidence from all over the world. A nineteenth-century ethnographic report from India, for example, recounts how, among the Kookies, "if a tiger even kills any of them, near a village, the whole tribe is up in arms, and goes in pursuit of the animal; when, if he is killed, the family of the deceased gives a feast of his flesh, in revenge of his having killed their relation. And should the tribe fail to destroy the tiger, in this first general pursuit of him, the family of the deceased must still continue the chase; for until they have killed either this, *or some other tiger,* and have given a feast of his flesh, they are in disgrace in the village, and not associated with by the rest of the inhabitants."

It is tempting to write off these acts as isolated holdovers from an earlier, more barbaric time, when people punished out of vengeance. We think we know what motivates us to punish now. We punish to deter would-be offenders and incapacitate dangerous people. And, in general, we punish only those individuals who can control themselves and are smart enough to know better. We are fair and just, after all.

With our modern outlook, we see where the historical examples fell short. An ox lacks many of the characteristics that our justice system claims are necessary to find an entity worthy of blame and punishment: the ability to appreciate the moral wrongness of its behavior, to act with bad intent, and to conform to rules. To suppose otherwise is to engage in "superstition"—as a 1916 Tennessee court put it, in the context of a fatal wagon accident, "The implication that the cart or the ox drawing it ... [i]s morally affected for having caused the death ... [is] repugnant to our ideas of justice." An oxcart can cause a terrible harm, but to consider the ox to be a moral agent of any kind is magical thinking—primitive foolishness long since rejected by modern society.

This story of twentieth-century enlightenment, though, is dubious. At the same time that the Tennessee court was offering its pronouncement, the citizens of neighboring Kentucky were gearing up for a series of cases that seemed quite in keeping with the past.

In 1918, Kentucky had passed a law abolishing "murder trials" for dogs accused of killing sheep. But the courts were slow to learn new tricks, and over the next decade a number of dogs were prosecuted.

When Bill, a collie, was "charged with being a dog of vicious character," in the winter of 1926, the Associated Press was there to report the story:

> "We, the jury, find the defendant guilty as charged," was the instructed verdict returned by a jury here yesterday in the case of the State of Kentucky versus Bill. . . .
>
> The death sentence was imposed by County Judge J.W. Pruitt, and Bill was legally executed.
>
> The dog was brought into court by the husband of his owner, Mrs. Sophia Stone.
>
> Witnesses testified as to Bill's character prior to his attack on a neighbor's daughter, the cause of the trial.
>
> Within a few minutes after the passing of sentence, Bill was electrocuted. His head was sent to a Lexington laboratory for examination.

This was not a farce designed to amuse the electorate. This was justice—the same justice that an accused man would receive. Which helps explain why two years later, W. C. Hamilton, the commonwealth's attorney, would tell the *New York Times* that a German shepherd with the slightly more aristocratic name of Kaiser Bill must be tried just as any other murderer would be.

Kaiser Bill would fare better than common Bill at court. Thanks—perhaps—to his royal moniker, he was able to get a more effective defense attorney. And although convicted three times and sentenced to death three times for killing sheep, he was eventually freed by the Kentucky Court of Appeals. Interestingly, it was not the absurdity of a murder trial for a dog that led Kaiser Bill's owner, Mrs. Henry Gay, to promise that she would spend "every cent" she had and appeal up to the Supreme Court if necessary to prevent the execution. It was, she explained, because he was innocent of the crime.

We would like to believe that we have finally achieved a modern, enlightened approach to justice—punishing only those with "guilty minds," and not because we like it, but because we must protect society. But even today our basic instincts bubble to the surface.

We, too, seem to feel vengeful toward animals from time to time. A surfer is dragged underwater off the coast of Australia, and we demand that the protected legal status of great white sharks be lifted so that they may be killed. A grizzly bear attacks a hiker in Yellowstone National Park, and we conduct a full investigation, reconstruct the crime scene, match the DNA, and execute the animal.

Occasionally we even feel the urge to punish inanimate objects. Be honest: Have you ever wanted to get back at your computer for losing a file or freezing up at a key moment? Have you kicked the chair that stubbed your toe?

And we sometimes take pleasure in the pain and suffering of those who have harmed us—bullies, pickpockets, terrorists—even when that misery does nothing to make us safer in the future.

What actually drives us to punish? It's not what we think.

When it comes to morality and punishment, we feel like we are rational deducers. If I ask you whether it is wrong to kill and eat your pet dog, you have an immediate response: of course! And when I press you on why it's wrong, you're quite capable of giving me reasons. But did those reasons lead you to that conclusion, or did you have a gut instinct that you then justified?

The best available evidence suggests that although many of our decisions reflect deliberation and reasoning, our moral compass often directs our behavior beyond our conscious awareness. In one famous experiment, people read descriptions of behaviors that are generally viewed as immoral, like two siblings having sex, and then told researchers what they thought. The trick was that the researchers carefully tailored the details of the scenarios to eliminate obvious reasons to object to the conduct. In the incest scenario, for example, the brother and sister were adults, used contraception, freely consented to the act, and experienced no resulting negative feelings. In addition, the incest never occurred again and was never disclosed. Study participants were quick to conclude that the sex was wrong, but they struggled to explain why when the experimenter pointed out that their grounds for objection (for example, that a baby with a genetic defect might be conceived) were nullified by the provided description (effective birth control was used). Even when they ran out of explanations, the participants did not change their opinions: around 80 percent clung to the idea that a wrong had been committed.

This work echoes a theme we've seen over and over again: although we have the capacity for careful analysis, we are not always the dispassionate, objective, and rational adjudicators we imagine ourselves to be. But it goes further, showing that none of our judgments are safe. Even our moral decision-making can be (and often is) guided by heuristic processing—quick, automatic mental shortcuts—rather than reason. In these moments, we are morally "dumbfounded." We arrive at a destination without knowing what guided us there, but with a keen ability to invent a plausible story to explain and justify our journey.

Psychologists, however, have the tools to expose our route.

When we engage in moral reasoning, we do not do so randomly. Patterns emerge if we look at a large number of people confronted with the same situation.

Take the decision of whether and how much a young man (let's call him David) should be punished for trying—but failing—to poison a chess master competing against him in an important competition. There are several potential rationales for punishing David. We might conclude that he is dangerous and want to incapacitate him so that he cannot kill anyone else. Or we might decide to punish David as an example, to deter other would-be poisoners from trying anything similar or to encourage David to change his own behavior. Or we might punish David simply because we feel that those who commit intentional wrongs ought to be given their just deserts—payback in proportion to the gravity of the offense.

When asked, people tend to focus on forward-looking, utilitarian considerations: they say they are driven to punish David in order to avoid harm in the future. But these self-reports don't tell us which motives are actually at work because, again, people often aren't aware of what's really guiding them. Could retribution—a hidden desire for payback—actually be playing a part?

Regrettably, that question is hard to sort out in experiments, because the elements that are likely to influence our desire to incapacitate a criminal or deter other would-be offenders—like the severity of the offense or how intentional it was—are also likely to influence our desire for retribution. If people are told that instead of trying to murder the competitor, David only tries to make him sick, they should be less motivated to disable him from acting again or deter others who might try something similar because the potential future harm is reduced. But people should also feel less retributive toward him: trying to make someone sick just doesn't call out for payback the way attempted murder does. So varying the gravity of David's crime does not allow us to isolate retribution as a distinct motive.

That was exactly the dilemma that led University of Pennsylvania psychologist Geoff Goodwin and me to try a novel experimental strategy: studying the punishment of animal offenders rather than humans. When we hunt down and kill a shark that has attacked a swimmer, we can't fool ourselves into thinking that the other sharks are somehow able to learn of the death, comprehend that it is punishment for killing a beachgoer, and then alter their behavior in the future to avoid similar punishment. So we can effectively take deterrence off the table as a potential motivation. Eliminating the possibility that our drive to punish comes down simply to a desire to incapacitate dangerous agents is more straightforward: we need only ensure that the perpetrator will be fully incapacitated regardless of what we choose to do.

Imagine two scenarios. In one, a shark attacks a young girl playing in the waves; in the other, a shark attacks a forty-eight-year-old pedophile. The shark has been hunted down and condemned to death by the authorities, and the only question is the method used to kill it. How much of a numbing agent should authorities give to the shark so that it does not feel any pain as the fatal poison does its work?

If your motivation is ensuring the future safety of the beach, the identity of the victim should not affect your answer, since the shark is going to be killed—that is, rendered unable to harm anyone in the future—no matter what. But your answer *should* change if you are motivated by retribution, because killing an innocent little girl is seen as a worse harm than killing an adult sex offender and thus would require a harsher response. Sure enough, that's what Geoff and I found: people provided more of the painkiller to the shark that killed the pedophile than to the shark that killed the girl.

We can alter the types of animal perpetrators and we can change the circumstances, but the effect holds. People are driven by retribution to punish attacking sharks, oxen, and dogs in ways that are not significantly different from how they are driven to punish human offenders guilty of comparable misdeeds.

On a purely rational level, it makes sense that the only reason we'd hunt down a shark that killed a surfer is to ensure the safety of the beach, not because we think the shark somehow deserves to be brought to justice and punished. But our true intentions are revealed in the data—findings that align with research by other scientists showing that there is often a disjunction between the punitive rationales that people give and their actual motives.

Indeed, there is a growing scientific consensus that it is a desire for retribution—not deterrence or incapacitation—that has the strongest influence on why we punish. This has led some psychologists to suggest that when some harm—say, a murder—has been committed, the motive to deliver payback to the perpetrator operates as a sort of automatic default. In their view, this is only sometimes overridden by a more deliberate reasoning process focused on how punishing the culprit will influence potential offenders and provide for a safer environment.

Though we are often unaware of its influence, our basic drive for retribution can create serious problems, undermining the laws we've carefully crafted over centuries to balance public safety, protection of the innocent, and fair treatment for the accused. We've worked, for instance, to eradicate punishment that turns on chance—whether a bullet happens to hit its intended target or the wall next to him, whether the victim of a pipe bomb turns out to be a movie star or a homeless person. And we've tried to construct a rational system for distinguishing between those who are acceptable targets for punishment and those who are not. But these protections can become meaningless in the face of our strong drive for payback.

To hold someone responsible for a crime under ancient English law, all you had to prove was that the person committed a "bad act." Roger murdered Charles with an ax? Case closed. But starting in the thirteenth century an additional requirement beyond the *actus reus* emerged: proof of *mens rea*. Did Roger possess a culpable state of mind when he drove that ax into Charles's skull? If not, Roger was worthy of neither blame nor punishment. Voluntarily swinging the ax that led to Charles's death did not in itself make Roger criminally liable—a court needed to know what Roger was thinking, intending, and understanding in the moment. Was he of sound mind, or did he suffer from a severe mental illness that prevented him from comprehending the nature and consequences of his actions? Was it Roger's purpose to kill Charles, or was he attempting to fell a tree when the ax accidentally slipped from his hand? The prudence of asking these questions seems obvious to us today. As the esteemed judge Oliver Wendell Holmes once wrote, "Even a dog distinguishes between being stumbled over and being kicked."

The requirement, in the words of the U.S. Supreme Court, that the state establish "an evil-meaning mind with an evil-doing hand" in order to convict someone means that certain entities cannot be targets of blame and punishment. Among those generally understood to lack criminal capacity—or, at least, to have diminished capacity—are young children, those with mental illness or severe intellectual disability, and animals. Of course, different legal systems around the world have adopted different thresholds for mental competency. In England, for example, the age of criminal responsibility for a youth—the point at which a child may be held accountable just like an adult—is ten years old, whereas it is fourteen in Italy, fifteen in Sweden, and eighteen in Belgium. Although state practice varies across America, at common law, children under seven cannot be held responsible for breaking the law at all, and those between age seven and fourteen are presumed to lack capacity, which the prosecution can rebut with evidence that the child knew what he was doing and realized it was wrong. As we saw earlier, even older teenagers receive special treatment on account of their not-yet-fully-developed brains, with those under eighteen barred from receiving the death penalty or life in prison without parole. The juvenile court system itself was started, in part, on the grounds that minors lack the culpability of adults and therefore ought to be handled differently. As Benjamin Lindsey, a pioneering juvenile court judge, wrote in 1910, "Our laws against crime are as inapplicable to children as they would be to idiots." Likewise, no matter how heinous the crime, it is unconstitutional in the United States to execute a criminal with "intellectual disability," and in states where the defense is recognized, someone with a serious mental illness who meets the criteria for insanity may not be punished at all.

While these legal frameworks are well intentioned, experiments that Geoff and I have conducted cast doubt on people's adherence to the bright lines they set out. Perceived blameworthiness does track with mental capacity, so participants tend to judge a high-IQ adult as more culpable than a low-IQ adult or a child (who are both seen as more culpable than a snake). But these judgments are sensitive to the grievousness of the harm committed and do not imply a categorical approach in which certain entities are deserving of punishment and others are not. People believe that a boy who throws a soda bottle off a bridge into high-speed traffic should be punished more harshly when he is described as fourteen years old than when he is described as eight, but the length of his sentence in a juvenile detention center depends on what happens to the bottle. If through *pure chance* it ends up causing an accident that kills a woman and her young daughters, the boy is given a much longer punishment, regardless of his age. What's more, on average, the eight-year-old whose bottle causes a fatal accident is assigned more than twice the amount of time in the detention center as the fourteen-year-old who takes the exact same action but doesn't happen to injure anyone. Indeed, people punish the unlucky child more than twice as much as a twenty-year-old perpetrator whose bottle falls harmlessly.

With so much discretion and flexibility built into the processes that govern how we treat people who have broken the law, these findings have very serious implications. Who qualifies for the insanity offense? It looks like an objective test, but in practice it's quite subjective. And the answer may have more to do with the nature of the offense than with the actual mental state or capacity of the accused. Which teenage offenders get transferred to adult court, and which remain in juvenile court? Again, law on the books purports to protect children categorically on the grounds of their mental immaturity, but it's easily disregarded. In this context, it is hardly a surprise to find that each year more than two hundred thousand juvenile offenders are tried as adults. And it is entirely expected that many states would exploit loopholes in recent Supreme Court cases barring automatic life sentences for juvenile murderers and life sentences without parole for juveniles convicted of lesser offenses. Our hidden drives help explain why state judges routinely skirt the core spirit of those decisions by refusing to resentence people previously given automatic life sentences and by condemning young adolescents, in new cases, to seventy or eighty years in prison without parole—not, technically, a life sentence.

We profess not to blame children in the same way that we blame adults, or to punish those whose mental illness kept them from understanding the nature of their criminal actions, but, in fact, we do exactly that.

If our moral processing always worked as we assume it does—assessing the relevant evidence in order to reach a conclusion about proper punishment, in a bottom-up fashion—we might do a better job of maintaining our commitment to judging children and mentally ill adults less harshly. But we often seem to be driven to punish first and seek justification second. We want to hold someone morally responsible when he commits a harm, and so, after the fact, we ratchet up our perceptions of control, intentionality, and even free will.

That is strange indeed: one would assume that a person believes in free will and then punishes according to that existing worldview. But our notions of human agency are surprisingly malleable. Studies show that when we reduce people's belief in free will (say, by having them attend a neuroscience course exploring the mechanistic causes of human behavior), they act less punitively. And the connection may run in the other direction as well: our desire to punish may drive our belief in free will. So, for example, after reading about a corrupt judge receiving kickbacks for sending innocent kids to a for-profit juvenile detention center, people reported a stronger general belief in free will than they reported after reading a neutral scenario about the recruitment of a new school superintendent. Wanting to punish the judge, they seem to have altered their understanding of human nature and responsibility to provide better support.

When it comes to our moral intuitions, the things that seem set in stone are not—even things that seem fundamental. In certain circumstances, we can even derive satisfaction from the punishment of an innocent party. That is remarkable, given that our legal system is predicated on the notion that an innocent person should never be punished for a crime. As Benjamin Franklin explained, "It is better 100 guilty Persons should escape than that one innocent Person should suffer." The famous English jurist William Blackstone put the ratio at ten to one but offered a similar sentiment, as have many other judges and scholars. Even the Bible says that God would not have destroyed Sodom if it had meant killing innocents. It is hard to think of a more foundational concept underlying the framework of our criminal laws and procedures.

But what about the Kookies? They would hunt for the tiger that had slaughtered a member of their village, but if they couldn't find the guilty animal, they'd just kill a different tiger. Could punishing an innocent ever bring us satisfaction?

In one set of experiments that Geoff and I conducted, we had participants read about three different scenarios following a deadly shark attack. In the first scenario, a shark that was subsequently caught and put to death was, upon autopsy, revealed to be the actual perpetrator. In the second scenario, the killed shark was revealed to be completely innocent but happened to be the exact same size and species as the actual perpetrator. In the third scenario, the killed shark was revealed to be a completely innocent shark of an equally dangerous but different species. Not surprisingly, participants showed notably more support for the killing of the actual perpetrator than for the killing of either of the innocent sharks. But they didn't see the killing of the two innocent sharks as equally wrong. The shark from the same species as the perpetrator was seen as more deserving of punishment, even though it was just as innocent as the shark from the other species, and no more dangerous.

The dynamic may be in play even when the stakes are much lower. In related work, researchers looked at the phenomenon of beanballs—the practice of a baseball pitcher targeting an innocent player in retaliation for one of his teammates having been hit by a pitch in an earlier at-bat. What they found was that nearly half of the baseball fans they surveyed found it morally acceptable for a pitcher to take such action in a hypothetical game between two Major League teams. When it was their team doing the retaliating, fans endorsed the targeting of an innocent opposing player even more strongly.

The implications of the research are troubling, suggesting that when a harm has been committed, our desire to find a culprit and reset the moral scales by inflicting punishment may sometimes override our commitment to fair treatment. In the back of our minds, we may already know this about ourselves—though we are loath to acknowledge it. The bloody unfairness stains our history books and our newspaper stories: a mob lynching of an innocent black man after police describe a rape suspect as black; the gangs that live by the motto "You take one of ours and we take one of yours"; the waterboarding of purported "enemy combatants" following the attack of September 11. When you look closely, these retaliatory acts look far less like accidents, anomalies, and collateral damage. They look like reflections of our true nature—who we really are.

If the elements deemed essential for just punishment can, in practice, be jettisoned, it is also the case that our drive to punish may be influenced by factors that are meant to be irrelevant. As an illustration, consider the sentencing of a hypothetical defendant, Pete Foster, who murdered a young white woman after she refused his sexual advances.

Change the color of the woman's skin from white to black, and you decrease the likelihood that Pete will face capital punishment. Numerous studies have shown that those who have murdered a white person are more likely to be sentenced to death than those who have murdered a black person. African Americans who end up on death row are also more likely to actually be executed.

But it is not just the race of the *victim* that matters. If we keep everything else the same and merely change Pete's race, we also see a large effect. Black defendants are considerably more likely to receive the death penalty. They also receive higher bails, face a greater incarceration rate, and are subject to longer sentences than white defendants. Black juveniles are not only more likely to be transferred to adult court but also end up with notably more severe sentences than their white peers.

This evidence of racial bias in punishment is supported by experiments using both mock jurors and real decision-makers. Juvenile probation officers, for instance, have been shown to view an offender as more violent, culpable, inclined to reoffend, and deserving of punishment when they are subliminally exposed to words associated with black people (such as *Harlem, dreadlocks, basketball*) than when exposed to race-neutral words (*heaven, loneliness*). It appears to be largely a matter of implicit bias rather than explicit bigotry.

Scientists think that the ultimate source of such unconscious bias is found in negative stereotypes that have percolated in our culture since the time of slavery and before and are stoked by a disproportionate number of news stories focused on African Americans and crime. These stereotypes provide a ready explanation for the black defendant's behavior: his violent and criminal nature. And when the focus is on the accused's evil disposition, rather than on circumstances not of his making, it is natural to treat him more harshly. In one recent experiment, researchers had two groups of participants read about a fourteen-year-old with seventeen prior juvenile convictions who raped an elderly woman. Participants were then asked to what extent, in general, they supported sentences of life without parole for juveniles in non-homicide cases. The texts given to the groups were identical, aside from one word: for the first group, the defendant was described as black; for the second group, he was described as white. Participants who had read about the black teenager expressed more support for the severe sentence and for the notion that kids are as blameworthy as adults.

It's upsetting to think that such a minor reference to race could have an impact. In a real trial, race may become salient in numerous ways, from the defendant's skin color to the coded language used by a prosecutor, judge, or a witness. Not everyone, though, is equally swayed by such cues. For some people, describing a defendant as a "violent inner-city criminal," as opposed to just a "violent criminal," causes them to favor harsher punishment, while others are not influenced by the racially tinged words at all. And there is some evidence to suggest that those who are aware that the issue of race is in play—either because they are particularly attuned to race or because the threat of discrimination is made explicit—may resist the tendency to act more punitively toward a black defendant so as not to appear racist.

The fact that referring to Pete as black rather than white could increase the severity of his punishment should not be surprising:

after all, many of us are familiar with lingering racial bias in the criminal justice system. But what if we now do something more subtle. Let's change the shape of Pete's nose, making his nostrils slightly wider and his nose flatter. Could that possibly make a difference?

In a word: yes. It's not just whether you are black; it's *how black* you are. The broadness of a defendant's nose, the thickness of his lips, and the darkness of his skin have all been correlated with capital-punishment decisions: in cases where the victim is white, the more stereotypically black a defendant's facial features, the more likely he is to receive the death penalty. The same dynamic is at work with non-capital sentences. One study found that felons with the most stereotypically black features spent up to eight months longer in prison than those with the least stereotypical faces.

Speaking of noses and lips, what if we gave Pete some good old-fashioned cosmetic surgery? Could making him better looking influence his punishment? The familiar story of the beautiful scofflaw who repeatedly bats her eyes out of speeding tickets is closer to the truth than we would care to admit. Research shows that the handsomeness of an offender can influence how harshly he is punished—not because people see the attractive defendant as innocent of the crime but because the beautiful are viewed as less blameworthy. In essence, when you have a pretty face, it can act as a halo, casting a more positive light on your actions. Cesare Lombroso and the other physiognomists we encountered earlier in the book are long since dead, but we still carry their torch. It's not only that we have preconceived notions about the bone structure of evil; it's also that we feel sure we know what virtue looks like.

But even without plastic surgery, Pete might influence those deciding his fate simply by changing his outward demeanor at trial. A man in Pete's position may not show emotion during proceedings for all sorts of reasons, including a sense that appearing contrite is pointless or may make him look guilty. But, in fact, psychologists have found that nonverbal displays of remorse, as well as apologies and statements of regret, can encourage a more positive view of a person accused of a crime. Indeed, when a person does not apologize or act remorseful, experimental participants tend to view him as having a worse character and being more likely to reoffend. In turn, this can lead participants to advocate less harsh punishment for a contrite or apologetic offender.

We see this in the real world, too, especially in capital trials. Prosecutors often hammer on the defendant's absence of regret, and jurors often cite it as a critical factor in their decision to impose the death penalty. And the hard data seems to suggest that those defendants who remain remorseless—who appear cocky or bored or cool, calculated, and controlled—fare worse than those who are emotionally contrite.

Of course, the power of remorse and apology is not reserved for those facing a death sentence. One recent study showed that people pulled over for speeding who said things to the officer like "I'm sorry" were given lower fines and were more likely to get off with just a warning.

We've been focusing on Pete's appearance, but let's zoom out: imagine that just before the jury was about to deliberate, there was a report on the morning news about an apparent terrorist bombing on the subway in Toronto. The tragic attack in Canada has no connection at all to Pete or to the trial, but a wealth of psychological research suggests that it may very well affect the way we punish.

Humans occupy a strange place in the animal kingdom: our instincts for self-preservation are similar to those of other species, but we are uniquely aware of our mortality. And thoughts of death are deeply unsettling. It is terrifying to think that we have only one life to live and that it could be snuffed out in an instant by any number of factors beyond our control: drunk drivers, sharks, lightning, cancer, and the Ebola virus, to name just a few.

Luckily, we have developed the means to quell this overwhelming terror, including our basic cultural belief systems, which provide our lives with purpose, stability, and order. Religions, for example, commonly tell us how to lead a meaningful life and avoid dangers, and offer reassurance that death is really not the end. Our legal institutions offer similar directions for how to be good citizens, protection from threats to our safety, and comfort that our way of life is lasting (even if our physical bodies are not).

The more terror we feel, the more we cling to these belief systems and the more vigorously we defend them. This is why the Canadian tragedy may affect Pete's sentence. A number of experiments have shown that thoughts of death, like those evoked by reading about a terrorist attack, can lead a person to act more punitively toward criminals—that is, those who already stand as a threat.

In one study, researchers asked a group of judges from Arizona to set bond in a hypothetical prostitution case. Before considering the facts of the case, however, half of the judges were given a personality test in which they were reminded of their own mortality. The judges who had been subconsciously induced to think about death set bond at $455, on average, whereas those who had not been so induced set bond at a small fraction of that figure—just $50. The researchers theorized that after being primed to consider their own mortality, judges were prompted to defend their worldviews and to treat someone who seemed to endanger the establishment more harshly. Had this been a real case, the impact on the defendant in question would most likely have been significant: for someone struggling to make ends meet, a higher bond can mean awaiting trial in jail.

While subtle reminders of death have been shown to increase the severity of punishment across a wide range of scenarios, from assaults to drunk driving, not all legal decision-makers are influenced in the same way. Those with very high self-esteem, for example, seem less susceptible to mortality cues, arguably because their strong sense of self helps them manage their fear. And some people simply do not view prostitutes and other criminals as particularly threatening. In fact, when an offense actually aligns with a decision-maker's worldview—think of a hate crime against a gay couple presided over by a vehemently anti-gay judge—that decision-maker may be more lenient to the offender.

As a general matter, though, when judges and jurors are faced with thoughts of death, it is often going to be at the expense of the accused. What is especially problematic for defendants is that there are so many ways in which decision-makers can be reminded of their mortality. An external event like a plane crash, epidemic, or war can certainly affect a verdict or sentence, but cues from inside the courtroom can be just as powerful. For one thing, many crimes involve interpersonal violence, and it is hard not to think about one's own vulnerability when hearing the details of a stickup, violent assault, or murder, like the one Pete was accused of committing.

Attorneys and witnesses regularly help the process along. A prosecutor may emphasize that two victims of a drunk-driving accident could have been killed, or may ask jurors to put themselves in the victim's place. Likewise, a witness may describe the impact of a murder on the victim's family.

The mortality dynamic may be strongest in capital cases. Not only are thoughts of death inevitable in such instances, but the defendants tend to be members of outgroups—the mentally ill, drug addicts, racial minorities, and the poor—who are naturally seen as greater threats. In addition, only those who are willing to impose the death penalty are allowed to serve on capital juries, and there is reason to believe that such individuals are more strongly affected by mortality-related prompts. Pro–death penalty juries are, indeed, more prone to convict. Logic would suggest that when a defendant's life is at stake, the checks we've built into the system would mitigate the effects of these hidden biases: jurors are aware of the heightened costs of erring, judges know that their decisions are more likely to be appealed and scrutinized by appellate courts, the attorneys involved in the case tend to be more experienced, and the proceedings generally receive greater attention from the public and the press. Yet the gravity of the situation provides no such salve to the accused; in fact, the seriousness of the crime can actually make things worse.

This dynamic may itself be amplified by something lurking in the background of every criminal law case—belief in evil. Recall our problematic "mug shot" view of criminality: when something horrible happens, we are inclined to see an evil person as the source. This notion allows us to maintain our reassuring belief in a just world, in which harms have a clear and recognizable origin that can be readily addressed. It is far more unsettling to think that most of us are capable of committing serious crimes—even though that is what research on the power of situational influences suggests.

In trying to understand the "myth of evil," researchers have catalogued the underlying assumptions that many of us share, including the idea that some people are born evil and that evil people derive pleasure from their bad acts. These beliefs inform our drives to punish: if you believe in the existence of pure evil, it stands to reason that you will tend to support harsh punishment and view efforts at reforming offenders as pointless. And that's exactly what the research shows, both when people are asked to consider matters in the abstract and when they're tasked with sentencing a real person. In one study, the potency of people's belief in evil predicted the likelihood that they would support the execution of Nidal Malik Hasan, the man responsible for shooting and killing thirteen people at Fort Hood.

Though much of the public believes that evil is an immutable trait, whether we view someone as evil can be influenced by subtle cues. Even seemingly insignificant things like an offender's wardrobe, taste in music, and favorite books (think Goth appearance, enjoyment of heavy metal, and interest in occult literature) can encourage some people to view the offender as more evil and prompt more severe punishment. Damien Echols, the accused ringleader of a group of teenagers convicted of murdering three eight-year-old boys in Arkansas in 1993, might have received the death penalty in any case—but in light of the research, it is hard to ignore the possible impact of his first name, black clothes, love of heavy metal, and interest in witchcraft, all of which were raised at trial.

The implications are disconcerting. People with an ardent belief in pure evil are active participants in determining sentences, reviewing punishments, and setting policy. It matters when a governor or president evaluating petitions for clemency from death-row inmates thinks—as George W. Bush did—that "good and evil are present in this world, and between the two there can be no compromise." And it matters when a sitting Supreme Court justice wholeheartedly believes that the Devil is a real person, as Justice Antonin Scalia does.

Such individuals are at a distinct disadvantage when it comes to appreciating the various forces outside of an offender's control that may have led him to commit a terrible act. And this creates a tragic paradox in which those who are more likely to see evil in others are more likely to commit evil acts themselves— supporting or perpetrating cruel acts against people whose crimes ultimately reflect not their corrupted dispositions but their genetic and environmental bad luck.

So, in light of all this, are our beliefs and motivations really that different from those of our medieval French counterparts who tried and executed a pig?

The Harvard psychologist Steven Pinker has offered a convincing argument that, viewed against the backdrop of human history, the modern world is relatively peaceful. One of the driving forces behind the decrease in violence, he argues, is the transfer of punishment responsibilities to a disinterested third party. And it seems obvious that the modern judicial system, with its judges, jurors, police, lawyers, and correctional officers, has indeed pre-empted much of the bloody individual and group retaliation that characterized our past. But if outward behavior has changed, it is less clear how our brains have fared.

We would very much like to believe that superstition has no place in our courthouses and that we are never driven by blood revenge. We would like to think that we take no pleasure in punishment. We want to believe that feelings of warmth toward our fellow man always outweigh feelings of disgust and hatred—that, in the words of Nelson Mandela, "deep down in every human heart, there [i]s mercy and generosity" and that "love comes more naturally to the human heart than its opposite." Mandela's words resonate because this is what we want to hear. But the reality of the matter sounds in dissonant chords.

It is true that, in the West, we no longer have public executions—for pigs or humans. It is true that we no longer break people on the rack or draw and quarter. But are we "better angels" on the inside, or have we merely constructed elaborate structures that camouflage the retributive drives within us? When we look closely at the *effects* of our punishments—the topic of the next chapter—we may find that our practices are not as enlightened as we might hope. What does our penal system actually do to people and for people—criminals, would-be offenders, victims, everyday citizens? Do we end up delivering payback to those who most deserve it? Does the suffering we dole out in the name of justice actually encourage people to swear off crime? Does it leave us safer?

# 10

# THROWING AWAY THE KEY

## The Prisoner

Eastern State Penitentiary is known today, first and foremost, for its premier haunted house. People line up down the block. It runs for weeks around Halloween, and purchasing advanced tickets is advisable. Each year it's meant to be a little more frightening— "Darker. Bloodier. *Terror* like you've never felt," according to the website. In 2013, the prison began offering visitors the option of being grabbed by the sadistic guards, deranged doctors, and murderous inmates who lurk about the eleven-acre compound. For an extra $70, there is even a VIP tour that includes a guided visit to death row, Al Capone's cell, and the underground punishment block. The "special Terror Behind the Walls LED flashlight" is included in the cost of admission.

Amidst the bars and bistros of Fairmont Avenue, the penitentiary, with its turrets and immense stone walls, seems strikingly out of place—a relic more fitting for a strategic medieval crossroads than the stroller-filled streets of modern Philadelphia. It is hard to imagine that the crumbling ruins and derelict cells once held men who could not wipe off the makeup and head home at night's end. But while the body has decayed and been repurposed, the spirit of Eastern State is more alive than ever, animating our current approach to punishment in the United States.

It may have been foreordained that Philadelphia's first European settlers would take the lead on corrections. Pennsylvania was, after all, the creation of a convict. Before setting off for the New World, the great William Penn achieved the unenviable distinction of having roomed in both the Tower of London and Newgate Prison. And many of his fellow Quakers—reluctant immigrants fleeing persecution—were all too aware of the ineffectiveness of English punishment and the suffering it caused.

As a result, the early penal code that Penn adopted sought a new path, largely eliminating the harsh corporal and capital punishments of England in favor of more civilized imprisonment. By the mid-eighteenth century, however, this noble vision had devolved into a detestable reality. While the lash had been effectively abandoned, the conditions of incarceration in Pennsylvania had grown squalid, overcrowded, and disorderly. It fell upon a new generation to reinvigorate Penn's legacy. Operating as the Society for Alleviating the Miseries of Public Prisons, these disciples—Philadelphia icons like Benjamin Franklin and Dr. Benjamin Rush, the father of American psychiatry—pushed through a series of reforms culminating in the building of what was arguably the world's first fully realized penitentiary, Eastern State.

The key innovation was solitary confinement. After touring Eastern State on behalf of the French government in 1831, Alexis de Tocqueville and Gustave de Beaumont explained the rationale in stark terms: "Thrown into solitude . . . [the prisoner] reflects. Placed alone, in view of his crime, he learns to hate it; and if his soul be not yet surfeited with crime, and thus have lost all taste for any thing better, it is in solitude, where remorse will come to assail him."

The first inmate at the prison was Charles Williams, admitted on October 25, 1829. He had light black skin, a broad mouth, and a scarred nose. He was a farmer by trade, but he could read. And he had been convicted of burglary—coming away with a twenty-dollar watch, a gold seal, a gold key. He was received by the first warden, Samuel Wood, who examined Charles from head (eyes: black) to toe (foot: 11 inches) and then watched as a hood was lowered over his carefully mapped face.

The hood was a critical component of this monastery of compulsion, designed to prevent communication, interaction, and knowledge of the surroundings. Whenever Charles was led from his cell, it would be in this hood. And when it was removed for the first time, he saw what lay ahead for the next twenty-four months of his life: whitewashed walls, an iron bedstead, a stool, a rack for clothes, and supplies for eating and cleaning. He was left alone. And so began the regimen of solitude: no chats with fellow prisoners or visits from children, no news of the world outside the walls, no whistling. He occasionally interacted with the prison staff, but even here there were rules. Charles was no longer Charles; he was addressed as "ONE"—the number sewn onto his clothing and hung over the door of his cell.

To contemporary reformers, this was not torture; indeed, it was the opposite. If the standard prison was a place of pointless suffering and cruelty—a refuse heap for the discarded to rot—the penitentiary, by contrast, was an institution of purpose, designed to cure the criminal and deter the future offender.

That did not mean coddling the inmate—far from it. Incarceration was designed to be exceedingly unpleasant: after all, inflicting extreme misery could be quite effective in discouraging criminal behavior. But barbarism was out. The interior of the prison, with its vaulted cellblocks and skylights, showed that this was not some medieval dungeon but a beacon of progress. At a time when the president of the United States had no running water in the White House, prisoners at Eastern Penitentiary had flush toilets and central heating.

The modern prison had arrived.

———

It is interesting to think what Tocqueville—who described Philadelphia, in 1831, as a city "infatuated ... with the penitentiary system"—would say today about the City of Brotherly Love, or these broader United States. America accounts for less than 5 percent of the world's population, but almost a quarter of all prisoners. Some 2.3 million individuals are behind bars across the country, and in excess of 6 million are under "correctional supervision"—more, by far, than in any other nation. Even at their height, the Gulag labor camps never came close to the number of our citizens currently on probation, in jail or prison, or on parole. Take one hundred thousand Americans, and 707 of them are languishing in a cell. By contrast, 284 out of every hundred thousand Iranians are locked up, 118 out of every hundred thousand Canadians, and only 78 out of every hundred thousand Germans.

A country that abolished slavery 150 years ago now has a greater number of black men in the correctional system than there were slaves in 1850 and a greater percentage of its black population in jail than was imprisoned in apartheid South Africa. Black, male, and no high school diploma? It's more likely than not that you will spend time in prison during your life.

Although there are many factors behind America's high incarceration rates, the ever-expanding list of criminal violations and the harshness of our sentencing are front and center.

When Illinois's criminal code was updated in 1961, it was 72 pages, but by 2000 it had grown to 1,200 pages. Illinois is no anomaly: in every state, we imprison people for relatively minor, nonviolent crimes—like using drugs or passing a bad check—that would receive a slap on the wrist in other countries. While no more than 10 percent of those convicted of crimes in Germany and the Netherlands are sentenced to prison, in the United States it's 70 percent. We also hand out much longer prison sentences than in other parts of the world. Burglarize a house in Vancouver, and on average you can expect five months in a Canadian facility.

But drive an hour south to Bellingham, Washington, and commit the same offense, and you'll spend more than three times as long in prison. The same pattern is true for serious crimes. In Norway, for example, no one can be given a sentence of more than twenty-one years, while in the United States we regularly lock people up and throw away the key.

Unlike many of our European counterparts, we also have all sorts of penalty enhancements and mandatory rules that can turn a seemingly small infraction into decades in prison. Forrest Heacock shared cocaine with three other people at a party, one of them accidentally overdosed and died, and Heacock was sentenced to forty years in jail for felony murder. Leandro Andrade shoplifted nine children's videotapes and received a sentence of fifty years to life because, twelve years earlier, he had been convicted of three counts of residential burglary. In California, the law said three strikes and you're out, even if that third strike was walking out of a Kmart with a copy of *Cinderella* tucked into your waistband. When the U.S. Supreme Court reviewed Leandro's case, in 2003, they said there was nothing cruel and unusual about his sentence. In many other countries the highest courts would have disagreed.

Our exceptionalism extends to the particular way we punish. While the United States is the only Western country to carry out capital punishment, what may set us apart even more is our embrace of solitary confinement. The practice was largely abandoned in the United States during the nineteenth and twentieth centuries, but over the last three or four decades we have found our way back to the model of Eastern State. Today, solitary confinement is widespread in American prisons, with more than eighty thousand people kept in isolation.

There are some positive recent signs that the gulf between America's correctional system and those of other industrialized democracies may be narrowing, at least slightly. Although there was a steady upward trend in the number of incarcerated Americans starting in the early 1970s, the prison population has actually dropped a little since its peak in 2009. Part of this reflects the ratcheting back of mandatory minimum sentences, expanded opportunities for inmates to apply for clemency, and efforts to reduce harsh charges for minor, nonviolent drug offenses. Other efforts at the state and federal levels have gone toward diverting more potential prisoners to treatment programs, releasing elderly prisoners who no longer pose a danger to the public, and eliminating the automatic parole-violation triggers that can send people back to prison for minimal infractions. In California, the harshest aspects of the three-strikes law were repealed—the third offense must now be a serious or violent felony for the law to come into play.

These are all important steps, but we need to realize that they were influenced by a unique confluence of events, including a precipitous drop in crime rates and a severe recession that left government officials scrambling to reduce costs. There is no guarantee that these trends will continue. Moreover, given the starting point, the absolute amount of progress is quite small. There are still five times as many inmates in state and federal prisons as there were in 1978. Three-strikes laws are still on the books in many states, including California. And although, today, shoplifting cannot send a man to prison for the rest of his life, these laws are far from lenient. If Leandro had stolen the videotapes by sticking his finger into the pocket of his sweatshirt and pretending to have a gun, the new reforms would have done him no good at all.

The truth is that we're not going to make much more progress until we realize that we are just as ignorant of the effects of our punishments as we are of what actually drives us to punish. Our favored tools of mass incarceration and solitary confinement do not do what we think they do. And we remain wedded to the same mistaken theories espoused some two hundred years ago by the Society for Alleviating the Miseries of Public Prisons.

Now, as then, the prisoner and potential prisoner are viewed as rational beings who make decisions to offend based on a cost-benefit analysis. To decrease crime, the thinking goes, you just need to increase the magnitude of the punishment until violating the law no longer seems to pay. The more distasteful the punishment—that is, the more we deprive criminals of the things that they normally enjoy—the less likely a person will be to choose to offend in the future. Harsh treatment is acceptable because it's directed only at people who deserve it in proportion to their wrongdoing. However, as moral individuals, we understand that we shouldn't cause a prisoner physical pain, which rules out various forms of abuse at the hands of the state. Tough prison sentences, then, are the optimal approach to punishment because they act as a strong deterrent without forcing us to "mistreat" the prisoner. They also provide a ready means for incapacitating people who just don't respond to the threat of being locked up. Prisoners who are uncontrollable are never let out; the rest, we can feel confident, will now steer clear of crime, knowing how unpleasant it is behind bars.

Put simply: our prisons are humane; our punishments are deserved; and our system makes us safer. That's what Eastern State's progenitors proclaimed, and that's what we believe. And we are dead wrong.


What is solitary confinement actually like?

To get a sense, walk into your bathroom, shut the door, lie down in your bathtub, and close your eyes. When you reopen them, imagine that this is where you will spend the next five years of your life. Take a look at your new kingdom.

Wake up in the morning and the fluorescent lights are already on, just as they have been all night. Roll from your bed and you can touch the walls—off-white or white. It may be thirteen by eight, or eight by ten, or fourteen by seven, but take a step and you touch the walls. There are no windows, but maybe you get a slit.

There is a toilet and a sink. This is where you sit for twenty-three hours each day for weeks and months and years on end. You get taken out only to shower and, on certain days, for a bit of movement in a slightly bigger cage—a narrow dog run.

In Maine, no radios or televisions are permitted. At California's Pelican Bay, those in solitary get a personal phone call only in the case of emergency. It is a bit softer in the Departmental Disciplinary Unit of the Walpole prison in Massachusetts: a radio after thirty days, a thirteen-inch black-and-white television after sixty, and up to four calls a month, if merited by good behavior. Human contact is virtually nonexistent. The doors are often solid metal, preventing you from talking with other inmates. For many, the opening of the door slot for the guard to push through a food tray is it for the entire day. If you want to feel a human touch, your only real chance is to break the rules—block out the lights to sleep or cover the opening in the door, and you can expect an "extraction." Officers with shields and helmets will rush into your cell, pin you to the ground, and shackle your arms and legs. Your clothes may be cut off your body as they kneel on your legs and back. You may then be strapped naked to a restraint chair.

More than 185 years after "ONE" walked through the gate of Eastern State, the experience of the solitary American inmate is surprisingly unchanged: a tiny cell, monotonous isolation, and a harsh response to any rule-breaking. Philadelphia's penitentiary had a "tranquilizing chair" a century before Walpole was even built. The big difference is that we now have far more evidence that solitary confinement is torture.

Humans need social contact—it's not a luxury, it's a necessity. Our brains are wired for connection, arguably because being part of a group provided an evolutionary advantage, allowing us to better avoid predators, garner resources, and find a mate, among other things. According to one theory, when ties are severed we experience the pain of loneliness in order to encourage us to reconnect with people. And evidence collected over the last several decades makes it clear that there are profound health consequences for those cut off from others. Infants die without food, but they also die without social interaction—a reality starkly presented in data from state-run orphanages in Eastern Europe during the second half of the twentieth century. More recently, researchers have found that social relationships are also critical for adults: over a given period of time, those with sound connections are 50 percent more likely to survive than those with weak ones. Put differently, having adequate social ties is comparable to quitting smoking in its effect. It hurts us to be alone; many studies have shown that isolation damages not only our physical health but our mental health and cognitive functioning as well.

When the U.S. military studied naval aviators captured and imprisoned during the Vietnam War, they found that the practices of solitary confinement by enemy forces produced suffering just as severe as that brought on by physical torture. As a POW, John McCain spent more than two years isolated in a tiny cell, during which time he was also physically abused. When he returned, he did not mince words: "It's an awful thing, solitary. It crushes your spirit and weakens your resistance more effectively than any other form of mistreatment."

Solitary confinement appears not only to aggravate existing mental illnesses but to breed new ones. A healthy person who has been locked alone in a cell for months or years may begin to exhibit depression, anxiety, and cognitive impairment. And many inmates in solitary show evidence of agitation, paranoia, memory lapses, hallucinations, irrational anger, and obsessive revengeful thoughts. A number of these psychological problems can appear within days. Self-mutilation is a regular occurrence, and roughly half of all prison suicides are by prisoners in isolation.

For all of our seeming progress, it is worth asking how much less barbaric our system is than the one that Philadelphia's founding fathers sought to replace. Nineteenth-century Philadelphians were no doubt pleased to learn from Tocqueville and Beaumont's report that of all the American prisons the men visited, only Eastern State's did not resort to the lash. But if you had asked "ONE" his preference, after months of silent loneliness, would he have chosen the penitentiary over corporal punishment?

In the modern United States, we have hacked away at the death penalty over the decades—prohibiting it for minors, those with an intellectual disability, and those guilty of rape—and fought hard for procedural reforms to better protect defendants, but have we actually reduced suffering? Are we more humane? Considering the raw numbers, it's hard to make that case. Our attention may be drawn to the fight against capital punishment, but only a few dozen people are executed each year in the United States. Meanwhile, thousands of our citizens are locked in boxes for months and years, and thousands more imprisoned for decades without the possibility of parole. Few of us stop to consider whether burying people alive is really such an enlightened alternative to lethal injection.

Yet there have been prominent people exposing the heinousness of the American model of corrections from the very start. On March 8, 1842, during his tour of the United States, Charles Dickens visited Eastern State, remarking to the prison inspectors that "the Falls of Niagara and your Penitentiary are two objects I might almost say I most wish to see." He subsequently "passed the whole day in going from cell to cell, and conversing with the prisoners." But despite his initial excitement, he found the whole Philadelphia experiment to be revolting: "I believe that very few men are capable of estimating the immense amount of torture and agony which this dreadful punishment, prolonged for years, inflicts upon the sufferers. . . . I hold this slow and daily tampering with the mysteries of the brain, to be immeasurably worse than any torture of the body."

According to Dickens, it was not a sadistic streak in the Pennsylvania populace that was behind the awfulness. The prison staff, in fact, seemed friendly and "really anxious . . . to do right."

The problem was not intention to torture; it was inattention in the face of torture. As Dickens wrote, "I am persuaded that those who devised this system of Prison Discipline, and those benevolent gentlemen who carry it into execution, do not know what it is that they are doing." That we can sleepwalk through atrocity is as true today as it was then. Something "cruel and wrong" can be created and run by people without cruelty in their hearts.

Our centuries-long somnolence has a lot to do with the comparative invisibility of the harms that arise from solitary confinement and long-term incarceration. In modern Saudi Arabia, punishment for armed robbery can entail beheading with a sword, followed by crucifixion. In Indonesia, a man can be publicly caned for gambling. The brutality and cruelty are flagrant. Dickens was correct: one of the reasons we aren't compelled to eliminate solitary confinement is that "its ghastly signs and tokens are not so palpable to the eye and sense of touch as scars upon the flesh; . . . its wounds are not upon the surface, and it extorts few cries that human ears can hear." It is "a secret punishment which slumbering humanity is not roused up to stay." But of course the damage is there—and with the aid of modern science, we can now see the once-hidden "signs" in the brain. When researchers studied prisoners of war who had been held captive in the former Yugoslavia, they found abnormalities in two particular types of prisoners: those who had suffered a traumatic brain injury and those who had been kept in solitary confinement.

Another reason that the suffering created by our prisons fosters so little sympathy is that it happens at a remove and doesn't seem to implicate us directly. Once again, our reluctance to hurt others can be reduced by distancing ourselves—physically, emotionally, or psychologically—from the person being harmed. It is much more difficult to administer a painful jolt of electricity to someone when you must hold his hand against the shock plate than when you can deliver it remotely from an adjoining room. Similarly, we are more hesitant when we are the ones pressing the button than when we are more tangentially involved in the shocking (if we are simply reading the test questions that prompt the electrical "feedback," for example). With incarceration, the person suffering is not only in another room, but he is hidden behind massive walls and fences, with little or no contact with anyone outside.

Moreover, the harm from solitary confinement, in contrast to corporal punishment, happens over time. We know that it's easier to deliver pain to a stranger when the threshold is reached incrementally—for instance, increasing the voltage by just 15 volts for each wrong answer up to 450 volts, as compared with giving a single 450-volt shock at the outset. And because the injury to the prisoner is not the result of some clear government action like whipping or beating, we take it less seriously. Studies show that harm caused by omission is viewed as less immoral than equivalent harm caused by commission. The notable thing about isolation, of course, is not the infliction of direct suffering; it's the withholding of the things people need in order not to suffer—in particular, human contact.

The result is that few of us will ever feel much guilt, even when we learn that an inmate committed suicide in prison. He's the one who took the razor blade to his wrists, not a prison guard (and certainly not us). Just as important, he committed the crime that landed him in jail in the first place, which leads us to the second myth about prison: that even if the conditions of incarceration are brutal, the inmates "deserve" it.

The payback narrative helps us accept treatment that, in any other context, would be considered an atrocity. The Department of Justice estimates that well over two hundred thousand prisoners are sexually abused while in custody each year—with almost a third subjected to rape by force or threat of force. Many of these victims are assaulted multiple times.

The data no longer seems shocking. Prison rape is a mainstay of television shows, like *Oz*, and movies, like *The Shawshank Redemption*. Inmate sexual-assault riffs are completely fair game for standups and late-night talk show hosts. And the fact is that no one really gets upset when the son of the Secretary of Health and Human Services—the department charged with protecting the health of all Americans—is selling a board game called Don't Drop the Soap, in which you "fight your way through 6 different locations in hopes of being granted parole" and "where no one playing enters through the front door!"

A big part of why we feel it's okay to laugh is that going to prison is conceived of as a choice: since you chose to commit a crime, you get what you deserve. But that justification, as we've seen, ignores the situational factors that lead to criminal behavior and the troubling fact that in the United States you can land yourself a lengthy prison term without having done anything likely to seriously harm anyone.

Think back to Leandro Andrade trying to make it out of the Kmart with *Free Willy 2, Cinderella, The Santa Clause,* and *Little Women* stuck into his pants. As a heroin addict stealing so that he could buy drugs, how much control did he have over his actions? And what does this military veteran and father of three truly deserve? The threat of sexual assault? By amending California's three-strikes law, the voters of California ensured that a shoplifter like Leandro would no longer be condemned to sit in prison for fifty years without the possibility of parole. But he would still be locked up and would still face the all-too-prevalent physical dangers of incarceration.

And it is hard to maintain that narrative of "deserved" suffering when the inmates who are raped in prison are not the worst criminals. They are disproportionately nonviolent first-time offenders. They are disproportionately young and physically small. They are disproportionately mentally disabled. They tend to have histories of being sexually abused as children. And in a horrible twist, those who would seem most deserving of brutal treatment not only avoid the worst abuse in prison but are given carte blanche to act as perpetrators. There is something unquestionably perverse about a system of justice that tacitly sanctions as part of punishment the very abuses that it condemns as mandating punishment.

Nor is it only the "worst of the worst" who end up in solitary confinement. Given how much more damaging it can be than normal incarceration, it is shocking to see how cavalier a warden can be in deciding to place an inmate in solitary, how little oversight there is from other administrators or judges, and what types of activities can cause a transfer. In some prisons, it is enough to get caught with a bit of marijuana under your mattress, have your name show up on a list of gang members, or receive a prohibited tattoo.

It is particularly unsettling to learn how many people with psychological problems end up in solitary confinement—and in prison more generally. The percentage of inmates who meet the criteria for a mental health disorder is five times greater than in the adult U.S. population as a whole. More than half of the prisoners in supermax facilities in Maine are classified as having a serious mental illness.

Psychologists have documented that people with psychological disorders often find it difficult to follow rules, which is why many end up incarcerated in the first place. Keeping such people apart from mainstream society makes some sense, in certain cases, because those who struggle with self-restraint can be dangerous. But it seems bizarre to then place these individuals in a world of total control, where every regulation is to be followed strictly and where failure to fall into line is punished harshly. That, however, is the reality: in the United States, there are more than three times as many people suffering from significant mental illness locked in our prisons and jails as there are in our mental health facilities. And only about a third of those individuals have received treatment since their incarceration began.

When it comes to being model prisoners, these people are doomed to fail. State inmates with mental illness are twice as likely to have been injured in a fight as those with no mental problems, and over half of them end up charged with violating facility rules. When that happens, they can be sent to solitary, which, again, frequently aggravates the symptoms of mental illness. More egregious still, when that person's psychological condition deteriorates—leading him to throw food or feces or act out against guards—we punish him with more isolation, adding years or even decades onto his sentence.

So, it is not only that severity of punishment is influenced by factors that we claim are irrelevant, like the thickness of the defendant's lips, but also that severity of punishment fails to track factors that we do deem relevant, like the egregiousness of the crime. Even the death penalty—arguably the most scrutinized aspect of our correctional system—is crippled by both afflictions. I've touched on how race influences the decision to inflict capital punishment, but we also fall short on attending to the criteria we've declared essential in passing sentence.

In 2005, the Supreme Court held that "capital punishment must be limited to those offenders who commit 'a narrow category of the most serious crimes' and whose extreme culpability make them 'the most deserving of execution.'" But in a recent survey of all of the murder cases in Connecticut between 1973 and 2007, the system turned out not to be delivering "just deserts" at all: murderers who had committed the most heinous crimes frequently did not receive the death penalty, and there was no legitimate principle that distinguished those on death row from those who escaped capital sentences.

Our forebears set out to design a system that was consistent, fair, and proportional. And it is with those aims that we have added new mechanisms—such as uniform sentencing guidelines for judges—designed to get rid of lingering arbitrariness and bias. But in fact we still punish in a way that is deeply inconsistent and often perverse.

If we accept that our system of punishment is not humane and that it fails to inflict deserved suffering in proportion to wrongdoing, perhaps it might still be justified if it makes us safer.

On a very general level, it seems uncontroversial that our criminal justice system reduces crime: take away our laws and punishments, and more people would drive drunk, steal from old ladies, and wallop line cutters at the supermarket. And on first glance, the numbers seem to show the effectiveness of our current approach to corrections. The rise of mass imprisonment has coincided with a significant decrease in criminal activity in the United States. Over the last twenty or so years, both property crime and violent crime have fallen by more than 40 percent. New York City stands out as a success story. A savvy visitor to the Big Apple once avoided walking back to the hotel at night and skipped the subway altogether, but today Manhattan is a destination of relative safety. It seems clear that the get-tough-on-crime efforts that began around the country in the 1970s have finally paid off: millions of criminals have been taken off the streets and millions of others deterred.

But the real story is not that simple.

First, there are many other plausible explanations for the decrease in criminal activity, from more-effective policing tactics to an aging population to low inflation that has undercut the market for stolen goods. If the expansion of our harsh incarceration practices really reduced crime rates, we would expect to see clear evidence that released offenders were being dissuaded from committing new crimes. But for the last twenty years our recidivism rates have been stuck at around 40 percent, and in certain states more than 60 percent of offenders are locked up again within three years of release. Three-strikes laws, in particular, appear to have had no notable impact on crime rates. We would also expect similarly situated countries that didn't experience an imprisonment boom to have missed out on the massive decrease in crime that occurred in the United States. But that is not the case either: while Canada has maintained a fairly stable rate of incarceration, its crime rate has generally gone up and down in step with that of its neighbor to the south. And although the top thirty-five countries in Europe *combined* continue to have fewer inmates than the United States, they have not been overrun by crime.

Second, these statistics often omit the massive amount of crime that now takes place *within* prisons. Indeed, some scholars and journalists have asserted that it is not so much that crime has dried up as that it has simply moved from one location to another. Prisons are rife with drug dealing, assaults, and rapes, but these transgressions happen—literally—behind closed doors, which creates a false impression of overall crime reduction.

Third, to determine if our prison system is actually keeping us safe from crime, we need to know what the effects would be of alternatives. This problem has long plagued research on the death penalty. When the Supreme Court reinstated capital punishment in 1976, after a four-year moratorium, it was on the grounds that it deterred murderers. A number of empirical studies since then have appeared to back this up. But when the National Research Council convened a committee of leading experts in 2011 to assess the last thirty-five years of research, they concluded that the work didn't actually show that the death penalty reduced homicides. For proof of deterrence, you really need to compare two numbers—the murder rate in State X with the death penalty in force and the murder rate in State X *without* the death penalty in force—covering the same time frame. That's impossible, of course.

So, to get a sense of whether our system of punishment actually accomplishes its stated goals, we need to take another approach. Instead of trying to find the answer by looking at broad statistics, let's consider our correctional framework from the perspective of someone on the cusp of committing a crime—say, Leandro Andrade, just before entering that Kmart back in 1995—and see what might have gone into his thinking.

One of the reasons California passed its three-strikes law was to act as a deterrent in just this type of situation. The idea was that a repeat offender would weigh the benefits of committing the additional crime against the significant costs entailed in that third strike. Making the strike very harsh would mean that people like Leandro would ultimately decide not to take the videotapes. But how straightforward is that calculus?

Understanding the law is the starting point—but, unfortunately, the law is often complex, nuanced, or obscure. Here, Leandro needed to know that even though shoplifting is normally a misdemeanor, it can be prosecuted as a felony if you have a prior conviction for a property crime. And although two counts of such a felony are normally punishable by a maximum of three years and eight months in prison, if you have two "serious" or "violent" previous felonies on your record, you are looking at fifty years in prison with no possibility of parole. In essence, Leandro needed to know that breaking into three homes one day twelve years earlier—crimes that were not "violent" in any real sense of the word, as no one was even home, and for which he had served his time behind bars—had left him walking a tightrope without a net.

But even complete awareness of the law isn't sufficient. To conduct a true cost-benefit analysis, Leandro also needed to understand how Kmart uses security cameras, how likely the staff were to notice his shoplifting, how quick they would be to catch him, and whether they would call the police. And he had to have an idea of whether a prosecutor would decide to prosecute, the chances a jury would convict, and the conditions of the prison he might be sent to. Though it required projecting many years in the future, it was equally important to estimate the probability that a court of appeals might overturn his mandatory sentence as unconstitutional and that the voters of California might eventually pass a proposition reforming the three-strikes law and allowing for a reduction of his sentence. Perhaps most critical, Leandro had to anticipate how it would feel to be locked up again and consider the various opportunities and experiences he would be forgoing during his incarceration.

There are so many moving parts and unknown variables that even a prize-winning economist would struggle to calculate the tradeoffs. And, of course, Leandro was not an economist at all. He was a heroin addict.

Even those of us who don't have a mental illness or substance abuse problem are subject to cognitive limitations, emotional states, and other distorting influences that make it hard to assess the cost of committing a crime. If motivated reasoning can lead a judge to disregard research that conflicts with what he believes to be true, it can also lead a potential criminal to ignore information that suggests he'll end up with a heavy prison sentence. Add in optimism bias magnified by the extreme uncertainty built into the system, and a person may conclude that he is likely to avoid punishment altogether, regardless of the threat he actually faces.

Recent research suggests that people may even struggle with the basic task of judging the severity of a punishment. Which sanction is worse: (a) a $750 fine or (b) a $750 fine *and* two hours of community service? In a stunning finding, those assuming the identity of a potential lawbreaker are inclined to view the enhanced penalty with the community service as *less* severe than the fine alone! The reason is that people in Leandro's position don't tend to evaluate the punishment using the correct *additive* approach—adding together the major unpleasantness of paying the fine with the minor unpleasantness of doing the community service. Instead, they evaluate it through a misleading *averaging* process: if you take the major unpleasantness of paying the fine and the minor unpleasantness of doing the community service and average them, you come up with a punishment that seems less harsh than the fine alone. So, a legislature may aim to make it less appealing to break the law by adding community service to a big fine or jail time, but because potential offenders can't do the math, increasing the sentence with the small extra penalty may actually encourage crime.

It doesn't help that none of us are very good at predicting how punishment might make us feel—what scientists call "affective forecasting." And even if we could foresee what it would be like watching the cell door slam shut on our first day in prison, the emotions of that moment are almost certainly temporary. Indeed, the experience of imprisonment shifts over time as people adapt to the conditions of incarceration. This means that ten years in prison is not twice as unpleasant as five years in prison and ten times as unpleasant as one year in prison. Many life changes— from winning the lottery to losing a limb in a car accident—turn out, in the long term, to have much less of an influence on our well-being than we expect. People can get used to anything, even prison. As Ellis Boyd "Red" Redding, Morgan Freeman's character in *The Shawshank Redemption,* who is serving a life sentence for murder, explains, "These walls are funny. First you hate 'em, then you get used to 'em. Enough time passes, you get so you depend on them. That's institutionalized." The fact that people get "institutionalized" before returning to society is a major problem for deterrence. With long sentences, we end up releasing people at moments when the prospect of another year of prison seems least unpleasant.

In fact, from a psychological perspective, our current system does everything wrong in terms of optimal deterrence. Deterrence works when potential offenders think that they are almost certain to be caught and given a clear, immediate punishment. Our system, by contrast, offers a low probability of getting caught and a hazy potential punishment far in the distant future.

In the United States, only 40.3 percent of reported forcible rapes, 28.2 percent of robberies, and 12.4 percent of burglaries result in charges being filed. A serial burglar, then, should expect to be arrested and charged for only one out of every eight houses he breaks into. That's a real problem, given that the likelihood of being apprehended by the police appears to have the single biggest impact on deterrence. It doesn't help that conviction rates are well below 100 percent in America—69 percent for burglary—or that sentences are highly uncertain. The death penalty is a prime example: how can it serve as an effective additional deterrent (beyond life in prison) when the chances of, say, a young black male actually being executed once he's on death row are only slightly higher than his chances of being killed as a result of an accident or violence outside of prison?

Likewise, despite our admission that "justice delayed is justice denied," our judicial process is often dragged out over a series of months. In Brooklyn, the average wait time for a trial is 243 days; in the Bronx it is 408 days. Some cases take three, four, or five years. Even when punishment is certain, the greater the delay between the violation and the punishment, the less the penalty will act as a deterrent.

If we really wanted to deter crime, we would stop wasting our time with harsh mandatory minimums, three-strikes laws, and life without the possibility of parole, which have a minimal or nonexistent impact on offending. We are almost always better served by putting resources into increasing police presence—magnifying the perception that crimes will be detected—than we are by passing new laws that add years on to sentences. A punishment needs to be distasteful, but it doesn't need to be long. That's true both for deterring would-be offenders and for nullifying the effects of "institutionalization." The added benefit of brevity is that when a person commits a crime that carries a relatively short sentence, he is more likely to be convicted and actually receive his punishment: research has shown that the greater the potential sanction, the higher the standard of proof mock jurors require in order to find someone guilty.

The few judicial systems that have embraced a deterrence approach grounded in psychology have shown how effective it can be. For many years, probation violations were routine in Hawaii because the punishment for breaking the rules came either months later or not at all, as the sanctions were so severe that judges were reluctant to impose them. But in 2004, the state launched a new initiative focused on making sanctions clear, certain, and immediate. In Hawaii's Opportunity Probation with Enforcement (HOPE) program, substance-abusing probationers know exactly how they should behave and what to expect if they don't follow orders. Every morning they have to call an automated drug-testing hotline, and if they're randomly selected, they have to report for testing by the early afternoon. If they test positive, they are arrested on the spot and put in jail for a few days.

The results have been impressive: HOPE probationers are far less likely than regular probationers to be rearrested for a new crime, have their probation revoked, miss a probation appointment, or abuse drugs. Seventeen states have now adopted programs modeled on the initiative, and these limited experiments with probation could be stepping-stones to a more effective overall corrections system.

As we consider the broader expanse, however, we see a world of criminal justice still mired in false and harmful notions of how best to treat offenders to discourage crime. Unfortunately, exposing the ineffectiveness of our approach does not tell the whole story. It is not simply that our mechanisms of justice fail to deter; it is that they actually *increase* the likelihood of future criminal behavior. You'd imagine that taking a bunch of criminals and placing them in an extremely controlled setting—and then culling the particularly dangerous ones from the herd and placing them in solitary—would be a great formula for limiting problem behavior. But the truth is that our prison environments actually engender violence.

That makes sense when you consider the sheer numbers. The

influx of inmates over the last few decades has left prisons woefully overcrowded and—as a consequence—without the funding needed to continue many educational and occupational programs. Pack people in and give them nothing to do and you will have individuals acting out, often violently. I saw that as a thirteen-year-old, watching the fights, vandalism, and abuse that occurred in the Longfellow Middle School cafeteria, where 1,200 of us were corralled each morning before classrooms opened at 7:30. If it can happen with a bunch of kids at a good public school in Falls Church, Virginia, what do you suppose happens with a pool of criminals?

When the U.S. attorney in Manhattan reviewed the experience of male teenagers held at Rikers Island in 2013, he found a "pervasive" and "deep-seated culture of violence." Although the average daily adolescent population at Rikers was just 692, there were 845 reported inmate-on-inmate fights, not to mention the many unreported ones. Harsh abuse by staff was routine: 44 percent of those in custody had been beaten at least once. And many of the resulting injuries were serious: head trauma, facial fractures, cuts requiring sutures. Conditions were so bad that some inmates requested isolation just to escape. There's similar data from all over the country. In Georgia between 2010 and 2014, for example, there were thirty-four murders that occurred *inside* state prisons. Our correctional facilities are incubators for brutality.

What is particularly disturbing is that the vast majority of the individuals crammed into our troubled correctional facilities are then released back into society. The notion that our penal system keeps the dangerous incapacitated is a myth. This year, 13.5 million people will spend time in jail or prison, and 95 percent of them will eventually return to the outside world. Inmates in long-term isolation are no exception: more than half will rejoin the communities from which they came.

It is often not a happy reunion. Many inmates acquire drug habits, communicable diseases (such as hepatitis and HIV), and gang affiliations, which they bring with them as they walk out the penitentiary gates. The nonviolent offender learns to be vicious. And the lone criminal may gain a network of future accomplices.

The losses, too, are staggering. After being locked up for months or years, many inmates have lost the very things that might allow them to return as productive and peaceful members of society: family ties, friendships, years of job training and experience. They are thrown back into the rough sea of life without the anchors, rudders, and charts of safe passage needed to avoid a wreck.

And many must navigate their new surroundings without the mental faculties they once enjoyed. Those kept in solitary usually face the greatest deficits upon release, and many struggle to initiate or manage relationships on the outside. Moreover, when you can no longer participate in normal social exchanges, holding a job and staying on the straight and narrow becomes nearly impossible. It should come as no surprise, really, that extended isolation has been linked to increases—not decreases—in recidivism. This is one of the reasons that the Commission on Safety and Abuse in America's Prisons, a bipartisan task force convened in 2006, concluded that there were no notable benefits to isolation of more than ten days or so, and that long-term seclusion caused obvious harm.

We are so obsessed with the idea that the experience inside prison must not be like the experience outside that we overlook how much harder that makes it for inmates to rejoin society once they are released. Depriving people of normal human contact does not eliminate criminal behavior; it eliminates the capacity to engage in normal human contact. Losing the stimulation of work, entertainment, or socialization does not prompt people to make better choices in the future; it leaves them unprepared to get a job or interact with the outside world when they are released.

One of the strangest side effects of our ineffective and unfair incarceration system is that it may also make people less likely to follow the law in the first place. To many policymakers, severe mandatory sentences seem to offer a powerful incentive to follow the rules. But the extreme harshness of our punishments may actually increase the likelihood of malfeasance because they suggest that the law is not worthy of respect. If a couple of garage break-ins over the summer and a stolen car can land a nineteen-year-old in prison for life, then it is hard to trust the system, believe in its rules, and rely on its processes and officers. Research has shown that citizens are more willing to defer to the decisions of legal authorities and more willing to follow the law when they see those authorities and legal rules as legitimate. In one study, a group of participants read about a proposed law that seemed unjust because it raised civil liberties concerns or hurt certain citizens, while another cohort read about a seemingly just law. Those who had read about an unjust provision were more likely to report that they planned to disregard other completely unrelated criminal laws in their day-to-day lives.

The same dynamics play out in the real world. One of the reasons that Hawaii's HOPE program has been so successful is that it has bucked the trend and made procedural justice a key component of its deterrence approach. From the outset, Hawaiian offenders understand that judges and probation officers want them to succeed. And although the punishments are consistently enforced, they are not overly harsh (a failed drug test often means simply a few days in jail), so defendants view the penalties as fair and legitimate. This perception, in turn, seems to encourage program participants to show greater respect for the law.

Yet the HOPE initiative is the rare exception, and while the program has done an admirable job of crafting an approach that more effectively deters, there is serious reason to question whether deterrence should remain a major focus of our correctional system. Ultimately, it is not enough to ask whether our current approach to punishment deters some set of criminals (or whether it could be properly reformed to deter more); we must also ask whether any benefits that accrue are worth the costs.

A trip to the pokey doesn't come cheap; nor does an execution. The total bill for our correctional system is some $60 billion each year. A year in a New Jersey prison costs more than a year at Princeton University. The trends are equally disheartening: state spending on prisons has outpaced spending on higher education in the last twenty years, increasing at six times the rate. And the cost of building and managing a supermax facility is generally two or three times the cost for other kinds of prisons. The irony is that spending money on education—in particular to keep male high school students from dropping out—appears to be a far more effective way to combat crime. Time in the classroom reduces the opportunity to get into trouble, helps instill positive values, and provides skills that lead to better jobs, diminishing the need to offend and increasing the perceived cost of being caught and imprisoned.

None of this, of course, takes into account the broader costs of our current punishment regime. As the Commission on Safety and Abuse in America's Prisons explained, "Many of those who are incarcerated come from and return to poor African-American and Latino neighborhoods, and the stability of those communities has an effect on the health and safety of whole cities and states."

In the end, the biggest cost may come to the values we say we hold dear. We say we want a system that is humane, but we deliver unimaginable suffering. We say we want to punish only those who deserve it and to punish in proportion to their wrongdoing, but we end up punishing randomly or, worse still, delivering the harshest experiences to those who least deserve it. We say we want to protect ourselves and reform prisoners, but instead we teach them brutality and leave ourselves less safe.

If we were somehow able to remove our cognitive blinders, we would never design our system of punishment as it currently stands. We would forget Eastern State. We would start again.

---

Halden is one of Norway's highest-security prisons. It houses murderers and rapists. But there are no bars on the windows. You cannot see the huge wall that surrounds the prison—just trees.

It was not built to intimidate or deter or separate. It was built to rehabilitate.

The facility has a sleek, minimalist aesthetic. Each prisoner is given a room with a flat-screen television, a toilet (behind a door), a shower, a fridge, and a desk. Linked to every ten or twelve rooms is a common living space.

Prisoners are locked in their cells only during the evening, with the day open for educational, vocational, and leisure activities. The prison has several workshops and sports facilities, as well as a library, a chapel, and a school. The inmates often save up their money to buy ingredients—including wasabi and garam masala—for communal cooking. There are tablecloths on the tables.

The prison staff aren't cast as unyielding enforcers, as in the United States; their role is to help inmates overcome their criminality and change their lives. And effort goes into fostering family ties (including permitting overnight stays in a house located at the facility) and preparing prisoners to reintegrate back into society.

It makes sense, according to Halden's governor, because everyone is eventually going to be released. A monstrous prison will create monsters. And what is the point of that?

Halden will never be repurposed as a haunted house or host dozens of paranormal investigations because, unlike Eastern State, it isn't scary, and it wasn't designed for suffering. It is hard to think of a model more different from our own. When Eastern State's architect, John Haviland, put his pen to paper, it was to "strike fear into the hearts of those who thought of committing a crime." And the grim fortress that he engendered has left a frightening legacy: in the United States, we are still wedded to the belief that the best way to protect the public is through harsh punitive sanctions and incapacitation. But times have changed. If once Europeans flocked to Pennsylvania to learn about its novel penitentiary, it is now time for Americans to look across the Atlantic.

In 2013, more than 150 years after Tocqueville and Dickens visited Eastern State, a delegation from Pennsylvania traveled to northern Europe to tour prison facilities, meet with inmates, and talk to correctional officials. What they found startled them. At the German and Dutch prisons they visited, inmates were making meals, wearing their own clothes, and locking their cells with keys when they went to work or study. Women with children under three had them by their side in special mother-baby units. And prisoners were provided with frequent home leave. Solitary confinement was very rare—a last resort—and restricted to short amounts of time (just hours or a few days), with provision made for regular human contact and the opportunity, with good behavior, for an early return to the general population. To encourage proper conduct, positive reinforcement was used far more often than harsh discipline. And when offenders were released, they were not permanently excluded—as is commonly the case in the United States—from voting, receiving government benefits, or enjoying other normal rights of citizenship. They were free.

The reason is simple: Germany and the Netherlands, like Norway, have organized their penal system around resocialization and rehabilitation. It's right there in their laws. Germany's Prison Act, for example, makes rehabilitating the inmate the *sole* aim of incarceration; protecting the public is simply a natural outgrowth of ensuring the inmate's successful transition back into society upon release. To help inmates with that eventual transition, the conditions inside the prison resemble the conditions outside as closely as possible. The rehabilitation model brings special benefits to mentally ill offenders. Incarcerating them makes little sense in this context, so in Germany they are instead placed in psychiatric hospitals, where they can get the specialized care they need to get better.

It is easy to think that there must be a catch or a trick. But the numbers suggest that the northern European model works. Norway has one of the lowest recidivism rates in the world—20 percent after two years. And reoffending in neighboring countries is also far lower than in North America. Do some prisoners take advantage of the comparative leniency? No doubt, but the numbers seem small indeed. In Germany, only one percent of prisoners fail to report back to prison after being given home leave.

Could America ever give up its punitive bent and focus on rehabilitation? There are plenty who would point to our unique culture to suggest that it's a fool's endeavor. The public wouldn't stand for it, they warn. Our criminals are more dangerous. We've always been a sink-or-swim nation: freedom to succeed and freedom to fail. No handouts. No tears for the wicked. And it's true that the success of European prisons is facilitated by a much more robust social safety net and a political environment in which civil treatment of offenders is more widely accepted. But the differences can be overdrawn. Britain, which managed to turn away from long-term solitary confinement starting in the 1980s, had—like us—a history of prison attacks on staff, murderous psychopaths, and inmate groups intent on undermining the correctional system. But British leaders found the courage to pull their punches, to give those behind bars more command over their lives, and things didn't get worse—they got better.

Even stronger evidence that American innovation is possible comes from new experiments in Pennsylvania and elsewhere that divert offenders into mental health programs, restrict inmate isolation, and provide transitional housing. In just the last five years, some states, including Mississippi and Colorado, have drastically cut their solitary populations, with encouraging results.

And, in fact, it is our unique culture that ought to propel reform, not stymie it. For a country that trumpets its commitment to freedom as exceptional and so willingly accepts risk in the name of protecting fundamental liberties, our maximally coercive and restrictive approach is baffling, even ludicrous.

We will fight tirelessly to protect the rights of those who spew hate in the public square, stockpile weapons capable of wiping out classrooms of children, and flood our airwaves with lies to sway elections, but we draw the line at permitting a man convicted of stealing videotapes a door to his toilet, the chance to spend a night with his family, or the experience of preparing his own dinner in his own shirt. If ensuring freedom for those who may harm us is worth the risk when the costs are high, that must certainly be the case when protecting their rights leaves us safer.

# PART IV

# Reform

# 11

# WHAT WE MUST OVERCOME

## The Challenge

Shortly after I became a law professor, I received a jury summons. I knew that law professors rarely make it onto juries; attorneys regularly strike them out of a fear that they will dominate the jury's decision-making—and also, I hear, because no attorney wants to feel like she is back in law school, with a professor analyzing her every word. However, I held out hope that I might pass through the gauntlet of background questions and find myself among the chosen twelve.

The first step was to fill out a juror information questionnaire with demographic information and then answer some "yes/no" questions. "Would you be more likely to believe the testimony of a police officer or any other law enforcement officer just because of his or her job?" "Would you have any problem following the Court's instruction that the defendant in a criminal case does not have to take the stand or present evidence, and it cannot be held against the defendant if he or she elects to remain silent or present no evidence?" "Is there any other reason you could not be a fair juror in a criminal case?"

If you checked "yes" for any of the boxes, the judge asked you some follow-up questions. For example, if you indicated that you were more likely to believe the testimony of a police officer, he explained to you that your job as a juror required you to treat every witness the same regardless of his or her position, race, gender, or the like. Then he asked whether you still thought you would have a problem being impartial. Everyone who had checked the "yes" box on that question changed his or her answer to "no." The judge was satisfied, and we moved on.

Many people would view this interaction as a perfect example of what works in our criminal justice system. Here, it would seem, we have not put our heads in the sand—we've acknowledged that there are prejudices certain jurors bring to court, and we've directly addressed them. We haven't shied away from asking awkward questions, and we've followed up to make our expectations clear. Just as important, we've gone big: every jury in every criminal case is taken through the screening. Even if they don't make it onto a panel, those in the jury pool leave with an understanding of what impartiality means and how to achieve it. Isn't this meaningful, honest progress?

In fact, our approach to juror screening provides a good illustration of precisely what we are doing wrong in our quest to eliminate unfairness from the law. It represents the first of three serious challenges we face in realizing science-based reform.

The problem with our questions and instructions isn't the underlying intention to ensure neutral and objective justice, nor is it the general formula offered to accomplish this worthy goal: define bias, screen for bias, correct bias. Both would seem to be quite in keeping with the spirit of this book. The trouble comes in the details.

While we purport to address bias, what we actually do is reinforce a false narrative of what bias is, where it comes from, and how it can be remedied. And this puts us in a worse spot than if our system took no position on bias at all.

Take the matter of introspection. There's a wealth of research suggesting that many biases can't be detected through soul-searching. And while it's one thing for us all to walk around believing that it's possible to self-reflect and identify all of our hidden proclivities, it's quite another thing to have the legal establishment confirm that intuition. Unfortunately, that is exactly what many of our rules and procedures do.

In the Third Circuit, for instance, jurors are asked questions to determine if they "have any beliefs, feelings, life experiences, or any other reasons that might influence [them] in rendering a verdict." Does the fact that the defendant was born in Guatemala matter to you? Would you discriminate against someone based on the color of his skin? As a juror, you think about the person you are—someone who believes deeply in equality—and you answer, "No, of course not." You know you're not racist. Case closed: there is no threat of bias toward the Hispanic defendant.

What's so damaging about this is not just that a juror may end up mistakenly believing that he's capable of objectivity, but that by weighing in, the Third Circuit stacks the cards against addressing the scourge of implicit racial bias. Now, to enact reform, we must overcome not only people's inherent skepticism but also the fact that they have been told repeatedly that such bias does not exist: if you know you are completely egalitarian, you cannot discriminate.

The same thing happens when our legal system bolsters the myth that being impartial is simply a choice. Over and over, during the trial process, jurors are instructed to switch off their irrelevant thoughts, emotions, and beliefs. "Do not allow sympathy, prejudice, fear, or public opinion to influence you," Third Circuit jurors are told. "You should also not be influenced by any person's race, color, religion, national ancestry, or gender." Likewise, whenever the judge sustains an objection, "you must disregard the question or the exhibit entirely. Do not think about or guess what the witness might have said in answer to the question; do not think about or guess what the exhibit might have shown." And if the judge orders evidence to be stricken or removed from the record, "you must not consider [it] or be influenced [by it] in any way."

Knowing how little control we have over the many automatic processes in our brains, such directives seem almost laughable. But this is no farce: these are the instructions that guide those participating in our legal system every single day. Out of thin air, the Third Circuit has conjured up a magical remote control for the brain, allowing jurors to erase, pause, and mute on command.

As amazing as our minds actually are, our legal rules, regulations, interpretations, and instructions make them out to be many times as impressive. To hear the law tell it, we are supermen and wonder women, able to rise above our prejudices, see through lies, and recall past events with crystal clarity. Every juror and every witness in every case is encouraged to have faith in his or her basic intuitions. Every judge on every court has been told that judicial bias can be controlled simply by making good choices. And every police officer and prosecutor has been trained to avoid misconduct with the same mantra of moral integrity through self-discipline. So, we vanquish our misgivings. Yes, we are able to set aside our political beliefs to decide this case. Yes, we are 100 percent certain that this man was the perpetrator. Yes, in carrying out our duties, we will treat every victim as equally worthy of respect.

Being aware of our natural limitations isn't a cure-all. But it's a necessary first step. As we saw when Judge Frank Barbaro revisited a decision he'd made years earlier: doubt is the friend of fairness. Without it, you cannot convince anyone that they really do have it wrong or that change is urgently needed. We'll need to go further, though, to overcome the second significant threat to progress, reexamining the basic framework for protecting the public from mistreatment by the government that we've constructed over centuries.

There is no question that the way in which cops, prosecutors, and judges exercise their ample discretion has an enormous impact on whether private citizens receive justice or injustice. In addressing this concern, the law has stuck to the notion that police officers, district attorneys, and judges make decisions in a rational, conscious way. So, to ensure proper behavior, it all comes down to establishing robust rules that clearly spell out what is permitted and what is not, and that provide incentives for following protocol. Most cops, D.A.s, and judges then toe the line, and the few wayward individuals who don't can be culled from the herd. This has been the model in the United States for many decades.

When significant injustice has come to light, our instinct has been to turn to our Bill of Rights and reaffirm our commitment to fair processes and procedures. In the 1960s, for instance, as attorneys and activists drew attention to police abuse of suspects, the Supreme Court articulated a set of precise constitutional constraints on law enforcement officers. Faced with the specter of coerced confessions leading to wrongful convictions, the justices established that, prior to being questioned, a person in custody must be told "that he has the right to remain silent, that anything he says can be used against him in a court of law, that he has the right to the presence of an attorney, and that if he cannot afford an attorney one will be appointed for him prior to any questioning if he so desires." The so-called *Miranda* warning has become a standard feature of cop shows, but there are now numerous other process-oriented rules that govern how police officers, prosecutors, and judges interact with the public.

In recent decades, law professors, lawyers, and judges have battled tirelessly over the minutiae of these regulations. Does the Constitution's prohibition on unreasonable searches bar a police officer from squeezing a bus passenger's canvas bag or looking at files on a home computer after a houseguest says it's okay? Can a person invoke his right not to incriminate himself in refusing to disclose his name to a police officer?

The result of these efforts is a thicket of extremely nuanced procedural protections. In the case of *Miranda* rights, for example, it is now settled that the privilege against self-incrimination must be invoked by the person being questioned. If the police begin to interrogate you, you must clearly claim your rights—if you don't, what you say can be used against you in a case. Likewise, the Supreme Court has stated that you have no right against self-incrimination if you are not under arrest. If the police ask you to come down to the station to answer a few questions and you go, you can't then decide you don't want to answer one of their questions without risking that your refusal will be used as evidence of your guilt at a later trial.

Do all of these thorny branches keep the legal establishment in check? The reality is that our procedural hedge offers a false sense of protection. Far from ensuring our goal of substantive justice, our rules of process may actually undermine it.

For one thing, many of the procedural rules do not actually constrain officers, prosecutors, and judges very much at all; they only appear to do so. The Supreme Court's handling of peremptory challenges is a good example. Allowing counsel on both sides to strike a certain number of jurors prior to trial without having to provide justification was meant to protect the integrity of the system—to allow attorneys to use their instincts and experience to identify subtle, hidden prejudices that might corrupt the verdict. But in practice the rule was often used to *introduce* bias: for decades, attorneys disproportionately excluded certain groups, based on their gender or the color of their skin. Facing significant criticism, the Supreme Court finally decided to address the problem, barring peremptory challenges based solely on the race of the juror and forcing attorneys to provide a race-neutral reason for excluding a juror if challenged by the opposing side. A deep societal value was under threat, so the Court fashioned a procedural remedy to tighten the discretion enjoyed by attorneys.

Many cheered this decision as a victory for the bedrock principle of nondiscrimination and for the right of citizens to serve as jurors and be tried by a representative group of their peers. Unfortunately, it has not been much of a constraint at all. The problem, as Justice Thurgood Marshall—the first African American appointed to the Supreme Court—foresaw, is that "any prosecutor can easily assert facially neutral reasons for striking a juror, and trial courts are ill equipped to second-guess those reasons." Today, in many instances, all that a prosecutor has to do to strike a black person from a death-penalty jury is to come up with a justification that's not explicitly about race. "The juror worked as a plumber and I'm concerned that he will be biased in favor of the defendant who also worked in the service industry" or "He said that he only made it through the eighth grade and I'm afraid that the complexity of the case may be beyond his capacities" or "She was chewing gum and did not seem to be paying attention to the questions being asked"—any of those will do. It need not be persuasive or even plausible.

How are judges to sort out whether the explanation is mere pretext? Members of the judiciary are rarely equipped to make such determinations. Experimental research involving practicing attorneys and students reveals that although race influences peremptory challenges, people typically justify their actions in race-neutral terms, which makes it impossible to tell whether race is the reason a juror has been excluded. And since racial biases often operate at an implicit level, the lawyers themselves may not even know.

As a result, in many areas of the country, it is hard to see progress. Between 2005 and 2009, prosecutors in Houston County, Alabama, struck approximately four out of five blacks in capital-case jury panels. About half of the resulting juries were all white, and the other half had only a single black juror. Despite all of the effort put into fashioning the proper procedural framework, we have not in fact dealt with the core problem of discrimination.

And important though it is, the failure of the peremptory challenge is just one example of a much broader phenomenon: we expend so much energy battling, reforming, and strictly enforcing our procedural protections that we lose sight of the fact that they are merely a means to an end. A judge will let you off of your shoplifting charge if the police stepped into your home and seized evidence without a warrant, but a court will rarely intervene in the obviously unjust situation of a man being sent to prison for the rest of his life for stealing a few DVDs. And a court will almost never overturn a sentence on the grounds that it is inherently wrong for someone to face the threat of gang rape while under the sole control of the state.

What if, during an interrogation, a detective continues probing after you've requested an attorney and you confess to a heinous murder? It doesn't matter if it's the only evidence in the case and proves without a doubt that you are the perpetrator; a judge won't let it before a jury. But if you *waive* your *Miranda* rights—as roughly 80 percent of suspects end up effectively doing—the fact that your confession is false will be treated as irrelevant: the waiver itself is taken as proof that your admission of guilt was uncoerced and reliable. Check the procedural box at the outset and the legal system is satisfied.

If we were truly concerned about substantive justice, that would never be the case. To begin with, it would matter that suspects don't understand their constitutional rights in about one million criminal cases—about 10 percent of the total—each year. We would address the fact that roughly one out of every three pretrial defendants believes incorrectly that if he remains silent after being arrested, his silence can be used against him at trial. And we would care that the vast majority of those who waive their rights are the innocent, the young, and those with mental disabilities: these are the people, after all, that we claim to most want to protect. Most critically, we would pay attention to what happens after a *Miranda* warning is read, and we would not stand for interrogation procedures that routinely produce false confessions.

But we seem to have forgotten that the purpose of guaranteeing the form of justice—the procedure to be followed, each and every time—was to ensure substantive rights, like liberty, privacy, security, and equality. We are now all form, substance be damned. We sleepwalk through the motions. All that matters is whether the right regulation was followed. And that allows for truly absurd results, like the false-confession case of Eddie Joe Lloyd, whose answers to police questioning were considered voluntary because he had been advised of his rights—even though his interview took place inside a mental hospital where he had been involuntarily committed with debilitating mental illness.

Worse still, when following protocol is the sole concern, it becomes acceptable to work around the rules in ways that deeply infringe the principles that motivated the creation of the protocol in the first place. Police departments, for instance, teach investigators how to deliver a *Miranda* warning so that it is most likely to be misunderstood and ignored. Officers are encouraged to bring up the warning as a casual aside—and not at the moment of arrest, when a person is most likely to be considering his rights. When the *Miranda* doctrine was first introduced, cops were worried that it would severely limit their ability to gain confessions, but in fact it has turned out to have a minimal effect on police work, precisely because it is so easy to work around.

The same may be said of the historic ruling that ended stop-and-frisk practices by the NYPD: the decision was met with strong resistance by law enforcement and cheered by rights activists, but the new requirements are easily evaded. There is nothing preventing an officer from picking out a black man on the street and frisking him for weapons; he just has to make sure that he checks the right procedural boxes related to "reasonable suspicion" (for example, is the man standing in a high-crime neighborhood, and did he run away when the officer approached?).

The complexity of our procedural rules—and the work we have put into developing them—creates the illusion of fairness. And that makes it all the more difficult to address the problems that plague our system. Ironically, it may be harder to eliminate false confessions when there is an ineffective set of procedural rules aimed at preventing them than it would be if there were no protections at all. With elaborate structures in place, it appears that we've addressed the issue, and anything that is not barred at the gates is given little or no scrutiny—it's assumed to be legitimate. The horrible truth is that in prohibiting the torture of suspects and requiring that arrestees be Mirandized, courts made lying to suspects seem more justified—a necessary tool for the police whose work of keeping us safe became more difficult.

If we heeded the evidence on false confessions or focused on core principles of justice, we would never let detectives lie to a suspect, telling him that an accomplice fessed up or that DNA evidence connected him to the crime. And it is revealing that most people don't understand that detectives are allowed to do this. When the general population assumes that a popular police practice is prohibited because it's unfair, it should raise a red flag. When rapists and murderers—the least rule-abiding among us—assume the same thing, it should set off fireworks.

Not everyone, though, is naïve about the "real" legal system—the manipulations, the loopholes, the human weaknesses and quirks. And the final challenge to addressing the hidden unfairness in our midst has to do with inequality: specifically, the unequal access to the truth about how legal actors perceive, think, and behave.

Some participants in criminal law cases are much savvier than others when it comes to human behavior. And these powerful individuals and institutions are already exploiting the weaknesses in our legal system for their own gain. What does that mean in practice? If you are rich and connected, you go free. If you are poor and uneducated, you go to prison.

A major source of the disparity has to do with how knowledge is disseminated in society. As we've seen, researchers are producing an ever-expanding pool of data about what really moves police officers, judges, jurors, and others. The problem is that for much of the population, there is no point of entry.

For one thing, the commercial publishing industry has adopted a model based on amassing and then holding back this valuable resource for all but the most elite consumers. In recent decades, large companies have swallowed up many previously nonprofit scientific journals, and prices have soared. When a single journal subscription can cost more than $40,000 a year, most of the public is kept on the other side of the paywall.

This wouldn't matter so much if there were a serious effort to summarize the findings for a broader audience and draw connections to active policy debates. But the translation project is stymied by legitimate concerns about taking scientific data to the public "too soon." Many researchers are reluctant to point to the practical applications of their work, lest they be accused of going beyond their data. And there will always be a danger that when journalists report on studies, they will distort the findings or omit important nuance. Many academics also worry about the appearance of bias that can creep in once one is associated with a particular policy recommendation. A scientist who advocates changes to the system based on her research is often seen as a scientist who brings an agenda to her data collection and analysis. Better to keep one's attention on the science and focus on reaching other academics, at least until the research is firmly established.

But as the public waits for replications, others are carefully reading the preliminary findings. They are trial consultants, members of a rapidly growing half-a-billion-dollars-a-year industry focused on bringing the insights and methods of social science to the world of litigation. Before the 1970s there was no such thing as a jury expert or a witness preparation guru, but today there are over six hundred firms in existence, and they exert a significant force on our criminal and civil legal systems. In major litigation, trial consultants are now used as a matter of course.

Interestingly, these consultants are not primarily lawyers: in one survey, only 5 percent of consultants had a JD, and only 11 percent reported any background in law. Rather, they are social scientists: about half of trial consultants hold a PhD, and about half are trained as psychologists (with obvious overlap between the two groups). As one litigation consultant explained, "Basically, jury consulting is applied psychology. . . . We'll read studies from *The Journal of Applied Psychology* or *Law and Human Behavior.* We are practitioners but pretty much everyone here could flip and become an academic."

And, in fact, it is academics who are credited with launching the field. One of the first and most prominent cases involving consultants was the 1974 trial of Joan Little, a young African American woman from North Carolina who was charged with murder in the death of a white prison guard at Beaufort County Jail, where she was locked up. Little claimed that the guard had raped her and that she had stabbed him with an ice pick in self-defense. A group of scientists led by John McConahay, a psychology professor at Duke, decided to offer their services. The first step they took was to survey county residents concerning their feelings about the case, as well as their general attitudes on matters like whether black women are inclined toward violence. By providing evidence that potential Beaufort County jurors were twice as likely as those in other jurisdictions to have made up their mind that Little was guilty, McConahay and his colleagues helped get the trial moved to Wake County, a significant benefit to the defense. In addition, the team collected data in order to figure out which traits and preferences suggested that a juror would side with the defendant and used this information to strike jurors with authoritarian views who were older, Republican, and less educated.

Although the trial dragged on for five weeks, the jury acquitted Little in just over an hour. Some critics now question the ultimate impact of the jury research, given the seeming weakness of the prosecution's case against Little, but McConahay's team helped pave the way for modern trial consultants.

The team's methods live on. It is still standard practice before a trial begins for consultants to collect information on the *potential* jury pool, discover any correlations that exist, and then target a sympathetic jury. Actual jurors are generally scored and ranked in terms of how closely their responses align with the ideal pro-prosecution or pro-defense panel member.

Today, though, trial consultants provide many other services, including assisting with overall strategy development, presentation effectiveness, deposition preparation, media relations, and negotiation. Their advice is based not only on existing psychological and marketing research but also on their own data collection in a case. Trial consultants may put together focus groups or stage full mock trials to test out particular approaches, theories, witnesses, or pieces of evidence; employ shadow jurors to watch the actual proceedings and provide feedback; and conduct post-trial interviews to better understand juror decision-making and develop strategies for future cases.

This all seems beneficial—a natural development in the pursuit of more effective and complete legal representation. So what's the problem?

Historically, the big concern has been charlatanism and the difficulty of assessing whether trial consultants make a significant difference to the outcome of trials. But with the industry rapidly becoming more sophisticated and honing its practices, the major issue for the future is access: who will get to enjoy consultants' services and who won't?

The expansion of the industry has been fueled by attorneys representing corporations in complex civil suits with hundreds of millions or billions at stake. The result is that trial services are now very pricey, with fees averaging around $250 an hour and some significantly higher. Jury consultants are commonplace when the rich and famous are dragged into court: O.J. Simpson, Martha Stewart, Calvin Broadus (aka Snoop Dogg), Robert Blake, and the Menendez brothers all used trial consultants for their criminal cases. And it's part of the standard defense package for high-rolling white-collar defendants. But those with fewer resources have often been left to fend for themselves. That's fundamentally unfair. Justice Hugo Black was right when he wrote, more than a half century ago, that "there can be no equal justice where the kind of trial a man gets depends on the amount of money he has."

And the gap between the haves and have-nots is only going to widen. For those at the top, crime really does pay—and the more you make, the more access you have to those who can help you game the system. And the more you have that power, the less likely the government is to investigate you, prosecute you, or take a hard line in plea bargaining, because they know that they aren't going to win at trial. There's a reason that this book about unfairness hasn't talked about white-collar crime: those who engage in corporate self-dealing, illegal accounting schemes, and securities fraud get more than a fair deal.

For those at the bottom, by contrast, the lack of access initiates a devastating downward cycle. You can't stop losing, because every time you return from prison, you are in a worse position to gain the help you need. Each new sentence keeps you away longer from gainful employment, education, and personal connections. You never have the chance to build up the necessary capital to buy in to the secret world that hedge-fund fraudsters take for granted. And you pass on the curse to your children: when you're incarcerated, they, too, are less likely to go to college or rise out of poverty. Entire inner-city communities become locked into this self-reinforcing inequity, while gated ones across the river are able to secure wealth and success for generations to come.

The cruel irony is that the trailblazers of the trial-consulting industry were motivated by a desire to defend the poor and vulnerable. Like those who assisted Joan Little, the sociologists involved in the first example of modern trial consulting two years earlier sought to ensure basic fairness for others, not to make money. Seven antiwar activists—six of whom were Catholic priests or nuns—stood charged with conspiring to raid federal offices, blow up steam tunnels in Washington, D.C., and kidnap Henry Kissinger to bring an end to U.S. involvement in Vietnam. The government elected to stage the trial in Harrisburg, Pennsylvania, a strongly conservative city with a low percentage of Catholics. Jay Schulman and his team, concerned that the jury pool would be heavily biased in favor of the prosecution, initiated a pretrial research study to try to learn which characteristics of community members were most closely linked to their likely verdicts. The purpose was simply to negate the government's unfair advantage—to even the scales.

But much has changed in the intervening decades. Trial consulting's tether to social justice has been severed, and balance is no longer the aim. With clients paying tens of thousands of dollars—or even, in the case of high-profile murder trials, hundreds of thousands of dollars—for the services, delivering a fair trial isn't enough. Clients want the verdict to go their way. In some ways, then, the goal of the trial consultant has been entirely reversed. If once the aim was to bring to light unappreciated biases and eliminate them, the focus now is on using social science to catalogue, control, and all too often accentuate biases. In fact, from the perspective of a trial consultant, a system that is predictably unfair, in ways that are hidden from most court participants, is the best possible situation. It presents a golden business opportunity.

Of course, there are still some in the industry who see their role as serving justice by helping lawyers and experts explain complex concepts to jurors, counteracting biases that courtroom actors may bring to trial, and identifying people with undisclosed prejudices. Yet these well-intentioned individuals are extremely vulnerable. When you possess the scientific knowledge to bend legal processes, judges, jurors, and witnesses to your ends, it's hard to say no to the easy money. What's more, the scope of distortion is immense: almost every finding I have described in this book could be used both to foster justice and to stymie it.

Take the research on eyewitness memory. Today, witness preparation is a key service offered by trial consultants, and it is often quite extensive, with informational interviews in which the lawyer explains the overall picture of the case and learns everything the witness knows, as well as simulations on the stand with feedback from a mock jury. This preparation carries a number of benefits, allowing a lawyer to better construct her arguments, decide whether a witness is credible, and help a nervous witness become more comfortable with the process. Yet, given what we now know about the fragility of memory, a trial consultant could easily conclude that this type of preparation is likely to contaminate the witness's memory and is therefore unethical to pursue. Realistically, though, how often will that happen?

The research on memory tells a consultant or lawyer that robust witness preparation makes it more likely that the verdict will go in favor of the client: witnesses who have been thoroughly rehearsed are more likely to adopt facts they've been given as their own memories, and they are more likely to express confidence in those memories, which jurors are then inclined to take as a sign that they are accurate. Unscrupulous consultants, then, will clearly prep their witnesses vigorously, but so will many consultants who are simply trying to be dedicated advocates for their clients. And there's little stopping them: trial consultants are not directly regulated and the standards set by the American Society of Trial Consultants are extremely general and easily met.

Lawyers are responsible for the consultants they hire, but in a perverse twist, failing to earnestly prepare a witness may be significantly more likely to earn sanction than readying your witness in a way that warps his recollection. In fact, a defendant can actually bring an "ineffective assistance of counsel" claim under the Sixth Amendment on such grounds. The American Bar Association and the judiciary have not only failed to seriously address dubious witness preparation, they've actually sanctioned practices that research shows lead to memory distortions. As the

North Carolina Supreme Court explained: "It is not improper for an attorney to prepare his witness for trial, to explain the applicable law in any given situation and to go over before trial the attorney's questions and the witness' answers so that the witness will be ready for his appearance in court, will be more at ease because he knows what to expect, and will give his testimony in the most effective manner that he can. Such preparation is the mark of a good trial lawyer . . . and is to be commended." Members of the United States Supreme Court have characterized the " 'coaching' of Government witnesses prior to their testimony" as "inevitable." And they have repeatedly emphasized the value of cross-examination as an effective tool for dealing with coaching, despite research from psychology suggesting that it almost certainly is not.

All of this means that few trial consultants or lawyers will see problematic witness preparation as problematic at all. And because such preparation invariably occurs in private and is often protected by attorney "work product privilege"—preventing the other side from accessing the materials a lawyer has prepared in anticipation of trial—outsiders will almost never find out when a witness's testimony has been tainted.

We make it easy for trial consultants and attorneys to use the insights from psychology and neuroscience to the detriment of accuracy, fairness, and justice. But weak ethical guidelines and loose professional constraints are only part of the story. Increasingly, research studies offer ways to directly influence the outcome of trial, with no need to extrapolate or read between the lines. Take a recent set of experiments in which scientists decided to see if they could use the juror screening process not to detect and remove bias—as intended—but to prejudice real people. In the experiment, every mock juror was asked two neutral questions, but some people were asked an additional question about whether they would be able to act impartially if the defendant turned out to be a gang member. Even when it was made explicit that the question was merely hypothetical, it had a powerful biasing effect: participants who were asked the question were significantly more likely to reach a guilty verdict than those who did not. According to the researchers, because gangs are associated with criminal behavior, exposure to the hypothetical question made that negative stereotype readily accessible and encouraged participants to find the defendant guilty.

Is it any surprise, then, that trial consultants now use *voir dire* not only to select favorable jurors but also to establish impressions that influence juror perceptions and judgments once the trial begins? In some ways, research like this can be read as a how-to manual for unscrupulous attorneys. Yet it need not be; it has just as much potential as a powerful force to eliminate bias in our system. For this transformation to take place, however, we need to be committed to reshaping how trial consultants and lawyers do their work. This does not mean changing who we are; it means reaffirming the principles upon which our criminal justice system is based. The purpose of *voir dire* is to pick a fair jury; when it is being used, instead, to stack the deck, then we have truly lost our way.

There is no reason to think that the people who make their living in the trial-consulting industry are somehow less moral than the rest of us. But they are creatures of their environment, and the current environment tells them that using knowledge of the human mind to manipulate legal actors is not only permissible but commendable. Not going the extra mile for your client is letting your client down. Witness preparation and juror analysis are all just part of the modern trial. Thus, few of these good people—trained scientists, lawyers, and others—ever stop to consider the far-reaching effects of their actions. We are selling jurors' and judges' minds to the highest bidder. It's time for honest reflection. Justice should not be a commodity.

# 12

# WHAT WE CAN DO

## The Future

A little over one hundred years ago, the English writer G. K. Chesterton was called for jury duty. After taking his oath, Chesterton sat back and observed the various characters in the unfolding drama: a woman accused of neglecting her children, a bicycle thief, a judge, assembled lawyers. From that intimate vantage point, he realized something that he had previously failed to grasp: "The horrible thing about all legal officials, even the best, about all judges, magistrates, detectives and policemen, is not that they are wicked (some of them are good), not that they are stupid (some of them are quite intelligent), it is simply that they have got used to it."

As he explained, the problem with the system was that those in it were so acclimated to their surroundings, so set in their ways and assumptions, that "they do not see the prisoner in the dock; all they see is the usual man in the usual place. They do not see the awful court of judgment; they only see their own workshop." For Chesterton, the solution was laymen jurors—outsiders, like him, who could "see the court and the crowd, and coarse faces of the policemen and the professional criminals, the wasted faces of the wastrels, the unreal faces of the gesticulating counsel—and see it all as one sees a new picture or a ballet hitherto unvisited."

As this book has suggested, Chesterton's faith in jurors was most likely misplaced—they are subject to many of the same cognitive limitations as the judges, police officers, and attorneys he criticized—but he was exactly right about the problem with our criminal justice system. We have gotten used to it. It is so familiar that we cannot see its true nature—what is moving its gears and gumming up the works. The main enemy of justice does not lie in the corrupt dispositions of a few bigoted cops, stupid jurors, or egotistical judges. It is found inside the mind of each of us.

The starting point of any reform comes in understanding and accepting this reality. We all need to look at the criminal justice system through new eyes. So, raising awareness about psychology and neuroscience research is critical. This work maps our flaws and shows us the way forward. It will take perseverance and courage, but our judicial system is flexible enough to respond to the new scientific evidence.

The good news is that researchers are devoting more and more attention not only to cataloguing our biases but also to controlling for them and even eliminating them. There's now evidence, for example, that implicit racial bias puts unarmed blacks at a significantly greater risk of being shot than unarmed whites, as well as evidence that police simulator training that emphasizes not shooting until certain can reduce errors. The training doesn't remove the underlying racial bias, however. To do that, scientists have been exploring an array of promising tactics. One successful approach is to show people images of well-known blacks with strong positive associations (like Martin Luther King Jr.) and well-known whites with strong negative associations (like Charles Manson) in order to disrupt racial stereotypes. Another involves presenting a vivid story in which participants are encouraged to imagine being badly hurt by a white assailant and rescued by a black man. Now that we know some of the key features of successful interventions, the challenge is to figure out how to make the debiasing stick. What's encouraging about this trend in research is that it greatly facilitates reform by explicitly testing solutions to the problems identified in this book.

Along with these new studies, a number of important real-world innovations are already under way—we've seen some in the preceding chapters—and others can be made right now. The fact that certain police departments have successfully switched to videotaping all interrogations from a third-party perspective, begun using cognitive-interview techniques when speaking to witnesses, and eliminated suggestive lineup procedures is proof that change is possible today. But we also need to devote attention to a broader reconceptualization of our criminal justice system in light of scientific insights, even as we acknowledge that this future-oriented work is inevitably somewhat speculative.

This book has explored the things about us that lead to unfairness, but we won't get where we want to go by focusing only on the ways we come up short. Human nature, while deeply flawed in some ways, is also a source of profound goodness. We are all capable of transformative compassion. And our greatest opportunity for achieving true justice is learning when to override our basic instincts and when to draw on our deep well of empathy.

Just because humans created the criminal justice system doesn't mean that we are ideal operators of its processes and institutions. Our natural limitations can prevent us from living up to our principles and achieving our goals. And the implication is that we need to reduce our legal system's reliance on human perception, memory, and judgment.

Many other fields—from election forecasting to traffic planning to eye surgery—have undergone a similar reckoning and realignment. Baseball teams that once picked players based on the intuitions of scouts now rely increasingly on statistical analyses to field winning teams. Pharmacists who once avoided dangerous drug interactions and allergies by relying on their memories and those of their customers now depend on programs that track prescription histories and offer automatic alerts.

Visit the Martin guitar factory in Nazareth, Pennsylvania, and you will learn that the company, which has prided itself on its handmade woodwork since 1833, decided a number of years ago that, in pursuit of the finest possible product, it should invest in a robot. The lacquer on the exterior of a guitar is only about twice the thickness of a human hair, which means that even a highly experienced worker who bears down just a little too hard on the polishing pad can easily burn right through to the raw wood, requiring a costly refinishing of the entire instrument. With its pressure-sensitive wheel and ability to execute exactly the same movements for each instrument, the polishing robot never makes that error. It was hard giving up human control, but to accomplish the company's core mission, it was the right decision, and those in charge weren't afraid to make it. As Dick Boak, a longtime employee, explains, "Because we have such a long heritage of hand craftsmanship we are always a little skeptical of new technologies. But where it makes sense for new technology to really work or improve the product we try to be open-minded."

We need to be similarly flexible in our quest for a more effective and enlightened criminal justice system. One of the best ways to address the unfairness that comes from the limitations of the human brain is simply to stop depending on human faculties. If we know that eyewitnesses are not very reliable and that judges often struggle to be objective, we need to think about how we can improve eyewitness identifications and reduce judicial bias, but we should also consider how we might avoid needing an eyewitness or a trial in the first place. Are there processes that we could simply do without?

One prime candidate, mentioned earlier, is the in-court witness identification. It is highly suggestive, regularly corrupted by earlier identification procedures, and given undue weight by jurors. Even prosecutors realize it's pure show. So let's cut the act.

Another candidate is the right of lawyers to remove jurors without cause before trial. The evidence suggests that rather than culling particularly biased jurors, attorneys use their peremptory strikes to tilt the jury to their side. Little would be lost by simply eliminating this ability. To address the failure of prosecutors to turn over evidence to the defense, we could have forensic reports automatically sent from the crime lab to the prosecution and defense at the same time, or have all police reports entered into an open-access file with no input or revision by the prosecution. You don't have to worry about dishonesty when there is no opportunity to be dishonest.

In many cases, we need to realize that technologies already exist that can reduce our dependence on fallible human faculties. When a murder occurred a few blocks from my house in Philadelphia, it was solved within a few days, not because witnesses came forward, but because several cameras captured the murderer going into the victim's house and driving by the home in his truck. With a proliferation of security cameras, an army of private citizens armed with smartphones, and more recording in interrogation rooms, squad cars, and prisons, the need to rely on the vagaries of human memory is greatly reduced. And the less dependent we are on eyewitness identifications and testimony, the less we have to place our trust in the ability of jurors to assess credibility. Although, as we've seen, videos are not panaceas, the broader benefits in combating wrongful convictions are significant: a video showing the license plate of the perpetrator's vehicle largely eliminates the possibility of a false confession or the chance that a photo of the bloody crime scene will sway a jury toward condemning an innocent man.

Improved forensic analysis may also play an important role. The closer we come to a world in which we can analyze DNA and other trace evidence in real time, based on limited or corrupted samples, the less we need to worry about many of the problems we've already discussed. Promising new technologies that can quickly close cases are already hitting the streets.

A few cities, for example, are experimenting with equipment that can pinpoint the precise location of a gunshot and automatically trigger a camera to swivel and record the perpetrator, freeing officers from having to rely on neighbors' flawed perceptions and foggy recollections, as well as ensuring that the police capture all incidents of gun violence.

Likewise, knowing that detectives often overlook critical evidence in the frenetic period following a crime and that memories of the scene can easily be distorted or quickly fade, in 2009 the New York Police Department began using the Panoscan, which captures a 360-degree view of the crime environment in high resolution. Months after a man is found bound and stabbed in his bed, the police can go back to the panoramic image and re-inspect every square inch of the room, from the shirts and jackets visible through the open closet door to the placement and condition of the five cigarette butts and cocaine on the table.

In another New York City innovation, the police department recently launched a smartphone pilot program that allows officers in the field to check, among other things, whether an apartment on a hallway they are walking down has been involved in an earlier domestic-violence report and whether a resident is a registered gun owner. Coming across an individual on the street, the officers in the program can immediately pull up her DMV and police records. With this technology, cops can get clear answers rather than having to rely on their faulty memories and dubious intuitions.

An officer who is called to an apartment because a neighbor has heard screaming, for instance, may have a vague recollection of a violent fight involving a PCP-addled man at that address. So, when the door is opened and a man shouts some expletives at him, the officer may assume that the man is a threat and take action that endangers both of them. With the smartphone, however, the officer can immediately look up the apartment number and see that he was wrong about the PCP incident—that was on the seventh floor. *This* apartment, according to the details recorded the last time the police were summoned, has a resident with severe Tourette's and schizophrenia who has no history of violence. With this data, the officer can properly address the situation without anyone getting hurt. Such technology does raise civil liberties concerns, but the tradeoff may be worth it if we can prevent officers from acting upon gut feelings that turn out to be baseless. Those mistakes often lead to liberty deprivations that are far more severe and lasting.

All that said, the best way to avoid known human biases or predictable errors in our criminal justice system may be to make changes outside of it. When confronted with a question like how to reduce the murder rate, we tend to recite the standard set of commonsense solutions: increase the number of officers in high-crime neighborhoods, crack down on drug gangs, and develop better tests to predict future violent behavior. But there may be other, less obvious responses that are more cost-effective and easily implemented. For example, a city could invest in trauma kits containing materials developed by the military for treating battlefield wounds and train all officers in how to address the major causes of preventable death in combat (a collapsed lung, airway obstruction, and hemorrhage from a limb), which also happen to be extremely common when someone has been shot in a drive-by or wounded in a robbery. Or we could have all hospitals and ambulances carry the inexpensive generic drug tranexamic acid, which is used to slow the bleeding of wounded soldiers—it's estimated that every year this simple change could save the lives of up to four thousand Americans who are the victims of violence. Before we go down the road of sanctioning invasive and problematic police actions to try to reduce gun violence (like "stop and frisk") or invest immense time and energy in developing neuro-recidivism predictors that may never be accurate, we should see if there's a simpler way to achieve our ultimate end: saving lives.

There are numerous opportunities for creative crime control

if we take a broader view of the problem. Researchers recently found that one of the major contributors to the decrease in robberies during the 1990s had to do with a seemingly unrelated policy change. The federal government had begun requiring states to disburse welfare payments through the Electronic Benefit Transfer system, which greatly reduced the amount of cash on the street, as beneficiaries started relying on debit cards. Less cash in circulation meant fewer cash-related crimes. The lesson? Sometimes those closest to the problem—cops, prosecutors, judges, and jurors—aren't in the best position to fix it.

Another promising approach is to limit the discretion of legal actors. As we've seen, when Supreme Court justices do research, they tend to sort through information in a biased fashion, finding exactly what they are looking for while avoiding and discounting contradictory data. Amicus briefs—filled with self-serving and misleading data—only make matters worse. So why not create an independent group, like Congress's Congressional Research Service, to provide reports on relevant topics to all the justices? This simple fix could combat judicial tunnel vision and ensure that all of the justices have access to the same data, which would make it harder to ignore conflicting evidence.

Likewise, given the tendency of experts to align their opinions with the side paying their fees, why not eliminate partisan expert witnesses? We could turn instead to independent witness panels funded jointly by the parties as part of normal court costs. And why not give those independent expert panels the ability to make binding decisions? We know that jurors don't understand the factors that can lead to memory distortions, so why do we allow them to decide whether a witness's identification or testimony is credible? If we care about accuracy, it makes little sense to give jurors the ability to decide for themselves whether to accept an expert opinion whole cloth or discard it entirely. Indeed, when a defendant invokes the insanity defense, it seems odd to permit expert testimony by psychologists on the key question of whether the accused was incapable of appreciating the nature of his criminal action, but then leave it to the jury (or, in some cases, the judge) to make the ultimate determination.

We should also consider establishing new protocols to channel behavior in the many situations where independent panels aren't feasible. With strong default best practices, cops, judges, prosecutors, and others could deviate where required but would know that they'd have to justify their actions later. Responding to the scene of a school shooting, for instance, police officers might stray from protocol by having a witness identify the man they had caught, but they would do so knowing that they would later have to articulate their reasons ("We needed to immediately determine if a killer was still active on the campus," for instance), and if the reasons were deemed insufficient (if, say, the crime scene was completely secure), the identification would not come before a jury. All too often people end up engaging in practices that we know are problematic—like using highly suggestive show-ups rather than live lineups—simply because it is convenient. We need to disrupt automatic behavior known to lead to bad outcomes and force people to challenge their working assumptions.

Computer programs can help by effectively "thinking" for legal actors during the moments when biases tend to arise and errors most often occur. So, for example, a smartphone app might guide a patrol officer securing a crime scene through an established set of procedures, with prompts at the points when errors are commonly made, much as a GPS program helps a driver navigate through an unknown city to a particular destination. Given the diffusion of responsibility in such hectic situations, the smartphone could force an officer to identify which other team members are in charge of various critical duties (recording the identities of witnesses at the scene, ensuring that evidence is preserved until detectives arrive, and so on) and then, in real time, list these officers' duties on their smartphones. An officer collecting witness information could then be prompted to take headshots, record initial statements, and enter names and phone numbers. An officer helping an injured victim could be walked through a series of quick checks designed to rule out life-threatening medical problems, avoiding the myopia that doomed David Rosenbaum.

This isn't science fiction; it only feels that way. Faced with a similarly grave threat, the aviation industry developed rigorous protocols and automated processes designed to avoid pilot error. Today, jetliner captains can disengage various autopilot functions and certain alerts when unusual circumstances call for a tailored approach. But for routine matters, they let established processes guide things, greatly reducing the risk of disaster. Yes, there is less human agency in the picture—many planes can now follow a flight path specified before takeoff without any intervention from the pilot—but few of us would complain that this is a step in the wrong direction. Indeed, it seems misguided to fret about the impact of such technology when the consequences of a mistake are so high. If we are comfortable with an e-mail program that warns us when we've forgotten to include an attachment we mentioned, why should we worry about technology that helps avoid plane crashes, accidental shootings, and wrongful convictions?

In the decades and centuries to come, we will have to decide how far we are willing to go in the quest to reduce our reliance on human cognition. One possibility is to dispose of live trials. I know this sounds radical, but hear me out.

If jurors and judges can be swayed by the attractiveness of a witness, a defendant's skin color, or the prosecutor's mannerisms, might it not make sense to one day move proceedings to a virtual environment, where participants interact through avatars designed to eliminate these biases? In most trials, there is no compelling reason for jurors to inspect the defendant, witness, or attorney in the flesh. And preventing jurors from doing so might yield significant benefits.

As was highlighted earlier, one way to reduce the possibility of jurors using inaccurate "tells" (like gaze aversion or jittery knees) to determine the credibility of a witness is to stop instructing them to focus on demeanor evidence. But a potentially more effective approach is simply to bar them from observing demeanor altogether. When there are no eyelids to monitor for excessive blinking, a juror or judge is forced to focus on what the witness actually says. And when you don't know if the defendant is black or white, slim or obese, old or young, attractive or unattractive, it is far less likely that biases grounded in these interpersonal differences will exert an influence. If you cannot hear a person's slow Southern drawl, you are much less likely to assume that the person is unintelligent or carries prejudices against African Americans.

It should not matter that the prosecutor has a particularly commanding presence in the courtroom or a charming way of speaking, or that the defendant has a generally dour expression or a strangely shaped head. And we should be willing to take bold action to address such a serious problem.

The virtual trial would help eliminate bias on the part of lawyers and judges as well. If they didn't know the demographic characteristics of the jurors, they would be less likely to make assumptions and treat them differently. And with the jury unable to see the lawyers, both prosecutors and defense attorneys might focus on making stronger arguments and probing more deeply into inconsistencies in witness statements rather than using body language, voice inflection, and wardrobe for maximum effect.

Introducing virtual trials would also be a boon for courtroom safety—eliminating the possibility of violence between defendants, witnesses, lawyers, and observers—as well as reducing the psychological strain entailed in providing in-court testimony or sitting on a jury. When I was called for jury service in Philadelphia, hearing the details of the crime—an alleged brutal beating that caused the victim brain damage—left me thinking about my own security. What was stopping one of the defendant's associates from following me home? And I realize that the discomfort I felt on that occasion is trivial compared with the fear experienced by victims and witnesses forced to testify face to face with the perpetrators of horrific acts of violence. As any district attorney will tell you, one of the major reasons that rape prosecutions are so difficult is that victims refuse to testify because they don't want to be in the same room as their attackers. With virtual testimony provided through avatars, the otherwise reluctant might feel comfortable enough to help put away dangerous individuals. And since all witnesses would likely feel less intimidated or nervous, it would also reduce the need for the rigorous rehearsal that can distort memories.

That comfort could be bolstered by standardizing the virtual environment of jurors, judges, witnesses, and attorneys. The simulated space of each trial—including the jury's vantage point on the witnesses, the color of the courtroom walls, the amount of light from windows, and the height of the judge's bench—would be uniform, so that all court participants would know exactly what to expect. There are almost certainly many other things besides the timing of lunch that affect verdicts and sentences—we just haven't yet identified them. The goal would be to remove all variability among trials, save for the particular facts and the law—the elements that are meant to determine the outcome.

All virtual trials could be recorded, which would greatly benefit appellate judges, who would be able to review exactly what jurors saw and heard. Today, they usually get only a typed transcript of lower court proceedings, and it can be very difficult to get a sense of the vital nuances of what happened at trial. Along with the recordings, we might consider instituting additional safeguards for the accused, such as the option of presenting the trial to multiple juries (possibly in lieu of an appeal). From a societal perspective, this would allow us the best possible opportunity to see whether our trials yield consistent results. And it might provide for more community engagement and increased transparency, by permitting far more people to observe the trial as it actually happens. In fact, criminal trials could even be broadcast through a court's website, supplementing the spotty error- and bias-checking done by attorneys and judges with crowdsourced oversight.

Even better, we could control juror bias directly by adopting a time delay between when attorneys present evidence and when it is broadcast. That way, if a lawyer's objection to particular testimony or a particular line of questioning is sustained, it wouldn't be presented to the jury at all. And a delay would allow judges to consider matters more deliberately, which could cut down on errors that lead to overturned verdicts and new trials.

The hurdles facing virtual adjudication are much lower than you might imagine. For one thing, the startup costs are likely to be dwarfed by the long-term benefits. With virtual courtrooms, major expenses like transportation and security would be drastically reduced. Indeed, when Pennsylvania officials elected to begin using video conferencing for some preliminary arraignments, warrant proceedings, and bail and sentencing hearings, they found that they saved $1.7 million each month. Freed from the logistical constraints of a physical courthouse, more cases could be heard each day, so poor defendants would spend less time locked up before trial, and the correctional system wouldn't have to spend so much to house them.

Similar technology already exists for conducting meetings and conferences, and virtual interactions are becoming commonplace. Increasingly, individuals separated by thousands of miles negotiate the details of multi-billion-dollar deals, manage international incidents, and coordinate military operations in real time. The sophistication and fluidity of exchanges can be astonishing. A soldier sitting at a computer in Nevada can help a Marine patrol take cover in the mountains of Afghanistan, monitor their exact movements with the help of infrared uniform patches, and instantly launch a missile from a Predator drone hovering fifteen thousand feet above them to take out an approaching pickup truck. On a smaller scale, surgeons working remotely have used robots to perform heart surgery, and every day psychologists see patients on Skype.

So, we must ask ourselves, if a doctor no longer needs to be in the same room with her patient, why is it so critical that a defendant be in the same room as the person he allegedly raped or shot or robbed? The traditional justifications—particularly that judges and jurors need to be able to take in a witness's entire demeanor—just do not stack up against the science. If our current legal rules prevent us from taking advantage of technological progress to remedy unfairness, we should reconsider those rules.

It is true that a virtual courtroom would remove a lot of the drama and excitement from the trial. But that is exactly the point: the elements that make for good television—bombastic attorneys, witnesses with shaky hands, and defendants seemingly unmoved by the tearful testimony of the victim—make for poor justice.

Of course, the virtual courtroom is but one of the criminal justice venues that could benefit from a redesign. Interrogations could also be conducted virtually, allowing for much better control over the factors that correlate with false confessions, as well as those that promote truthful testimony. The same is true of interviews with witnesses. Plus, with virtual technology, witnesses could be interviewed quickly and effectively wherever they happened to be.

Some virtual spaces are already being developed, with the virtual identification procedure leading the way. Lineups created, chosen, and administered by computers remove a major source of human bias. And there are yet other intriguing possibilities. What if we eliminated the prison and created a virtual corrections environment? Those convicted of crimes might continue to live in their homes and work at their jobs but be required to spend two hours every day in an immersive online space tailored to serve whatever ends we deemed best, whether deterrence, rehabilitation, or something else. The eventual payoff could be enormous. For one thing, we would no longer have to house, feed, and clothe most inmates, which would drastically reduce correctional costs. More critically, only the convict would experience the punishment, not his children, spouse, parents, and friends, as in the current system, and it would be only the punishment that we directly intended, not the assaults that plague today's prisons. Alternatively, what if we allowed the public access to virtual crime scenes in cold cases to encourage crowdsourced detective work? Some facts could be withheld for strategic purposes, but why not tap into the creative problem-solving abilities of millions of Americans? Leaving a case to a single cop seems ludicrous in this light. We need to look in new directions if we want to make a meaningful change to our system. We're limited only by our imaginations and our stubborn adherence to the way things have "always" been done.

If we are going to make our system of criminal justice fairer, we need to be less reliant on faulty human processes, but we also have to be more compassionate. We need to stop viewing the people we arrest, prosecute, convict, and imprison as evil and less than human, for that toxic combination drives us to hate and hurt, makes our brutish treatment seem justified, and does little to make us safer. We must challenge the structures that prevent us from seeing our commonalities, hide our shared goals, and dampen our empathy for our fellow human beings. And we must build new mechanisms that encourage us to understand the perspectives and situations of others.

Our criminal justice system is pervaded by powerful group divisions and defined by conflict: criminals versus cops, prosecutors versus defense attorneys, prisoners versus guards, the incarcerated versus the general public. And these dynamics are behind some of the worst injustice in our system. When police officers view the suspects they confront as despised enemies, with values that are diametrically opposed to their own, it makes it much easier to mistreat them, just as when prison guards view convicts in dehumanizing ways. Similarly, for all of its proclaimed benefits, the adversarial trial system also promotes an "us" versus "them" attitude that can encourage lawyers to cut corners and behave immorally. And our system of imprisonment itself acts as a potent force in confirming our sense that those inside are fundamentally different from the rest of us, and that we are locked in an eternal struggle: right versus wrong, good versus bad, order versus disorder.

It can be no surprise that members of the public fail to raise an eyebrow when a new, harsh mandatory sentence is handed down, or when a study suggesting endemic prison rape or deplorable living conditions is released, or when legislation is enacted that prevents parolees from living within the confines of a city, deprives them of their ability to vote, or stamps them with a permanent badge of ignominy. But these are terrible things. And if we stopped to think about our common humanity and shared destiny, we'd realize that they are directly at odds with our values and we would not stand for them.

How do we make an inherently adversarial system less adversarial?

We might start by helping police officers think differently about their mandate: rather than "Lock people up," it ought to be "Improve safety within communities." Some urban police forces have already found that recasting the role of the police officer from law enforcer to security promoter increases the willingness of private citizens to aid the police in their work. And encouraging understanding and sharing serves not only to help solve crimes but also to keep them from happening in the first place.

One recent example comes from what was once ground zero for antagonism between the police and the community: Watts, an impoverished neighborhood in South Los Angeles long known for its gang warfare and brutal confrontations between cops and residents. Hoping to reverse the tide, in 2011 the LAPD launched a new Community Safety Partnership to facilitate communication between concerned residents (including some former gang leaders) and police leadership. The two groups began coming together every Monday to discuss the status of gang feuds, investigations, and other safety matters affecting the neighborhood. The new level of understanding, trust, and respect has yielded tangible benefits, helping to defuse conflicts and reduce violent crime. In 2013, in fact, Los Angeles saw its lowest number of homicides since 1966. There are many factors at work, of course, but positive engagement between law enforcement and the public has been essential: treating people with respect and fairness really does make them more likely to respect the law in return.

We should continue to consider new ways to encourage police officers to see things from the perspective of the people in the districts they serve. And we ought to rethink certain well-intended policies that inadvertently reinforce powerful divisions between community members and police officers, including rules prohibiting police officers from serving in neighborhoods where they live or grew up (designed to avoid potential conflicts in which an officer must take an enforcement action against someone she knows).

We could adopt a similar approach in realigning the relationship between detectives and suspects. As we've seen, the commonly used Reid technique casts the two as adversaries. The resulting interrogations tend to be highly confrontational, focused on battering a suspect into submission and lying to him if necessary until he fesses up, which we know greatly increases the likelihood of a false confession. So, what if we recast the investigator's objective, from obtaining an admission of guilt to simply gathering reliable information? Rosy claims to the contrary, the emphasis in our current approach is not on reaching an accurate account of what happened. That's why detectives are permitted to offer the suspect potential motives and descriptions of how the crime went down—

even if they're entirely made up—to make it more psychologically palatable for him to accept responsibility. It's an effective way to get to "I did it," but it's a terrible way to get to the truth.

We need a renewed focus on accuracy. During the initial stages of an interview, a detective should simply ensure that the suspect provides a complete description of events. Even if the story begins to sound implausible, the detective shouldn't switch to trying to extract a confession but should instead redouble his efforts to gather as much information as possible by pointing out inconsistencies in the suspect's version of events. Those who are most vulnerable to suggestion and coercion—the young, the mentally ill, and those with intellectual disabilities—should be identified and treated with special care. As part of a collaboration between the police and psychologists, the United Kingdom revamped its own investigative questioning procedures along these lines. The reforms have not only reduced the likelihood of a suspect admitting to a crime he didn't commit, they've actually increased the amount of useful information that guilty suspects reveal.

It will be harder to alter our adversarial trial system because of the elaborate structures that it has spawned, but there is a promising way forward. One of the first steps is to reaffirm the existing principle that lawyers serve not only their clients but the system of justice as well. Prosecutors and defense attorneys are, in many ways, seeking the same thing: Innocent people should be exonerated. Guilty people should be convicted, but their sentences should be just. And all defendants should enjoy the most impartial and respectful treatment possible. Somehow that powerful common purpose—to figure out what really happened and reach a fair outcome through a fair process—has been lost. In the roar of the adversarial juggernaut, the prosecutor forgets that the defendant is a real person, and the defense comes to ignore the fact that a victim has been seriously hurt. Each side is encouraged to engage in dishonesty, and experts are used to mislead rather than clarify, which can lead to disastrous verdicts.

One solution is to remove the legal work of collecting and probing the evidence from partisan actors and place it in the hands of one or more independent authorities. Other countries show what's possible. In Germany, for instance, a prosecutor, tasked with uncovering evidence of both the defendant's guilt *and his innocence,* prepares a dossier of the case, but the presiding judge enjoys primary responsibility for gathering and sorting through the facts at trial, including examining witnesses. The adversarial approach is not a necessary component of a just legal system, and it's easy to overlook the fact that the spectacle of lawyerly confrontation, with shouted objections, opposing motions, and fiery speeches, is actually a rather late addition to Anglo-American criminal procedure. It was developed to ensure fairness, but in many respects it has had the opposite effect.

Most notably, the adversarial system has played an important role in the shift from quick and relatively straightforward proceedings to trials that are long and extremely complicated. And with lawyers constantly wrangling over procedural rules, it's no longer possible to provide regular trials to everyone charged with a crime. We just don't have the resources, which has led us to rely heavily on the plea bargain. In nine out of ten cases today, as we've seen, the accused waives his right to trial in exchange for a lighter punishment. That means that only one person in ten gets an independent judgment of his case. Only one in ten enjoys the presumption of innocence and the right to cross-examine his accusers. Only one in ten is provided with the privilege against self-incrimination.

Constitutional protections do not apply in plea negotiations. And this is particularly consequential because, in plea bargaining, the prosecutor enjoys a tremendous amount of discretion, taking on all the key roles: accuser, investigator, adjudicator, and sentencer. This concentration of authority inevitably leads to unequal treatment and unfairness. Blacks taking pleas end up with harsher sentences than if they were white. People committing a crime in one area of the state receive probation, while those perpetrating the same acts a few miles away are incarcerated. And, as we've seen, innocent parties can be compelled to plead guilty if they perceive the risk of going to trial as too high. When that happens, not only do we send an innocent person to prison, but we also close the case, which means that the police stop looking for the guilty party.

The plea bargain, then, is best likened not to a shortcut but to a short circuit of our constitutional guarantees of due process. This presents a profound irony: while the adversarial system was introduced to protect defendants, the overwhelming resource requirements of that system have helped to drive a shift to plea bargaining, which has far fewer safeguards than a non-adversarial trial.

In light of this reality, we need to abandon the widely held belief that the truth is best revealed through a vigorous clash of zealous partisans armed with an imposing arsenal of technical legal rights, rules, and procedures. The resulting battles are dramatic, but they do not lead inevitably to justice—particularly given that their costly nature has forced us to resort to ugly backroom deal-making. It seems no coincidence that in countries with largely non-adversarial systems, plea bargains tend to be much rarer.

To begin to address the negative effects of the adversarial process, we should not only bolster existing norms that encourage lawyers to think of the common good but also develop new professional rules that firmly articulate that winning is not the ultimate end for prosecutors or defense attorneys. Causing an innocent man to be convicted is clearly wrong and shameful, yes, but so is helping a guilty man go free. Avoiding these outcomes should be a primary concern for lawyers on both sides. Indeed, a prosecutor who discovers and reveals evidence that a defendant is innocent should be celebrated and congratulated. As part of this process, it may be helpful to look, again, at Germany, where the prosecutor is seen as the "watchman of the law," with the role of providing an objective presentation of the facts.

With respect to prison guards and prisoners, too, we might find inspiration across the Atlantic. In the United States, the job of the corrections officer is akin to that of a kennel worker or zoo-keeper. The division between the keeper and the kept is absolute, and the task is clear: secure the animals in their cages. According to the Texas Department of Criminal Justice, the "essential functions" of a guard include counting, feeding, and supervising the inmates; restraining those who are combative, using force when necessary; and responding to emergencies like escapes and injuries. As we've seen, in northern Europe, by contrast, corrections officers are more like social workers. They take courses in educational theory, ethics, psychology, and conflict management, which help them to serve as mentors and role models. Rather than minimize direct contact with inmates, they seek opportunities for engagement: corrections officers play sports and music with those they supervise; they offer counseling and provide learning opportunities. Most important, they treat inmates with respect. We need to embrace a similar ethos in the United States: that guards and prisoners are united in a shared endeavor to help the prisoner remedy the harm he has inflicted, address the underlying causes of his criminal behavior, and prepare him to reintegrate into society. Our corrections hiring should target people well suited to rehabilitative work rather than disciplinarians ready for a fight.

We should also reduce the impenetrable divide between the public and the prison population. Although certain types of offenders are quite appropriately kept separate from the general public, many would benefit from closer ties with outside society. And the rest of us would benefit, too. If those convicted of crimes will walk among us again, we must begin preparing them today. We ought to help prisoners maintain family connections, allowing frequent interaction with loved ones so that they have support when they return. There is no justification for callous and shortsighted policies like limiting an inmate to a single phone call to his kids once every two weeks. Destroying families doesn't prevent crime; it engenders it.

We should also foster links between offenders and employers so that most inmates have jobs when they reenter the labor market. There is strong evidence that ensuring stable employment is one of the best ways to prevent reoffending: former inmates with steady jobs are up to 40 percent less likely to end up back in prison. Employment does more than allow a person to support himself without returning to crime; it also enables him to build connections with those who model conventional, law-abiding behavior. Day-pass employment of prisoners in local businesses, leading to permanent positions after their release, is realistic if we make it safe and profitable with the aid of government subsidies or insurance.

On a related note, we should make full restoration of the rights of citizenship a goal for every prisoner. Today, even after someone has repaid his debt to society, his criminal record continues to hold him back in countless ways. Roughly nine out of ten employers look into the criminal histories of the people they are considering hiring. And criminal records are also used to deny people welfare benefits, rental housing, loans, and voting rights. The problem is that although a person's criminal record stays with him forever, its usefulness in predicting reoffending decreases significantly over time. Across a range of offenses, experts have tracked what they call the "point of redemption"—usually three to seven years after the crime—at which time a previous arrest ceases to make an individual more likely to be rearrested than someone in the general population. We can't tie anchors around people's waists, toss them in the deep end, and expect them to swim. If our goal really is for those who have committed crimes to become productive citizens, we've got to give them *more* help than other people, not less.

Eliminating the sharp, adversarial divisions within our criminal justice system and cultivating empathy raises an intriguing question: why not get rid of blame as an organizing principle altogether? Why not instead treat crime like a public-health issue—an epidemic that we are all fighting together?

The more we understand the genetic and environmental factors that shape criminal behavior, the more it looks like a disease, and the less our current framework of ascribing moral responsibility appears justifiable. We're told that horrible acts reflect wicked dispositions and bad, but voluntary, choices. We're told that offenders are worthy of condemnation because they knowingly disregard the rules in pursuit of their own repugnant desires. But that just doesn't mesh with a nuanced understanding of human behavior.

It is not a coincidence that roughly a third to a half of the American prison population suffers from serious mental disorders. It is not a coincidence that those who are incarcerated are disproportionately uneducated, poor, and survivors of childhood abuse and neglect. And while we already acknowledge that some harmful acts are not the product of free will—the man whose sudden seizure causes him to drop his baby cannot be said to have chosen to assault his child—the lines we draw between compelled behavior and voluntary, intentional conduct are a convenient fiction. They simply reflect the divide between the unmistakable, documented influences on human actions and the determinants that remain hidden. The fact that it is very difficult to figure out the particular nexus of factors that led a person to pull that trigger, kick in that back door, or write that bad check does not mean that he freely chose to commit a crime.

We need to quit wasting our time trying to sort out who *really* deserves blame. But how might we proceed? There is no quick and easy path through the thicket of laws, practices, and beliefs that take the existence of rational actors, good and evil, as a given.

We can start by acknowledging that removing blame from our

criminal justice system doesn't mean that harmful conduct would suddenly become acceptable or that people who commit crimes would suddenly be free from sanction. The idea that if we stopped vilifying the criminal we'd have to treat rape victims and rapists exactly the same way is entirely false. Even without a legal framework grounded in personal volition and culpability, a serial rapist has still committed terrible acts that we would rightfully denounce, and we might very well prevent that person from interacting with society for the rest of his life. But we'd no longer subject individuals to poor treatment and contempt on the grounds that they're bad people who deserve it. We'd get out of the payback business. Instead, we'd focus on remedying the harm, rehabilitating the criminal, discouraging others from taking similar actions, and treating the conditions that precipitated the crime in the first place.

This may sound revolutionary, but it's really not so different from how we handle outbreaks of disease. When a dangerous virus overwhelms a town, causation is relevant, but blame isn't. We don't treat someone who has contracted Ebola or dengue fever as sinful. We get to work restoring the person's health, preventing new cases, and trying to eliminate root causes.

As we've seen, that basic model is already being embraced in certain countries. Innovative prisons like Halden show us what's possible. And Americans, too, might come to view prisons more as hospitals, with the focus on "treating" the underlying factors that lead to offending and quarantining certain individuals who pose a particular threat to the public and are incurable.

Indeed, there is strong precedent in the United States for moving the criminal justice system away from blame. In the early twentieth century, juvenile courts were created with the idea that the state should not be a retributive punisher of delinquent children but rather a guardian of their interests. The moral responsibility of the child became irrelevant; the focus was placed instead on rehabilitation. Unfortunately, in the intervening decades, juvenile proceedings lost this compassionate edge and came to look much like their adult counterparts.

Yet there are hopeful signs that the impulse to deemphasize blame may again be catching on. In response to the failure of our legal system to address drug relapses, mental health problems, and high levels of reoffending, a number of jurisdictions have begun experimenting with community-based programs that reject a model of corrections focused on vigorous prosecution and harsh punishment. One of the most notable developments has been the emergence over the last two decades of problem-solving courts, which divert offenders away from the single revolving door of the prison toward a forum where they receive tailored treatment based on their history of mental illness, drug abuse, or prostitution. The underlying theory is that you cannot prevent reoffending unless you work to understand and address the true sources of criminal behavior, like addiction or schizophrenia. So, rather than acting as adversaries, keeping one another at arm's length, the prosecutor, defense attorney, and judge work collaboratively to come up with a plan of treatment and monitoring. Offenders are not seen as evil people who deserve to suffer, but rather as individuals with serious long-term problems, who merit realistic expectations and compassion. Drugs courts, for example, treat addiction as a disease and accept that those who are addicted to drugs will, in all likelihood, relapse. As a result, the zero tolerance and harsh reprimand systems inside prisons—and built into normal parole procedure—make little sense. Problem-solving courts instead use empirically validated techniques to modify behavior, like ratcheting up minor sanctions after repeated failures (including community service, more drug testing, fees, homework, and occasional jail time) and employing simple reinforcement techniques.

And it works. Research shows that the more humane approach of problem-solving courts—based not on hurting offenders in proportion to their wrongdoing but on helping them according to their needs—is more effective than highly punitive alternatives.

Those who come before mental health courts are less likely to reoffend, less likely to commit more serious offenses when they do, and more likely to experience improvement in their mental health. Drug courts get similarly high marks on reducing recidivism and drug use, as well as on cost-effectiveness.

With more than three thousand problem-solving courts now operating in the United States—and others in countries as diverse as Jamaica, Brazil, New Zealand, and England—the future looks bright. Yet they still handle only a very small fraction of the people who come through the criminal justice system. And the major question is why all offenders don't deserve similar treatment. We need to make a better case for reform across the board.

One of the great benefits of removing blame from the system is that it allows us to turn to things we've been neglecting, like ensuring the healing of those harmed by crimes, including victims and their families, witnesses, and community members. Victims shouldn't be pushed to the side and treated as mere pieces of evidence—they should be respected as integral parts of the proceedings. It makes little sense that the U.S. Constitution focuses so much attention on the rights of the accused and convicted but fails to offer any protections to victims. They should be permitted an active role in the various parts of a case, from initial hearings to plea bargains to sentencing and even post-conviction. The legal system should ask victims what they need to mend and work to achieve those ends. In some cases, that may mean facilitating apologies and aiding victims in forgiving those who have committed crimes against them. Recent research suggests that such actions can be far more effective at repairing the harm than retributive punishment of the offender. In fact, granting forgiveness may provide a victim with a heightened sense of justice and fairness, as well as improved psychological well-being. In other cases, catering to a victim's needs may mean figuring out how the perpetrator can provide restitution. Even if offenders are not treated as blameworthy, they ought to mitigate the impact of what they've done. If you broke a glass while visiting a friend, it wouldn't matter if it was a complete accident: you would still help pick up the pieces, and if it had any real value, you would probably offer to replace it.

Perhaps the biggest consequence of moving away from a blame-based criminal justice system is a shift in societal resources from punishing crime to preventing it. Giving up a blame mindset lays the groundwork for transferring tax dollars from prisons and courts to schools, neighborhood improvement initiatives, and mental health care. A single death-penalty case, from arrest to execution, costs a state government between $1 million and $3 million. The average cost of housing an inmate in a supermax prison is approximately $75,000 a year. Justice is a finite resource: we have only so much money, so much time, and so much empathy. Should we spend such a large portion of what we have on trials and punishments? The fact that we still err despite our massive investments only strengthens the case for intervening before crimes are ever committed.

When we prevent a crime from occurring, we avoid nearly every one of the problems identified in this book. Yet we tend to think about criminal justice only after the fact. We wait for the shot to be fired. We wait for the claim of police brutality or the allegation of prosecutorial misconduct. We convince ourselves that reacting is just as good—that executing a criminal balances the scales of justice for the loss of the murder victim; that providing an appeal ensures that any error made during an investigation or trial can be set right. But that is always wrong. By focusing on responding, our criminal justice system always comes up short. Ask any murder victim's parent: no punishment can make up for what has been lost. And many criminals are never caught at all.

Moreover, we can expect to identify only a tiny percentage of the mistakes, biases, and acts of dishonesty marring the work of police officers, judges, jurors, and others. Most who have been wronged will never know it. Even if they do find out, the opportunity to remedy the problem is severely restricted: people often aren't aware of their rights, there aren't enough competent attorneys to file complaints and appeals, and there's frequently no hard evidence to convince a judge to address the issue. In only 5 to 10 percent of all cases, for example, is there a biological sample for DNA testing. And if a judge, two decades down the line, by some miracle, does acknowledge a suggestive eyewitness identification or a coercive interrogation and overturns a sentence, we still can't call it justice, for we placed an innocent man in a closet-sized cell for twenty years of his life.

The strongest argument for shifting resources toward prevention is simple fairness: we profess to care deeply about equality, but certain people have a much greater chance of ending up as criminals, and as victims. There is nothing inevitable about this. It is a lie to say that a significant rate of crime is unavoidable and that we must simply accept the status quo of thousands of people being shot and robbed and raped. The question is, how much do we care about other people—the unlucky ones? And how willing are we to invest in changing the environments that encourage criminality? Eliminating blame from our criminal justice system will push us in the right direction, because blame is often our best excuse for doing nothing.

The reforms I have suggested are only a small fraction of the possibilities, and whether we choose to pursue them will have less to do with our natural limitations than with our commitment to equal justice under the law. While some solutions require significant restructuring and long-term planning, many innovations in police protocol, rules of procedure, courtroom design, and our legal code are well within our reach today.

Unfortunately, when it comes to law, we have a particularly strong resistance to change and tend to believe that those before us were more enlightened and less fallible. We fetishize our Founding Fathers and the learned jurists of old. We treat the frameworks they developed as optimal, incapable of improvement, and we therefore deny the very possibility of reform. But if they were alive today, the visionaries of yesteryear would have quite different visions. And our laws and legal practices are just as likely to benefit from the centuries of progress—and, yes, science—as building design, medicine, and transportation. To think that Henry Ford would build the same Model T today is absurd. And yet we convince ourselves that James Madison would deliver an identical copy of the Bill of Rights—and that other modernizers of the criminal justice system would choose to disregard the latest research on human behavior if they were our contemporaries. But why? Why should law be different?

In Montgomery, Alabama, in 1965, Martin Luther King Jr. asserted that "the arc of the moral universe is long, but it bends toward justice." And it might seem safe to assume that the unfairness explored in this book will be stamped out in society's ceaseless and inevitable march forward. Ten thousand years ago, there was no court or trial to ensure that a man accused of murder received due process—justice was the end of a spear. One thousand years ago, proof of guilt was revealed when a woman's hand festered after being burned with a hot iron. One hundred years ago, black citizens could be barred from the jury box, bar, and bench on account of the color of their skin. And ten years ago, it was legal in the United States to execute someone who had committed his crime before he was eighteen. Progress, certainly—but this has been no unbroken advance. It has been a journey, uphill and against the wind. It has entailed detours and backtracking—and our current vantage point has much to do with chance. History makes clear that our next destination may, or may not, lie up the mountain.

The decline of the trial by ordeal—the starting point of this book—was not brought about because people suddenly realized that dipping men and women into water to see if they float was a poor way to assess innocence. It disappeared because the Catholic Church hierarchy decided that commanding God to work miracles in the service of a human judicial system violated biblical principles. And what replaced the ordeal was not a system of evidence and reason but something arguably less accurate and humane than what had come before: judicial torture. For roughly the next half millennium, when a person was strongly suspected of a serious crime, but there were no witnesses, he would be broken on the rack or subjected to the thumbscrew to elicit a confession. Like those who had administered the ordeal, the officials in charge did not see themselves as cruel or unjust. Like us, they constructed an elaborate structure of seemingly objective rules and procedures that affirmed their righteousness and impartiality.

Yet we are different from those who came before. And what sets us apart is not the virtue of our current laws—our plea-bargain system, for one, gives innocent defendants a "choice" that's not so different from that offered under judicial torture—but rather our *potential* for virtue.

It would have taken an exceptional person to stand in the common crowd at Soissons as Clement was thrown into the vat and spot injustice. What would have inspired doubt? And what resources would he have had to nurture it and help it spread afield? What evidence could he have mustered? Who would have listened? At a time without mass communication or centralized government, even the most passionate and resolute reformer could not have expected to have much of an impact.

We enjoy magnificent advantages over our forebears in the quest to remedy unfairness. We know much more than they did about human behavior, we possess amazing technologies to track, address, and prevent problems, and we have a greatly enhanced capacity to coordinate actions that affect millions of people.

But for it to matter, we must act.

The arc of history does not bend toward justice unless we bend it.

# Acknowledgments

*Nobody cares about criminal law except theorists
and habitual criminals.*
—SIR HENRY MAINE

If you go by the last century of news stories, novels, and movies, Sir Henry's statement ranks up there with the 1962 Decca Records verdict that "the Beatles have no future in show business." But Sir Henry was right on a certain level: although people may be enthralled by criminal law, they don't really *care* about it. On a list of major concerns, the state of our criminal justice system has, until very recently, come well down the line. A string of highly publicized errors, failures, and abuses has drawn sudden attention to the topic. But most people don't know what's really going on.

I set out to write this book because I became convinced that the truth about our legal system could not remain confined to the academics who studied it or those unfortunate souls who suffered under it; the general public needed to confront the hidden unfairness.

My path was greatly facilitated by numerous scientists and scholars whose work grounds this book. In this illustrious group, Jon Hanson deserves special mention: he introduced me to the field of law and mind sciences and opened my eyes to an array of problems I had never considered. His kindness, brilliance, and generosity changed the trajectory of my professional life: without him, I wouldn't be a law professor.

I am also deeply grateful to my editor, Amanda Cook. It is hard to imagine a more dedicated, tireless, and thoughtful guardian for this project. Her efforts—and those of her star assistant editor, Emma Berry—have made the book sharper, clearer, and more engaging. With her deft touch and keen instincts, Katya Rice taught me the value of a terrific copyedit. And I owe much to the entire team at Crown who brought the book to market.

I thank Will Lippincott, my agent and friend, whose constant support, strong advocacy, and wise counsel have helped me navigate the world of publishing, and everyone at Lippincott Massie McQuilkin for keeping things on course.

I am indebted to the efforts of a true honor roll of research assistants: Jessica Acheson, Justine Baakman, Kathleen Bichner, Louis Casadia, John Corcoran, Nathaniel Crider, Andrew Davis, Mallory Deardorff, Tudor Farcas, Kyle Gray, Claudia Hage, Seth Haynes, William Holland, Rachel Horton, Patrick Mulqueen, Alexandra Rogin, and Patrick Woolford. Their enthusiasm and hard work kept me going when the mountains of research studies and books seemed to grow taller with each step I took. More broadly, I thank students in my Criminal Law course and my Law and Mind Sciences seminar who challenged me to rethink my assumptions and look at old material with fresh eyes.

I am also grateful for the diligent assistance of the librarians and staff of the Drexel Legal Research Center, including Sunita Balija, John Cannan, Steven Thorpe, and especially Lindsay Steussy, for helping track down a wide range of material with admirable speed and efficiency. Jerry Arrison deserves special accolades for his assistance in making my dream of online endnotes a reality.

For their help and encouragement, I thank my colleagues at Drexel and Brooklyn Law, as well as an army of friends who read parts of the proposal and manuscript, guided me toward useful sources, and provided invaluable advice, in particular Adam Alter, Dena Gromet, Peter Leckman, Catherine Price, Dominic Tierney, and Benjamin Wallace-Wells. My collaborator Geoff Goodwin has played an especially prominent role in shaping my thoughts on the book's core topics. He is as rigorous and bright a scientist as I've met, and I have learned a tremendous amount from him, not because we always agree on things, but because frequently we don't. Our research on punishment was supported by a generous grant from the National Science Foundation, to which I am very grateful.

One of the corollaries to the discussion on the biological and environmental causes of criminal behavior is that our *positive* actions are also indelibly shaped by our families. This book is no exception. I know how lucky I am to have been born into such a wonderful, encouraging, and loving home. Jay, Beth, and Nate, I would not have had the diverse interests, grit, and intelligence to write this book without your presence in my life. I also thank my extended family for their support, including my grandmother, Lenore, a poet, who at ninety still writes me weekly letters: whether genetic or learned, her passion for the written word runs in my veins.

This book is dedicated to my wife, Brooke, and my daughter, Mira. Brooke, you are an amazing woman, my greatest champion, and my greatest comfort. Mira, you are the most wondrous person I've ever met. I love you both more than you can know. My major regret is that my sacrifices in writing this book fell on your shoulders as well. But they were also sacrifices for you: I want you both to live in a better world than the one we have.

# A Note on Sources

Authors of nonfiction for a general audience face a difficult trade-off as they put together their endnotes and bibliographies: brevity (*but* a lack of completeness and reduced usefulness for those who seek additional insight) or thoroughness (*but* lots of extra pages that can scare readers away and push up the price)? The vast majority choose brevity, but after thinking hard about this dilemma, I realized that I didn't actually have to choose.

In the pages that follow, I include a comprehensive list for each chapter of the sources that I drew upon directly or consulted while writing the book. I've also created a set of detailed endnotes that are available online. These notes are designed to provide exact citations as well as added nuance—including supplemental facts, counterevidence, and related research. I've tried to include active links wherever possible so that readers can access sources with ease.

I think transparency is an important value in both science and law. And I hope the result is a book that provides far more information on sources than most offerings aimed at a broad audience while being easier to use than academic books that require frequent flipping between main text and endnotes.

To access the extended notes, just go to www.adambenforado .com/unfair.

# Bibliography

INTRODUCTION

Almanzar, Yolanne. "27 Years Later, Case Is Closed in Slaying of Abducted Child." *New York Times*, December 16, 2008.

Aviv, Rachel. "The Science of Sex Abuse." *New Yorker*, January 14, 2013.

Balko, Radley. "Trial by Ordeal: The Surprising Accuracy of the Dark Ages' Trial by Fire Rituals." Reason.com, February 1, 2010. http://reason.com/archives/2010/02/01/trial-by-ordeal.

Bartlett, Robert. *Trial by Fire and Water: The Medieval Judicial Ordeal.* Oxford: Clarendon, 1986.

Benton, John F., ed. *Self and Society in Medieval France: The Memoirs of Abbot Guibert of Nogent (1064?–c. 1125).* New York: Harper & Row, 1970.

Brown, Peter. "Society and the Supernatural: A Medieval Change." *Daedalus* 104, no. 2 (1975): 133–51.

Cancer.net. "Brain Tumor: Symptoms and Signs." Last modified June 2013. http://www.cancer.net/cancer-types/brain-tumor/symptoms-and-signs.

Center for Sex Offender Management. *What You Need to Know About Sex Offenders.* Center for Effective Public Policy, 2008.

Centers for Disease Control and Prevention. *10 Leading Causes of Death by Age Group Highlighting Unintentional Injury Deaths, United States: 2011.* Accessed November 2, 2014. http://www.cdc.gov/injury/wisqars/pdf/10lcid_unintentional_deaths_2010-a.pdf.

Colman, Rebecca V. "Reason and Unreason in Early Medieval Law." *Journal of Interdisciplinary History* 4, no. 4 (1974): 571–91.

Cooper, Alexia, and Erica L. Smith. U.S. Department of Justice. *Homicide Trends in the United States, 1980–2008: Annual Rates for 2009 and 2010.* November 2011.

Diamond, Jared. "That Daily Shower Can Be a Killer." *New York Times*, January 28, 2013.

Eagleman, David. "What Our Brains Can Teach Us." *New York Times*, February 22, 2013.

Feresin, Emiliano. "Italian Court Reduces Murder Sentence Based on Neuroimaging Data." *Nature News Blog,* September 1, 2011. http://blogs.nature.com/news/2011/09/italian_court_reduces_murder_s.html.

Garrett, Brandon L. *Convicting the Innocent: Where Criminal Prosecutions Go Wrong.* Cambridge, MA: Harvard University Press, 2012.

Glaberson, William. "Man at Heart of Megan's Law Convicted of Her Grisly Murder." *New York Times,* May 31, 1997.

Greely, Henry T. "Law and the Revolution in Neuroscience: An Early Look at the Field." *Akron Law Review* 42 (2009): 687–715.

Greene, Joshua, and Jonathan Cohen. "For the Law, Neuroscience Changes Nothing and Everything." *Philosophical Transactions of the Royal Society B: Biological Sciences* 359 (2004): 1775–85.

Gross, Samuel R., Barbara O'Brien, Chen Hu, and Edward Kennedy. "Rate of False Conviction of Criminal Defendants Who Are Sentenced to Death." *Proceedings of the National Academy of Sciences* (2014): 7230–35.

Gross, Samuel R., and Michael Shaffer. *Exonerations in the United States, 1989–2012.* National Registry of Exonerations, June 2012.

Hamzelou, Jessica. "Brain Scans Reduce Murder Sentence in Italian Court." *New Scientist,* September 1, 2011.

Howland, Arthur C., ed. *Ordeals, Compurgation, Excommunication, and Interdict.* Philadelphia: University of Pennsylvania, 1901.

Innocence Project. "DNA Exonerations Nationwide." Accessed March 18, 2014. http://www.innocenceproject.org/Content/DNA_Exonerations_Nationwide.php.

Innocence Project. "DNA Exoneree Case Profiles." Accessed March 18, 2014. http://www.innocenceproject.org/know/.

Innocence Project. *200 Exonerated, Too Many Wrongfully Convicted.* New York: Benjamin N. Cardozo School of Law, Yeshiva University.

Innocence Project. "Unreliable or Improper Forensic Science." Accessed May 28, 2014. http://www.innocenceproject.org/understand/Unreliable-Limited-Science.php.

Kahneman, Daniel. *Thinking, Fast and Slow.* New York: Farrar, Straus & Giroux, 2011.

Kang, Jerry. "Trojan Horses of Race." *Harvard Law Review* 118 (2005): 1489–1593.

Kassin, Saul M., Steven A. Drizin, Thomas Grisso, Gisli H. Gudjonsson, Richard A. Leo, and Allison D. Redlich. "Police-Induced Confessions: Risk Factors and Recommendations." *Law and Human Behavior* 34 (2010): 3–38.

Kerr, Margaret H., Richard D. Forsyth, and Michael J. Plyley. "Cold Water and Hot Iron: Trial by Ordeal in England." *Journal of Interdisciplinary History* 22, no. 4 (1992): 573–94.

Kuran, Timur, and Cass R. Sunstein. "Availability Cascades and Risk Regulation." *Stanford Law Review* 51 (1999): 683–768.

Lancaster, Roger N. "Sex Offenders: The Last Pariahs." *New York Times*, August 20, 2011.

Lea, Henry Charles. *The Ordeal*. Philadelphia: University of Pennsylvania Press, 1973.

Leeson, Peter. "Justice, Medieval Style: The Case That 'Trial by Ordeal' Actually Worked." *Boston Globe*, January 31, 2010.

Leeson, Peter T. "Ordeals." *Journal of Law and Economics* 55 (2012): 691–714.

Levenson, Jill S., and Leo P. Cotter. "The Effect of Megan's Law on Sex Offender Reintegration." *Journal of Contemporary Criminal Justice* 21, no. 1 (2005): 49–66.

Loewenstein, George F., Elke U. Weber, Christopher K. Hsee, and Ned Welch. "Risk as Feelings." *Psychological Bulletin* 2 (2001): 267–86.

McAlhany, Joseph. Monodies *and* On the Relics of Saints: *The Autobiography and a Manifesto of a French Monk from the Time of the Crusades*. Translated by Jay Rubenstein. New York: Penguin, 2011.

"Megan's Law Website." Pennsylvania State Police. Accessed November 2, 2014. http://www.pameganslaw.state.pa.us/History.aspx?dt=.

National Conference of State Legislatures. *State Statutes Related to Jessica's Law*. Accessed November 3, 2014. http://www.leg.state.vt.us/WorkGroups/sexoffenders/NCSLs_Jessicas_Law_Summary.pdf.

Palmer, Robert C. "Trial by Ordeal." *Michigan Law Review* 87 (1989): 1547–56.

Pilarczyk, Ian C. "Between a Rock and a Hot Place: The Role of Subjectivity and Rationality in the Medieval Ordeal by Hot Iron." *Anglo-American Law Review* 25 (1996): 87–112.

Prichard, James C. *The Life and Times of Hincmar, Archbishop of Rheims*. London: A. A. Masson, 1849.

Rottenstreich, Yuval, and Christopher K. Hsee. "Money, Kisses, and Electric Shocks: On the Affective Psychology of Risk." *Psychological Science* 12 (2001): 185–90.

Rubenstein, Jay. *Guibert of Nogent: Portrait of a Medieval Mind*. New York: Routledge, 2002.

Sample, Ian. "US Courts See Rise in Defendants Blaming Their Brains for Criminal Acts." *Guardian*, November 10, 2013.

"Sex Laws Unjust and Ineffective." *Economist*, August 6, 2009.

Slovic, Paul. " 'If I Look at the Mass I Will Never Act': Psychic Numbing and Genocide." *Judgment and Decision Making* 2 (2007): 79–95.

Slovic, Paul. *The Perception of Risk*. London: Earthscan, 2000.

Slovic, Paul. "Perception of Risk." *Science* 236 (1987): 280–85.

Slovic, Paul, John Monahan, and Donald G. MacGregor. "Violence Risk Assessment and Risk Communication: The Effects of Using Actual Cases, Providing Instruction, and Employing Probability Versus Frequency Formats." *Law and Human Behavior* 24 (2000): 271–96.

Slovic, Paul, and Ellen Peters. "Risk Perception and Affect." *Current Directions in Psychological Science* 15 (2006): 322–25.

Slovic, Paul, and Daniel Västfjäll. "The More Who Die, the Less We Care: Psychic Numbing and Genocide." In *Behavioural Public Policy*, edited by Adam J. Oliver. Cambridge: Cambridge University Press, 2013.

Sunstein, Cass R. "Book Review: Misfearing: A Reply." *Harvard Law Review* 119 (2006): 1110–25.

Sunstein, Cass R. "Terrorism and Probability Neglect." *Journal of Risk and Uncertainty* 26 (2003): 121–36.

Tewksbury, Richard, and Matthew Lees. "Perceptions of Sex Offender Registration: Collateral Consequences and Community Experiences." *Sociological Spectrum* 26 (2006): 309–34.

U.S. Department of Transportation. *Traffic Safety Facts: 2012 Data: Children*. Washington, DC: National Highway Traffic Safety Administration, 2014.

U.S. Sentencing Commission. *Sentence Length in Each Primary Offense Category*. 2011.

*United States v. Garsson*. 291 F. 646 (S.D.N.Y. 1923).

"Witch Village." *Monty Python and the Holy Grail*. DVD. Directed by Terry Gilliam and Terry Jones. Culver City, CA: Columbia TriStar Home Entertainment, 2001.

Youth Villages. "In Child Sex Abuse, Strangers Aren't the Greatest Danger, Experts Say." *Science Daily*, April 13, 2014. http://www.sciencedaily.com/releases/2012/04/120413100854.htm.

Zgoba, Kristen. *Megan's Law: Assessing the Practical and Monetary Efficacy*. New Jersey Department of Corrections, 2008.

## 1. THE LABELS WE LIVE BY ~ THE VICTIM

Accuracy Project. "David Rosenbaum." Last modified January 1, 2012. http://www.accuracyproject.org/cbe-Rosenbaum,David.html.

Adams, Cindy. "Trayvon Martin Killing to Be Investigated by Federal

Authorities." Examiner.com, March 19, 2012. http://www.examiner.com/article/trayvon-martin-killing-to-be-investigated-by-federal-authorities.

Alter, Adam. "Why It's Dangerous to Label People." *Psychology Today,* May 17, 2010. http://www.psychologytoday.com/blog/alternative-truths/201005/why-its-dangerous-label-people.

Blockshopper.com. "3824 Harrison Street NW in Washington-Friendship Heights Sold for $1,000,000." December 18, 2006. http://dc.blockshopper.com/sales/cities/washington-friendship_heights/property/18510064/3824_harrison_street_nw/1351355.

Brainline.org. "What Is the Glasgow Coma Scale?" Accessed February 13, 2014. http://www.brainline.org/content/2010/10/what-is-the-glasgow-coma-scale.html.

Briggs, Steven, and Tara Opsal. "The Influence of Victim Ethnicity on Arrest in Violent Crimes." *Criminal Justice Studies: A Critical Journal of Crime, Law, and Society* 25, no. 2 (2012): 177–89.

Callan, Mitchell J., Rael J. Dawtry, and James M. Olson. "Justice Motive Effects in Ageism: The Effects of a Victim's Age on Observer Perceptions of Injustice and Punishment Judgments." *Journal of Experimental Social Psychology* 48 (2012): 1343–49.

Cohen, Claudia E. "Person Categories and Social Perception: Testing Some Boundaries of the Processing Effects of Prior Knowledge." *Journal of Personality and Social Psychology* 40, no. 3 (1981): 441–52.

D'Amato, Erik. "Mystery of Disgust." *Psychology Today,* January 1, 1998. http://www.psychologytoday.com/articles/200909/mystery-disgust.

Darley, John M., and Paget H. Gross. "A Hypothesis-Confirming Bias in Labeling Effects." *Journal of Personality and Social Psychology* 44, no. 1 (1983): 20–33.

*D.C. Fire and Medical Services Department v. D.C. Office of Employee Appeals.* 986 A.2d 419 (D.C. 2010).

Dean, Michael Allan. "Images of the Goddess of Justice." Last modified April 1, 2013. http://mdean.tripod.com/justice.html.

District of Columbia Task Force on Emergency Medical Services. *Report and Recommendations.* Washington, DC: January 27, 2007.

Dooley, Pamela A. "Perceptions of the Onset Controllability of AIDS and Helping Judgments: An Attributional Analysis." *Journal of Applied Social Psychology* 25, no. 10 (1995): 858–69.

Duggan, Paul. "Report Scolds D.C. Agencies in Response to Assault." *Washington Post,* June 17, 2006.

Eberhardt, Jennifer L., Nilanjana Dasgupta, and Tracy L. Banaszynski. "Believing Is Seeing: The Effects of Racial Labels and Implicit Beliefs on Face Perception." *Personality and Social Psychology Bulletin* 29 (2003): 360–70.

Fisher, Marc. "Doctor's Deposition Details Fatal Night at Howard ER." *Washington Post,* April 6, 2008.

Gamboa, Suzanne, and Sonya Ross. "Prosecutor in FL Shooting Known as Victim Advocate." Foxnews.com, April 12, 2012. http://www.foxnews.com/us/2012/04/12/prosecutor-in-fl-shooting-known-as-victim-advocate/.

Ganim, Sara. "Alleged Jerry Sandusky Victim Leaves School Because of Bullying, Counselor Says." *Patriot-News,* November 20, 2011. http://www.pennlive.com/midstate/index.ssf/2011/11/alleged_jerry_sandusky_victim.html.

Goldstein, Joseph. "F.B.I. Audit of Database That Indexes DNA Finds Errors in Profiles." *New York Times,* January 24, 2014.

Goodwin, Geoffrey P., and Justin F. Landy. "Valuing Different Human Lives." *Journal of Experimental Psychology: General* 143, no. 2 (2014): 778–803.

Gorman, James. "Survival's Ick Factor." *New York Times,* January 23, 2012.

Green, Susan. "George Zimmerman Makes First Court Appearance at Bond Hearing." Examiner.com, April 12, 2012. http://www.examiner.com/article/george-zimmerman-makes-first-court-appearance-at-bond-hearing.

Harris, Lasana T., and Susan T. Fiske. "Dehumanizing the Lowest of the Low: Neuroimaging Responses to Extreme Out-Groups." *Psychological Science* 17, no. 10 (2006): 847–53.

Inbar, Yoel, and David Pizarro. "Grime and Punishment: How Disgust Influences Moral, Social, and Legal Judgments." *Jury Expert* 21, no. 2 (March 2009): 12–18.

Innocence Project. "DNA Exonerations Nationwide." Accessed February 15, 2014. http://www.innocenceproject.org/Content/DNA_Exonerations_Nationwide.php.

Innocence Project. "51% of 300 DNA Exonerations Involved Use of Improper/Unvalidated Forensic Science: Breakdown by Discipline." Accessed February 15, 2014. http://www.innocenceproject.org/docs/FSBreakdownDiscipline.pdf.

Janofsky, Michael. "Official Washington Pays Tribute to Reporter Who Was Killed." *New York Times,* January 14, 2006.

Janofsky, Michael. "Suspect Said to Confess Killing Times Reporter." *New York Times,* January 13, 2006.

Jones, Cathaleene, and Elliot Aronson. "Attribution of Fault to a Rape Victim as a Function of Respectability of the Victim." *Journal of Personality and Social Psychology* 26, no. 3 (1973): 415–19.

Jones, Dan. "The Depths of Disgust." *Nature* 447, no.14 (June 2007): 768–71.

*Jordan v. United States.* Brief for Appellant. 18 A.3d 703 (2011) (No. 07-CF-340), 2010 WL 7359337.

*Jordan v. United States.* Brief for Appellee. 18 A.3d 703 (2011) (No. 07-CF-340), 2010 WL 7359345.

Kahneman, Daniel. *Thinking, Fast and Slow.* New York: Farrar, Straus & Giroux, 2011.

Kassin, Saul M., Itiel E. Dror, and Jeff Kukucka. "The Forensic Confirmation Bias: Problems, Perspectives, and Proposed Solutions." *Journal of Applied Research in Memory and Cognition* 2 (2013): 42–52.

King, Colbert I. "The Death of David Rosenbaum." *Washington Post*, February 25, 2006.

Kiume, Sandra. "Disgust and Social Tolerance." *Psych Central.* Accessed February 15, 2014. http://psychcentral.com/blog/archives/2007/01/04/disgust-and-social-tolerance/.

Lange, Nick D., Rick P. Thomas, Jason Dana, and Robyn M. Dawes. "Contextual Biases in the Interpretation of Auditory Evidence." *Law and Human Behavior* 35 (2011): 178–87.

Lemonick, Michael D. "Why We Get Disgusted." *Time*, May 24, 2007.

Mamet, David. *Faustus.* New York: Dramatists Play Service, 2007.

McGreal, Chris. "Somalian Rape Victim, 13, Stoned to Death." *Guardian*, November 2, 2008.

McNerney, Sam. "A Nauseating Corner of Psychology: Disgust." *Big Think*, December 9, 2012. http://bigthink.com/insights-of-genius/a-nauseating-corner-of-psychology-disgust.

MedlinePlus. "Do Not Resuscitate Orders." Last modified February 3, 2014. http://www.nlm.nih.gov/medlineplus/ency/patientinstructions/000473.htm.

Milk, Leslie, and Ellen Ryan. "Washingtonians of the Year 2007: The Rosenbaums." *Washingtonian*, January 1, 2008.

Morales, Andrea C., and Gavan J. Fitzsimons. "Product Contagion: Changing Consumer Evaluations Through Physical Contact with 'Disgusting' Products." *Journal of Marketing Research* 44, no. 2 (May 2007): 272–83.

National Institute of Justice. "What Is CODIS?" Last modified July 16, 2010. http://nij.gov/journals/266/Pages/backlogs-codis.aspx.

Noble, Andrea. "D.C. Fire Chief's Changes Ignore Earlier EMS Task Force Recommendation." *Journal of Emergency Medical Services,* August 28, 2013.

Penn, William. *Some Fruits of Solitude in Reflections and Maxims.* London: Freemantle, 1901.

Pennsylvania Attorney General. "Child Sex Charges Filed Against Jerry Sandusky; Two Top Penn State University Officials Charged with Perjury and Failure to Report Suspected Child Abuse." News release. November 5, 2011. http://www.attorneygeneral.gov/press.aspx?id=6270.

Purdum, Todd S. "David Rosenbaum, Reporter for Times Who Covered Politics, Dies at 63." *New York Times,* January 9, 2006.

Randall, Eric. "Bullies Force an Alleged Sandusky Victim to Leave His High School." *Wire,* November 21, 2011. http://www.theatlantic wire.com/national/2011/11/bullies-forced-alleged-sandusky-victim -leave-his-high-school/45267/.

Riedel, Marc. "Homicide Arrest Clearances: A Review of the Literature." *Sociology Compass* 2, no. 4 (2008): 1150–59.

Roberts, Aki. "The Influences of Incident and Contextual Characteristics on Crime Clearance of Nonlethal Violence: A Multilevel Event History Analysis." *Journal of Criminal Justice* 36 (2008): 61–71.

Robinson, Amanda L., and Meghan S. Chandek. "Differential Police Response to Black Battered Women." *Women and Criminal Justice* 12 (2000): 29–61.

*Rosenbaum v. District of Columbia.* Complaint for Damages. 2006 CA 008405 M (D.C. Super. Ct. dismissed Nov. 30, 2007).

Rozin, Paul, Larry Hammer, Harriet Oster, Talia Horowitz, and Veronica Marmora. "The Child's Conception of Food: Differentiation of Categories of Rejected Substances in the 16 Months to 5 Year Age Range." *Appetite* 7 (1986): 141–51.

Rozin, Paul, Maureen Markwith, and Clark McCauley, "Sensitivity to Indirect Contacts with Other Persons: AIDS Aversion as a Composite of Aversion to Strangers, Infection, Moral Taint and Misfortune." *Journal of Abnormal Psychology* 103 (1994): 495–504.

Schaffer, Amanda. "The Moral Dilemmas of Doctors During Disaster." *New Yorker,* September 13, 2013.

Schnall, Simone, Jonathan Haidt, Gerald L. Clore, and Alexander H. Jordan. "Disgust as Embodied Moral Judgment." *Personality and Social Psychology Bulletin* 34 (2008): 1096–1109.

*Selena Walker v. D.C. Fire and Emergency Medical Services.* OEA Matter No. 1601-0133-06 (D.C. June 26, 2007).

Sherman, Gary D., Jonathan Haidt, and Gerald L. Clore. "The Faintest Speck of Dirt: Disgust Enhances the Detection of Impurity." *Psychological Science* 23 (2012): 1506–14.

Silverman, Elissa. "Don't Split Department, Task Force Tells Fenty." *Washington Post,* September 21, 2007.

Simon, Dan. *In Doubt: The Psychology of the Criminal Justice Process.* Cambridge, MA: Harvard University Press, 2012.

*Situationist* Staff. "The Situation of Donations." *Situationist,* May 29, 2011. http://thesituationist.wordpress.com/2011/05/29/the-situation-of-donations/.

Smith, Douglas A., Christy A. Visher, and Laura A. Davidson. "Equity and Discretionary Justice: The Influence of Race on Police Arrest Decisions." *Journal of Criminal Law and Criminology* 75, no.1 (1984): 234–49.

Sommers, Sam. *Situations Matter.* New York: Riverhead, 2011.

Substance Abuse and Mental Health Services Administration, Office of Applied Studies. "Appendix B: Tables of Model-Based Estimates (50 States and the District of Columbia)." Accessed February 15, 2014. http://www.oas.samhsa.gov/2k8state/AppB.htm#TabB-9.

"Sudan: Gang Rape Victim Found Guilty of 'Indecent Acts.'" *Sudan Tribune,* February 21, 2014.

"Suspect in Northern Liberties Shooting ID'd." ABC.com, November 18, 2011. http://abclocal.go.com/wpvi/story?section=news/crime&id=8437751.

Thompson, Tisha, and Rick Yarborough. "I-Team: Seeing Through the Smoke." *NBC Washington,* August 27, 2013. http://www.nbcwashington.com/investigations/I-Team-Seeing-Through-the-Smoke-220734681.html.

USHistory.org. "Brief History of William Penn." Accessed February 8, 2014. http://www.ushistory.org/penn/bio.htm.

Vergano, Dan. "Jamestown Cannibalism Confirmed by Skull from 'Jane.'" *USA Today,* May 1, 2013.

Wilber, Del Quentin, and Debbi Wilgoren. "Medical Condition Suspected at First in Journalist's Fall." *Washington Post,* January 10, 2006.

Williams, Clarence, and Allan Lengel. "Report Faults Response to Assault." *Washington Post,* June 16, 2006.

Willoughby, Charles J. Government of the District of Columbia, Office of the Inspector General. *Summary of Special Report: Emergency Response to the Assault on David E. Rosenbaum.* June 2006.

Zagefka, Hanna, Masi Noor, Rupert Brown, Georgina Randsley de Moura, and Tim Hopthrow. "Donating to Disaster Victims: Responses to Natural and Humanly Caused Events." *European Journal of Social Psychology* 41 (2011): 353–63.

## 2. DANGEROUS CONFESSIONS ~ THE DETECTIVE

Black, Lisa, and Ruth Fuller. "3rd Life Sentence for Girl's Murder." *Chicago Tribune,* June 26, 2009.

*Bram v. United States.* 168 U.S. 532 (1897).

*Bruton v. United States.* 391 U.S. 123 (1968).

"Central Park Jogger (1989)." *New York Times,* October 3, 2012.

*Chambers v. Florida.* 309 U.S. 227 (1940).

*Colorado v. Connelly.* 479 U.S. 157 (1986).

Dervan, Lucian E., and Vanessa A. Edkins. "The Innocent Defendant's Dilemma: An Innovative Empirical Study of Plea Bargaining's Innocence Problem." *Journal of Criminal Law and Criminology* 103 (2013): 1–48.

Devers, Lindsey. U.S. Department of Justice. *Plea and Charge Bargaining.* January 24, 2011.

Drizin, Steven A., and Richard A. Leo. "The Problem of False Confessions in the Post-DNA World." *North Carolina Law Review* 82 (2004): 891–1007.

*Frazier v. Cupp.* 394 U.S. 731 (1969).

Garrett, Brandon L. *Convicting the Innocent: Where Criminal Prosecutions Go Wrong.* Cambridge, MA: Harvard University Press, 2011.

Garrett, Brandon L. "Introduction: *New England Law Review* Symposium on 'Convicting the Innocent.'" *New England Law Review* 46 (2012): 671–87.

Gross, Samuel R., Kristen Jacoby, Daniel J. Matheson, Nicholas Montgomery, and Sujata Patil. "Exonerations in the United States, 1989 Through 2003." *Journal of Criminal Law and Criminology* 95, no. 2 (2005): 523–60.

Guyll, Max, Stephanie Madon, Yueran Yang, Daniel G. Lannin, Kyle Scherr, and Sarah Greathouse. "Innocence and Resisting Confession During Interrogation: Effects on Physiologic Activity." *Law and Human Behavior* 37 (2013): 366–75.

Inbau, Fred E., John F. Reid, Joseph P. Buckley, and Brian C. Jayne. *Criminal Interrogation and Confessions,* 5th ed. Burlington, MA: Jones & Barlett Learning, 2013.

Innocence Project. "DNA Exonerations Nationwide." Accessed May 6, 2014. http://www.innocenceproject.org/Content/DNA_Exonerations_Nationwide.php.

Innocence Project. "James Ochoa." Accessed May 6, 2014. http://www.innocenceproject.org/Content/James_Ochoa.php.

Jones, Edward, and Victor Harris. "The Attribution of Attitudes." *Journal of Experimental Social Psychology* 3 (1967): 1–24.

"Juan Rivera, Center on Wrongful Convictions." *Northwestern Law.* Accessed May 6, 2014. http://www.law.northwestern.edu/legalclinic/ wrongfulconvictions/exonerations/il/juan-rivera.html.

"Juan Rivera Exhibit 2." *Northwestern Law.* Accessed May 5, 2014. http://www.law.northwestern.edu/legalclinic/wrongfulconvictions/ exonerations/documents/RiveraPCExhibit2.pdf.

Karlsen, Carol F. *The Devil in the Shape of a Woman: Witchcraft in Colonial New England.* New York: W. W. Norton, 1998.

Kassin, Saul M., Steven A. Drizin, Thomas Grisso, Gisli H. Gudjons- son, Richard A. Leo, and Allison D. Redlich. "Police-Induced Confes- sions: Risk Factors and Recommendations." *Law and Human Behavior* 34 (2010): 3–38.

Kassin, Saul M., and Gisli H. Gudjonsson. "The Psychology of Con- fessions: A Review of the Literature and Issues." *Psychological Science in the Public Interest* 5 (2004): 33–67.

Kassin, Saul M., Richard A. Leo, Christian A. Meissner, Kimberly D. Richman, Lori H. Colwell, Amy May-Leach, and Dana La Fon. "Police Interviewing and Interrogation: A Self-Report Survey of Police Practices and Beliefs." *Law and Human Behavior* 31 (2007): 381–400.

Kassin, Saul M., and Karlyn McNall. "Police Interrogations and Con- fessions: Communicating Promises and Threats by Pragmatic Implica- tion." *Law and Human Behavior* 15 (1991): 233–51.

Kassin, Saul M., Christian A. Meissner, and Rebecca J. Norwick. "'I'd Know a False Confession if I Saw One': A Comparative Study of College Stu- dents and Police Investigators." *Law and Human Behavior* 34 (2005): 211–27.

Langbein, John H. "Torture and Plea Bargaining." *University of Chi- cago Law Review* 46 (1978): 3–22.

Le, Phuong. "Testimony of Girl IDs Defendant in Slaying." *Chicago Tribune,* September 18, 1998.

Leo, R. A. "The Third Degree and the Origins of Psychological Po- lice Interrogation in the United States." In *Interrogations, Confessions, and Entrapment,* edited by G. Daniel Lassiter. New York: Kluwer Aca- demic Publishers, 2004.

Martin, Andrew. "Baby-sitter's Murder Victimizes 2 Families." *Chi- cago Tribune,* October 23, 1992.

Martin, Andrew. "Court Reverses Conviction of Man Jailed for 19 Years in Rape and Murder." *New York Times,* December 10, 2011.

Martin, Andrew. "Illinois: Inmate Cleared by DNA Is Freed." *New York Times,* January 6, 2012.

Martin, Andrew. "The Prosecution's Case Against DNA." *New York Times,* November 25, 2011.

Mills, Steve, and Dan Hinkel. "DNA Links Murder and Rape of Holly Staker, 11, to Second Murder 8 Years Later." *Chicago Tribune,* June 10, 2014.

Moxley, R. Scott. "The Case of the Dog That Couldn't Sniff Straight." *OC Weekly,* November 5, 2005.

Moxley, R. Scott. "CSI Games: If DNA Evidence Doesn't Fit in Orange County, Alter It?" *OC Weekly,* March 13, 2008.

Moxley, R. Scott. "Oops." *OC Weekly,* October 26, 2006.

National Registry of Exonerations. "Juan Rivera." Accessed May 8, 2014. https://www.law.umich.edu/special/exoneration/Pages/casedetail .aspx?caseid=3850.

Possley, Maurice. "DNA Tests Give Hope to Convict in 1992 Murder." *Chicago Tribune,* March 26, 2005.

Russano, Melissa B., Christian A. Meissner, Fadia M. Narchet, and Saul M. Kassin. "Investigating True and False Confessions Within a Novel Experimental Paradigm." *Psychological Science* 16, no. 6 (2005): 481–86.

Shipler, David K. "Why Do Innocent People Confess?" *New York Times,* February 23, 2012.

Simon, Dan. *In Doubt: The Psychology of the Criminal Justice Process.* Cambridge, MA: Harvard University Press, 2012.

Sommers, Sam. *Situations Matter.* New York: Riverhead, 2011.

*State v. Rivera.* 962 N.E. 2d 53 (Ill. App. Ct. 2011).

*State v. Rivera.* Brief for Defendant. 962 N.E. 2d 53 (Ill. App. Ct. 2011) (No. 2-09-1060).

Toris, Carol, and Bella M. DePaulo. "Effects of Actual Deception and Suspiciousness of Deception on Interpersonal Perceptions." *Journal of Personality and Social Psychology* 47 (1984): 1063–73.

White, Welsh S. *Miranda's Waning Protections: Police Interrogation Practices After Dickerson.* Ann Arbor: University of Michigan Press, 2006.

Wigmore, John Henry. *A Treatise on the Anglo-American System of Evidence in Trials at Common Law,* 2nd ed., vol. 2. Boston: Little, Brown, 1923.

Wrightsman, Lawrence S., and Saul M. Kassin. *Confessions in the Courtroom.* Newbury Park, CA: Sage, 2003.

## 3. THE CRIMINAL MIND ~ THE SUSPECT

*Alick Evan McGregor.* 1887. Photograph. New Zealand Police Museum, Porirua.

American Psychiatric Association. *Diagnostic and Statistical Manual of Mental Disorders,* 5th ed. Arlington, VA: American Psychiatric Publishing, 2013.

American Psychological Association. "Mental Illness Not Linked to Crime, Research Finds." Last modified April 21, 2014. http://www.apa.org/news/press/releases/2014/04/mental-illness-crime.aspx.

Baird, Abigail A., and Jonathan A. Fugelsang. "The Emergence of Consequential Thought: Evidence from Neuroscience." *Philosophical Transactions of the Royal Society of London, Series B: Biological Sciences* 359, no. 1451 (2004): 1797–1804.

Batts, Shelley. "Brain Lesions and Their Implications in Criminal Responsibility." *Behavioral Sciences and the Law* 27 (2009): 261–72.

Benforado, Adam. "The Geography of Criminal Law." *Cardozo Law Review* 31, no. 3 (2010): 823–904.

Bigler, Erin D., Mark Allen, and Gary K. Stimac. "MRI and Functional MRI." In *Neuroimaging in Forensic Psychiatry*, edited by Joseph Simpson. Oxford: John Wiley, 2012.

Blass, Thomas. "The Milgram Paradigm After 35 Years: Some Things We Now Know About Obedience to Authority." *Journal of Applied Social Psychology* 29, no. 5 (1999): 955–78.

Boffey, Phillip M. "The Next Frontier Is Inside Your Brain." *New York Times*, February 23, 2013.

Braverman, Irus. "Governing Certain Things: The Regulation of Street Trees in Four North American Cities." *Tulane Environmental Law Journal* 22, no. 1 (2008): 35–59.

Brown University. "'Warrior Gene' Predicts Aggressive Behavior After Provocation." Last modified January 19, 2009. http://news.brown.edu/pressreleases/2009/01/hotsauce.

Burns, Jeffrey M., and Russell Swerdlow. "Right Orbitofrontal Tumor with Pedophilia Symptom and Constructional Apraxia Sign." *Archives of Neurology* 60 (2003): 437–40.

"Celebrity Mugshots." CNN.com. Last updated March 20, 2013. http://www.cnn.com/2013/03/19/showbiz/celebrity-news-gossip/bruno-mars-mugshot-smile-gq.

Chinlund, Christine, Dick Lehr, and Kevin Cullen. "Senate President: A Mix of Family, Southie, Power." *Boston Globe*, September 18, 1988.

Cohen, Elizabeth. "North Carolina Lawmakers OK Payments for Victims of Forced Sterilization." CNN.com, July 28, 2013. http://www.cnn.com/2013/07/26/us/north-carolina-sterilization-payments.

Cohen, Nick. "Where Be Monsters?" *Observer*, January 17, 2004. Accessed September 27, 2014. http://www.theguardian.com/uk/2004/jan/18/ukcrime.guardiancolumnists.

Coid, Jeremy, Min Yang, Simone Ullrich, Amanda Roberts, Paul

Moran, Paul Bebbington, Traolach Brugha, Rachel Jenkins, Michael Farrell, Glyn Lewis, Nicola Singleton, and Robert Hare. "Psychopathy Among Prisoners in England and Wales." *International Journal of Law and Psychology* 32, no. 3 (2009): 134–41.

Cole, Simon A. *Suspect Identities: A History of Fingerprinting and Criminal Identification.* Cambridge, MA: Harvard University Press, 2001.

Cook, Gareth. "Secrets of the Criminal Mind." *Scientific American,* May 7, 2013. http://www.scientificamerican.com/article/secrets -criminal-mind-adrian-raine/.

Cox, James A. "Bilboes, Brands, and Branks: Colonial Crimes and Punishments." *Colonial Williamsburg Journal,* Spring 2003.

"Criminal Sittings." *Evening Post,* October 5, 1888.

Davie, Neil. "Lombroso and the 'Men of Real Science': British Reactions, 1886–1918." In *The Cesare Lombroso Handbook,* edited by Paul Knepper and P. J. Ystehede. New York: Routledge, 2013.

Davie, Neil. *Tracing the Criminal: The Rise of Scientific Criminology in Britain, 1860–1918.* Oxford: Bardwell Press, 2005.

Dobbs, David. "Beautiful Brains." *National Geographic,* October 2011.

Durose, Matthew R., Alexia D. Cooper, and Howard N. Snyder. U.S. Department of Justice. *Recidivism of Prisoners Released in 30 States in 2005: Patterns from 2005 to 2010.* April 2014.

Eagleman, David. "What Our Brains Can Teach Us." *New York Times,* February 22, 2013.

Eckholm, Erik. "Juveniles Facing Lifelong Terms Despite Rulings." *New York Times,* January 1, 2014.

*Encyclopedia Britannica Online.* "Cesare Lombroso." Accessed May 18, 2014. http://www.britannica.com/EBchecked/topic/346759/Cesare-Lombroso.

Farah, Martha J. "Neuroethics: The Practical and Philosophical." *Trends in Cognitive Sciences* 9, no. 1 (2005): 34–40.

Federal Bureau of Investigation. "James 'Whitey' Bulger Captured: Media Campaign Leads to Top Ten Arrest." Last modified June 23, 2011. http://www.fbi.gov/news/stories/2011/june/bulger_062311/bulger _062311.

Filipovic, Jill. "The Conservative Philosophy of Tragedy: Guns Don't Kill People, People Kill People." *Guardian,* December 21, 2012.

Finn, Jonathan. *Capturing the Criminal Image: From Mug Shot to Surveillance Society.* Minneapolis: University of Minnesota Press, 2009.

Fiske, Alan Page, Shinobu Kitayama, Hazel Rose Markus, and Richard E. Nisbett. "The Cultural Matrix of Social Psychology." In *The Handbook of Social Psychology,* 4th ed., vol. 2, edited by Daniel T. Gilbert, Susan T. Fiske, and Gardner Lindzey. New York: Oxford University Press, 1998.

Fletcher, Robert. "The New School of Criminal Anthropology." Address, Anthropological Society of Washington, Washington, DC, April 21, 1861.

"Francis Galton, Prevalent Features Among Men Convicted of Larceny (Without Violence)." Accessed October 10, 2014. http://galton.org/composite.htm.

*Frank Masters.* 1890. Photograph. New Zealand Police Museum, Porirua.

*Graham v. Florida.* 560 U.S. 48 (2010).

Greely, Henry T. "Law and the Revolution in Neuroscience: An Early Look at the Field." *Akron Law Review* 42 (2009): 687–715.

Harcourt, Bernard E. "Reflecting on the Subject: A Critique of the Social Influence Conception of Deterrence, the Broken Windows Theory, and Order-Maintenance Policing New York Style." *Michigan Law Review* 97 (1998): 291–389.

Harmon, Katherine. "Brain Injury Rate 7 Times Greater Among U.S. Prisoners." *Scientific American,* February 4, 2012.

Hirstein, William. "What Is a Psychopath?" *Psychology Today,* January 30, 2013. Accessed September 26, 2014. http://www.psychologytoday.com/blog/mindmelding/201301/what-is-psychopath-0.

*John Powell.* 1889. Photograph. New Zealand Police Museum, Porirua.

Jones, Kathleen B. "The Trial of Hannah Arendt." *Humanities* 35, no. 2 (March/April 2014). http://www.neh.gov/humanities/2014/march april/feature/the-trial-hannah-arendt.

Kalichman, Michael, Dena Plemmons, and Stephanie J. Bird. "Editor's Overview: Neuroethics: Many Voices and Many Sources." *Science and Engineering Ethics* 18, no. 3 (September 2012): 423–32.

Kean, Sam. "Phineas Gage: Neuroscience's Most Famous Patient." *Slate,* May 6, 2014. http://www.slate.com/articles/health_and_science/science/2014/05/phineas_gage_neuroscience_case_true_story_of_famous_frontal_lobe_patient.html.

Keizer, Kees, Siegwart Lindenberg, and Linda Steg. "The Spreading of Disorder." *Science* 322 (2008): 1681–85.

Kelling, George L., and James Q. Wilson. "Broken Windows: The Police and Neighborhood Safety." *Atlantic Monthly,* March 1, 1982.

Kennedy, Helen. "Notorious Gangster Whitey Bulger Was Inspiration for Jack Nicholson's Character in 'The Departed.'" *Daily News,* June 23, 2011.

Khalid, Asma. "Whitey and Billy: A Tale of Two Boston Brothers." WBUR, June 2, 2013. http://www.wbur.org/2013/06/02/whitey-billy -bulger-brothers.

Kiehl, Kent A., and Joshua W. Buckholtz. "Inside the Mind of a Psychopath." *Scientific American Mind,* September/October 2010.

Kitzhaber, John. "Proclamation of Human Rights Day, and Apology for Oregon's Forced Sterilization of Institutionalized Patients." Speech. Salem, OR, December 2, 2002.

Knapp, Alex. "How Lead Caused America's Violent Crime Epidemic." *Forbes,* January 3, 2013.

Kuo, Frances E., and William C. Sullivan. "Environment and Crime in the Inner City: Does Vegetation Reduce Crime?" *Environment and Behavior* 33, no. 3 (May 2001): 343–67.

Langan, Patrick A., and David J. Levin. U.S. Department of Justice. *Recidivism of Prisoners Released in 1994.* June 2, 2002.

Lehr, Dick, and Girard O'Neill. "Whitey Bulger: Secrets Behind the Capture of the FBI's Most Wanted Man." *Salon,* February 24, 2013. http://www.salon.com/2013/02/24/whitey_bulger_secrets_behind_the _capture_of_the_fbis_most_wanted_man/.

Lehrer, Jonah. "The Crime of Lead Exposure." *Wired,* June 1, 2011. http://www.wired.com/2011/06/the-crime-of-lead-exposure/.

Leistedt, Samuel J., and Paul Linkowski. "Psychopathy and the Cinema: Fact or Fiction?" *Journal of Forensic Sciences* 59 (2014): 167–74.

Lilienfeld, Scott O., and Hal Arkowitz. "What 'Psychopath' Means." *Scientific American,* November 28, 2007. http://www.scientificamerican .com/article/what-psychopath-means/.

Logan, Wayne A. "Policing Identity." *Boston University Law Review* 92 (2012): 1561–1611.

Lombroso-Ferrero, Gina. *Criminal Man According to the Classification of Cesare Lombroso.* New York: Knickerbocker, 1911.

Mayo Clinic. "Antisocial Personality Disorder." Accessed May 21, 2014. http://www.mayoclinic.org/diseases-conditions/antisocial-personality -disorder/basics/definition/con-20027920.

Mayo Clinic. "Position Emission Tomography (PET) Scan." Accessed May 21, 2014. http://www.mayoclinic.org/tests-procedures/pet-scan/ basics/definition/prc-20014301.

Medline Plus. "Antisocial Personality Disorder." Accessed May 21, 2014. http://www.nlm.nih.gov/medlineplus/ency/article/000921.htm.

Medline Plus. "Brain PET Scan." Accessed May 21, 2014. http://www.nlm.nih.gov/medlineplus/ency/article/007341.htm.

Medline Plus. "PET Scan." Accessed May 21, 2014. http://www.nlm.nih.gov/medlineplus/ency/article/003827.htm.

Milgram, Stanley. "Behavioral Study of Obedience." *Journal of Abnormal and Social Psychology* 67, no. 4 (1963): 371–78.

Milgram, Stanley. *Obedience to Authority: An Experimental View.* New York: Harper & Row, 1974.

Miller, Arthur G., ed. *The Social Psychology of Good and Evil.* New York: Guilford, 2004.

Miller, D. W. "Poking Holes in the Theory of 'Broken Windows.'" *Chronicle of Higher Education* 31, no. 17 (2001).

*Miller v. Alabama.* 132 S. Ct. 2455 (2012).

Mitchell, D. V. B., S. B. Anvy, and R. J. R. Blair, "Divergent Patterns of Aggressive and Neurocognitive Characteristics in Acquired Versus Developmental Psychopathy." *Neurocase* 12, no. 3 (2006): 164–78.

Mobbs, Dean, Hakwan C. Lau, Owen D. Jones, and Christopher D. Frith. "Law, Responsibility, and the Brain." *PLOS Biology* 5, no. 4 (April 2007): 693–700.

Monterosso, John, and Barry Schwartz. "Did Your Brain Make You Do It?" *New York Times,* July 27, 2012.

Morse, Stephen J. "Neuroimaging Evidence in Law: A Plea for Modesty and Relevance." In *Neuroimaging in Forensic Psychiatry,* edited by Joseph Simpson. Oxford: John Wiley, 2012.

Muskal, Michael. "Exterminator Charged with Murder in Death of Philadelphia Doctor." *Los Angeles Times,* January 24, 2013.

Nadelhoffer, Thomas, and Walter Sinnott-Armstrong. "Neurolaw and Neuroprediction: Potential Promises and Perils." *Philosophy Compass* 7, no. 9 (2012): 631–42.

News from the National Academies. "Juvenile Justice Reforms Should Incorporate Science of Adolescent Development." Last modified November 13, 2012. http://www8.nationalacademies.org/onpinews/newsitem.aspx?RecordID=14685.

Pearl, Sharrona. *About Faces: Physiognomy in Nineteenth-Century Britain.* Cambridge, MA: Harvard University Press, 2010.

Pease, Ken. "Crime Reduction." In *The Oxford Handbook of Criminology,* 3rd ed., edited by Mike Maguire, Rod Morgan, and Robert Reiner. Oxford: Oxford University Press, 2002.

Peterson, Jillian K., Jennifer Skeem, Patrick Kennealy, Beth Bray, and Andrea Zvonkovic. "How Often and How Consistently Do Symptoms Directly Precede Criminal Behavior Among Offenders with Mental Illness?" *Law and Human Behavior* 38, no. 5 (2014): 439–49.

Psych Central Staff. "Antisocial Personality Disorder Symptoms." *Psych Central.* Accessed May 21, 2014. http://psychcentral.com/disorders/antisocial-personality-disorder-symptoms/.

Raine, Adrian. *The Anatomy of Violence: The Biological Roots of Crime.* Toronto: Random House, 2013.

Reeves, Hope. "I See . . . Hemorrhoids in Your Future." *New York Times,* March 10, 2013.

Reyna, Valerie F. "How People Make Decisions That Involve Risk: A Dual-Processes Approach." *Current Directions in Psychological Science* 13, no. 2 (2004): 60–66.

Reyna, Valerie F., and Frank Farley. "Risk and Rationality in Adolescent Decision Making." *Psychological Science in the Public Interest* 7, no. 1 (2006): 1–44.

*Roper v. Simmons.* 543 U.S. 551 (2005).

Ross, Lee, and Donna Shestowsky. "Contemporary Psychology's Challenges to Legal Theory and Practice." *Northwestern University Law Review* 97, no. 3 (2003): 1081–1114.

Royal Society. *Brain Waves Module 4: Neuroscience and the Law.* London: Royal Society, 2011.

Rushing, Susan E., Daniel A. Pryma, and Daniel D. Langleben. "PET and SPECT." In *Neuroimaging in Forensic Psychiatry,* edited by Joseph Simpson. Oxford: John Wiley, 2012.

Sabol, S. Z., Stella Hu, and D. Hamer. "A Functional Polymorphism in the Monoamine Oxidase A Gene Promoter." *Human Genetics* 103, no. 3 (September 1998): 273–79.

Schuessler, Jennifer. "Book Portrays Eichmann as Evil, but Not Banal." *New York Times,* September 2, 2014.

Shader, Michael. U.S. Department of Justice. *Risk Factors for Delinquency: An Overview.* 2004.

"This Day: An Extraordinary Scene." *Evening Post,* December 4, 1889.

This Day in History. "Dachau Liberated: April 29, 1945." History.com. Accessed May 19, 2014. http://www.history.com/this-day-in-history/dachau-liberated.

University of Massachusetts. "UMass Presidents: William M. Bulger." Last modified June 30, 2011. http://www.massachusetts.edu/presidents/bulger.html.

University of Texas at Dallas. "Criminologist's Research Shows Genes

Influence Criminal Behavior." Last modified January 24, 2012. http://www.utdallas.edu/news/2012/1/24-15201_Criminologists-Research-Shows-Genes-Influence-Crim_article-wide.html.

University of Washington. "Brain Facts and Figures." Accessed May 20, 2014. http://faculty.washington.edu/chudler/facts.html.

"Urgent Private Affairs." *Evening Post,* June 10, 1886.

Valencia, Milton J., Shelley Murphy, and Martin Finucane. "Whitey Bulger, Boston Gangster Found Responsible for 11 Murders, Gets Life in Prison." *Boston Globe*, November 14, 2013.

Valeo, Tom. "Legal-Ease: Is Neuroimaging a Valid Biomarker in Legal Cases?" *Neurology Today* 12, no. 8 (2012): 38–40.

Vedantam, Shankar. "Behind a Halloween Mask, Even 'Good' Kids Can Turn into Candy Thieves." NPR, October 31, 2012. http://www.npr.org/blogs/thesalt/2012/10/31/164030718/behind-a-halloween-mask-even-good-kids-can-turn-into-candythieves.

Victorian Web. "Victorian Science: An Introduction." Last modified December 6, 2008. http://www.victorianweb.org/science/intro.html.

Wheeler, Mark. "UCLA Researchers Map Damaged Connections in Phineas Gage's Brain." *UCLA Newsroom*, May 16, 2012. http://newsroom.ucla.edu/releases/embargoed-for-release-until-wednesday-233846.

"Whitey Bulger Biography." *Bio.* Accessed May 21, 2014. http://www.biography.com/people/whitey-bulger—328770#capture-and-trial&awesm=~oEWyGCLDWfHOKb.

Wiebking, Christine, Alexander Sartorius, Harald Dressing, and Greg Northoff. "Pedophilia." In *Neuroimaging in Forensic Psychiatry,* edited by Joseph Simpson. Oxford: John Wiley, 2012.

Wikimedia Commons. "File: De Humana Physiognomia-Kuh und Mann.jpg." Last modified August 1, 2008. http://commons.wikimedia.org/wiki/File:De_Humana_Physiognomia_-_Kuh_und_Mann.jpg/.

*William Johnston.* 1887. Photograph. New Zealand Police Museum, Porirua.

Witt, Jessica, and James Brockmole. "Action Alters Object Identification: Wielding a Gun Increases the Bias to See Guns." *Journal of Experimental Psychology: Human Perception and Performance* 38, no. 5 (2012): 1159–67.

Wolfe, Mary K., and Jeremy Mennis. "Does Vegetation Encourage or Suppress Urban Crime? Evidence from Philadelphia, PA." *Landscape and Urban Planning* 108 (November–December 2012): 112–22.

Zimbardo, Philip G., and Michael R. Leippe. *The Psychology of Attitude Change and Social Influence.* New York: McGraw-Hill, 1991.

4. BREAKING THE RULES ~ THE LAWYER

"A Cheating Crisis in America's Schools." ABC News, April 29, 2012. http://abcnews.go.com/Primetime/story?id=132376&page=1.

Ariely, Dan. The (Honest) Truth About Dishonesty. New York: Harper-Collins, 2012.

Asimow, Michael. "Embodiment of Evil: Law Firms in the Movies." UCLA Law Review 48 (2001): 1341–92.

Bandes, Susan. "The Lone Miscreant, The Self-Training Prosecutor, and Other Fictions: A Comment on Connick v. Thompson." Fordham Law Review 715 (2012): 715–36.

Barber, Elizabeth. "Dallas Targets Wrongful Convictions, and Revolution Starts to Spread." Christian Science Monitor, May 25, 2014.

Bazelon, Emily. "Playing Dirty in the Big Easy." Slate, April 18, 2012. http://www.slate.com/articles/news_and_politics/crime/2012/04/new_orleans_district_attorney_leon_cannizzaro_is_being_questioned_for_his_ethics_in_pursuing_convictions_.html.

Biography.com. "Harry Connick Jr." Accessed May 13, 2014. http://www.biography.com/people/harry-connick-jr-5542.

Brady v. Maryland. 373 U.S. 83 (1963).

Bryan, Christopher J., Gabrielle S. Adams, and Benoît Monin. "When Cheating Would Make You a Cheater: Implicating the Self Prevents Unethical Behavior." Journal of Experimental Psychology: General 142, no. 4 (2013): 1001–5.

Chance, Zoë, Michael I. Norton, Francesca Gino, and Dan Ariely. "Temporal View of the Costs and Benefits of Self-Deception." Proceedings of the National Academy of Sciences 108 (2011): 15655–59.

Cohen, Taya R., A. T. Panter, and Nazli Turan. "Guilt Proneness and Moral Character." Current Directions in Psychological Science 21 (2012): 355–59.

Connick v. Thompson. 131 S. Ct. 1350 (2011).

Dallas County District Attorney's Office. "Conviction Integrity Unit." Accessed April 26, 2014. http://www.dallasda.com/division/conviction-integrity-unit/.

Davidson, Adam, Jacob Goldstein, Caitlin Kenney, and Dan Kedmey. "What's the Easiest Way to Cheat on Your Taxes?" New York Times, April 3, 2012.

"Failure of Empathy and Justice." New York Times, March 31, 2011.

Fisher-Giorlando, Marianne. "Louisiana." In The Social History of Crime and Punishment in America: An Encyclopedia, edited by Wilbur R. Miller. Los Angeles: Sage, 2012.

Florida Innocence Project. "Conviction Integrity Units: Righting the Wrongs or a Waste of Time?" *Plain Error*, September 18, 2012. http://floridainnocence.org/content/?tag=conviction-integrity-units.

Garrett, Brandon L. *Convicting the Innocent: Where Criminal Prosecutions Go Wrong*. Cambridge, MA: Harvard University Press, 2011.

Gino, Francesca, and Dan Ariely. "The Dark Side of Creativity: Original Thinkers Can Be More Dishonest." *Journal of Personality and Social Psychology* 102 (2011): 445–59.

Gino, Francesca, Maurice E. Schweitzer, Nicole L. Mead, and Dan Ariely. "Unable to Resist Temptation: How Self-Control Depletion Promotes Unethical Behavior." *Organizational Behavior and Human Decision Processes* 115 (2011): 191–203.

Gino, Francesca, Shahar Ayal, and Dan Ariely. "Contagion and Differentiation in Unethical Behavior." *Psychological Science* 20, no. 3 (2009): 393–98.

Graves, Lucia. "Which Types of Students Cheat Most?" *U.S. News and World Report*, October 3, 2008.

Harris Interactive. "Confidence in Congress Stays at Lowest Point in Almost Fifty Years." May 21, 2012. http://www.harrisinteractive.com/NewsRoom/HarrisPolls/tabid/447/ctl/ReadCustom%20Default/mid/1508/ArticleId/1068/Default.aspx.

History.com. "Nuremberg Trials." Accessed April 21, 2014. http://www.history.com/topics/world-war-ii/nuremberg-trials.

Hollway, John, and Ronald M. Gauthier. *Killing Time: An 18-Year Odyssey from Death Row to Freedom*. New York: Skyhorse Publishing, 2010.

Indvik, Lauren. "U.S. Internet Piracy Is on the Decline." *USA Today*, March 25, 2011.

Innocence Project. "Conviction Integrity Unit Reviews Possible Wrongful Convictions." *Innocence Blog*, March 26, 2013. http://www.innocenceproject.org/Content/Conviction_Integrity_Unit_Reviews_Possible_Wrongful_Convictions.php.

Innocence Project. "Conviction Integrity Unit to Review 50 Brooklyn Murder Cases." *Innocence Blog*, May 13, 2013. http://www.innocenceproject.org/Content/Conviction_Integrity_Unit_to_Review_50_Brooklyn_Murder_Cases.php.

Innocence Project. "The Exonerator." *Innocence Blog*, November 17, 2008. http://www.innocenceproject.org/Content/The_Exonerator.php.

Internal Revenue Service. "Tax Gap." Last modified December 3, 2013. http://www.irs.gov/uac/The-Tax-Gap.

"Ira Sorkin, Lawyer for Bernie Madoff, Leaves Dickstein Shapiro."

*JD Journal,* November 3, 2010. http://www.jdjournal.com/2010/11/03/ ira-sorkin-lawyer-for-bernie-madoff-leaves-dickstein-shapiro/.

IRS Oversight Board. *2011 Taxpayer Attitude Survey.* Washington, DC: IRS Oversight Board, 2012.

Jarvis, Rebecca. "America at Tax Time: What Cheaters Cost Us." CBS News, April 16, 2012. http://www.cbsnews.com/8301-3445_162-57414288/ america-at-tax-time-what-cheaters-cost-us/.

Josephson Institute of Ethics. *2012 Report Card on the Ethics of American Youth.* Los Angeles: Josephson Institute for Ethics, 2012.

Keenan, David, Deborah Jane Cooper, David Lebowitz, and Tamar Lerer. "The Myth of Prosecutorial Accountability After *Connick v. Thompson:* Why Existing Professional Responsibility Measures Cannot Protect Against Prosecutorial Misconduct." *Yale Law Journal Online* 121 (2011).

"Lawyer Joke Collection." Last modified October 31, 2010. http:// www.iciclesoftware.com/LawJokes/IcicleLawJokes.html.

Liptak, Adam. "$14 Million Jury Award to Ex-Inmate Is Dismissed." *New York Times,* March 29, 2011.

Liptak, Adam. "Prosecutor Becomes Prosecuted." *New York Times,* June 24, 2007.

Lithwick, Dahlia. "Cruel but Not Unusual: Clarence Thomas Writes One of the Meanest Supreme Court Decisions Ever." *Slate,* April 11, 2011. http://www.slate.com/articles/news_and_politics/jurisprudence/ 2011/04/cruel_but_not_unusual.single.html.

Mazar, Nina, On Amir, and Dan Ariely. "The Dishonesty of Honest People: A Theory of Self-Concept Maintenance." *Journal of Marketing Research* 45 (2008): 633–44.

Mazar, Nina, and Dan Ariely. "Dishonesty in Everyday Life and Its Policy Implications." *Journal of Public Policy and Marketing* 25, no. 1 (2006): 1–21.

McCabe, Donald L., Kenneth D. Butterfield, and Linda Klebe Treviño. "Academic Dishonesty in Graduate Business Programs: Prevalence, Causes, and Proposed Action." *Academy of Management Learning and Education* 5 (2006): 294–305.

McCoy, Kevin. "IRS Struggling to Combat Rise in Tax Fraud." *USA Today,* April 15, 2012.

McLaughlin, Michael. "National Registry of Exonerations: More Than 2,000 People Freed After Wrongful Convictions." Last modified May 22, 2012. http://www.huffingtonpost.com/2012/05/21/national -registry-of-exonerations_n_1534030.html.

"McVeigh's Former Lawyer Speaks Out." CBS News, June 11, 2001. http://www.cbsnews.com/news/mcveighs-former-lawyer-speaks-out/.

Menkel-Meadow, Carrie. "Can They Do That? Legal Ethics in Popular Culture." *UCLA Law Review* 48 (2001): 1305–37.

Moore, Terri. "Prosecutors Reinvestigate Questionable Evidence: Dallas Establishes 'Conviction Integrity Unit.'" *Criminal Justice* 26 (2011): 1–6.

Novotney, Amy. "Beat the Cheat." *Monitor on Psychology* 42 (2011): 54.

"Orleans Parish District Attorney." Accessed April 21, 2014. http://orleansda.com/the-d-a/.

Pérez-Peña, Richard. "Studies Find More Students Cheating, with High Achievers No Exception." *New York Times*, September 7, 2012.

Pinker, Steven. "The Sugary Secret of Self-Control." Review of *Willpower: Rediscovering the Greatest Human Strength*, by Roy F. Baumeister and John Tierney. *New York Times*, September 2, 2011.

Possley, Maurice, and Ken Armstrong. "The Flip Side of a Fair Trial." *Chicago Tribune*, January 11, 1999.

Recording Industry Association of America. "Student FAQ." Accessed April 21, 2014. http://www.riaa.com/toolsforparents.php?content_selector=resources-for-students.

Ridgeway, James, and Jean Casella. "14 Years on Death Row. $14 Million in Damages?" *Mother Jones*, October 6, 2010. http://www.motherjones.com/politics/2010/09/connick-v-thompson.

Salisbury, David. "Breakdown of White-Matter Pathways Affects Decisionmaking As We Age." *Research News at Vanderbilt*, April 11, 2012. http://news.vanderbilt.edu/2012/04/declining-decisionmaking/.

Shu, Lisa L., Francesca Gino, and Max H. Bazerman, "Dishonest Deeds, Clear Conscience: When Cheating Leads to Moral Disengagement and Motivated Forgetting." *Personality and Social Psychology Bulletin* 37 (2011): 330–49.

Simon, Dan. *In Doubt: The Psychology of the Criminal Justice Process.* Cambridge, MA: Harvard University Press, 2012.

Siwek, Stephen E. "The True Cost of Sound Recording Piracy to the U.S. Economy." August 21, 2007. http://www.ipi.org/ipi_issues/detail/the-true-cost-of-sound-recording-piracy-to-the-us-economy.

Smith, Abbe. "Can You Be a Good Person and a Good Prosecutor?" *Georgetown Journal of Legal Ethics* 14 (2001): 355–400.

Stern, Walter. "Dershowitz Defends His Defense of Bad People." *Yale Herald*, February 5, 1999.

Takeuchi, Hikaru, Yasuyuki Taki, Yuko Sassa, Hiroshi Hashizume,

Atsushi Sekiguchi, Ai Fukushima, and Ryuta Kawashima. "White Matter Structures Associated with Creativity: Evidence from Diffusion Tensor Imaging." *NeuroImage* 51 (2010): 11–18.

Thompson, John. "The Prosecution Rests, But I Can't." *New York Times*, April 9, 2009.

Tierney, John. "Be It Resolved." *New York Times*, January 5, 2012.

Xu, Xiaomeng, Kathryn E. Demos, Tricia M. Leahey, Chantelle N. Hart, Jennifer Trautvetter, Pamela Coward, Kathryn R. Middleton, and Rena R. Wing. "Failure to Replicate Depletion of Self-Control." *PLOS ONE* 9, no. 10 (2014): 1–5.

Zeleny, Jeff. "Daschle Ends Bid for Post, Obama Concedes Mistake." *New York Times*, February 3, 2009.

Zimmerman, Isaiah M. "Stress and the Trial Lawyer." *Litigation* 9 (1983): 37.

## 5. IN THE EYE OF THE BEHOLDER ~ THE JURY

"About the IAT." Project Implicit. Accessed May 13, 2014. https://implicit.harvard.edu/implicit/iatdetails.html.

Alfano, Sean. "Court Sides with Cops on High-Speed Chase." CBS News, April 30, 2007. http://www.cbsnews.com/stories/2007/04/30/supremecourt/main2743124.shtml.

Benforado, Adam. "Frames of Injustice: The Bias We Overlook." *Indiana Law Journal* 85 (2010): 1334–78.

Bornstein, Brian H., and Edie Greene. "Jury Decision Making: Implications For and From Psychology." *Current Directions in Psychological Science* 20, no. 1 (2011): 63–67.

Egan, Timothy. "Not Guilty: The Jury." *New York Times*, October 4, 1995.

Gibbs, Jewelle Taylor. *Race and Justice: Rodney King and O.J. Simpson in a House Divided*. San Francisco: Jossey-Bass, 1996.

Goffman, Alice. *On the Run: Fugitive Life in an American City*. Chicago: University of Chicago Press, 2014.

Greely, Henry T. "Law and the Revolution in Neuroscience: An Early Look at the Field." *Akron Law Review* 42 (2009): 687–715.

"Homer Badman." *The Simpsons*. Directed by David Mirkin. November 27, 1994.

Kahan, Dan M. "Culture, Cognition, and Consent: Who Perceives What, and Why, in Acquaintance-Rape Cases." *University of Pennsylvania Law Review* 158 (2010): 729–813.

Kahan, Dan M., David A. Hoffman, and Donald Braman. "Whose

Eyes Are You Going to Believe? *Scott v. Harris* and the Perils of Cognitive Illiberalism." *Harvard Law Review* 122 (2009): 837–906.

Korn, Harrison A., Micah A. Johnson, and Marvin M. Chun. "Neurolaw: Differential Brain Activity for Black and White Faces Predicts Damage Awards in Hypothetical Employment Discrimination Cases." *Social Neuroscience* 7 (2012): 398–409.

Kotlowitz, Alex. "Deep Cover: Alice Goffman's 'On the Run.'" *New York Times*, June 26, 2014.

Lassiter, G. Daniel. "Illusory Causation in the Courtroom." *Current Directions in Psychological Science* 11 (2002): 204–8.

Lassiter, G. Daniel. "Videotaped Confessions: The Impact of Camera Point of View on Judgments of Coercion." *Journal of Applied Sociology* 3 (1986): 268–76.

Lassiter, G. Daniel, Shari Seidman Diamond, Heather C. Schmidt, and Jennifer K. Elek. "Evaluating Videotaped Confessions: Expertise Provides No Defense Against the Camera Perspective Effect." *Psychological Science* 18 (2007): 224–26.

Lassiter, G. Daniel, and Andrew L. Geers. "Bias and Accuracy in the Evaluation of Confession Evidence." In *Interrogations, Confessions, and Entrapment*, edited by G. Daniel Lassiter. New York: Springer, 2004.

Lassiter, G. Daniel, Andrew L. Geers, Ian M. Handley, Paul E. Weiland, and Patrick J. Munhall. "Videotaped Interrogations and Confessions: A Simple Change in Camera Perspective Alters Verdicts in Simulated Trials." *Journal of Applied Psychology* 87 (2002): 867–74.

Lassiter, G. Daniel, Andrew L. Geers, Patrick J. Munhall, Ian M. Handley, and Melissa J. Beers. "Videotaped Confessions: Is Guilt in the Eye of the Camera?" *Advances in Experimental Social Psychology* 33 (2001): 198–254.

Lassiter, G. Daniel, Patrick J. Munhall, Andrew L. Geers, Paul E. Weiland, and Ian M. Handley. "Accountability and the Camera Perspective Bias in Videotaped Confessions." *Analysis of Sociological Issues and Public Policy* 1 (2001): 53–70.

Lewis, Paul. "Every Step You Take: UK Underground Centre That Is Spy Capital of the World." *Guardian*, March 2, 2009.

Lovett, Ian. "In California, a Champion for Police Cameras." *New York Times*, August 21, 2013.

Nadelhoffer, Thomas, and Walter Sinnott-Armstrong. "Neurolaw and Neuroprediction: Potential Promises and Perils." *Philosophy Compass* 7, no. 9 (2012): 631–42.

Phelan, Sean M., John F. Dovidio, Rebecca M. Puhl, Diana J. Burgess, David B. Nelson, Mark W. Yeazel, Rachel Hardeman, Sylvia Perry, and Michelle van Ryn. "Implicit and Explicit Weight Bias in a National Sample of 4,732 Medical Students: The Medical Student CHANGES Study." *Obesity* 22 (2014): 1201–8.

"Police Chase: *Scott v. Harris.*" YouTube video, 6:00. Posted July 19, 2007. http://www.youtube.com/watch?v=DBY2y2YsmNo.

Ratcliff, Jennifer J., G. Daniel Lassiter, Heather C. Schmidt, and Celeste J. Snyder. "Camera Perspective Bias in Videotaped Confessions: Experimental Evidence of Its Perceptual Basis." *Journal of Experimental Psychology* 12 (2006): 197–206.

Rattan, Aneeta, Cynthia S. Levine, Carol S. Dweck, and Jennifer L. Eberhardt. "Race and the Fragility of the Legal Distinction Between Juveniles and Adults." *PLOS ONE* 7, no. 5 (2012): 1–7.

Rose, Reginald. *12 Angry Men.* Directed by Sidney Lumet. Metro-Goldwyn-Mayer, 1957. 96 min.

Ross, Lee, and Andrew Ward. "Naïve Realism in Everyday Life: Implications for Social Conflict and Misunderstanding." In *Values and Knowledge,* edited by Edward S. Reed, Elliot Turiel, and Terrance Brown. Mahwah, NJ: Lawrence Erlbaum, 1996.

Schmidt, Michael S. "In Policy Change, Justice Dept. to Require Recordings of Interrogations," *New York Times,* May 22, 2014.

Schvey, Natasha, Rebecca Puhl, Katherine Levandoski, and Kelly Brownell. "The Influence of a Defendant's Body Weight on Perceptions of Guilt." *International Journal of Obesity* 37, no. 9 (September 2013): 1275–81.

*Scott v. Harris.* 550 U.S. 372 (2007).

*Scott v. Harris.* Brief for Respondent. 550 U.S. 372 (2007) (No. 05-1631).

*Scott v. Harris.* Oral Argument Transcript. 550 U.S. 372 (2007) (No. 05-1631).

"Should Police Wear Cameras?" *New York Times,* October 22, 2013.

Storms, Michael D. "Videotape and the Attribution Process: Reversing Actors' and Observers' Points of View." *Journal of Personality and Social Psychology* 27 (1973): 165–75.

Timoney, John F. "The Real Costs of Policing the Police." *New York Times,* August 19, 2013.

"Why I Ran." YouTube video, 9:37. Posted December 8, 2009. http://www.youtube.com/watch?v=JATVLUOjzvM&feature=related.

"Young People of Color Mistrust Police, Legal System, Report Finds." *ScienceDaily,* August 16, 2014. http://www.sciencedaily.com/releases/2014/08/140816204417.htm.

6. THE CORRUPTION OF MEMORY ~ THE EYEWITNESS

Association for Psychological Science. "Having to Make Quick Decisions Helps Witnesses Identify the Bad Guy in a Lineup." August 28, 2012. http://ow.ly/djveA.

Association for Psychological Science. "Unusual Suspects: How to Make Witnesses More Reliable." March 5, 2012. http://www.psychologicalscience.org/index.php/news/unusual-suspects-how-to-make-witnesses-more-reliable.html#hide.

Brewer, Neil, and Gary Wells. "Eyewitness Identification." *Current Directions in Psychological Science* 20 (2011): 24–27.

Brigham, John C., and Robert K. Bothwell. "The Ability of Prospective Jurors to Estimate the Accuracy of Eyewitness Identifications." *Law and Human Behavior* 7 (1983): 19–30.

Castel, Alan, Michael Vendetti, and Keith J. Holyoak. "Fire Drill: Inattentional Blindness and Amnesia for the Location of Fire Extinguishers." *Attention, Perception, and Psychophysics* 74 (2012): 1391–96.

Clark, Steven E., Ryan T. Howell, and Sherrie L. Davey. "Regularities in Eyewitness Identification." *Law and Human Behavior* 32 (2008): 198–218.

Darwin, Charles. *On the Origin of Species.* London: John Murray, 1859.

Deffenbacher, Kenneth A., Brian H. Bornstein, Steven D. Penrod, and E. Kiernan McGorty. "A Meta-Analytic Review of the Effects of High Stress on Eyewitness Memory." *Law and Human Behavior* 28 (2004): 687–706.

Downey, Maureen. Georgia Innocence Project. "Sharper Eyewitnessing." December 21, 2007. http://www.ga-innocenceproject.org/Articles/Article_95.htm.

"Editorial: Georgia Should Have Eyewitness ID Protocol." *Athens Banner Herald,* September 23, 2011.

Eldridge, Margery A., Philip J. Barnard, and Debra A. Bekerian. "Autobiographical Memory and Daily Schemas at Work." *Memory* 2 (1994): 51–74.

"File: US10dollarbill-Series 2004A.jpg." *Wikimedia Commons.* Accessed May 15, 2014. http://en.wikipedia.org/wiki/File:US10dollarbill-Series_2004A.jpg.

Fisher, Ronald, Rebecca Milne, and Ray Bull. "Interviewing Cooperative Witnesses." *Current Directions in Psychological Science* 20 (2011): 16–19.

Frenda, Steven, Rebecca Nichols, and Elizabeth Loftus. "Current Issues and Advances in Misinformation Research." *Current Directions in Psychological Science* 20 (2011): 20–23.

Garrett, Brandon L. *Convicting the Innocent: Where Criminal Prosecutions Go Wrong.* Cambridge, MA: Harvard University Press, 2011.

Garrett, Brandon L. "Introduction: *New England Law Review* Symposium on 'Convicting the Innocent.'" *New England Law Review* 46 (2012): 671–87.

Goode, Erica, and John Schwartz. "Police Lineups Start to Face Fact: Eyes Can Lie." *New York Times,* August 28, 2011.

Gurney, Daniel J., Karen J. Pine, and Richard Wiseman. "The Gestural Misinformation Effect: Skewing Eyewitness Testimony Through Gesture." *American Journal of Psychology* 126 (2013): 301–14.

Haines, Errin. Georgia Innocence Project. "Man Cleared by DNA Eager for Christmas in Freedom." December 20, 2007. http://www.ga -innocenceproject.org/Articles/Article_94.htm.

Harley, Erin M., Keri A. Carlsen, and Geoffrey R. Loftus. "The 'Saw-It-All-Along' Effect: Demonstrations of Visual Hindsight Bias." *Journal of Experimental Psychology: Learning, Memory, and Cognition* 30 (2004): 432–38.

Harvard University Press. "Understanding Eyewitness Misidentifications." March 14, 2011. http://harvardpress.typepad.com/hup_publicity /2011/03/understanding-eyewitness-misidentifications.html.

Hasel, Lisa E., and Saul M. Kassin. "On the Presumption of Evidentiary Independence: Can Confessions Corrupt Eyewitness Identifications?" *Psychological Science* 20 (2009): 122–26.

Hope, Lorraine, William Lewinski, Justin Dixon, David Blocksidge, and Fiona Gabbert. "Witnesses in Action: The Effects of Physical Exertion on Recall and Recognition." *Psychological Science* 23 (2012): 386–90.

"Hugo Munsterberg." Accessed May 18, 2014. http://www.famous psychologists.org/hugo-munsterberg/.

Hulse, Lynn M., and Amina Memon. "Fatal Impact? The Effects of Emotional and Weapon Presence on Police Officers' Memories for a Simulated Crime." *Legal and Criminological Psychology* 11 (2006): 313–25.

Innocence Project. "John Jerome White." Accessed May 12, 2014. http://www.innocenceproject.org/Content/John_Jerome_White.php.

Innocence Project. *Reevaluating Lineups: Why Witnesses Make Mistakes and How to Reduce the Chance of Misidentification.* New York: Benjamin N. Cardozo School of Law, Yeshiva University.

Konkol, Mark. "Chicago Police Solve More Murders with New Strategy, Witness Cooperation." *DNAinfo Chicago,* July 24, 2013. http://

www.dnainfo.com/chicago/20130724/loop/chicago-police-solve-more
-murders-with-new-strategy-witness-cooperation.

Krug, Kevin. "The Relationship Between Confidence and Accuracy: Current Thoughts of the Literature and a New Area of Research." *Applied Psychology in Criminal Justice* 3 (2007): 7–41.

Lindsay, D. Stephen, J. Don Read, and Kusum Sharma. "Accuracy and Confidence in Person Identification: The Relationship Is Strong When Witnessing Conditions Vary Widely." *Psychological Science* 9 (1998): 215–18.

Liptik, Adam. "34 Years Later, Supreme Court Will Revisit Witness IDs." *New York Times,* August 22, 2011.

Loftus, Elizabeth F., and John C. Palmer. "Reconstruction of Automobile Destruction: An Example of the Interaction Between Language and Memory." *Journal of Verbal Learning and Verbal Behavior* 13 (1974): 585–89.

Malpass, Roy S., Colin G. Tredoux, and Dawn McQuiston-Surrett. "Lineup Construction and Lineup Fairness." In *Handbook of Eyewitness Psychology,* vol. 2, *Memory for People,* edited by R. C. L. Lindsay, David F. Ross, J. Don Read, and Michael P. Toglia. Mahwah, NJ: Lawrence Erlbaum, 2007.

Megreya, Ahmed M., and A. Mike Burton. "Matching Faces to Photographs: Poor Performance in Eyewitness Memory (Without the Memory)." *Journal of Experimental Psychology: Applied* 14 (2008): 364–72.

Meissner, Christian A., and John C. Brigham. "Thirty Years of Investigating the Own-Race Bias in Memory for Faces: A Meta-Analytic Review." *Psychology, Public Policy, and Law* 7 (2001): 3–35.

Memon, Amina, Lorraine Hope, James Bartlett, and Ray Bull. "Eyewitness Recognition Errors: The Effects of Mugshot Viewing and Choosing in Young and Old Adults." *Memory and Cognition* 30 (2002): 1219–27.

Münsterberg, Hugo. *On the Witness Stand: Essays in Psychology and Crime.* New York: Doubleday, Page, 1908.

Nauert, Rick. "Ability to Recognize Faces Is Hardwired." *Psych Central.* Accessed December 5, 2011. http://psychcentral.com/news/2011/12/05/ability-to-recognize-faces-is-hardwired/32196.html.

Opfer, Chris. "The Problem with Police Line-Ups." *Atlantic,* February 19, 2013. http://www.theatlanticcities.com/politics/2013/02/problem-police-line-ups/4724/.

Rabin, Roni Caryn. "A Memory for Faces, Extreme Version." *New York Times,* May 25, 2009.

Rankin, Bill. "Innocent Man's Conviction Show's Flaws in Line-

Ups." Georgia Innocence Project, December 13, 2007. http://www.ga
-innocenceproject.org/Articles/Article_90.htm.

Rhodes, Matthew G., and Jeffrey S. Anastasi. "The Own-Age Bias in
Face Recognition: A Meta-Analytic and Theoretical Review." *Psychological Bulletin* 138 (2012): 146–74.

Sacchi, Dario, Franca Agnoli, and Elizabeth Loftus. "Changing History: Doctored Photographs Affect Memory for Past Public Events." *Applied Cognitive Psychology* 21 (2007): 1005–22.

Schmechel, Richard S., Timothy P. O'Toole, Catharine Easterly, and
Elizabeth Loftus. "Beyond the Ken? Testing Jurors' Understanding of
Eyewitness Reliability Evidence." *Jurimetrics* 46 (2006): 177–214.

Searcy, Jean H. "Age Differences in Accuracy and Choosing in Eyewitness Identification and Face Recognition." *Memory and Cognition* 27
(1999): 538–52.

Simon, Dan. *In Doubt: The Psychology of the Criminal Justice Process.* Cambridge, MA: Harvard University Press, 2012.

Simon, Dan. "The Limited Diagnosticity of Criminal Trials."
*Vanderbilt Law Review* 64 (2011): 143–223.

Simons, Daniel J., and Christopher F. Chabris. "Gorillas in Our
Midst: Sustained Inattentional Blindness for Dynamic Events." *Perception* 28 (1999): 1059–74.

Simons, Daniel J., and Christopher F. Chabris. "What People Believe
About How Memory Works: A Representative Survey of the U.S. Population." *PLOS ONE* 6, no. 8 (2011): 1–7.

Sledge, Kaffie. Georgia Innocence Project. "Adjusting to Freedom."
April 21, 2008. http://www.ga-innocenceproject.org/Articles/Article
_104.htm.

State of New Jersey, Office of the Attorney General. "Attorney General Guidelines for Preparing and Conducting Photo and Live Lineup
Identification Procedures." April 18, 2001.

*State v. Henderson.* 27 A.3d 872 (N.J. 2011).

*State v. White.* Transcript of Record. No. 314 (Ga. Super. Ct. May 29,
1980).

Steblay, Nancy M. "A Meta-Analytic Review of the Weapon Focus
Effect." *Law and Human Behavior* 16 (1992): 413–24.

Thompson, Jennifer. "I Was Certain, But I Was Wrong." *New York
Times,* June 18, 2000.

Tomes, Jennifer L., and Albert N. Katz. "Confidence-Accuracy Relations for Real and Suggested Events." *Memory* 8 (2000): 273–83.

Turner, Dorie. "DNA Test Clears Man After 27 Years." *Washington
Post,* December 11, 2007.

University of California, Los Angeles. "Did You See That? How Could You Miss It?" *ScienceDaily*, November 26, 2012. http://www.sciencedaily.com/releases/2012/11/121126151058.htm.

Valentine, Tim, and Jan Mesout. "Eyewitness Identification Under Stress in the London Dungeon." *Applied Cognitive Psychology* 23 (2009): 151–61.

Valentine, Tim, Alan Pickering, and Stephen Darling. "Characteristics of Eyewitness Identification That Predict the Outcome of Real Lineups." *Applied Cognitive Psychology* 17 (2003): 969–93.

Vredeveldt, Annelies, and Steven D. Penrod. "Eye-Closure Improves Memory for a Witnessed Event Under Naturalistic Conditions." *Psychology, Crime, and Law* 1 (2012): 893–905.

*Watkins v. Sowders.* 449 U.S. 341 (1981).

Weiser, Benjamin. "In New Jersey, Rules Are Changed on Witness IDs." *New York Times*, August 24, 2011.

Wells, Gary. "The Mistaken Identification of John Jerome White." Accessed May 18, 2015. http://www.psychology.iastate.edu/~glwells/The_Misidentification_of_John_White.pdf.

Wells, Gary L. "The Psychology of Lineup Identifications." *Journal of Applied Social Psychology* 14 (1983): 89–103.

Wells, Gary L., and Amy L. Bradfield. " 'Good You Identified the Suspect': Feedback to Eyewitnesses Distorts Their Reports of the Witnessing Experience." *Journal of Applied Psychology* 83 (1998): 360–76.

Wells, Gary L., Steve D. Charman, and Elizabeth A. Olson. "Building Face Composites Can Harm Lineup Identification Performance." *Journal of Experimental Psychology: Applied* 11 (2005): 147–56.

Wells, Gary L., and Elizabeth A. Olson. "Eyewitness Identification: Information Gain from Incriminating and Exonerating Behaviors." *Journal of Experimental Psychology: Applied* 8 (2002): 155–67.

Wise, Richard A., Clifford S. Fishman, and Martin A. Safer. "How to Analyze the Accuracy of Eyewitness Testimony in a Criminal Case." *Connecticut Law Review* 42 (2009): 435–513.

Wise, Richard A., Martin A. Safer, and Christina M. Moro. "What U.S. Law Enforcement Officers Know and Believe About Eyewitness Interviews and Identification Procedures." *Applied Cognitive Psychology* 25 (2011): 488–500.

"Witnesses Given New Tool to Fight Gang Crime." *UoP News*, March 19, 2013. http://www.port.ac.uk/uopnews/2013/03/19/witnesses-given-new-tool-to-fight-gang-crime/.

Yuille, John C. "Research and Teaching with Police: A Canadian Example." *International Review of Applied Psychology* 33 (1984): 5–23.

Yuille, John C., Graham Davies, Felicity Gibling, David Marxsen, and Stephen Porter. "Eyewitness Memory of Police Trainees for Realistic Role Plays." *Journal of Applied Psychology* 79 (1994): 931–36.


7. HOW TO TELL A LIE ~ THE EXPERT

Akehurst, Lucy, Gunter Kohnken, Aldert Vrij, and Ray Bull. "Lay Persons' and Police Officers' Beliefs Regarding Deceptive Behavior." *Applied Cognitive Psychology* 10 (1996): 461–71.

Allison, Helen E., and Richard J. Hobbs. *Science and Policy in Natural Resource Management: Understanding System Complexity.* New York: Cambridge University Press, 2006.

*Anderson v. Bessemer City.* 470 U.S. 564 (1985).

Aspinwall, Lisa G., Teneille R. Brown, and James Tabery. "The Double-Edged Sword: Does Biomechanism Increase or Decrease Judges' Sentencing of Psychopaths?" *Science* 337 (2012): 846–49.

Aspinwall, Lisa G., Teneille R. Brown, and James Tabery. "Supplementary Materials for 'The Double-Edged Sword: Does Biomechanism Increase or Decrease Judges' Sentencing of Psychopaths?'" *Science,* August 17, 2012, 1–29. http://www.sciencemag.org/content/suppl/2012/08/15/337.6096.846.DC1/1219569.Aspinwall.SM.pdf.

Associated Press. "Judge Says Remarks on 'Gorillas' May Be Cited in Trial on Beating." *New York Times,* June 12, 1991.

Association for Psychological Science. "Forensic Experts May Be Biased by the Side That Retains Them." *ScienceDaily,* August 28, 2013. http://www.sciencedaily.com/releases/2013/08/130828092302.htm.

Balmer, Andy. "*Gary James Smith v. State of Maryland.*" *Reasonable Excuse* (blog), August 30, 2012. http://andybalmer.wordpress.com/tag/no-lie-mri/.

Baskin, Deborah R., and Ira B. Sommers. "Crime-Show-Viewing Habits and Public Attitudes Toward Forensic Evidence: The 'CSI Effect' Revisited." *Justice System Journal* 31, no. 1 (2010): 97–113.

"Beyond Good Cop/Bad Cop: A Look at Real-Life Interrogations." NPR, December 5, 2013. http://www.npr.org/2013/12/05/248968150/beyond-good-cop-bad-cop-a-look-at-real-life-interrogations.

Bloom, Floyd E., Howard L. Fields, Michael S. Gazzaniga, Scott T. Grafton, Kent Kiehl, Helen Mayberg, Read Montague, Louis J. Ptacek, Marcus Raichle, Adina Roskies, and Anothony Wagner. *A Judge's Guide to Neuroscience: A Concise Introduction.* Santa Barbara: University of California, 2010.

Bond, Charles F., Jr., and Bella M. DePaulo. "Accuracy of Deception

Judgments." *Personality and Social Psychology Review* 10, no. 3 (2006): 214–34.

 *Boyd v. U.S.* 116 U.S. 616 (1886).

 Boyes-Watson, Carolyn. *Crime and Justice: Learning Through Cases.* Lanham, MD: Rowman & Littlefield, 2014.

 "Brains Scan for Lie Detection." *Washington Post,* August 26, 2012.

 Brainwave Science. "Brain Fingerprinting Advantages." Accessed May 16, 2014. http://www.brainwavescience.com/product-advantages.html.

 Brainwave Science. "Product Application for Law Enforcement." Accessed May 16, 2014. http://www.brainwavescience.com/law-advantages .html.

 Brainwave Science. "Product Applications." Accessed May 16, 2014. http://www.brainwavescience.com/technology.html.

 Brickell, Wendy. "Is It the CSI Effect or Do We Just Distrust Juries?" *Criminal Justice* 23 (2008): 10–18.

 Bright, David A., and Jane Goodman-Delahunty. "Gruesome Evidence and Emotion: Anger, Blame, and Jury Decision-Making." *Law and Human Behavior* 30, no. 2 (2006): 183–202.

 Canli, Turhan, Susan Brandon, William Casebeer, Philip J. Crowley, Don DuRousseau. Henry T. Greely, and Alvaro Pascual-Leone. "Neuroethics and National Security." *American Journal of Bioethics* 7, no. 5 (May 2007): 3–13.

 Cannon, Lou. "Prosecution Rests Case in Rodney King Beating Trial." *Washington Post,* March 16, 1993.

 Carey, Benedict. "Decoding the Brain's Cacophony." *New York Times,* October 31, 2011.

 Chermak, Steven, and Frankie Y. Bailey, eds. *Crimes and Trials of the Century,* vol. 1, *From the Black Sox Scandal to the Attica Prison Riots.* Westport, CT: Greenwood, 2007.

 Cognitive Neuroscience Society. "Memory, the Adolescent Brain, and Lying: The Limits of Neuroscientific Evidence in the Law." *ScienceDaily,* April 16, 2013. http://www.sciencedaily.com/releases/2013/ 04/130416180039.htm.

 Cook, Michael. "Liar, Liar, Brain on Fire!" *Mercatornet,* June 17, 2010. http://www.mercatornet.com/articles/view/liar_liar_brain_on_fire.

 Cutler, Brian L., and Margaret Bull Kovera. "Expert Psychological Testimony." *Current Directions in Psychological Science* 20, no. 1 (2011): 53–57.

 *Daubert v. Merrell Dow Pharmaceuticals.* 509 U.S. 579 (1993).

 Defoe, Daniel. *An Effectual Scheme for the Immediate Preventing of Street Robberies, and Suppressing All Other Disorders of the Night.* London: J. Wilford, 1731.

DePaulo, Bella M., Kelly Charlton, Harris, James J. Lindsay, and Laura Muhlenbruck. "The Accuracy-Confidence Correlation in the Detection of Deception." *Personality and Social Psychology Review* 1, no. 4 (1997): 346–57.

DePaulo, Bella M., Brian E. Malone, James J. Lindsay, Laura Muhlenbruck, Kelly Charlton, and Harris Cooper. "Cues to Deception." *Psychological Bulletin* 129, no. 1 (2003): 90–106.

Deutsch, Linda. "Witness Denies Being Influenced by Gates." *Los Angeles Times,* April 14, 1992.

Dickens, Charles. "The Demeanour of Murderers." In *The Works of Charles Dickens,* vol. 36. New York: Charles Scribner's Sons, 1908.

*Donelly v. California.* 228 U.S. 243 (1913).

Duhigg, Charles. "How Companies Learn Your Secrets." *New York Times,* February 16, 2012.

Eldeib, Duaa. "Polygraphs and False Confessions in Chicago." *Chicago Tribune,* March 10, 2013.

Eldeib, Duaa. "3 Disputed Polygraph Exams in Wrongful Conviction Cases." *Chicago Tribune,* March 10, 2013.

"Excerpts from the LAPD Officers' Trial." *Famous Trials.* Accessed August 27, 2014. http://law2.umkc.edu/faculty/projects/ftrials/lapd/kingtranscript.html.

Farrell, Brian. "Can't Get You Out of My Head: The Human Rights Implications of Using Brain Scans as Criminal Evidence." *Interdisciplinary Journal of Human Rights Law* 4 (2010): 89–95.

Fed. R. Evid. 702.

Feldman, Allen. "On Cultural Anesthesia: From Desert Storm to Rodney King." *American Ethnologist* 21, no. 2 (May 1994): 404–18.

*Fox v. Tomczak.* Fourth Amended Complaint. No. 04 C 7309 (N.D. Ill. Apr. 26, 2006), 2006 WL 1157466.

Frank, Mark G., Thomas Hugh Feeley, Nicole Paolantonio, and Timothy J. Servoss. "Individual and Small Group Accuracy in Judging Truthful and Deceptive Communication." *Group Decision and Negotiations* 13, no.1 (January 2004): 44–59.

*Frye v. United States.* 293 F. 1013 (D.C. Cir. 1923).

*Galloway v. Superior Court.* 816 F.Supp. 12 (D.D.C. 1993).

Gatowski, Sophia I., Shirley A. Dobbin, James T. Richardson, Gerald P. Ginsburg, Mara L. Merlino, and Veronica Dahir. "Asking the Gatekeepers: A National Survey of Judges on Judging Expert Evidence in a Post-*Daubert* World." *Law and Human Behavior* 25, no. 5 (2001): 433–58.

Ghorayshi, Azeen. "This Is Your Brain on the Department of Defense." *Blue Marble* (blog), *Mother Jones,* April 3, 2012. http://www

.motherjones.com/blue-marble/2012/04/department-of-defense
-neuroscience-bioethics-brains-law.

Giridharadas, Anand. "India's Use of Brain Scans in Courts Dismays Critics." *New York Times,* September 15, 2008.

Goldstein, Michael. "The Other Beating." *Los Angeles Times,* February 19, 2006.

Granhag, Pär Anders, and Leif A. Strömwall. "Effects of Preconceptions on Deception Detection and New Answers to Why Lie-Catchers Often Fail." *Psychology, Crime, and Law* 6 (2000): 197–218.

Granhag, Pär Anders, and Leif A. Strömwall. "Repeated Interrogations: Verbal and Non-verbal Cues to Deception." *Applied Cognitive Psychology* 16 (February 2002): 243–57.

Greely, Hank. "To Tell the Truth: Brain Scans Should Not Be Used for Lie Detection Unless Their Reliability Is Proven." *Scientific American,* December 2010.

Greely, Henry T. "Law and the Revolution in Neuroscience: An Early Look at the Field." *Akron Law Review* 42 (2009): 687–715.

Greely, Henry T., and Judy Illes. "Neuroscience-Based Lie Detection: The Urgent Need for Regulation." *American Journal of Law and Medicine* 33 (2007): 377–431.

Grubin, Don, and Lars Madsen. "Lie Detection and the Polygraph: A Historical Review." *Journal of Forensic Psychiatry and Psychology* 16, no. 2 (June 2005): 357–69.

Gurley, Jessica R., and David K. Marcus. "The Effects of Neuroimaging and Brain Injury on Insanity Defenses." *Behavioral Sciences and the Law* 26 (2008): 85–97.

Hanna, Aura, and Roger Remington. "The Representation of Color and Form in Long-Term Memory." *Memory and Cognition* 24, no. 3 (1996): 322–30.

Hansen, Mark. "True Lies." *ABA Journal,* October 1, 2009.

Harris, Mark. "MRI Lie Detectors: Can Magnetic-Resonance Imaging Show Whether People Are Telling the Truth?" *IEEE Spectrum,* July 30, 2010. http://spectrum.ieee.org/biomedical/imaging/mri-lie -detectors/0.

Hartwig, Maria, Pär Anders Granhag, Leif A. Strömwall, and Ola Kronkvist. "Strategic Use of Evidence During Police Interviews: When Training to Detect Deception Works." *Law and Human Behavior* 30 (2006): 603–19.

Inbau, Fred E., John E. Reid, Joseph P. Buckley, and Brian C. Jayne. *Criminal Interrogation and Confessions.* Burlington, MA: Jones & Bartlett Learning, 2011.

Jones, Owen D., Anthony D. Wagner, David L. Faigman, and Marcus E. Raichle. "Neuroscientists in Court." *Nature Review Neuroscience* 14 (2013): 730–36.

"Judicial Seminars on Emerging Issues in NeuroScience." American Association for the Advancement of Science. Last updated July 22, 2014. http://www.aaas.org/page/judicial-seminars-emerging-issues-neuroscience.

Kleisner, Karel, Lenka Priplatova, Peter Frost, and Jaroslav Flegr. "Trustworthy-Looking Face Meets Brown Eyes." *PLOS ONE* 8, no. 1 (2013): 1–7.

*Koon v. United States.* 518 U.S. 81 (1996).

Kovera, Margaret Bull, and Bradley D. McAuliff. "The Effects of Peer Review and Evidence Quality on Judge Evaluations of Psychological Science: Are Judges Effective Gatekeepers?" *Journal of Applied Psychology* 85, no. 4 (2000): 574–86.

Kuperberg Lab. "Functional Magnetic Resonance Imaging (fMRI)." *Massachusetts General Hospital.* Accessed May 16, 2014. http://www.nmr.mgh.harvard.edu/kuperberglab/volunteers/fMRI.htm.

Laris, Michael. "Debate on Brain Scans as Lie Detectors Highlighted in Maryland Murder Trial." *Washington Post,* August 26, 2012.

Laris, Michael. "Ex-Army Ranger Gary Smith Sentenced to 28 Years in Prison in Retrial." *Washington Post,* October 15, 2012.

Laris, Michael. "Gary Smith Guilty of Involuntary Manslaughter in 2006 Shooting of Fellow Army Ranger." *Washington Post,* September 19, 2012.

"Law and Neuroscience." Vanderbilt University, 2014. http://www.psy.vanderbilt.edu/courses/neurolaw/.

Linder, Douglas. "The Rodney King Beating Trials." *Jurist,* December 2001. http://jurist.law.pitt.edu/famoustrials/king.php.

"Los Angeles Riots Fast Facts." CNN.com. Last modified May 3, 2014. http://www.cnn.com/2013/09/18/us/los-angeles-riots-fast-facts/.

MacArthur Foundation Research Network on Law and Neuroscience. "Education and Outreach." Vanderbilt University, 2014. http://www.lawneuro.org/outreach.php.

*Maharashtra v. Sharma.* Sessions Case No. 508/07. June 12, 2008 (India).

Margolick, David. "As Venues Are Changed, Many Ask How Important a Role Race Should Play." *New York Times,* May 23, 1992.

*Mattox v. United States.* 156 U.S. 237 (1895).

McCabe, David P., and Alan D. Castel. "Seeing Is Believing: The Effect of Brain Images on Judgments of Scientific Reasoning." *Cognition* 107 (2008): 343–52.

McCabe, David P., Alan D. Castel, and Matthew G. Rhodes. "The Influence of fMRI Lie Detection Evidence on Juror Decision-Making." *Behavioral Sciences and the Law* 29 (2011): 566–77.

Megerian, Chris. "N.J. Parole Board Says Polygraph Tests Effective in Detecting, Preventing Violations by Sex Offenders." NJ.com, November 18, 2009. http://www.nj.com/news/index.ssf/2009/11/nj_parole_board_study_says_pol.html.

Merriman, C. D. "Biography of Daniel Defoe." Literature Network. Accessed May 15, 2014. http://www.online-literature.com/defoe/.

Miller, Greg. "Brain Exam May Have Swayed Jury in Sentencing Convicted Murderer." *ScienceInsider*, December 14, 2010. http://news.sciencemag.org/technology/2010/12/brain-exam-may-have-swayed-jury-sentencing-convicted-murderer.

Minzner, Max. "Detecting Lies Using Demeanor, Bias, and Context." *Cardozo Law Review* 29 (2008): 2557–81.

Model Criminal Jury Instructions: Credibility of Witnesses § 3.04. 3d Cir. 2012.

Model Criminal Jury Instructions: Opinion Evidence (Expert Witnesses) § 2.09. 3d Cir. 2012.

Model Criminal Jury Instructions: Role of the Jury § 1.02. 3d Cir. 2012.

Monterosso, John, and Barry Schwartz. "Did Your Brain Make You Do It?" *New York Times*, July 27, 2012.

Monterosso, John, Edward B. Royzman, and Barry Schwartz. "Explaining Away Responsibility: Effects of Scientific Explanation on Perceived Culpability." *Ethics and Behavior* 15, no. 2 (2005): 139–58.

Moreno, Joëlle Anne. "The Future of Neuroimaged Lie Detection and the Law." *Akron Law Review* 42 (2009): 717–37.

Morse, Dan. "The Long Life of a MoCo Homicide Case: Two Trials, Two Appeals, Third Trial on the Horizon." *Washington Post*, August 31, 2014.

Murphy, Emily. "Update on Indian BEOS Case: Accused Released on Bail." *Law and Biosciences Blog, Stanford Law School*, April 2, 2009. http://blogs.law.stanford.edu/lawandbiosciences/2009/04/02/update-on-indian-beos-case-accused-released-on-bail/.

Murrie, Daniel C., Marcus T. Boccaccini, Lucy A. Guarnera, and Katrina A. Rufino. "Are Forensic Experts Biased by the Side That Retained Them?" *Psychological Science* 24, no. 10 (2013): 1889–97.

Mydans, Seth. "Los Angeles Policemen Acquitted in Taped Beating." *New York Times*, April 30, 1992.

Mydans, Seth. "The Police Verdict." *New York Times*, April 30, 1992.

Mydans, Seth, Richard W. Stevenson, and Timothy Egan. "Seven Minutes in Los Angeles." *New York Times*, March 18, 1991.

Nadelhoffer, Thomas, and Walter Sinnott-Armstrong. "Neurolaw and Neuroprediction: Potential Promises and Perils." *Philosophy Compass* 7, no. 9 (September 2012): 631–42.

National Research Council of the National Academies. *Reference Manual on Scientific Evidence,* 3rd ed. Washington, DC: National Academies Press, 2011.

Nichols, Bill. *Blurred Boundaries: Questions of Meaning in Contemporary Culture.* Bloomington: Indiana University Press, 1994.

No Lie MRI. "New Truth Verification Technology." Accessed May 16, 2014. http://www.noliemri.com/index.htm.

Occupational Safety and Health Administration. "Safety and Health Regulations for Construction." Accessed May 18, 2014. https://www.osha.gov/pls/oshaweb/owadisp.show_document?p_table=standards&p_id=10839.

O'Sullivan, Maureen. "The Fundamental Attribution Error in Detecting Deception: The Boy-Who-Cried-Wolf Effect." *Personality and Social Psychology Bulletin* 29, no. 10 (2003): 1316–27.

Pelisek, Christine. "L.A. Riots Anniversary: Stacey Koon's Disturbing Testimony." *Daily Beast,* April 28, 2012.

Public Library of Science. "Brown-Eyed People Appear More Trustworthy Than Blue-Eyed People: People Judge Men's Trustworthiness Based on Face Shape, Eye Color." *ScienceDaily,* January 9, 2013. http://www.sciencedaily.com/releases/2013/01/130109185850.htm.

Pulice, Erin B. "The Right to Silence at Risk: Neuroscience-Based Lie Detection in the United Kingdom, India, and the United States." *George Washington International Law Review* 42 (2010): 865–96.

Rawls, John. *A Theory of Justice.* Cambridge, MA: Belknap Press, 1971.

Reardon, Sara. "Courtroom Neuroscience Not Ready for Prime Time." *ScienceInsider* (blog), *American Association for the Advancement of Science,* December 12, 2011. http://news.sciencemag.org/scienceinsider/2011/12/courtroom-neuroscience-not-ready.html?rss=1.

"The Reid Technique." John E. Reid & Associates, Inc. Accessed May 18, 2014. http://www.reid.com/educational_info/critictechnique.html.

Robertson, Christopher T., and David V. Yokum. "The Effect of Blinded Experts on Juror Verdicts." *Journal of Empirical Legal Studies* 9, no. 4 (2012): 765–94.

Robinson, Paul H., Robert Kurzban, and Owen Jones. "The Origins of Shared Intuitions of Justice." *Vanderbilt Law Review* 60 (2007): 1633–88.

*The "Rodney King" Case: What the Jury Saw in* California v. Powell. Directed by Dominic Palumbo. Courtroom Television Network, 1992. Videocassette (VHS), 116 min.

*The Rodney King Incident: Race and Justice in America.* Directed by Michael Pack. Princeton, NJ: Films for the Humanities and Sciences, 1998. Videocassette (VHS), 56 min.

Rosenthal, Andrew. "Bush Calls Police Beating 'Sickening.'" *New York Times,* March 22, 1991.

Royal Society. *Brain Waves Module 4: Neuroscience and the Law.* London: Royal Society, 2011.

Saini, Angela. "The Brain Police: Judging Murder with an MRI." *Wired UK,* May 27, 2009. http://www.wired.co.uk/magazine/archive/2009/06/features/guilty?page=all.

Schauer, Frederick. "Can Bad Science Be Good Evidence? Neuroscience, Lie Detection, and Beyond." *Cornell Law Review* 95 (2010): 1191–1220.

Schuller, Regina A., and Patricia A. Hastings. "Trials of Battered Women Who Kill: The Impact of Alternative Forms of Expert Evidence." *Law and Human Behavior* 20, no. 2 (1996): 167–87.

Schweitzer, N. J., Michael J. Saks, Emily R. Murphy, Adina L. Roskies, Walter Sinnott-Armstrong, and Lyn M. Gaudet. "Neuroimages as Evidence in a *Mens Rea* Defense: No Impact." *Psychology, Public Policy, and Law* 17, no. 3 (2011): 357–93.

Scripps Research Institute. "Possibility of Selectively Erasing Unwanted Memories." *ScienceDaily,* September 10, 2013. http://www.sciencedaily.com/releases/2013/09/130910140941.htm.

Serrano, Richard A. "LAPD Officers Reportedly Taunted King in Hospital." *Los Angeles Times,* March 23, 1991.

Simon, Dan. "The Limited Diagnosticity of Criminal Trials." *Vanderbilt Law Review* 64 (2011): 143–223.

Slobogin, Christopher. *Proving the Unprovable: The Role of Law, Science, and Speculation in Adjudicating Culpability and Dangerousness.* New York: Oxford University Press, 2007.

Sporer, Siegfried L., and Barbara Schwandt. "Moderators of Nonverbal Indicators of Deception: A Meta-Analytic Synthesis." *Psychology, Public Policy, and Law* 13, no. 1 (2007): 1–34.

Stanley, Jay. "High-Tech 'Mind Readers' Are Latest Effort to Detect Lies." *Free Future* (blog), American Civil Liberties Union, August 29, 2012. https://www.aclu.org/blog/technology-and-liberty/high-tech-mind-readers-are-latest-effort-detect-lies.

Texas Department of Criminal Justice Parole Division. *Sex Offender Treatment and Polygraph Guidelines.* January 28, 2014.

Tierney, John. "At Airports, a Misplaced Faith in Body Language." *New York Times,* March 23, 2014.

Tubman-Carbone, Heather. "An Exploratory Study of New Jersey's Sex Offender Polygraph Policy: Report to the New Jersey State Parole Board." November 13, 2009. http://media.nj.com/ledgerupdates _impact/other/11.18.09%20polygraph%20report.pdf.

United States Court of Appeals for the Third Circuit. "About the Court." Accessed May 14, 2014. http://www.ca3.uscourts.gov/about-court.

United States Courts. "Juror Qualifications, Exemptions, and Excuses." Accessed May 18, 2014. http://www.uscourts.gov/FederalCourts/ JuryService/JurorQualifications.aspx.

United States Government Accountability Office. *TSA Should Limit Future Funding for Behavior Detection Activities.* November 2013.

*United States v. Watson.* 483 F.3d 828 (D.C. Cir. 2007).

Vidmar, Neil. "The Psychology of Trial Judging." *Current Directions in Psychological Science* 20, no. 1 (2011): 58–62.

Vrij, Aldert, Samantha A. Mann, Ronald P. Fisher, Sharon Leal, Rebecca Milne, and Ray Bull. "Increasing Cognitive Load to Facilitate Lie Detection: The Benefit of Recalling an Event in Reverse Order." *Law and Human Behavior* 32 (2008): 253–65.

Warden, Rob. "Juan Rivera Freed After More Than 19 Years Behind Bars for a Crime It Had Long Been Obvious He Could Not Have Committed." *Bluhm Legal Clinic, Northwestern Law.* Accessed May 17, 2014. http://www.law.northwestern.edu/legalclinic/wrongfulconvictions/ exonerations/il/juan-rivera.html.

Weisberg, Deena Skolnick, Frank C. Keil, Joshua Goodstein, Elizabeth Rawson, and Jeremy R. Gray. "The Seductive Allure of Neuroscience Explanations." *Journal of Cognitive Neuroscience* 20, no. 3 (2008): 470–77.

Wiseman, Richard, Caroline Watt, Leanne ten Brinke, Stephen Porter, Sara-Louise Cooper, and Calum Rankin. "The Eyes Don't Have It: Lie Detection and Neuro-Linguistic Programming." *PLOS ONE* 7, no. 7 (2012): 1–6.

Young, Erica J., Massimiliano Aceti, Erica M. Griggs, Rita A. Fuchs, Zachary Zigmond, Gavin Rumbaugh, and Courtney A. Miller. "Selective, Retrieval-Independent Disruption of Methamphetamine-Associated Memory by Actin Depolymerization." *Biological Psychiatry Journal* 75 (2014): 96–104.

## 8. UMPIRES OR ACTIVISTS? ~ THE JUDGE

Achen, Christopher H., and Larry M. Bartels. "It Feels Like We're Thinking: The Rationalizing Voter and Electoral Democracy." Paper presented at the Annual Meeting of the American Political Science Association, Philadelphia, August 30–September 3, 2006. http://www.princeton.edu/~bartels/thinking.pdf.

"After Sending a Man to Prison, Judge Admits He Was Biased." NPR, June 14, 2014. http://www.npr.org/2014/06/14/321952967/after-sending-a-man-to-prison-judge-admits-he-was-biased.

American Bar Association. "Most Americans See 'Judicial Activism' Crisis." WND, September 20, 2005. http://www.wnd.com/2005/09/32620/.

Anderson, Kyle J., and David A. Pierce. "Officiating Bias: The Effect of Foul Differential on Foul Calls in NCAA Basketball." *Journal of Sports Sciences* 27 (2009): 687–94.

Askins, Robert L. "The Official Reacting to Pressure." *Referee* 3 (1978): 17–20.

Baker, Peter, and Neil A. Lewis. "Republicans Press Judge About Bias." *New York Times,* July 14, 2009.

Beck, Howard, and Michael S. Schmidt. "N.B.A. Referee Pleads Guilty to Gambling Charges." *New York Times,* August 16, 2007.

Benforado, Adam. "Color Commentators of the Bench." *Florida State University Law Review* 38 (2011): 451–79.

Berdejo, Carlos, and Noam M. Yuchtman. "Crime, Punishment, and Politics: An Analysis of Political Cycles in Criminal Sentencing." *Review of Economics and Statistics* 95, no. 3 (2013): 741–56.

Birnbaum, Phil. "A Guide to Sabermetric Research." Society for American Baseball Research. Accessed November 7, 2014. http://sabr.org/sabermetrics.

Bombardieri, Marcella, Jonathan Saltzman, and Thomas Farragher. "For Drunk Drivers, a Habit of Judicial Leniency." *Boston Globe,* October 30, 2011.

Boyd, Christina L., Lee Epstein, and Andrew D. Martin. "Untangling the Causal Effects of Sex on Judging." *American Journal of Political Science* 54 (2010): 389–411.

Canes-Wrone, Brandice, Tom S. Clark, and Jason P. Kelly. "Judicial Selection and Death Penalty Decisions." *American Political Science Review* 108, no. 1 (2014): 23–39.

Casarez, Jean. "Did Racial Bias Lead NYC Judge to Convict Man of Murder?" CNN.com, August 7, 2014. http://www.cnn.com/2014/08/06/justice/new-york-murder-conviction-revisited/.

Cinquegrana, R. J., and Diana K. Lloyd. *Report to the Supreme Judicial Court.* Boston: Choate, Hall & Stewart LLP, 2012.

*Confirmation Hearing on the Nomination of Elena Kagan to Be an As-*

*sociate Justice of the Supreme Court of the United States.* Before the Comm. on the Judiciary, 111th Cong. (2010).

*Confirmation Hearing on the Nomination of Hon. Sonia Sotomayor, to Be an Associate Justice of the Supreme Court of the United States.* Before the Comm. on the Judiciary, 109th Cong. (2009).

*Confirmation Hearing on the Nomination of John G. Roberts, Jr. to Be Chief Justice of the United States.* Before the Comm. on the Judiciary, 109th Cong. (2005).

*Confirmation Hearing on the Nomination of Robert H. Bork to Be Associate Justice of the United States.* Before the Comm. on the Judiciary, 100th Cong. (1987).

*Confirmation Hearing on the Nomination of Samuel A. Alito, Jr. to Be an Associate Justice of the Supreme Court of the United States.* Before the Comm. on the Judiciary, 109th Cong. (2006).

"Congressional Baseball Game 2012: Political Wounds Still Fresh." CBS News, June 29, 2012. http://www.cbsnews.com/8334-503544_162 -57463434-503544/congressional-baseball-game-2012-political-wounds -still-fresh/.

Danziger, Shai, Jonathan Levav, and Liora Avnaim-Pesso. "Extraneous Factors in Judicial Decisions." *Proceedings of the National Academy of Sciences* 108, no. 17 (2010): 6889–92.

Danziger, Shai, Jonathan Levav, and Liora Avnaim-Pesso. "Reply to Weinshall-Margel and Shapard: Extraneous Factors in Judicial Decisions Persist." *Proceedings of the National Academy of Sciences* 108, no. 42 (2010): E834.

Dawson, Peter, Stephen Dobson, John Goddard, and John Wilson. "Are Football Referees Really Biased and Inconsistent? Evidence of the Incidence of Disciplinary Sanction in the English Premier League." *Journal of the Royal Statistical Society: Series A* 170 (2007): 231–50.

"Drexel University School of Law Student Handbook: Academic Year 2013–2014." http://drexel.edu/law/studentLife/studentAffairs/ Student%20Handbook/.

Englich, Brite, Thomas Mussweiler, and Fritz Strack. "Playing Dice with Criminal Sentences: The Influence of Irrelevant Anchors on Experts' Judicial Decision Making." *Personality and Social Psychology Bulletin* 32 (2006): 188–200.

"Failure of Empathy and Justice." *New York Times*, March 31, 2011.

Fleming, Stephen M., Charlotte L. Thomas, and Raymond J. Dolan. "Overcoming Status Quo Bias in the Human Brain." *Proceedings of the National Academy of Sciences* 107, no. 13 (2009): 6005–9.

Fraga, Brian. "Nearly Two Dozen State Judges Acquit 95 Percent of OUI Defendants in Bench Trials, Report States." *Herald News* (Fall River, MA), November 1, 2012.

Frank, Jerome. *Law and the Modern Mind*. New York: Brentano's, 1930.

Garicano, Luis, Ignacio Palacios-Huerta, and Canice Prendergast. "Favoritism Under Social Pressure." *Review of Economics and Statistics* 87 (2005): 208–16.

Glynn, Adam N., and Maya Sen. "Identifying Judicial Empathy: Does Having Daughters Cause Judges to Rule for Women's Issues?" *American Journal of Political Science* (2014): 1–18.

Greely, Henry T., and Anthony D. Wagner. "Reference Guide on Scientific Evidence." In *Reference Manual on Scientific Evidence*, 3rd ed. Washington, DC: National Academies Press, 2011.

Greenhouse, Linda. "Evolving Opinions: Heartfelt Words from the Rehnquist Court." *New York Times*, July 6, 2013.

Guthrie, Chris, Jeffrey J. Rachlinski, and Andrew J. Wistrich. "Blinking on the Bench: How Judges Decide Cases." *Cornell Law Review* 93 (2007): 1–44.

Guthrie, Chris, Jeffrey J. Rachlinski, and Andrew J. Wistrich. "Inside the Judicial Mind." *Cornell Law Review* 86 (2001): 777–830.

Hagemann, Norbert, Bernd Strauss, and Jan Leibing. "When the Referee Sees Red." *Psychological Science* 19 (2008): 769–71.

Hall, Erika, and Robert Livingston. "The Hubris Penalty." *Journal of Experimental Social Psychology* 48 (2012): 899–904.

Hunt, Albert R. "Washington Flip Flops on Justice Roberts." *New York Times*, July 1, 2012.

Iaryczower, Matias, Garrett Lewis, and Matthew Shum. "To Elect or to Appoint? Bias, Information, and Responsiveness of Bureaucrats and Politicians." *Journal of Public Economics* 97 (2013): 230–44.

Irwin, John, and Daniel Real. "Unconscious Influences on Judicial Decision-Making: The Illusion of Objectivity." *McGeorge Law Review* 43 (2010): 1–18.

James, Bill. "Keynote Speech at the Conference on Empirical Studies." University of Pennsylvania Law School, Philadelphia, PA, October 25, 2013.

Jost, Kenneth. "Roberts' Confirmation Hearings Conclude." NPR, September 15, 2005. http://www.npr.org/templates/story/story.php?storyId=4850135.

Jost, Kenneth. "Roberts Says He Has 'No Agenda' on Bench." NPR, September 12, 2005. http://www.npr.org/templates/story/story.php?storyId=4843769.

Kahan, Dan M., Ellen Peters, Erica Cantrell Dawson, and Paul Slovic. "Motivated Numeracy and Enlightened Self-Government." The Cultural Cognition Project Working Paper No. 116 (2013).

Kastellec, Jonathan P. "Racial Diversity and Judicial Influence on Appellate Courts." *American Journal of Political Science* 57 (2013): 167–83.

Klein, Ezra. "Unpopular Mandate." *New Yorker*, June 25, 2012.

Kranjec, Alexander, Matthew Lehet, Bianca Bromberger, and Anjan Chatterjee. "A Sinister Bias for Calling Fouls in Soccer." *PLOS ONE* 5 (2010): 1–4.

*Kyllo v. United States.* 533 U.S. 27 (2001).

Landsman, Stephan, and Richard F. Rakos. "A Preliminary Inquiry into the Effect of Potentially Biasing Information on Judges and Jurors in Civil Litigation." *Behavioral Sciences and the Law* 12 (1994): 113–26.

Larsen, Allison Orr. "Confronting Supreme Court Fact Finding." *Virginia Law Review* 98 (2012): 1255–1312.

Larsen, Allison Orr. "The Trouble with Amicus Facts," *Virginia Law Review* 100 (2014): 1757–1818.

Lichtblau, Eric. "Advocacy Group Says Justices May Have Conflict in Campaign Finance Cases." *New York Times,* January 19, 2011.

Lichtblau, Eric. "Thomas Cites Failure to Disclose Wife's Job." *New York Times,* January 24, 2011.

Liptak, Adam. "Another Factor Said to Sway Judges to Rule for Women's Rights: A Daughter." *New York Times,* June 16, 2014.

Liptak, Adam. "Harsher Sentencing Guidelines Can't Be Used for Old Offenses, Justices Say." *New York Times,* June 10, 2013.

Liptak, Adam. "Seeking Facts, Justices Settle for What Briefs Tell Them." *New York Times,* September 1, 2014.

Liptak, Adam, and Allison Kopicki. "Approval Rating for Justices Hits Just 44% in New Poll." *New York Times,* June 7, 2012.

Mauro, Tony, and David Ingram. "The Sotomayor Confirmation Hearings: Sotomayor Pledges 'Fidelity to the Law.'" *National Law Journal,* July 13, 2009.

McKinley, James C., Jr. "Ex-Brooklyn Judge Seeks Reversal of His Verdict in 1999 Murder Case." *New York Times,* December 12, 2013.

McKinley, James C., Jr. "Prosecutor Questions Ex-Judge's Memory." *New York Times,* February 10, 2014.

"The Mechanisms of Choice." *Observer* 25, no. 1 (2012). http://www.psychologicalscience.org/index.php/publications/observer/2012/january-12/the-mechanics-of-choice.html.

Miller, S. A. "Kagan O'Care Bias Feared." *New York Post,* November 16, 2011.

Moskowitz, Tobias J., and L. Jon Wertheim. *Scorecasting: The Hidden Influences Behind How Sports Are Played and Games Are Won*. New York: Crown Archetype, 2011.

"MTA Fixing Trippy Brooklyn Subway Stairs After Dean Peterson's Hilarious Viral Video." *Huffington Post*, June 28, 2012. http://www.huffingtonpost.com/2012/06/28/mta-fixing-trippy-brooklyn-subway-stairs-dean-peterson_n_1634229.html.

Nelson, William E., Harvey Rishikof, I. Scott Messinger, and Michael Jo. "The Liberal Tradition of the Supreme Court Clerkship: Its Rise, Fall, and Reincarnation." *Vanderbilt Law Review* 62 (2009): 1749–1814.

"The Next Chief Justice." *New York Daily News*, September 16, 2005.

O'Brien, Keith. "Do the Math? Only if I Agree with It!" *Boston Globe*, October 20, 2013.

Pariser, Eli. *The Filter Bubble*. New York: Penguin, 2011.

Peterson, Dean. "New York Subway Stairs Gag: Dean Peterson Films Straphangers Enjoying Their 'Trip' (Video)." *Huffington Post*, July 5, 2012. http://www.huffingtonpost.com/2012/06/27/new-york-subway-stairs-dean-paterson_n_1631674.html?utm_hp_ref=new-york.

Pew Research Center for the People and the Press. "Supreme Court's Favorable Rating Still at Historical Low." March 25, 2013. http://www.people-press.org/2013/03/25/supreme-courts-favorable-rating-still-at-historic-low/.

Posner, Richard A. "The Incoherence of Antonin Scalia." *New Republic*, August 24, 2012. http://www.tnr.com/article/magazine/books-and-arts/106441/scalia-garner-reading-the-law-textual-originalism?page=0,0.

Price, Joseph, and Justin Wolfers. "Biased Referees? Reconciling Results with the NBA's Analysis." *Contemporary Economic Policy* 30, no. 3 (2011): 320–28.

Pullman, Sandra. "Ginsburg and WRP Staff." ACLU, March 7, 2006. http://www.aclu.org/womens-rights/tribute-legacy-ruth-bader-ginsburg-and-wrp-staff.

Rachlinski, Jeffrey J., Sheri Lynn Johnson, Andrew J. Wistrich, and Chris Guthrie. "Does Unconscious Racial Bias Affect Trial Judges?" *Notre Dame Law Review* 84 (2009): 1195–1246.

"Researchers Find Appointed Justices Outperform Elected Counterparts." *ScienceDaily*, February 22, 2013. http://www.sciencedaily.com/releases/2013/02/130222121049.htm.

Roberts, Roxanne, and Amy Argetsinger. "A Truly Exclusive Washington Party: Antonin Scalia Hosts Justices to Toast New Henry Friendly Bio." *Washington Post*, May 1, 2012.

Rothman, Josh. "Supreme Court Justices: Addicted to Google." *Boston Globe,* June 7, 2012.

Rowland, C. K., and Bridget Jeffery Todd. "Where You Stand Depends on Who Sits: Platform Promises and Judicial Gatekeeping in the Federal District Courts." *Journal of Politics* 53, no. 1 (1995): 175–85.

Saltzman, Jonathan, Marcella Bombardieri, and Thomas Farragher. "A Judicial Haven for Accused Drunk Drivers." *Boston Globe,* November 6, 2011.

Samuels, Dorothy J. "Scalia's Gay Marriage Problem." *New York Times,* March 15, 2013.

Scalia, Antonin, and Bryan A. Garner. Interview by Stephen Adler. *Thompson Reuters Newsmaker,* September 17, 2012.

Schwartz, Robert. "Like They See 'Em." *New York Times,* October 6, 2005.

Senior, Jennifer. "In Conversation: Antonin Scalia." *New York,* October 6, 2013.

Simonsohn, Uri, and Francesca Gino. "Daily Horizons: Evidence of Narrow Bracketing in Judgment From 10 Years of M.B.A. Admissions Interviews." *Psychological Science* 24 (2013): 219–41.

Smelcer, Susan Navarro. *Supreme Court Justices: Demographic Characteristics, Professional Experience, and Legal Education, 1789–2010.* CRS Report R40802. Washington, DC: Library of Congress, Congressional Research Service. April 9, 2010.

Sotomayor, Sonia. "A Latina Judge's Voice." *Berkeley La Raza Law Journal* 13 (2002): 87–92.

Stanford Encyclopedia of Philosophy. "Feminist Philosophy of Law." May 19, 2009. http://plato.stanford.edu/entries/feminism-law/.

*Statement of the Justices of the Supreme Judicial Court.* November 1, 2012.

"Stern: Bet Probe 'Worst Situation That I Have Ever Experienced." ESPN.com, July 25, 2007. http://sports.espn.go.com/nba/news/story?id=2947237.

Stevenson, Richard W. "President Names Roberts as Choice for Chief Justice." *New York Times,* September 6, 2005.

Sunstein, Cass R. "Judicial Partisanship Awards." *Washington Independent,* July 31, 2008.

Sunstein, Cass R., and Thomas Miles. "Depoliticizing Administrative Law." *Duke Law Journal* 58 (2008): 2193–2230.

Supreme Court of the United States. "Biographies of Current Justices of the Supreme Court." http://www.supremecourt.gov/about/biographies.aspx.

Sutter, Matthias, and Martin G. Kocher. "Favoritism of Agents: The Case of Referees' Home Bias." *Journal of Economic Psychology* 25 (2004): 461–69.

Tierney, John. "Do You Suffer from Decision Fatigue?" *New York Times*, August 17, 2011.

Torres-Spelliscy, Ciara, Monique Chase, Emma Greenman, and Susan M. Liss. "Improving Judicial Diversity." Brennan Center for Justice, 2010. http://www.brennancenter.org/publication/improving -judicial-diversity.

Totenberg, Nina. "Robert Bork's Supreme Court Nomination 'Changed Everything, Maybe Forever.'" NPR, March 19, 2012. http:// www.npr.org/blogs/itsallpolitics/2012/12/19/167645600/robert-borks -supreme-court-nomination-changed-everything-maybe-forever.

Tur, Katy. "MTA Blocks Staircase After Viral Video Shows People Tripping on Same Subway Station Step." NBC.com, June 29, 2012. http://www.nbcnewyork.com/news/local/Subway-Stair-Tripping -People-Fall-Steps-Brooklyn-Station-36-Street-Sunset-Park-MTA -160629545.html.

Tversky, Amos, and Daniel Kahneman. "Judgment Under Uncertainty: Heuristics and Biases." *Science* 185 (1974): 1124–31.

United States Courts. "Code of Conduct for United States Judges." Last revised March 20, 2014. http://www.uscourts.gov/RulesAnd Policies/CodesOfConduct/CodeConductUnitedStatesJudges.aspx.

United States Courts. "Judicial Conference Regulations: Gifts." http://www.uscourts.gov/RulesAndPolicies/CodesOfConduct/Judicial ConferenceRegulationsGifts.aspx.

United States Senate Committee on the Judiciary. "Nomination of John G. Roberts." http://www.judiciary.senate.gov/meetings/ nomination-of-john-g-roberts.

*United States v. Booker.* 543 U.S. 220 (2005).

*United States v. Jones.* 132 S. Ct. 945 (2012).

*United States v. Sykes.* 131 S. Ct. 2267 (2011).

U.S. Const. amend. IV.

Vallone, Robert P., Lee Ross, and Mark R. Lepper. "The Hostile Media Phenomenon: Biased Perception and Perceptions of Media Bias in Coverage of the Beirut Massacre." *Journal of Personality and Social Psychology* 49, no. 3 (1985): 577–85.

Van Quaquebeke, Niels, and Steffen R. Giessner. "How Embodied Cognitions Affect Judgments: Height-Related Attribution Bias in Football Foul Calls." *Journal of Sport and Exercise Psychology* 32 (2010): 3–22.

Weber, Bruce. "Umpires v. Judges." *New York Times*, July 11, 2009.

Weinshall-Margel, Keren, and John Shapard. "Overlooked Factors in the Analysis of Parole Decisions." *Proceedings of the National Academy of Sciences* 108, no. 2 (2011): E833.

Whitney, David, Nicole Wurnitsch, Byron Hontiveros, and Elizabeth Louie. "Perceptual Mislocalization of Bouncing Balls by Professional Tennis Referees." *Current Biology* 18 (2008): R947–49.

Wistrich, Andrew J., Chris Guthrie, and Jeffrey J. Rachlinski. "Can Judges Ignore Inadmissible Information? The Difficulty of Deliberately Disregarding." *University of Pennsylvania Law Review* 153 (2005): 1251–1345.

Zelinsky, Aaron S. J. "The Justice as Commissioner: Benching the Judge-Umpire Analogy." *Yale Law Journal* 199 (2010): 113.

## 9. AN EYE FOR AN EYE ~ THE PUBLIC

Abwender, David A., and Keyatta Hough. "Interactive Effects of Characteristics of Defendant and Mock Juror on U.S. Participants' Judgment and Sentencing Recommendations." *Journal of Social Psychology* 141 (2001): 603–15.

Aharoni, Eyal, and Alan J. Fridlund. "Punishment Without Reason: Isolating Retribution in Lay Punishment of Criminal Offenders." *Psychology, Public Policy, and Law* 18, no. 4 (2012): 599–625.

Alicke. Mark D. "Culpable Causation." *Journal of Personality and Social Psychology* 63, no. 3 (1992): 368–78.

Alicke, Mark D. "Culpable Control and Psychology of Blame." *Psychological Bulletin* 126 (2000): 556–74.

"Animals: Kaiser Bill." *Time,* November 18, 1929.

Arndt, Jamie, Jeff Greenberg, Tom Pyszczynski, and Sheldon Solomon. "Subliminal Exposure to Death-Related Stimuli Increases Defense of the Cultural Worldview." *Psychological Science* 8, no. 5 (1997): 379–85.

Arndt, Jamie, J. D. Lieberman, A. Cook, and S. Solomon. "Terror Management in the Courtroom." *Psychology, Public Policy, and Law* 11, no. 3 (2005): 407–38.

Aspinwall, Lisa G., Teneille R. Brown, and James Tabery. "The Double-Edged Sword: Does Biomechanism Increase or Decrease Judges' Sentencing of Psychopaths?" *Science* 337, no. 6096 (2012): 846–49.

*Atkins v. Virginia.* 536 U.S. 304 (2002).

Aviv, Rachel. "No Remorse." *New Yorker,* January 2, 2012.

Ayres, Ian, and Joel Waldfogel. "A Market Test for Race Discrimination in Bail Setting." *Stanford Law Review* 46 (1994): 987–1047.

Baldus, David, George Woodworth, David Zuckerman, Neil Alan

Weiner, and Barbara Broffitt. "Racial Discrimination and the Death Penalty in the Post-Furman Era: An Empirical and Legal Overview, with Recent Findings from Philadelphia." *Cornell Law Review* 83 (1998): 1638–1770.

Baumeister, Roy F., and Aaron Beck. *Evil: Inside Human Violence and Cruelty.* New York: Henry Holt, 1999.

Benforado, Adam. "Quick on the Draw: Implicit Bias and the Second Amendment." *Oregon Law Review* 89, no. 1 (2010): 1–80.

Bennett, Mark, and Deborah Earwaker. "Victim's Responses to Apologies: The Effects of Offender Responsibility and Offense Severity." *Journal of Social Psychology* 134, no. 4 (1994): 457–64.

Bloom, Paul. *Just Babies: The Origins of Good and Evil.* New York: Crown, 2013.

Bondeson, Jan. *The Feejee Mermaid and Other Essays in Natural and Unnatural History.* Ithaca, NY: Cornell University Press, 1999.

Bucciarelli, Monica, Sangeet Khemlani, and Philip N. Johnson-Laird. "The Psychology of Moral Reasoning." *Judgment and Decision Making* 3, no. 2 (2008): 121–39.

Burke, Brian L., Andy Martens, and Erik H. Faucher. "Two Decades of Terror Management Theory: A Meta-Analysis of Mortality Salience Research." *Personality and Social Psychology Review* 14, no. 10 (2010): 155–95.

Burris, Christopher T., and John K. Rempel. " 'Just Look at Him': Punitive Responses Cued by 'Evil' Symbols." *Basic and Applied Social Psychology* 33 (2011): 69–80.

Campbell, Maggie, and Johanna Ray Vollhardt. "Fighting the Good Fight: The Relationship Between Belief in Evil and Support for Violent Policies." *Personality and Social Psychology Bulletin* 40, no. 1 (2014): 16–33.

Carlsmith, Kevin M., and John M. Darley. "Psychological Aspects of Retributive Justice." *Advances in Experimental Psychology* 40 (2008): 193–236.

Carlsmith, Kevin M., John M. Darley, and Paul H. Robinson. "Why Do We Punish? Deterrence and Just Deserts as Motives for Punishment." *Journal of Personality and Social Psychology* 83, no. 2 (2002): 284–99.

Carlsmith, Kevin M., and Avani Mehta Sood. "The Fine Line Between Interrogation and Retribution." *Journal of Experimental Psychology* (2008): 191–96.

Cave, Stephen. "Imagining the Downside of Immortality." *New York Times,* August 27, 2011.

Clark, Cory J., Jamie B. Luguri, Peter H. Ditto, Joshua Knobe, Azim F.

Shariff, and Roy F. Baumeister. "Free to Punish: A Motivated Account of Free Will Belief." *Journal of Personality and Social Psychology* 106, no. 4 (2014): 501–13.

Cohen, Esther. "Law, Folklore, and Animal Lore." *Past and Present* 110 (1986).

"Condemned Dog Faces Kentucky Court Today." *New York Times*, January 16, 1928.

Cushman, Fiery. "Crime and Punishment: Distinguishing the Roles of Causal and Intentional Analyses in Moral Judgment." *Cognition* 108 (2008): 353–80.

Cushman, Fiery. "Punishment in Humans: From Intuitions to Institutions." *Philosophy Compass* (2015): 117–33.

Cushman, Fiery, A. J. Durwin, and Chaz Lively. "Revenge Without Responsibility? Judgments About Collective Punishment in Baseball." *Journal of Experimental Social Psychology* 48, no. 5 (2012): 1106–10.

Darby, Bruce W., and Barry R. Schlenker. "Children's Reactions to Transgressions: Effects of the Actor's Apology, Reputation, and Remorse." *British Journal of Social Psychology* 28, no. 4 (1989): 353–64.

Darley, John. M., Kevin M. Carlsmith, and Paul H. Robinson. "Incapacitation and Just Deserts as Motives for Punishment." *Law and Human Behavior* 24, no. 6 (2000): 659–83.

Day, Martin V., and Michael Ross. "The Value of Remorse: How Drivers' Responses to Police Predict Fines for Speeding." *Law and Human Behavior* 35, no. 3 (2011): 221–34.

Ditto, Peter H., David A. Pizarro, and David Tannenbaum. "Motivated Moral Reasoning." In *Moral Judgment and Decision Making*, edited by Daniel M. Bartels, Christopher W. Bauman, Fiery Cushman, David A. Pizarro, and A. Peter McGraw. Burlington, MA: Academic Press, 2009.

Donahue, John, III. "Capital Punishment in Connecticut, 1973–2007: A Comprehensive Evaluation from 4866 Murders to One Execution." Working Paper, Stanford Law School, National Bureau of Economic Research, June 8, 2013.

Dressler, Joshua. *Understanding Criminal Law*, 6th ed. New Providence, NJ: LexisNexis, 2012.

Eberhardt, Jennifer. "The Race Factor in Trying Juveniles as Adults." *New York Times*, June 5, 2012.

Eberhardt, Jennifer L., Paul G. Davies, Valerie J. Purdie-Vaughns, and Sheri Lynn Johnson. "Looking Deathworthy: Perceived Stereotyping of Black Defendants Predicts Capital-Sentencing Outcomes." *Psychological Science* 17, no. 5 (2006): 383–86.

Eckholm, Erik. "Juveniles Facing Lifelong Terms Despite Rulings." *New York Times,* January 19, 2014.

Ellard, John H., Christina D. Miller, Terri-lynne Baumle, and James M. Olson. "Just World Processes in Demonizing." In *The Justice Motive in Everyday Life,* edited by M. Ross and D. T. Miller. New York: Cambridge University Press, 2002.

Evans, E. P. *The Criminal Prosecution and Capital Punishment of Animals.* New York: Dutton, 1906.

Exodus 21:28 (King James).

Franklin, Benjamin. *The Writings of Benjamin Franklin,* vol. 9. Edited by Albert Henry Smyth. London: Macmillan, 1906.

Frazer, Sir James George. "The Ox That Gored." In *Folk-Lore in the Old Testament,* vol. 3. London: Macmillan, 1919.

Girgen, Jen. "The Historical and Contemporary Prosecution and Punishment of Animals." *Animal Law* 9 (2003): 97–103.

Gold, Gregg J., and Bernard Weiner. "Remorse, Confession, Group Identity, and Expectancies About Repeating a Transgression." *Basic and Applied Social Psychology* 22, no. 4 (2000): 291–300.

Goodwin, Geoffrey P., and Adam Benforado. "Judging the Goring Ox." *Cognitive Science* (2014).

Graham, Sandra, and Brian S. Lowery. "Priming Unconscious Racial Stereotypes About Adolescent Offenders." *Law and Human Behavior* 28, no. 5 (2004): 483–504.

Greenberg, Jeff, Tom Pyszczynski, and Sheldon Solomon. "The Causes and Consequences of a Need for Self-Esteem: A Terror Management Theory." In *Public Self and Private Self,* edited by Roy F. Baumeister. New York: Springer-Verlag, 1986.

Greenberg, Jeff, Tom Pyszczynski, Sheldon Solomon, Linda Simon, and Michael Breus. "Role of Consciousness and Accessibility of Death-Related Thoughts in Mortality Salience Effects." *Journal of Personality and Social Psychology* 67, no. 4 (1994): 627–37.

Greene, Joshua D., Leigh E. Nystrom, Andrew D. Engell, John M. Darley, and Jonathan D. Cohen. "The Neural Bases of Cognitive Conflict and Control in Moral Judgment." *Neuron* 44, no. 2 (2004): 389–400.

Greene, Joshua D., R. Brian Sommerville, Leigh E. Nystrom, John M. Darley, and Jonathan D. Cohen. "An fMRI Investigation of Emotional Engagement in Moral Judgment." *Science* 293, no. 5537 (2001): 2105–8.

Gromet, Dena, Geoff Goodwin, and John M. Darley. "Taking Pleasure in Doing Harm: The Influence of Hedonic States on Judgments of Immorality and Evil." Unpublished manuscript.

Grose, Jessica. "A Death in Yellowstone." *Slate,* April 2, 2012. http://

www.slate.com/articles/health_and_science/death_in_yellowstone /2012/04/grizzly_bear_attacks_how_wildlife_investigators_found_a _killer_grizzly_in_yellowstone_.single.html.

Haidt, Jonathan. "The Emotional Dog and Its Rational Tail: A Social Intuitionist Approach to Moral Judgment." *Psychological Review* 108, no. 4 (2001): 814–34.

Haidt, Jonathan. *The Righteous Mind: Why Good People Are Divided by Politics and Religion.* New York: Pantheon, 2012.

Haidt, Jonathan, Frederick Björklund, and Scott Murphy. "Moral Dumbfounding: When Intuition Finds No Reason." Unpublished manuscript, August 10, 2000.

Harlow, Robert E., John M. Darley, and Paul H. Robinson. "The Severity of Intermediate Penal Sanctions: A Psychophysical Scaling Approach for Obtaining Community Perceptions." *Journal of Quantitative Criminology* 11 (1995): 71–95.

Holmes, Oliver Wendell. *The Common Law.* Boston: Little, Brown, 1881.

Hurwitz, John, and Mark Peffley. "Playing the Race Card in the Post–Willie Horton Era." *Public Opinion Quarterly* 69, no. 1 (Spring 2005): 99–112.

Hyde, Walter Woodburn. "The Prosecution and Punishment of Animals and Lifeless Things in the Middle Ages and Modern Times." *University of Pennsylvania Law Review* 64, no. 7 (1916): 696–730.

"The Infancy Defense." 'Lectric Law Library. Accessed May 27, 2014. http://www.lectlaw.com/mjl/cl032.htm.

Jehle, Alayna, Monica K. Miller, and Markus Kemmelmeier. "The Influence of Accounts and Remorse on Mock Jurors' Judgments of Offenders." *Law and Human Behavior* 33, no. 5 (2009): 393–404.

Kelsen, Hans. *General Theory of Law and State.* Translated by A. Wedberg. New York: Russell & Russell, 1945.

"Kentucky Dog Murder Trials Held Repealed." *Washington Post,* January 25, 1929.

"Kentucky Jury Convicts Dog: Death Sentence Carried Out." *New York Times,* January 11, 1926.

Kirchmeier, Jeffrey. "Our Existential Death Penalty: Judges, Jurors, and Terror Management." *Law and Psychology Review* 32 (2008): 55–107.

Kleinke, Chris L., Robert Wallis, and Kevin Stalder. "Evaluation of a Rapist as Function of Expressed Intent and Remorse." *Journal of Social Psychology* 132, no. 4 (1992): 525–37.

Knobe, Joshua. "Intentional Action and Side Effects in Ordinary Language." *Analysis* 63 (2003): 190–93.

Liebman, James S. "The Overproduction of Death." *Columbia Law Review* 100 (2000): 2030–2156.

Liptak, Adam. "Justices Bar Mandatory Life Sentences for Juveniles." *New York Times,* June 25, 2012.

Macrae, John. "Account of the Kookies of Lunctas." *Asiatic Researches* 7 (1803): 11–22.

Malle, Bertram F., Steve Guglielmo, and Andrew E. Monroe. "A Theory of Blame." *Psychological Inquiry: An International Journal for the Advancement of Psychological Theory* 25, no. 2 (2014): 147–86.

Mandela, Nelson. *Long Walk to Freedom: The Autobiography of Nelson Mandela.* Boston: Little, Brown, 2008.

Martin, J. R., and David Rose. *Working with Discourse.* London: Bloomsbury Academic, 2003.

McFatter, Robert M. "Purposes of Punishment: Effects of Utilities of Criminal Sanctions on Perceived Appropriateness." *Journal of Applied Psychology* 67, no. 3 (1982): 255–67.

McNamara, Joseph P. "Curiosities of the Law: Animal Prisoner at the Bar." *Notre Dame Law* 3, no. 30 (1927): 30–36.

Miller, Arthur G. *The Social Psychology of Good and Evil.* New York: Guilford, 2004.

Milman, Oliver. "Shark Attacks Prompt Calls to Review the Great White's Protected Status." *Guardian,* July 16, 2012.

Mitchell, Tara L., Ryann M. Haw, Jeffrey E. Pfeifer, and Christian A. Meissner. "Racial Bias in Mock Juror Decision-Making: A Meta-Analytic Review of Defendant Treatment." *Law and Human Behavior* 29, no. 6 (2005): 621–37.

Monterosso, John, Edward B. Royzman, and Barry Schwartz. "Explaining Away Responsibility: Effects of Scientific Explanation on Perceived Culpability." *Ethics and Behavior* 15 (2005): 139–58.

*Morisette v. United States.* 342 U.S. 246 (1952).

Mustard, David B. "Racial, Ethnic, and Gender Disparities in Sentencing: Evidence from the U.S. Federal Courts." *Journal of Law and Economics* 44 (2001): 285–314.

Newheiser, Anna-Kaisa, Takuya Sawaoka, and John F. Dovidio. "Why Do We Punish Groups? High Entitativity Promotes Moral Suspicion." *Journal of Experimental Social Psychology* 48 (2012): 931–36.

Ohbuchi, Ken-ichi, Masuyo Kameda, and Nariyuki Agarie. "Apology as Aggression Control: Its Role in Mediating Appraisal of and Response to Harm." *Journal of Personality and Social Psychology* 56, no. 2 (1989): 219–27.

"Old Enough to Be a Criminal?" UNICEF. Accessed May 27, 2014. http://www.unicef.org/pon97/p56a.htm.

*Parker-Harris Co. v. Tate.* 188 S.W. 54 (Tenn. 1916).

Paxton, Joseph M. and Joshua D. Greene. "Moral Reasoning: Hints and Allegations." *Topics in Cognitive Science* 2, no. 3 (2010): 511–27.

Pinker, Steven. *The Better Angels of Our Nature: Why Violence Has Declined.* New York: Viking, 2011.

Pizarro, David A. and Paul Bloom. "The Intelligence of the Moral Intuitions: Comment on Haidt (2001)." *Psychological Review* 110 (2003): 193–96.

Plato. *The Laws of Plato.* Translated by A. E. Taylor. London: J. M. Dent, 1934.

Pyszczysnki, Tom, Sheldon Solomon, and Jeff Greenberg. *In the Wake of 9/11: The Psychology of Terror.* Washington, DC: American Psychological Association, 2003.

Rattan, Aneeta, Cynthia S. Levine, Carol S. Dweck, and Jennifer L. Eberhardt. "Race and the Fragility of the Legal Distinction Between Juveniles and Adults." *PLOS ONE* 7, no. 5 (2012): 1–6.

Robinson, Dawn T., Lynn Smith-Lovin, and Olga Tsoudis. "Heinous Crime or Unfortunate Accident? The Effects of Remorse on Responses to Mock Criminal Confessions." *Social Forces* 73, no. 1 (1994): 175–90.

Robinson, Paul H., Sean E. Jackowitz, and Daniel M. Bartels. "Extralegal Punishment Factors: A Study of Forgiveness, Hardship, Good Deeds, Apology, Remorse, and Other Such Discretionary Factors in Assessing Criminal Punishment." *Vanderbilt Law Review* 65 (2012): 737–826.

Robinson, Paul H., Robert Kurzban, and Owen D. Jones. "The Origins of Shared Intuitions of Justice." *Vanderbilt Law Review* 60 (2007): 1633–88.

*Roper v. Simmons.* 543 U.S. 551 (2005).

Rosenblatt, Abram, Jeff Greenberg, Sheldon Solomon, Tom Pyszczynski, and Deborah Lyon. "Evidence for Terror Management Theory I. The Effects of Mortality Salience on Reactions to Those Who Violate or Uphold Cultural Values." *Journal of Personality and Social Psychology* 57, no. 4 (1989): 681–90.

Royal Society. *Brain Waves Module 4: Neuroscience and the Law.* London: Royal Society, 2011.

Rucker, Derek D., Mark Polifroni, Phillip E. Tetlock, and Amanda L. Scott. "On the Assignment of Punishment: The Impact of General-Societal Threat and the Moderating Role of Severity." *Personality and Social Psychology Bulletin* 30, no. 6 (2004): 673–84.

Senior, Jennifer. "In Conversation: Antonin Scalia." *New York*, October 6, 2013.

Shariff, Azim F., Joshua D. Greene, Johan C. Karremans, Jamie B. Luguri, Cory J. Clark, Jonathan W. Schooler, Roy F. Baumeister, and Kathleen D. Vohs. "Free Will and Punishment: A Mechanistic View of Human Nature Reduces Retribution." *Psychological Science* 25 (2014): 1563–70.

Stevenson, Margaret C., and Bette L. Bottoms. "Race Shapes Perceptions of Juvenile Offenders in Criminal Court." *Journal of Applied Social Psychology* 39, no. 7 (2009): 1660–89.

Streater, Scott. "Yellowstone Bear Euthanized After DNA Evidence Links Two Fatal Attacks." *New York Times*, October 7, 2011.

Sundby, Scott E. "The Capital Jury and Absolution: The Intersection of Trial Strategy, Remorse, and the Death Penalty." *Cornell Law Review* 83, no. 4 (1998): 1557–98.

Sweeney, Sarah. "On the Side of the Angels." *Harvard Gazette*, November 10, 2011.

Taylor, Christy, and Chris L. Kleinke. "Effects of Severity of Accident, History of Drunk Driving, Intent, and Remorse on Judgments of a Drunk Driver." *Journal of Applied Social Psychology* 22 (1992): 1641–55.

Tyler, Tom R., and Robert J. Boeckmann. "Three Strikes and You Are Out, but Why? The Psychology of Public Support for Punishing Rule Breakers." *Law and Society Review* 31, no. 2 (1997): 237–65.

Volokh, Alexander. "*n* Guilty Men." *University of Pennsylvania Law Review* 146 (1997): 173–218.

Walster, Elaine. "Assignment of Responsibility for an Accident." *Journal of Personality and Social Psychology* 3 (1996): 73–79.

Warr, Mark, Robert F. Meier, and Maynard L. Erickson. "Norms, Theories of Punishment, and Publicly Preferred Penalties for Crimes." *Sociological Quarterly* 24 (1983): 75–91.

Webster, Russell J., and Donald A. Saucier. "Angels and Demons Are Among Us: Assessing Individual Differences in Belief in Pure Evil and Belief in Pure Good." *Personality and Social Psychology Bulletin* 39 (2013): 1455–70.

## 10. THROWING AWAY THE KEY ~ THE PRISONER

"A New Probation Program in Hawaii Beats the Statistics: Transcript." PBS, February 2, 2014. Originally broadcast on November 24, 2013. http://www.pbs.org/newshour/bb/law-july-dec13-hawaiihope_11-24/.

"The Abuse of Solitary Confinement." *New York Times*, June 20, 2012.

Adams, William Lee. "Norway Builds the World's Most Humane Prison." *Time*, May 10, 2010.

Alexander, Michelle. *The New Jim Crow: Mass Incarceration in the Age of Colorblindness*, rev. ed. New York: New Press, 2010.

Amnesty International. *Death Sentences and Executions, 2013*. London: Amnesty International Publications, 2014.

Amnesty International. "Indonesian Government Must Repeal Caning Bylaws in Aceh." May 22, 2011. https://www.amnesty.org/en/news-and-updates/indonesian-government-must-repeal-caning-bylaws-aceh-2011-05-20.

Amnesty International. "Saudi Arabia: Five Beheaded and 'Crucified' Amid 'Disturbing' Rise in Executions." May 21, 2013. http://www.amnesty.org/en/news/saudi-arabia-five-beheaded-and-crucified-amid-disturbing-rise-executions-2013-05-21.

Apuzzo, Matt. "Holder Endorses Proposal to Reduce Drug Sentences in Latest Sign of Shift." *New York Times*, March 13, 2014.

Baron, Jonathan, and Ilana Ritov. "Omission Bias, Individual Differences, and Normality." *Organizational Behavior and Human Decision Processes* 94 (2003): 74–85.

Boston Review. "Supermax Prison Cell Extraction." YouTube video, 12:44. Posted December 16, 2010. http://youtu.be/3jUfK5i_lQs.

Briggs, Chad S., Jody L. Sundt, and Thomas C. Castellano. "The Effect of Supermaximum Security Prisons on Aggregate Levels of Institutional Violence." *Criminology* 41 (2003): 1341–76.

Bureau of Justice Statistics. "FAQ Detail: What Is the Probability of Conviction for Felony Defendants?" Accessed May 25, 2015. http://www.bjs.gov/index.cfm?ty=qa&iid=403.

Butler, Paul. "On Trayvon Martin and Racial Profiling." *Daily Beast*, March 26, 2012. http://www.thedailybeast.com/articles/2012/03/26/paul-butler-on-trayvon-martin-and-racial-profiling.html.

Cacioppo, John T., and Louise C. Hawkley. "Perceived Social Isolation and Cognition." *Trends in Cognitive Sciences* 13, no. 10 (2009): 447–54.

Cal. Penal Code § 1170.12 (West 2014).

Cannon, Carl M. "Petty Crime, Outrageous Punishment." *Reader's Digest,* October 2005.

Caplan, Lincoln. "The Random Horror of the Death Penalty." *New York Times,* January 7, 2012.

Carlsmith, Kevin M., and John M. Darley. "Psychological Aspects of Retributive Justice." *Advances in Experimental Psychology* 40 (2008): 193–236.

Carson, E. Ann. U.S. Department of Justice. *Prisoners in 2013*. September 2014.

Carson, E. Ann, and Daniela Golinelli. U.S. Department of Justice. *Prisoners in 2012: Trends in Admissions and Releases, 1991–2012*. December 2013.

Chemerinksy, Erwin. "Cruel and Unusual: The Story of Leandro Andrade." *Drake Law Review* 52 (2003): 1–24.

Chemerinsky, Erwin. "3 Strikes Reform in CA: 'Victory for Common Sense.'" *Crime Report*, December 6, 2012. http://www.thecrimereport .org/viewpoints/2012-12-three-strikes-reform-in-california-a-victory -for-hum.

Darley, John, Sol Fulero, Craig Haney, and Tom Tyler. "Psychological Jurisprudence." In *Taking Psychology and Law into the Twenty-First Century*, edited by James R. P. Olgoff. New York: Kluwer Academic Publishers, 2004.

Death Penalty Information Center. "Executions by Year Since 1976." Accessed May 24, 2014. http://www.deathpenaltyinfo.org/executions -year.

Devereaux, Ryan. "Prisoners Challenge Legality of Solitary Confinement Lasting More Than a Decade." *Guardian*, May 31, 2012.

Dickens, Charles. *American Notes*. London: Chapman and Hall, 1842.

Donahue, John J., III. "Capital Punishment in Connecticut, 1973–2007: A Comprehensive Evaluation from 4866 Murders to One Execution." Working Paper, Stanford Law School, National Bureau of Economic Research, June 8, 2013.

Eastern State Penitentiary. "Facade: Online 360 Tour." Accessed May 25, 2014. http://www.easternstate.org/explore/online-360-tour.

Eastern State Penitentiary. "FAQ, Terror Behind the Walls." Accessed May 13, 2014. http://www.easternstate.org/halloween/visit/faq.

Eastern State Penitentiary. "History of Eastern State: General Overview." Accessed May 16, 2014. http://www.easternstate.org/learn/ research-library/history.

Eastern State Penitentiary. "Home, Terror Behind the Walls." Accessed May 13, 2014. http://www.easternstate.org/halloween.

Eastern State Penitentiary. "Timeline." Accessed May 15, 2014. http://www.easternstate.org/learn/timeline.

Eastern State Penitentiary. "2013 Schedule and Prices, Terror Behind the Walls." Accessed May 13, 2014. http://www.easternstate.org/ halloween/visit/schedule-prices.

Eastern State Penitentiary. "VIP Experiences, Terror Behind the Walls." Accessed May 13, 2014. http://www.easternstate.org/halloween/ eastern-state-after-dark-vip-tour.

"Eastern State Penitentiary." USHistory.org. Accessed May 15, 2014. http://www.ushistory.org/tour/eastern-state-penitentiary.htm.

*Ewing v. California*. 538 U.S. 11 (2003).

Federal Bureau of Investigation. "Offenses Cleared." In *Uniform*

*Crime Report: Crime in the United States, 2010.* Washington, DC: U.S. Department of Justice, Federal Bureau of Investigation, 2011.

Folger, Robert, and S. Douglas Pugh. "The Just World and Winston Churchill: An Approach/Avoidance Conflict About Psychological Distance When Harming Victims." In *The Justice Motive in Everyday Life,* edited by Michael Ross and Dale T. Miller. Cambridge: Cambridge University Press, 2002.

Fried, Barbara H. "Beyond Blame: Would We Be Better Off in a World Without Blame?" *Boston Review,* June 28, 2013.

Friends of HOPE. "Hope: Hawaii's Opportunity Probation with Enforcement." Accessed May 25, 2014. http://hopehawaii.net/index.html.

Gawande, Atul. "Hellhole: The United States Holds Tens of Thousands of Inmates in Long-Term Solitary Confinement. Is This Torture?" *New Yorker,* March 30, 2009.

Gayathri, Amrutha. "US Only Western Country to Carry Out Capital Punishment Last Year, Ranks 5th Worldwide." *International Business Times,* March 27, 2012.

Gentleman, Amelia. "Inside Halden, the Most Humane Prison in the World." *Guardian,* May 18, 2012.

Getty, J. Arch, Gabor Rittersporn, and Victor Zemskov. "Victims of the Soviet Penal System in the Pre-War Years: A First Approach on the Basis of Archival Evidence." *American Historical Review* 98 (Oct. 1993): 1017–49.

Gibbons, John J., and Nicholas de B. Katzenbach. *Confronting Confinement: A Report of the Commission on Safety and Abuse in America's Prisons.* New York: Vera Institute of Justice, 2006.

Glaberson, William. "For 3 Years After Killing, Evidence Fades as a Suspect Sits in Jail." *New York Times,* April 15, 2013.

Glazek, Christopher. "Raise the Crime Rate." *N+1 Magazine,* Winter 2012.

Goode, Erica. "Senators Start a Review of Solitary Confinement." *New York Times,* June 19, 2012.

Goode, Erica. "U.S. Prison Populations Decline, Reflecting New Approach to Crime." *New York Times,* July 25, 2013.

Gopnik, Adam. "The Caging of America." *A Critic at Large* (blog). *New Yorker,* January 30, 2012.

"Grandstanding on Prisons in Texas." *New York Times,* April 4, 2014.

*Gregg v. Georgia.* 428 U.S. 153 (1976).

Guttel, Ehud, and Doron Teichman. "Criminal Sanctions in the Defense of the Innocent." *Michigan Law Review* 110 (2012): 597–645.

Harmon, Katherine. "Brain Injury Rate 7 Times Greater Among U.S. Prisoners." *Scientific American,* February 4, 2012.

Hawaii State Judiciary. "HOPE Probation." Accessed May 25, 2014. http://www.courts.state.hi.us/special_projects/hope/about_hope _probation.html.

Hawken, Angela, and Mark Kleiman. *Managing Drug Involved Probationers with Swift and Certain Sanctions: Evaluating Hawaii's Hope.* Washington, DC: National Criminal Justice Reference Services, 2009.

Hawkley, Louise C., and John T. Cacioppo. "Loneliness Matters: A Theoretical and Empirical Review of Consequences and Mechanisms." *Annals of Behavioral Medicine* 40 (2010): 218–27.

*Heacock v. Commonwealth.* 323 S.E.2d 90 (Va. 1984).

Holt-Lunstad, Julianne, Timothy B. Smith, and J. Bradley Layton. "Social Relationships and Morality Risk: A Meta-analytic Review." *PLOS Med* 7 (2010): 1–23.

Hrenchir, Tim. "Sebelius' Son Sells Game Out of Cedar Crest." *Topeka Capital-Journal,* January 26, 2008.

International Centre for Prison Studies. "Canada, World Prison Brief." Accessed May 16, 2014. http://www.prisonstudies.org/country/ canada.

International Centre for Prison Studies. "Germany, World Prison Brief." Accessed May 16, 2014. http://www.prisonstudies.org/country/ germany.

International Centre for Prison Studies. "Highest to Lowest." Accessed May 18, 2014. http://www.prisonstudies.org/highest-to-lowest (filtered by Prison Population Rate).

International Centre for Prison Studies. "Iran, World Prison Brief." Accessed May 18, 2014. http://www.prisonstudies.org/country/iran.

International Centre for Prison Studies. "United States, World Prison Brief." Accessed May 16, 2014. http://www.prisonstudies.org/country/ united-states-america.

Internet Movie Database. *"The Shawshank Redemption* (1994): Quotes." Accessed May 24, 2014. http://www.imdb.com/title/tt0111161/ quotes?item=qt0470719.

James, Doris J., and Lauren E. Glaze. U.S. Department of Justice. *Mental Health Problems of Prison and Jail Inmates.* September 2006.

John Sebelius Art & Design. "Don't Drop the Soap." Accessed May 24, 2014. http://www.johnsebelius.com/dontdropthesoap.html.

Johnston, Norman. *Eastern State Penitentiary: Crucible of Good Intentions.* Philadelphia: Philadelphia Museum of Art for the Eastern State

Penitentiary Task Force of the Preservation Coalition of Greater Philadelphia, 1994.

Justice Center: The Council of State Governments. *Improving Outcomes for People with Mental Illnesses Involved with New York City's Criminal Court and Correction Systems.* December 2012.

Kahan, Paul. *Eastern State Penitentiary: A History.* Charleston, SC: History Press, 2008.

Kaiser, David, and Lovisa Stannow. "Prison Rape and the Government." *New York Review of Books,* March 24, 2011.

Katz, Lawrence, Steven D. Levitt, and Ellen Shustorovich. "Prison Conditions, Capital Punishment, and Deterrence." *American Law and Economics Review* 5 (2003): 318–43.

Keim, Brandon. "Solitary Confinement: The Invisible Torture." *Wired,* April 29, 2009. http://www.wired.com/2009/04/solitaryconfinement/.

Kohn, David. "Three Strikes: Penal Overkill in California?" CBS News, October 28, 2002. http://www.cbsnews.com/news/three-strikes-28-10-2002/.

Lappi-Seppälä, Tapio. "Penal Policy in Scandinavia." *Crime and Justice* 36 (2007): 217–93.

Lieberman, Matthew D. *Social: Why Our Brains Are Wired to Connect.* New York: Random House, 2013.

Liptak, Adam. "Inmate Count in U.S. Dwarfs Other Nations'." *New York Times,* April 23, 2008.

Llanos, Miguel. "Crime in Decline, but Why? Low Inflation Among Theories." NBC News. September 20, 2011. http://www.nbcnews.com/id/44578241/ns/us_news-crime_and_courts/t/crime-decline-why-low-inflation-among-theories/#.U4EH_V4tpcN.

*Lockyer v. Andrade.* 538 U.S. 63 (2003).

Mauer, Marc. "Is the 'Tough on Crime' Movement on Its Way Out?" MSNBC.com, May 5, 2014. http://www.msnbc.com/msnbc/sentencing-reform-the-end-tough-crime.

McCleland, Jacob. "The High Costs of High Security at Supermax Prisons." NPR, June 19, 2012. http://www.npr.org/2012/06/19/155359553/the-high-costs-of-high-security-at-supermax-prisons.

Mears, Daniel P. "Supermax Prisons: The Policy and the Evidence." *Criminology and Public Policy* 12 (2013): 681–719.

Milgram, Stanley. *Obedience to Authority: An Experimental View.* New York: Harper & Row, 1974.

Miller, John. "'A Suffering People': English Quakers and Their Neighbours, c. 1650–c. 1700." *Past and Present* 188 (2005): 71–103.

"The Myth of Deterrence." *New York Times,* April 27, 2012.

# Bibliography | 353

Nadler, Janice. "Flouting the Law." *Texas Law Review* 83 (2005): 1399–1441.

Nagin, Daniel S. "Deterrence in the 21st Century: A Review of the Evidence." In *Crime and Justice: An Annual Review of Research*, edited by Michael Tonry. Chicago: University of Chicago Press, 2013.

National Association for the Advancement of Colored People. *Misplaced Priorities: Over Incarcerate, Under Educate*, 2nd ed. Baltimore: National Association for the Advancement of Colored People, 2011.

National Institute of Justice. "Five Things About Deterrence." September 12, 2014. http://nij.gov/five-things/Pages/deterrence.aspx?utm_source=eblast-govdelivery&utm_medium=eblast&utm_campaign=five+things-deterrence.

National Institute of Justice. "Program Profile: Hawaii Opportunity Probation with Enforcement (HOPE)." Accessed May 25, 2015. http://www.crimesolutions.gov/ProgramDetails.aspx?ID=49.

National Research Council. *Deterrence and the Death Penalty*. Edited by Daniel S. Nagin and John V. Pepper. Washington, DC: National Academies Press, 2012.

National Standards to Prevent, Detect, and Respond to Prison Rape. 28 C.F.R. pt. 115 (2012).

"New York Rethinks Solitary Confinement." *New York Times*, February 20, 2014.

Penn Medicine. "Pennsylvania Hospital History: Stories: Dr. Benjamin Rush." Accessed May 15, 2014. http://www.uphs.upenn.edu/paharc/features/brush.html.

Pew Center on the States. *State of Recidivism: The Revolving Door of America's Prisons*. Washington, DC: Pew Center on the States, 2011.

Pew Charitable Trusts. *Collateral Costs: Incarceration's Effect on Economic Mobility*. Washington, DC: Pew Charitable Trusts, 2010.

Pizarro, Jesenia M., Kristen M. Zgoba, and Sabrina Haugebrook. "Supermax and Recidivism: An Examination of the Recidivism Covariates Among a Sample of Supermax Ex-Inmates." *Prison Journal* 94 (2014): 180–97.

Resnick, Brian. "Chart: One Year at Prison Costs More Than One Year at Princeton." *Atlantic*, November 1, 2011. http://www.theatlantic.com/national/archive/2011/11/chart-one-year-of-prison-costs-more-than-one-year-at-princeton/247629/.

Resnick, Judith, and Jonathan Curtis-Resnick. "Abolish the Death Penalty and the Supermax, Too." *Slate*, June 18, 2012. http://hive.slate.com/hive/how-can-we-fix-constitution/article/abolish-the-death-penalty-and-the-supermax-too.

"Reviving Clemency, Serving Justice." *New York Times*, April 23, 2014.

Ridgeway, James, Jean Casella, and Sal Rodriguez. "Senators Finally Ponder the Question: Is Solitary Confinement Wrong?" *Mother Jones*, June 19, 2012.

Robinson, Paul H., and John M. Darley. "The Role of Deterrence in the Formulation of Criminal Law Rules: At Its Worst When Doing Its Best." *Georgetown Law Journal* 91 (2003): 950–51.

Robinson, Paul H., Geoffrey P. Goodwin, and Michael D. Reisig. "The Disutility of Injustice." *New York University Law Review* 85 (2010): 1940–2033.

Robinson, Paul H., Sean E. Jackowitz, and Daniel M. Bartels. "Extralegal Punishment Factors: A Study for Forgiveness, Hardship, Good Deeds, Apology, Remorse, and Other Such Discretionary Factors in Assessing Criminal Punishment." *Vanderbilt Law Review* 65 (2012): 737–826.

*Roper v. Simmons.* 543 U.S. 551 (2005).

Savage, Charlie. "Justice Dept. Seeks to Curtail Stiff Drug Sentences." *New York Times*, August 12, 2013.

Savage, David G. "Supreme Court to Hear Three-Strikes Challenge." *Los Angeles Times*, April 2, 2002.

*The Shawshank Redemption.* Directed by Frank Darabont. Burbank, CA: Warner Brothers Pictures, 1994.

"Smarter Sentencing." *New York Times*, August 13, 2013.

Subramanian, Ram, and Alison Shames. *Sentencing and Prison Practices in Germany and the Netherlands: Implications for the United States.* New York: Vera Institute of Justice, 2013.

Tapley, Lance. "The Worst of the Worst: Supermax Torture in America." *Boston Review*, November 1, 2010.

Torrey, E. Fuller, Aaron D. Kennard, Don Eslinger, Richard Lamb, and James Pavle. *More Mentally Ill Persons Are in Jails and Prisons Than Hospitals: A Survey of the States.* Arlington, VA: Treatment Advocacy Center, 2010.

UNICEF, *Children at Risk in Central and Eastern Europe: Perils and Promises.* Florence, Italy: United Nations Children's Fund, International Child Development Centre, 1997.

Weaver, Kimberlee, Stephen M. Garcia, and Norbert Schwarz. "The Presenter's Paradox." *Journal of Consumer Research* 39 (2012): 445–60.

Weiser, Benjamin. "New York State in Deal to Limit Solitary Confinement." *New York Times*, February 19, 2014.

Wolfers, Justin. "Life in Prison, with the Remote Possibility of Death." *New York Times,* July 18, 2014.


11. WHAT WE MUST OVERCOME ~ THE CHALLENGE

"About the Advocates." *The Advocates.* Accessed May 4, 2014. http:// www.theadvocates.com/philosophy.htm.

Alcindor, Yamiche. "Officer Testimony No Slam Dunk for Zimmerman Prosecutors." *USA Today,* July 2, 2013.

American Society of Trial Consultants. "Areas of Consulting." Accessed May 4, 2014. http://www.astcweb.org/public/article.cfm/areas -of-consulting.

American Society of Trial Consultants. "History and Goals." Accessed May 4, 2014. http://www.astcweb.org/public/article.cfm/society -goals.

American Society of Trial Consultants. *The Professional Code of the American Society of Trial Consultants.* 2013.

Bloomberg News. "Stewart Sued by Jury Consultant for $74,047 in Fees." *Chicago Tribune,* November 18, 2005.

*Bond v. United States.* 529 U.S. 334 (2000).

Buckley, Cara. "State's Witnesses in Zimmerman Trial Put the Prosecution on the Defensive." *New York Times,* July 2, 2013.

Carbado, Devon W., Cheryl I. Harris, and Kimberle Williams Crenshaw. "Racial Profiling Lives On." *New York Times,* August 14, 2013.

*Corenevsky v. Superior Court.* 682 P.2d 360 (Cal. 1984).

Crocker, Caroline B., and Margaret Bull Kovera. "Systematic Jury Selection." In *Handbook of Trial Consulting,* edited by Richard L. Wiener and Brian H. Bornstein. New York: Springer, 2011.

Early, Kate. "The Impact of Pretrial Publicity on an Indigent Capital Defendant's Due Process Right to a Jury Consultant." *Roger Williams University Law Review* 16 (2011): 687–722.

Edwards, Tamsin. "Climate Scientists Must Not Advocate Particular Policies." *Guardian,* July 31, 2013.

Equal Justice Initiative. *Illegal Racial Discrimination in Jury Selection: A Continuing Legacy.* Montgomery, AL, 2010.

Frederick, Jeffrey T. "Social Science Involvement in Voir Dire: Preliminary Data on the Effectiveness of 'Scientific Jury Selection.'" *Behavioral Sciences and Law* 2 (1984): 375–94.

Garrett, Brandon L. *Convicting the Innocent: Where Criminal Prosecutions Go Wrong.* Cambridge, MA: Harvard University Press, 2011.

*Geders v. United States.* 425 U.S. 80 (1976).

*Gilliam v. State.* 629 A.2d 685 (Md. 1993).

Gobert, James J., Ellen Kreitzberg, and Charles H. Rose III. *Jury Selection: The Law, Art and Science of Selecting a Jury.* Eagen, MN: West, 2009.

Harmon, Rachel. "Promoting Policing at Its Best." *Virginia Journal* 15 (2012): 33–57.

Hartje, Rachel. "A Jury of Your Peers? How Jury Consulting May Actually Help Trial Lawyers Resolve Constitutional Limitations Imposed on the Selection of Juries." *California Western Law Review* 41 (2005): 479–506.

Hutson, Matthew. "Unnatural Selection." *Psychology Today* 40 (2007): 90–95.

Joy, Peter A., and Kevin C. McMunigal. "Witness Preparation: When Does It Cross the Line?" *Criminal Justice* 17 (2002): 48.

"Juror Information Questionnaire." 234 Pa. Code Rule 632. http://www.pacode.com/secure/data/234/chapter6/s632.html.

Kassin, Saul M., Richard A. Leo, Christian A. Meissner, Kimberly D. Richman, Lori H. Colwell, Amy-May Leach, and Dana La Fon. "Police Interviewing and Interrogation: A Self-Report Survey of Police Practices and Beliefs." *Law and Human Behavior* 31 (2007): 381–400.

Kressel, Neil J., and Dorit F. Kressel. *Stack and Sway: The New Science of Jury Consulting.* Cambridge, MA: Westview, 2002.

Lackey, Robert T. "Science, Scientists, and Policy Advocacy," *U.S. Environmental Protection Agency Papers.* Paper 142 (2007). http://digital commons.unl.edu/usepapapers/142.

Lattman, Peter. "Jury Is Seated in Rajat Gupta Trial." *New York Times,* May 21, 2012.

LeGrande, Nicole, and Kathleen Mierau. "Witness Preparation and the Trial Consulting Industry." *Georgetown Journal of Legal Ethics* 17 (2004): 947–60.

Leo, Richard A. "Inside the Interrogation Room." *Journal of Criminal Law and Criminology* 86 (1996): 266–303.

Leo, Richard A., Steven A. Drizin, Peter J. Neufeld, Bradley R. Hall, and Amy Vatner. "Bringing Reliability Back In: False Confessions and Legal Safeguards in the Twenty-First Century." *Wisconsin Law Review* 2 (2006): 479–539.

Lieberman, Joel D. "The Utility of Scientific Jury Selection: Still Murky After 30 Years." *Current Directions in Psychological Science* 20 (2011): 48–52.

Lieberman, Joel D., and Bruce D. Sales. *Scientific Jury Selection.* Washington, DC: American Psychological Association, 2007.

McDermott, Tricia. "The Jury Consultants." CBS News, June 2, 2004. http://www.cbsnews.com/8301-18559_162-620794.html.

*Miranda v. Arizona.* 384 U.S. 436 (1966).

Model Criminal Jury Instructions § 1.01–.19.

Model Rules of Professional Conduct Rule 3.4(b).

Moore, Sarah G., David T. Neal, Gavan J. Fitzsimons, and Baba Shiv. "Wolves in Sheep's Clothing: How and When Hypothetical Questions Influence Behavior." *Organizational Behavior and Human Decision Processes* 117 (2012): 168–78.

National Conference of Bar Examiners. "The Multistate Bar Examination (MBE)." http://www.ncbex.org/about-ncbe-exams/mbe/.

National Legal Aid and Defender Association. "Collected Quotes Pertaining to Equal Justice." *Communication Resources.* Accessed May 4, 2014. http://www.nlada.org/News/Equal_Justice_Quotes.

Noë, Alva. "When Science Becomes News, the Facts Can Go Up in Smoke." NPR, May 4, 2014. http://www.npr.org/blogs/13.7/2014/05/04/308926616/when-science-becomes-news-the-facts-can-go-up-in-smoke?utm_source=facebook.com&utm_medium=social&utm_campaign=npr&utm_term=nprnews&utm_content=20140504.

Oliver, Myrna. "R. D. Herman, 'Harrisburg 7' Trial Judge." *Los Angeles Times,* April 9, 1990.

O'Rourke, William. *The Harrisburg 7 and the New Catholic Left.* Notre Dame, IN: University of Notre Dame Press, 2012.

Owens, Simon. "Is the Academic Publishing Industry on the Verge of Disruption?" *U.S. News and World Report,* July 23, 2012.

Parascandola, Rocco, Jenna O'Donnell, and Larry McShane. "NYPD Stop-and-Frisks Drop 99% in Brooklyn, While Shootings Increase in Brownsville, East New York." *New York Daily News,* August 16, 2014.

Paterson, Stephen J., and Norma J. Silverstein. "Jury Research: How to Use It." *United States Attorneys' Bulletin* 48, no. 3 (2000): 1–29.

*People v. Lloyd.* Trial Transcript No. 85-00376 (Mich. Rec. Ct. May 2, 1985).

*People v. McGuirk.* 245 N.E.2d 917 (Ill.App. 1969).

Pielke, Robert A., Jr. *The Honest Broker: Making Sense of Science in Policy and Politics.* Cambridge: Cambridge University Press, 2007.

Posey, Amy J., and Lawrence S. Wrightsman. *Trial Consulting.* New York: Oxford University Press, 2005.

Robbennolt, Jennifer K., and Matthew Taksin. "Jury Selection, Peremptory Challenges, and Discrimination." *APA Monitor on Psychology* 40 (2009): 18.

Rogers, Richard. "Getting It Wrong About Miranda Rights: False

Beliefs, Impaired Reasoning, and Professional Neglect." *American Psychologist* 66 (2011): 728–36.

*Salinas v. Texas.* 133 S.Ct. 2174 (2013).

Serio, Steven C. "A Process Right Due? Examining Whether a Capital Defendant Has a Due Process Right to a Jury Selection Expert." *American University Law Review* 53 (2004): 1143–86.

Shipler, David. "Why Do Innocent People Confess?" *New York Times,* February 23, 2012.

Shipp, E. R. "Jay Schulman, Expert on Juries." *New York Times,* December 3, 1987.

Simon, Dan. *In Doubt: The Psychology of the Criminal Justice Process.* Cambridge, MA: Harvard University Press, 2012.

Sommers, Samuel, and Michael Norton. "Race-Based Judgments, Race-Neutral Justifications: Experimental Examination of Peremptory Use and the *Batson* Challenge Procedure." *Law and Human Behavior* 31 (2007): 261–73.

*State v. Earp.* 571 A.2d 1227 (Md. 1990).

*State v. McCormick.* 259 S.E.2d 880 (N.C. 1979).

*State v. Sobczak.* 347 Wis.2d 724 (2013).

*Swain v. Alabama.* 380 U.S. 202 (1965).

"Trial Consulting and Research." *DecisionQuest.* Accessed May 4, 2014. http://www.decisionquest.com/utility/showArticle/?objectID =1536.

"Trial Consulting for Criminal Cases." NJP Litigation Consulting. Accessed May 4, 2014. http://www.njp.com/notable_CriminalCases_cases.html.

*United States. v. MacDonald.* 456 U.S. 1 (1982).

*United States v. Sayakhom.* 186 F.3d 928 (1999).

"Use of Jury Consultants." USLegal.com. Accessed May 4, 2014. http://courts.uslegal.com/jury-system/selection-process-at-the-courthouse/use-of-jury-consultants/.

Wiener, Richard L., and Brian H. Bornstein. "Introduction: Trial Consulting from a Psycholegal Perspective." In *Handbook of Trial Consulting.* New York: Springer, 2011.

Wingrove, Twila, Angela L. Korpas, and Robert F. Belli. "The Use of Survey Research in Trial Consulting." In *Handbook of Trial Consulting,* edited by Richard L. Wiener and Brian H. Bornstein. New York: Springer, 2011.

Wydick, Richard C. "The Ethics of Witness Coaching." *Cardozo Law Review* 17 (1995): 1–52.

12. WHAT WE CAN DO ~ THE FUTURE

"A New Perspective on Crime Scenes: The Man on the Bed." *New York Times*, November 18, 2011.

Alliance for Excellent Education. *Saving Futures, Saving Dollars: The Impact of Education on Crime Reduction and Earnings.* Washington, DC: Alliance for Excellent Education, 2013.

Anderson, D. Mark. "In School and Out of Trouble? The Minimum Dropout Age and Juvenile Crime." *Review of Economics and Statistics* 96 (2014): 318–31.

Bartlett, Robert. *Trial by Fire and Water: The Medieval Judicial Order.* New York: Oxford University Press, 1986.

Baumeister, Roy F. *Evil: Inside Human Cruelty and Violence.* New York: W. H. Freeman, 1997.

Baumeister, Roy F., E. J. Masicampo, and C. Nathan DeWall. "Prosocial Benefits of Feeling Free: Disbelief in Free Will Increases Aggression and Reduces Helpfulness." *Personality and Social Psychology Bulletin* 35 (2009): 260–68.

Benforado, Adam. "Quick on the Draw: Implicit Bias and the Second Amendment." *Oregon Law Review* 89, no. 1 (2010): 1–80.

Benton, John F., ed. *Self and Society in Medieval France: The Memoirs of Abbot Guilbert of Nogent.* New York: Harper Torchbacks, 1970.

Berkowitz, Leonard. "Evil Is More Than Banal: Situationism and the Concept of Evil." *Personality and Social Psychology Review* 3 (1999): 246–53.

BI Incorporated. *Overview of the Illinois DOC High-Risk Parolee Reentry Program and 3-Year Recidivism Outcomes of Program Participants.* 2002.

Birnbaum, Phil. "A Guide to Sabermetric Research." Society for American Baseball Research. Accessed November 7, 2014. http://sabr .org/sabermetrics.

Block, Melissa. "Theodore Parker and the 'Moral Universe.'" NPR, September 2, 2010. http://www.npr.org/templates/story/story .php?storyId=129609461.

Blumstein, Alfred, and Kiminori Nakamura. "'Redemption' in an Era of Widespread Criminal Background Checks." *NIJ Journal* 263 (2009): 10–17.

Boak, Dick. "Welcome." 2008. http://www.dickboak.com/dickboak _website/Home.html.

Bono, Giacomo, Michael E. McCullough, and Lindsey M. Root. "For-

giveness, Feeling Connected to Others, and Well-Being: Two Longitudi-
nal Studies." *Personality and Social Psychology Bulletin* 34, no. 2 (2008):
182–95.

Bornstein, Brian, and Edie Greene. "Jury Decision Making: Implications For and From Psychology." *Current Directions in Psychological
Science* 20 (2011): 63–67.

Bowden, Mark. "The Killing Machines." *Atlantic,* August 14, 2013.
http://www.theatlantic.com/magazine/archive/2013/09/the-killing
-machines-how-to-think-about-drones/309434/.

Buntin, John. "What Does It Take to Stop Crips and Bloods from
Killing Each Other?" *New York Times,* July 10, 2013.

Cassell, Paul G. "Standing for Victims: They Need Their Own Constitutional Amendment." *Slate,* June 14, 2012. http://hive.slate.com/
hive/how-can-we-fix-constitution/article/standing-for-victims.

Chesterton, G. K. "G. K. Chesteron Empanels a Jury." *Lapham's
Quarterly.* Accessed May 20, 2014. http://www.laphamsquarterly.org/
voices-in-time/g-k-chesteron-empanels-a-jury.php?page=all.

Clark, Cory J., Jamie B. Luguri, Peter H. Ditto, Joshua Knobe, Azim
F. Shariff, and Roy F. Baumeister. "Free to Punish: A Motivated Account
of Free Will Belief." *Journal of Personality and Social Psychology* 106
(2014): 501–13.

Clarke, Randolph, and Justin Capes. "Incompatibilist (Nondeter-
ministic) Theories of Free Will." *Stanford Encyclopedia of Philosophy,*
August 17, 2000. http://plato.stanford.edu/entries/incompatibilism
-theories/.

Correll, Joshua, Bernadette Park, Charles M. Judd, and Bernd Wit-
tenbrink. "The Influence of Stereotypes on Decisions to Shoot." *European Journal of Social Psychology* 37 (2007): 1102–17.

Correll, Joshua, Bernadette Park, Charles M. Judd, and Bernd Wit-
tenbrink. "The Police Officer's Dilemma: Using Ethnicity to Disambig-
uate Potentially Threatening Individuals." *Journal of Personality and
Social Psychology* 83 (2002): 1314–29.

Correll, Joshua, Bernadette Park, Charles M. Judd, Bernd Witten-
brink, and Melody S. Sadler. "Across the Thin Blue Line: Police Officers
and Racial Bias in the Decision to Shoot." *Journal of Personality and
Social Psychology* 92, no. 6 (2007): 1006–23.

Correll, Joshua, Geoffrey R. Urland, and Tiffany A. Ito. "Event-
Related Potentials and the Decision to Shoot: The Role of Threat Perception and Cognitive Control," *Journal of Experimental Social Psychology*
42 (2006): 120–28.

"Cost." *National Coalition to Abolish the Death Penalty.* Accessed May 27, 2014. http://www.ncadp.org/pages/cost.

Council on Crime and Justice. *Low Level Offenses in Minneapolis: An Analysis of Arrests and Their Outcomes.* 2004.

Cournoyer, Caroline. "Courtroom Violence on the Rise." *Governing the States and Localities,* January 19, 2012. http://www.governing.com/blogs/view/courtroom-violence-on-the-rise.html.

Danzig, Christopher. "Video Arraignments Save Money and Make Judges Feel Safer." *Above the Law,* June 17, 2011. http://abovethelaw.com/2011/06/video-arraignments-save-money-and-make-judges-feel-safer/.

Darley, John M. "Social Organization for the Production of Evil." *Psychological Inquiry* 3 (1992): 199–218.

"Death Penalty Cost." Amnesty International. Accessed May 27, 2014. http://www.amnestyusa.org/our-work/issues/death-penalty/us-death-penalty-facts/death-penalty-cost.

DeMatteo, David, Casey LaDuke, Benjamin R. Locklair, and Kirk Heilbrun. "Community-Based Alternatives for Justice-Involved Individuals with Severe Mental Illness: Diversion, Problem-Solving Courts, and Reentry." *Journal of Criminal Justice* 41 (2013): 64–71.

DeMatteo, David, Sanjay Shah, Megan Murphy, and Julie Present Koller. "Treatment Models for Clients Diverted or Mandated into Drug Treatment." In *Addictions: A Comprehensive Guidebook,* 2nd ed., edited by Barbara S. McCrady and Elizabeth E. Epstein. New York: Oxford University Press, 2013.

Devers, Lindsey. U.S. Department of Justice. *Plea and Charge Bargaining Research Summary.* January 21, 2011.

Digital Media Law Project. "Recording Public Meetings and Court Hearings." Accessed May 23, 2014. http://www.dmlp.org/legal-guide/recording-public-meetings-and-court-hearings.

Digital Media Law Project. "State Law: Recording." Accessed May 23, 2014. http://www.dmlp.org/legal-guide/state-law-recording.

Dorf, Michael C., and Charles Frederick Sabel. "Drug Treatment Courts and Emergent Experimentalist Government." *Vanderbilt Law Review* 53, no. 3 (2000): 831–83.

Dubber, Markus Dirk. "American Plea Bargains, Germany Lay Judges, and the Crisis of Criminal Procedure." *Stanford Law Review* 49 (1997): 547–605.

Eagleman, David. "The Brain on Trial." *Atlantic,* June 7, 2011. http://www.theatlantic.com/magazine/archive/2011/07/the-brain-on-trial/308520/?single_page=true.

Eagleman, David. *Incognito: The Secret Lives of the Brain.* New York: Vintage, 2011.

Ellard, John H., Christina D. Miller, Terri-lynne Baumle, and James M. Olson. "Just World Processes in Demonizing." In *The Justice Motive in Everyday Life,* edited by Michael Ross and Dale T. Miller. New York: Cambridge University Press, 2002.

Emmets, Katie. "Local Police Use Blood-Clotting Agent to Save Lives." *Alligator,* January 30, 2009.

Exline, Julie Juola, Everett L. Worthington Jr., Peter Hill, and Michael E. McCullough. "Forgiveness and Justice: A Research Agenda for Social and Personality Psychology." *Personality and Social Psychology Review* 7, no. 4 (2003): 337–48.

Fallis, David S. "ShotSpotter Detection System Documents 39,000 Shooting Incidents in the District." *Washington Post,* November 2, 1013.

Farah, Martha. "Neuroethics: The Practical and the Philosophical." *Trends in Cognitive Sciences* 9 (2005): 34–40.

Flatley, Joseph L. "World's First Remote Heart Surgery Completed in Leicester, UK." *Engadget,* May 4, 2010. http://www.engadget.com/2010/05/04/worlds-first-remote-heart-surgery-completed-in-leicester-uk/.

Fried, Barbara H. "Beyond Blame." *Boston Review,* June 28, 2013.

Funk, Friederike, Victoria McGeer, and Mario Gollwitzer. "Get the Message: Punishment Is Satisfying If the Transgressor Responds to Its Communicative Intent." *Personality and Social Psychology Bulletin* 40, no. 8 (2014): 986–97.

Gowdy, J. D. "The Bill of Rights and James Madison's Statesmanship." *The Washington, Jefferson, and Madison Institute* (blog), June 9, 2013. http://wjmi.blogspot.com/2013/06/the-bill-of-rights-and-james-madisons.html.

Greenwald, Anthony G., Mark A. Oakes, and Hunter G. Hoffman. "Targets of Discrimination: Effects of Race on Responses to Weapons Holders." *Journal of Experimental Social Psychology* 39 (2003): 399–405.

Hastings, Michael. "The Rise of the Killer Drones: How America Goes to War in Secret." *Rolling Stone,* April 16, 2012.

Huddleston, C. West, Douglas B. Marlowe, and Rachel Casebolt. *Painting the Current Picture: A National Report Card on Drug Courts and Other Problem Solving Court Programs in the United States.* Alexandria, VA: National Drug Court Institute, 2008.

*In re* Devon T. 584 A.2d 1287 (Md. Ct. Spec. App. 1991).

Inbau, Fred E., John E. Reid, Joseph P. Buckley, and Brian C. Jayne.

*Criminal Interrogation and Confessions.* Burlington, MA: Jones & Bartlett Learning, 2011.

Innocence Project. *Reevaluating Lineups: Why Witnesses Make Mistakes and How to Reduce the Chance of a Misidentification.* New York: Benjamin N. Cardozo School of Law, Yeshiva University.

James, Erwin. "The Norwegian Prison Where Inmates Are Treated Like People." *Guardian,* February 24, 2013.

Kassin, Saul M., Steven A. Drizin, Thomas Grisso, Gisli H. Gudjonsson, Richard A. Leo, and Allison D. Redlich. "Police-Induced Confessions: Risk Factors and Recommendations." *Law and Human Behavior* 34 (2019): 3–38.

Kastre, Tammy, and David Kleinman. "Providing Trauma Care." *Police,* January 24, 2013. http://www.policemag.com/channel/patrol/articles/2013/01/trauma-care-the-first-five-minutes.aspx.

Krey, Volker F. "Characteristic Features of German Criminal Proceedings: An Alternative to the Criminal Procedure Law of the United States?" *Loyola of Los Angeles International and Comparative Law Review* 21 (1999): 591–603.

"L.A. Now Live: First Homicides of 2014 and L.A.'s Crime Statistics." *Los Angeles Times,* January 6, 2014.

Lai, Calvin K., Kelly M. Hoffman, and Brian A. Nosek. "Reducing Implicit Prejudice." *Social and Personality Psychology Compass* 7 (2013): 315–30.

Lai, Calvin K., Maddalena Marini, Steven A. Lehr, Carlo Cerruti, Jiyun-Elizabeth L. Shin, Jennifer A. Joy-Gaba, Arnold K. Ho, Bethany A. Teachman, Sean P. Wojcik, Spassena P. Koleva, Rebecca S. Frazier, Larisa Heiphetz, Eva E. Chen, Rhiannon N. Turner, Johnathan Haidt, Selin Kessebir, Carlee Beth Hawkins, Hilary S. Schaefer, Sandro Rubichi, Giuseppe Sartori, Christopher M. Dial, N. Sriram, Mahzarin R. Banaji, and Brian A. Nosek. "Reducing Implicit Racial Preferences: I. A Comparative Investigation of 17 Interventions." *Journal of Experimental Psychology: General* 143, no. 4 (2014): 1765–85.

Langan, Patrick A., and David J. Levin. U.S. Department of Justice. *Recidivism of Prisoners Released in 1994.* 2002.

Langbein, John H. "Torture and Plea Bargaining." *University of Chicago Law Review* 46 (1978): 3–22.

Larsen, Allison Orr. "Confronting Supreme Court Fact Finding." *Virginia Law Review* 98 (2012): 1255–1312.

Leeson, Peter T. "Ordeals." *Journal of Law and Economics* 55 (2012): 691–714.

Lehrer, Brian. "Following Up: Should Cops Live in the Same Neighborhoods They Police?" *WNYC*, April 18, 2013.

Lochner, Lance, and Enrico Moretti. "The Effect of Education on Crime: Evidence from Prison Inmates, Arrests and Self-Reports." *American Economic Review* 94 (2004): 155–89.

Machin, Stephen, Olivier Marie, and Sunčica Vujić. "The Crime Reducing Effect of Education." *Economic Journal* 121 (2011): 463–84.

MacLin, Otto H., Christian A. Meissner, and Laura A. Zimmerman. "PC_Eyewitness: A Computerized Framework for the Administration and Practical Application of Research in Eyewitness Psychology." *Behavior Research Methods* 37 (2005): 324–34.

MacLin, Otto H., Laura A. Zimmerman, and Roy S. Malpass. "PC_Eyewitness and the Sequential Superiority Effect: Computer-Based Lineup Administration." *Law and Human Behavior* 29 (2005): 303–21.

Marlowe, Douglas B., David S. DeMatteo, and David S. Festinger. "A Sober Assessment of Drug Courts." *Federal Sentencing Reporter* 16 (2003): 113–28.

"Martin Guitar Factory Tour Part 3 (of 6)." YouTube video, 13:57. Posted April 14, 2010. http://www.youtube.com/watch?v=e4K1ec2n_M8.

Martin, Steven S., Clifford A. Butzin, Christine A. Saum, and James A. Inciardi. "Three-Year Outcomes of Therapeutic Community Treatment for Drug Involved Offenders in Delaware." *Prison Journal* 79 (1999): 294–320.

McNeil, Donald G., Jr. "A Cheap Drug Is Found to Save Bleeding Victims." *New York Times*, March 20, 2012.

Nadelhoffer, Thomas, and Walter Sinnott-Armstrong. "Neurolaw and Neuroprediction: Potential Promises and Perils." *Philosophy Compass* 7 (2012): 631–42.

Natividad, Michelle, and Maurice Emsellem. *65 Million "Need Not Apply": The Case for Reforming Criminal Background Checks for Employment.* New York: National Employment Law Project, 2011.

New York Police Department. "Panoscan." In Michael Wilson, "Crime Scene Investigation: 360 Degrees." *New York Times*, November 18, 2011.

Neyfakh, Leon. "The Bias Fighters." *Boston Globe*, September 21, 2014.

Neyfakh, Leon. "The Custom Justice of 'Problem-Solving Courts.'" *Boston Globe*, March 23, 2014.

Pager, Devah. "The Mark of Criminal Record." *American Journal of Sociology* 108 (2003): 937–75.

Pager, Devah, Bruce Western, and Bart Bonikowski. "Discrimination in a Low-Wage Labor Market: A Field Experiment." *American Journal of Sociology* 74 (2009): 777–99.

Palmer, Robert. "Trial by Ordeal." *Michigan Law Review* 87 (1989): 1547–56.

Paul-Emile, Kimani. "Beyond Title VII: Rethinking Race, Ex-Offender Status and Employment Discrimination in the Information Age." *Virginia Law Review* 100 (2014). 893–952.

Plant, E. Ashby, and B. Michelle Peruche. "The Consequences of Race for Police Officers' Responses to Criminal Suspects." *Psychological Science* 16 (2005): 180–83.

Ranaivo, Yann. "Wilmington to Lease $415,000 Gunshot Sensor Network." *News Journal* (Wilmington, DE), February 19, 2014.

Reardon, Sara. "Mugshots Built from DNA Data." *Nature*, March 20, 2014.

Riggs, Mike. "The End of Car Chases." *Atlantic*, October 31, 2013. http://www.theatlanticcities.com/technollogy/2013/10/end-car-chases/7425/.

Rodriguez, Sal. *Fact Sheet: The High Cost of Solitary Confinement.* Solitary Watch, 2011.

*Roper v. Simmons.* 543 U.S. 551 (2005).

Rosen, Gideon. "Beyond Blame." *Boston Review*, July 10, 2013.

Ruderman, Wendy. "New Tool for Police Officers: Records at Their Fingertips." *New York Times*, April 11, 2013.

Sears, Greg J., Haiyan Zhang, Willi H. Wiesner, Rick D. Hackett, and Yufei Yuan. "A Comparative Assessment of Videoconferencing and Face-to-Fact Employment Interviews." *Management Decision* 51 (2013): 1733–52.

Simon, Dan. *In Doubt: The Psychology of the Criminal Justice Process.* Cambridge, MA: Harvard University Press, 2012.

Slobogin, Christopher. "Therapeutic Jurisprudence: Five Dilemmas to Ponder." *Psychology, Public Policy, and Law* 1 (1995): 193–219.

Southern Center for Human Rights. *The Crisis of Violence in Georgia's Prisons.* Atlanta, GA: Southern Center for Human Rights, 2014.

Sritharan, Rajees, R., and Bertram Gawronski. "Changing Implicit and Explicit Prejudice: Insights from the Associative-Propositional Evaluation Model." *Social Psychology* 41 (2010): 113–23.

Stanford Lucile Packard Children's Hospital. "What Cardiothoracic Surgery at the Children's Heart Center is Known For." Accessed May 22, 2014. http://www.lpch.org/clinicalSpecialtiesServices/COE/ChildrensHeartCenter/ctSurgery/knownFor.html.

StarChase. "How It Works: Overview." 2013. http://www.starchase.com/howitworks.html.

Steadman, H., and M. Naples. "Assessing the Effectiveness of Jail Diversion Programs for Persons with Serious Mental Illness and Co-Occurring Substance Use Disorders." *Behavioral Sciences and the Law* 23 (2005): 163–70.

Stillman, Tyler F., and Roy F. Baumeister. "Guilty, Free, and Wise: Belief in Free Will Facilitates Learning from Self-Conscious Emotions." *Journal of Experimental Social Psychology* 46 (2010): 951–60.

Subramanian, Ram, and Alison Shames. *Sentencing and Prison Practices in the Netherlands: Implications for the United States.* New York: Vera Institute of Justice, 2013.

Sunstein, Cass R. "Fighting Crime by Going Cashless." *BloombergView,* April 29, 2014. http://www.bloombergview.com/articles/2014 -04-29/fighting-crime-by-going-cashless.

Texas Department of Criminal Justice. "Correctional Officer Eligibility Criteria." January 9, 2014. http://www.tdcj.state.tx.us/hrextra/ coinfo/emp-co.html.

Texas Department of Criminal Justice. "Correctional Officer Essential Functions." April 1, 2014. http://www.tdcj.state.tx.us/hrextra/ coinfo/essentialfunctions.html.

Travis, Jeremy. *But They All Come Back: Facing the Challenges of Prisoner Reentry.* Washington, DC: Urban Institute Press, 2005.

Travis, Jeremy, Amy L. Solomon, and Michelle Waul. *From Prison to Home: The Dimensions and Consequences of Prisoner Reentry.* Washington, DC: Urban Institute, 2001.

Uggen, Christopher. "Work as a Turning Point in the Life Course of Criminals: A Duration Model of Age, Employment, and Recidivism." *American Sociological Review* 67 (2000): 529–46.

United States Attorney, Southern District of New York. *CRIPA Investigation of the New York City Department of Correction Jails on Rikers Island.* New York: U.S. Department of Justice, 2014.

U.S. Census Bureau. *Profile of General Population and Housing Characteristics: 2010.*

U.S. Const. amend. VI.

Vohs, Kathleen D., and Jonathon Schooler. "The Value of Believing in Free Will: Encouraging a Belief in Determinism Increases Cheating." *Psychological Science* 19 (2008): 49–54.

Wenzel, Michael, and Tyler G. Okimoto. "How Acts of Forgiveness Restore a Sense of Justice: Addressing Status/Power and Value Concerns Raised by Transgressions." *European Journal of Social Psychology* 40, no. 3 (2010): 401–17.

Werse, Valerie. "The Confrontation Clause in Video Conferencing." *Rutgers Computer and Technology Law Journal* (2012): 1–13.

*West's Encyclopedia of American Law.* S.v. "Insanity Defense." Accessed November 7, 2014. http://legal-dictionary.thefreedictionary.com/Insanity+Defense.

Wilson, Michael. "Crime Scene Investigation: 360 Degrees." *New York Times,* November 18, 2011.

Witvliet, Charlotte V.O., Everett L. Worthington, Lindsey M. Root, Amy F. Sato, Thomas E. Ludwig, and Julie J. Exline. "Retributive Justice, Restorative Justice, and Forgiveness: An Experimental Psychophysiology Analysis," *Journal of Experimental Social Psychology* 44, no. 1 (2008): 10–25.

Witvliet, Charlotte vanOyen, Thomas E. Ludwig, and Kelly L. Vander Laan. "Granting Forgiveness or Harboring Grudges: Implications for Emotion, Physiology, and Health." *Psychological Sciences* 12, no. 2 (2001): 117–23.

Wolf, Elaine M. "Systemic Constraints on the Implementation of a Northeastern Drug Court." In *Drug Courts in Theory and in Practice,* edited by James L. Nolan, Jr. New York: Aldine de Gruyter, 2002.

Wright, Richard, Erdal Tekin, Volkan Torpalli, Chandler McClellan, Timothy Dickinson, and Richard Rosenfeld. "Less Cash, Less Crime: Evidence from the Electronic Benefit Transfer Program." Working Paper, 2014. http://www.nber.org/papers/w19996.

"Written Testimony for Amy Solomon, Senior Advisor to the Assistant Attorney General, Office of Justice Programs, U.S. Department of Justice." *U.S. Equal Employment Opportunity Commission.* July 26, 2011. http://www.eeoc.gov/eeoc/meetings/7-26-11/solomon.cfm.

Yee, Amy. "In India, a Small Pill with Positive Side Effects." *New York Times,* April 4, 2012.

# Index

ADAM BENFORADO is an associate professor of law at Drexel University. A graduate of Yale College and Harvard Law School, he served as a federal appellate law clerk and an attorney at Jenner & Block. He has published numerous scholarly articles, and his op-eds and essays have appeared in a variety of publications including the *Washington Post*, the *Philadelphia Inquirer*, and *Legal Times*. He lives in Philadelphia with his wife and daughter.

Adam Benforado is available for select speaking engagements. To inquire about a possible appearance, please contact the Penguin Random House Speakers Bureau at speakers@penguinrandomhouse.com or visit www.prhspeakers.com.

# UNFAIR

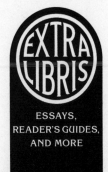

ESSAYS,
READER'S GUIDES,
AND MORE

# A Reader's Guide for *Unfair: The New Science of Criminal Injustice*

## BY ADAM BENFORADO

*For additional features, visit adambenforado.com.*

*Unfair* is the result of law professor Adam Benforado's deep research into the intersection of human psychology and our legal system. In it, he weaves together historical examples, scientific studies, and compelling court cases—from the collie put on trial in Kentucky to the five teenagers who falsely confessed in the Central Park Jogger case—to show how our judicial processes fail to uphold our values and endanger society's most vulnerable members.

Laying out the scope of our system's dysfunction—where the outcomes of legal cases turn on factors as small as the facial features of the defendant or the number of photos in a mug-shot book—Benforado provides a wealth of innovative and practical reforms to help prevent future miscarriages of justice.

Eye-opening and galvanizing, *Unfair* is sure to spark dialogue in your book club. We hope this guide will enhance your discussion.

## QUESTIONS AND TOPICS FOR DISCUSSION

1. Has your understanding of the legal system changed as a result of reading *Unfair*? How about your idea of what "justice" means?

2. In chapter 2, Benforado tells the story of Juan Rivera, who falsely confessed to the brutal rape and murder of an eleven-year-old girl. False confessions also played a role in the infamous Central Park Jogger case. What were your reactions to reading about this phenomenon?

3. If victims of a carjacking identified you as their assailant and you had two choices—either plead guilty and spend two years in prison, or try your luck at trial, with a potential sentence of twenty-five years to life—which would you choose if you knew you were innocent? Were you surprised to learn that nine out of ten people charged with a crime end up taking a plea bargain? Do you think our criminal justice system should rely so heavily on plea bargains?

4. What do you think of the solutions Benforado proposes to reform our laws, practices, and procedures? What solutions do you think would be most and least effective? Why?

5. In the year *Unfair* was first published, series like *The Jinx*, *Serial*, and *Making a Murderer* garnered a lot of attention and brought into question the

accuracy and effectiveness of our criminal justice system. How has reading *Unfair* shaped your understanding of these cases?

6. Benforado provides evidence that our approach to punishment fails to achieve our societal goals. Has the book changed your opinion on issues like the death penalty, three-strikes laws, or solitary confinement?

7. Which real-life story or study in the book surprised you most? Why?

8. Benforado outlines how race can dramatically affect everything from the treatment of victims to the harshness of punishment. What do you think of his argument that racial discrimination today is more about implicit bias than explicit racial hatred? What do you think can be done to address racial disparities in the justice system? Will we ever have "equal justice" for all Americans?

9. Have you ever been called for jury duty or summoned as a witness? Discuss your experience. Do Benforado's observations about the limitations of jurors and witnesses ring true for you? Why or why not?

10. Benforado explores the genetic and environmental forces that influence criminal behavior and argues against the idea that criminals are evil people who freely choose to commit greedy, lustful, or hateful acts. Do you agree with him? Why or why not?

11. Judges are meant to be impartial moderators, and yet, as Benforado shows, they are susceptible to numerous biases. How does this affect your view

of judges (including members of the Supreme Court)? Would you rather be tried by a judge or by a jury of your peers?

12. "Each of us believes that we see the world exactly as it is and that other reasonable people will see things similarly" (page 94). Discuss this statement in the context of the justice system as well as in everyday life.

13. *Unfair* challenges us to examine how our backgrounds and beliefs shape our perceptions and judgments. Which aspects of your identity might inhibit your ability to be fair during a trial? If a judge asked you to set aside your biases, would you be able to do it?

14. Has *Unfair* changed the way you would pursue justice if you were the victim of a crime? Has it changed the way you would interact with police officers and attorneys working on your case?

15. In his introduction, Benforado makes the claim that, eventually, our current justice system will be perceived in the same way that we view medieval trials by ordeal. What did you think about his prediction when you read it, and did you agree? Did your opinion change as you read more of the book?

16. What can we learn from the legal systems of other countries around the world? Did any of the differences that Benforado described between our justice system and another country's surprise you?

17. In analyzing our criminal justice system, Benforado presents numerous psychological insights

about human behavior, but many of the research studies he cites—studies of memory, tunnel vision, dishonesty, racial bias, and other issues—have broader implications. Do you think any of these studies are relevant to your job? Your relationships? The business world? Health care? National security?

18. After reading the book, do you think everyday citizens have a responsibility to change the legal system, or is reform the responsibility of lawyers, judges, lawmakers, and other professionals? What can an individual do to make a difference?

# A Conversation with Adam Benforado

Q. Recent events in Baltimore and other cities have brought a lot of attention to inequities in our criminal justice system. What can we do to make it operate the way it was designed to, so that it's fair for everyone?

A. The first thing to realize is that even if we eliminated all of the problems we've identified—bigoted cops, corrupt prosecutors, foolish jurors, activist judges—we would still have terrible abuse, wrongful convictions, and unequal justice. The reason is that the design of our system itself is unfair because it's built on incorrect assumptions about human behavior. To make real progress, we need to understand the hidden forces that shape how people think and act when committing a crime, drawing a weapon on a suspect, deciding a witness is lying, or concluding that someone deserves the death penalty.

Q. How can a system based on the fact that people are rational operators guided by reason be flawed?

A. For centuries we didn't have the tools to appreciate the defects in that model. But recent groundbreaking work in psychology and neuroscience has allowed us to see our true selves: we are frequently guided by elements in our situation that we have little awareness of or control over. A judge, for instance, may feel certain that his decision in a case reflects an objective reading of the law, when in fact the outcome has been influenced by things as seemingly irrelevant as the time of day when the case was heard, the gender of his only child, or the shape of the defendant's nose.

Q. You cast doubt on the solidity of some of the cornerstones of our justice system, among them eyewitness identifications, forensic evidence, and suspect confessions. What has shaken your faith?

A. It's the data. We place great trust in eyewitness memory, charging tens of thousands of people with crimes each year after they are identified in police lineups, though research reveals that when eyewitnesses make a selection, they choose an innocent person roughly one out of three times. We assume that matching a fingerprint or DNA sample is immune to human error, but lab technicians interpret the evidence in front of them in accordance with what they already believe to be true. Likewise, it seems inconceivable to us that a person could confess to a brutal felony and be innocent, but exonerations have exposed the awful truth, and experiments have shown that the most widely used interrogation technique is largely to blame.

Q. In the book, you use some truly jaw-dropping actual cases to bring the science to life. Which story shocked you the most?

A. There were many times in the course of my research when I could hardly believe what I had come across: the formal trial and execution of a pig for murder; an innocent teenager who, under detectives' questioning, came to believe he'd actually stabbed his parents to death; an Indian woman convicted of murder based on a scan of her brain that purported to reveal her guilt. But one particular image stands out (and I've included it in the book): it's a photograph of a lineup taken in Meriwether County, Georgia, in 1979. What is startling is not just that the man in the middle was wrongly accused and spent over a decade imprisoned for a crime he didn't commit. It's that the actual rapist is standing in the same lineup just two spots to his right. By pure coincidence, he had been locked up in the jail for an unrelated offense, and detectives had pulled him in as a filler. The victim looked at the person who had brutally attacked her, whom she'd been face-to-face with, and picked out another guy. It's a powerful reminder of one of the book's core messages: good people with good intentions can produce terrible injustice.

Q. But sometimes there really are bad apples, right? Such as a prosecutor who withholds evidence that shows the defendant is innocent?

A. The theme holds, even here. For the most part, prosecutor misconduct is not about poor character; it's about lawyers being put in situations that provide opportunity and ready justifications for bending the rules. One of the reasons prosecutors are so vulnerable is not their desire to advance their own interests; rather, it's the pressure they're under to gain a conviction for the sake of the victim, the detectives who worked the case, and the general public. When we believe we are acting for the benefit of others we are more likely to engage in dishonesty than when we are just looking out for ourselves, because it's easier for us to rationalize our actions.

**Q. Inequality is a huge issue in America today. How do the flaws in our criminal justice system make things worse?**

**A.** Although most of the public is ignorant of the psychological dynamics that determine the outcomes of cases, there are certain people who understand what is really going on—trial consultants. They use their knowledge of juror, witness, and judicial behavior to gain a crucial edge in the proceedings. The wealthy can pay consultants to make sure that trials are as biased as possible in their favor, while the poor are left to fend for themselves.

**Q. With so much wrong with our system, how can it be fixed? Are there changes that could easily be implemented?**

**A.** One of the most important things to do is reduce our reliance on faulty human capacities. If implicit racial biases lead judges to set bail higher for a black man than for a white man, then we ought to either make the bail amount automatic or eliminate it altogether. If knowing the identity of the suspect leads police officers administering identification procedures unconsciously to steer witnesses, the person handling the lineup shouldn't have this information. And if jurors are poor at discerning whether someone is lying or telling the truth, we shouldn't give them the job of assessing credibility.

**Q. Would video cameras in interrogation rooms, and on the police, help matters?**
**A.** Yes and no. In the wake of recent citizen deaths at the hands of the police, a number of jurisdictions have rushed to purchase dash cams for squad cars and body cams for officers. And cameras can indeed be a great way to lessen our dependence on eyewitness memories and discourage abuse. But they can also introduce bias by offering a limited or one-sided perspective. In experiments, when people are shown a tape of an interrogation shot from behind the suspect, they are significantly more likely to find a resulting confession to be coerced than when they are offered the perspective of the detective doing the questioning.

**Q. What about our approach to corrections— how do we even begin to address the problem?**
**A.** I believe that the starting point for reform is to ask what actually motivates us to punish. A couple of years ago I received a grant from the National Science Foundation to look at whether it all comes down to a desire to make society safer, as many people believe. The results of those experiments showed that this

common perception is wrong. In fact, we are often driven by a motive for payback, even if the punishment does little to reduce future threats. And the power of our retributive instinct can help explain two of the ugliest secrets in our system: our tolerance for endemic rape within prisons and our willingness to try children as adults, even as we acknowledge that kids lack the brain development to be considered fully culpable.

**Q. Are you proposing that we go soft on crime? What about personal responsibility?**

**A.** I am a strong proponent of accountability, and I'm firmly committed to doing what it takes to eradicate crime, but I'm not going to defer to folk wisdom on either front: I want to know what the best available research says. And the evidence is clear: when society knowingly fails to protect children from heavy metals and abusive home environments that are linked to criminal behavior, when it decides to let inner-city schools crumble and neglects to provide urban youth with opportunities for advancement, it bears primary responsibility for the crimes that result. Putting our energy into blaming those who never really had a chance has gotten us nowhere. And our harsh punishments are at best ineffective and at worst leave us less secure, because the vast majority of those who experience the brutality and deprivation of prison—including those in solitary confinement—are eventually released.

Q. Are there any lessons we can take from how other countries treat prisoners?

A. Absolutely. In northern Europe, for instance, the emphasis tends to be largely on rehabilitating the prisoner, so the experience of incarceration is designed not to deliver suffering but to encourage healthy interactions and skill development that can help an offender be successful when he is released. And it works: although direct comparisons can be tricky, countries like Norway appear to have much lower recidivism rates than we do. Still, I believe that we ultimately need to go further in our reform project. We need a public-health model for dealing with crime—a model that enables us to shift from reacting after harms have already been committed to investing primarily in prevention.

For additional Extra Libris content from your other
favorite authors and to enter great book giveaways, visit
**ReadItForward.com/Extra-Libris.**

**ESSAYS, READER'S GUIDES, AND MORE**